Black Pris
and Their World, Alabama,
1865–1900

Carter G. Woodson Institute Series in Black Studies

REGINALD BUTLER, *Editor*

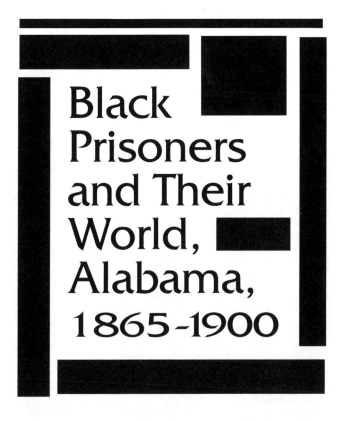

Black Prisoners and Their World, Alabama, 1865-1900

Mary Ellen Curtin

University Press of Virginia
Charlottesville and London

THE UNIVERSITY PRESS OF VIRGINIA
© 2000 by the Rector and Visitors of the University of Virginia
All rights reserved
Printed in the United States of America

First published in 2000

∞The paper used in this publication meets the minimum requirements of the
American National Standard for Information Sciences—Permanence of Paper for
Printed Library Materials, ANSI Z39.48-1984.

Library of Congress Cataloging-in-Publication Data
Curtin, Mary Ellen, 1961–
    Black prisoners and their world, Alabama, 1865–1900 / Mary Ellen Curtin.
        p.   cm.—(Carter G. Woodson Institute series in Black studies)
    Includes bibliographical references (p.) and index.
    ISBN 0-8139-1981-9 (cloth : alk. paper)—ISBN 0-8139-1984-3 (pbk. : alk. paper)
        1. Convict labor—Alabama—History.   2. Afro-American prisoners—Alabama—
Social conditions.   3. Coal mines and mining—Alabama—Birmingham Region—
History.   I. Title.
II. Series.

HV8929.A22 C87 2000
365'.65—dc21

00-028214

Contents

Illustrations

Acknowledgments

I have long looked forward to the day when I could formally thank the many friends, teachers, family members, fellow scholars, and institutions that have helped to bring this project to fruition. This book began as a doctoral dissertation at Duke University under the guidance of Raymond Gavins. Professor Gavins sparked my interest in African-American history and gave unstintingly of his time, knowledge, and insight while encouraging me to pursue my research in my own way. He was a model adviser, and in my own teaching and mentoring, I strive to match his example. I wish to thank him and the many other scholars in the Duke history department who inspired and assisted me. Jack Cell, William Chafe, David Barry Gaspar, Lawrence Goodwyn, Janet Ewald, Anne Firor Scott, and Peter Wood made Duke an exceptionally exciting place to study and research southern history and the black experience, and I feel privileged to have benefited from their teaching. Nancy Hewitt, now of Rutgers University, deserves a special thanks for being exceedingly generous with her time and encouragement. I have been enriched by the confidence she has always shown in me and in my work. I would also like to express my appreciation to Robert J. Norrell of the University of Knoxville at Tennessee for first calling my attention to the rich sources in prison history waiting to be used at the Alabama Department of Archives and History (ADAH).

The ADAH in Montgomery was a wonderful place to conduct long-term research. The friendly and knowledgeable staff consistently went out of their way to make me feel welcome in Montgomery. Without their help and expertise this book could not have been written. I would especially like to thank Debbie Pendleton, Mike Breedlove, Mark Palmer, Josephine Perry, Tracey Berezansky, Willie Maryland, Rickie Brunner, Frazine Taylor, and Edwin Bridges, Director of the Archives. I especially appreciated the friendship extended to me by Josie Perry and her five children (Kimmy, Tabitha, Ann, Joseph, and Jennifer) as well as the entire Maryland family. Other institutions and repositories that contributed to the success of this project include the Schomburg Center and the main branch of the New York Public Library, the Birmingham Public Library, the National Archives, Duke University, Howard University, and the Shelby, Greene, and Hale County Courthouses in Alabama.

A number of institutions gave financial support that enabled me to research and write this manuscript. Many thanks to Duke University for funding my graduate studies and providing a much-needed travel grant. A fellowship from the Charlotte Newcomb Foundation enabled me to extend my research time in Alabama. A predoctoral fellowship from the Carter G. Woodson Institute at the University of Virginia provided the scholarly and financial support needed to complete my dissertation. It was a joy to work with other fellows who included Constance Curry, Penny Russell, Zoe Strother, Daryl Scott, and Adam Fairclough. Armstead Robinson, the late Director of the Woodson Institute, enthusiastically supported this project; I owe him and the entire staff at the Woodson Institute a great deal. A Research Enhancement Grant from Southwest Texas State University in San Marcos, Texas, enabled me to explore sources outside of Alabama.

Portions of chapter 7 are reprinted from *Hidden Histories of Women in the New South,* edited by Virginia Bernhard, Betty Brandon, Elizabeth Fox-Genovese, Theda Perdue, and Elizabeth Hayes Turner, by permission of the University of Missouri Press. Copyright © 1994 by the Curators of the University of Missouri.

Those who helped me with the writing, and rewriting, of this manuscript deserve special mention. I would like to thank Kirsten Fischer, Vikki Bynum, Gregg Andrews, Michael Fitzgerald, Alex Lichtenstein, the anonymous readers for the University Press of Virginia, and Adam Fairclough for reading all or part of the manuscript and for offering thoughtful criticism that has improved this work enormously. Over too many years Richard Holway of the University Press of Virginia supported this project; I wish to thank him for his patience. My cohort in graduate school always provided warm friendship, camaraderie, and intellectual stimulation upon which I still rely. I owe more than I can say to Ann Farnsworth-Alvear, Kirsten Fischer, Christina Greene, Molly Mullin, and Andrew Neather. I also wish to thank the entire history department at Southwest Texas State University in San Marcos, Texas, for giving me my first academic home. I shall always remember my time there with fondness and gratitude. I would also like to thank Tony Badger, for giving me a forum for presenting my research in the United Kingdom, and my new colleagues at the University of Essex, for providing me with such an outstanding environment in which to teach and pursue intellectual work.

I also owe tremendous debts to my family on both sides of the Atlantic. For many years my husband Adam Fairclough endured a most unusual domestic arrangement with amazing patience and good cheer. No matter what the circumstances, he always gave me his unqualified love and encouragement and he never wavered in his certainty that this book would come to be. His wit, gentleness, and friendship have sustained me; the family that we share with Jenny Fairclough and our son Arthur gives me great joy. My six siblings in America, Ann, John, Pat, Eileen, Mark, and Bill, although scattered from coast to coast, give me a mental touchstone every day, and I thank them for shaping my interests and my life. Finally, I owe more than I can express to my parents, John and Jane Curtin, who have always provided me with love, humor, and two wonderful examples of how to live. To them this book is dedicated.

Black Prisoners
and Their World, Alabama,
1865–1900

Map of Alabama, highlighting the Black Belt

Introduction

■ This book traces the history of black prisoners in Alabama from the end of the Civil War to the turn of the twentieth century. It germinated when, as a graduate student, I began reading about Birmingham, Alabama, during the late nineteenth century and the African Americans who comprised nearly half of that city's mining force. Skilled and organized, black miners cooperated with whites and participated in numerous strikes. This interracial labor movement has made Birmingham of special interest to southern historians, and controversy continues to swirl around basic questions: Did industrialization dissolve racial tensions or heighten them? Was such cooperation a matter of short-lived convenience, or did it indicate that a labor movement could dislodge entrenched white supremacy?[1] The activities of these black miners, as well as the intellectual debates they generated, interested me. What positively intrigued me, however, was the discovery that many of these same black miners in late nineteenth-century Birmingham had previously been prisoners.[2]

Many ex-prisoners became miners because Alabama used prison labor extensively in its coal mines. By 1888 all of Alabama's able male prisoners were leased to two major mining companies: the Tennessee Coal and Iron Company (TCI) and the Sloss Iron and Steel Company. For a charge of up to $18.50 per month per man, these corporations "leased," or rented, prison laborers and worked them in coal mines.[3] Contrary to popular imagery, company-paid "wardens," not potbellied sheriffs, kept watch during

1

the day. Underground, two armed "mine bosses" guarded the exit and entrance. Six days a week, each prisoner mined a daily quota, or "task," of two to five tons of coal. Every day, while on his knees, the average convict miner shoveled 8,000 to 12,000 pounds of dead weight. Wardens, bosses, and prison guards inflicted brutal whippings, coercing prisoners relentlessly. Such brutality exacted a terrible human cost. Throughout the late nineteenth century, Alabama had the most profitable prisons in the nation; it also had the most deadly, with mortality rates that far outstripped any comparable state.[4]

It is one thing to describe this system as brutal; it is another, however, to convey how these men faced, and even overcame, this overwhelming challenge to their survival. Before entering the convict coal mines, most prisoners had worked only as farmers. Hands that had once grasped plows now gingerly cradled dynamite. Men accustomed to work outside now labored underground in cramped subterranean rooms; surrounded by rock and coal face, they rarely saw the sky and sun. Prisoners sometimes worked in water up to their necks, and they constantly breathed dangerous fumes. Furthermore, coal mining was a demanding skill; mastering it required practice, fearlessness, and ingenuity. "I am a physically strong man," prison inspector Dr. Albert T. Henley confided in a letter, "but if I had to go in a mine and cut and load three trams a day, I am sure that I could not do it if my life depended on it and I have a much more intelligent idea of it than the average negro."[5]

In fact, not every prisoner was a "negro," but Henley's remark shows the deep association between criminality, convict mining, and race. African-American prisoners dominated Alabama prison mines. In 1890 TCI leased 1,051 state prisoners; 894 of them were black. Among county convicts (prisoners convicted of misdemeanors), whites made up an even smaller percentage. In the entire state of Alabama, whites comprised less than 4 percent of all county prisoners. Throughout the 1880s the Black Belt counties of Bullock, Dallas, Greene, Hale, Lowndes, Marengo, Perry, and Sumter did not imprison or lease a single white county prisoner.[6]

Given the cruelty, racism, and high mortality endemic to this system, it seems strange to encounter black prisoners who survived and chose to remain as free miners. Nevertheless, many did. In the words of Reginald Heber Dawson, chief inspector of the Alabama Department of Corrections, nearly half of all convicts became free miners and "never became our prisoners again."[7] One prisoner who testified before a congressional committee was asked if he would ever return to farming, but Ezekiel Archey scoffed at the idea. "If I was ever so lucky to get free again," Archey told the senator, "I could make from $7 to $8 a day in the mines without a farm." A report by the U.S. Immigration Commission estimated that "50% of the negro coal miners in the district are ex-convicts." In 1889 a state legislative investigation stated that "the number of convicts annually released in Jefferson

County is quite a thousand. It is not to be disputed that a very large proportion of this number,—practically all who have become coal miners,—remain there, and bring their families to live with them." It was "the ex-convicts," stated an inspector in 1886, who were "the most blatant about the rights of free labor."[8]

This study asks some deceptively simple but vital questions: Why did the convict-leasing system emerge? Why did so many African Americans become prisoners? How did newly emancipated Alabama blacks respond to the convict lease? And how did their responses shape class formations and other social divisions both in Birmingham and in the rural Black Belt? The leasing system is most deeply associated with the flowering of late nineteenth-century segregation and industrialization—in other words, with the political economy of the New South. As I delved more deeply into these questions, however, I realized the significance of Reconstruction and emancipation conflicts for understanding the origins of the lease and its subsequent trajectory.

Black prisoners of late nineteenth-century Alabama were part of a new generation of former slaves, a group which the late Armstead L. Robinson saw as "members of an evolving working class." In an important article that examined the lives of newly emancipated African Americans in Memphis, Tennessee, Robinson drew upon the insights of community studies in the postemancipation South as well as the innovative approaches in working-class history pioneered by E. P. Thompson and Herbert Gutman that investigated life outside the workplace. Robinson focused on how former slaves adjusted to freedom and urban life without extensive government aid. Instead, he argued, freedpeople relied on indigenous infrastructures that included artisanal skills, their churches and benevolent associations, and entrepreneurial ambition. Robinson analyzed the resulting class tensions within the community, as well as the white "external oppression" that these activities produced.[9] More recent studies by Tera Hunter, Peter Rachleff, and Julie Saville also have stressed the links between emancipation, Reconstruction, and the challenges faced by black urban and rural workers.[10]

The conflicts created by the convict-leasing system, however, remain an unexplored dimension of the African-American transition out of slavery. In order to understand how newly freed blacks responded to forced prison mining, we must grasp the world they lived in before entering that institution. Part of that world involved complex community ties, thwarted economic aspirations, and political conflicts. Another dimension involved the new legal restrictions southern societies imposed that drew a disproportionate number of African Americans into prison. The history of Alabama's black working class is incomplete without consideration of the time many of them spent as free people, prisoners, and then prison laborers.

This study focuses on the pasts and aspirations of the imprisoned. The testimony of prisoners and other evidence encouraged me to imagine black prisoners as human beings with a past rooted in slavery and the limited promise of Reconstruction. Although incarcerated, black prisoners pursued a variety of goals that included gaining legal justice, returning home, learning mining, or simply surviving. Despite their pitiful status, Alabama's black prisoners influenced a multitude of events, including the shaping of prison policy. Their ordeal reveals the strivings, and conflicts, within black communities, sheds new light on the complex meaning of freedom for African Americans, and illuminates how prison contributed to the development of a new black working class.

A focus on black prisoners and their world distinguishes this book from previous studies of the convict-leasing system. In the past, scholars of the lease have emphasized the system's brutality, profitability, racism, and corruption. The abomination of the lease exposed the shallow paternalism of the era's white elite. As C. Vann Woodward has argued, "The convict lease system did greater violence to the moral authority of the Redeemers than did anything else. For it was upon the tradition of paternalism that the Redeemer regimes claimed authority to settle the race problem and 'deal with the Negro.'"[11] In addition to serving as a means of racial repression, the lease undoubtedly underpinned racial segregation and capitalism in the New South. A recent study stresses the lease's economic function and its key role in southern industrialization and modernization.[12] But in most existing narratives of the lease, prisoners appear only as workers who make occasional desperate attempts at resistance; little is revealed about their lives before, during, or after their incarceration. Until now, prisoners have been seen only as the casualties of a cruel system, not as historical actors in their own right.

Divorcing prisoners from the history and administration of the convict lease system, however, has distorted southern prison history. It has led, for example, to the near erasure of female prisoners, black and white, from the story. Until 1888, state female prisoners in Alabama cooked, cleaned, and worked as servants for prison contractors at the same mining camps and farms that employed male prisoners. They too were exploited by the convict-leasing system; they too developed strategies for survival, some unique to their gender. However, none of the published work on convict-leasing in Alabama mentions the existence of women prisoners.[13] Because of their gender, their fewer numbers, and their less profitable labor, female prisoners have fallen out of the narrative. Nevertheless, women prisoners were a source of labor—and frustration—for inspectors and contractors. Their "unruly" behavior provoked new prison policies, causing the sex segregation of prisoners. Their assertive acts—such as fighting off rape, wearing their own clothing, and verbal scorn—invite a comparison with the behavior of female slaves and call attention to how black women learned, over time, to defend and assert themselves, even in prison.

The emphasis on the administrative history of the convict-leasing system, as well as its role in the South's political economy, has also produced a distorted conception of power relations within prison. Contractors exerted authority, to be sure. But reforms enacted in Alabama after 1883 enabled prisoners to appeal to the new rules governing contractors and thus sometimes improve their situation.[14] Prisoners exploited the reforms introduced by Reginald Heber Dawson, head of Alabama's Department of Corrections, in order to gain early releases, inform upon contractor abuses, and establish certain "rights" for themselves, such as the rights to communicate with their families and to possess a "time card" which showed the expected date of their release. Not all of these privileges were bestowed from above; many were fought for from below. These struggles offer a glimpse into the world of black prisoners by telling us what they valued.

Furthermore, their growing skill as miners caused prisoners to perceive themselves as able, valuable workers, whose actions could influence daily mining operations. During the 1880s and 1890s, prisoners engaged in sabotage, strikes, arson, and other forms of outright resistance. These were not random acts of rebellion but responses to specific changes in the circumstances of the workplace. Prison "schooled" convicts in mining, but it also provided an opportunity to contest white power. Labor relations in prison were certainly more constrained than among free miners; nevertheless, the disputes of prisoners and mining contractors mirrored the issues free miners contested with their bosses. Through arguments over tramcars, safety, and the production process, many black prisoners developed new identities as miners, which enabled them to enter the world of free labor with confidence upon their release.

The transition from prisoner to coal miner was not just forced upon convicts from without, however: it also involved changes from within. Mining and prison life transformed individuals, to be sure, but black prisoners were not ciphers. Many entered prison with skills, such as literacy; they also originated from families who hoped for their return and communities that had endured the hardships of slavery and the unkept promises of Reconstruction. Before they became prisoners, their communities had shaped these men and women, for good and for worse. Certain characteristics that appear to transfer into prison include racial pride, acting in concert, expectations of justice, and a recognition of the potentially impartial power of the law. All of these qualities aided prisoners in their struggle to survive.

As I began to investigate why convicts came to be used in coal mines and the vicissitudes of the male and female convict experience, an equally important question loomed: why did a disproportionate number of African Americans come to be prisoners?[15] Studies of the lease have tended to treat prisoners in institutional isolation, yet the crimes of which prisoners were accused reveal the social conflicts endemic to emancipation and Reconstruction.

The story of Alabama's black prisoners began, ironically, with emancipation. With the end of the Civil War, 400,000 African Americans in Alabama gained their freedom. For the first time former slaves, in theory, could move without restraint, gain the fruits of their labor, and live with their families beyond a master's authority. The end of slavery promised great things, yet the meaning of freedom was uncertain and contested. The freedpeople had few possessions and no land. Their legal status was precarious, and it would be two years before men could vote. Furthermore, freedom subjected African Americans to new forms of legal control. Under slavery the prisoners in Alabama's penitentiary were 99 percent white.[16] But after emancipation the vast majority of all prisoners were black.

This shift was brought about, initially, by the Black Codes: laws that sought to restrain newly freed African Americans. The Black Codes made it a crime for a freedperson to have a gun, be out after a certain hour, or utter "offensive language" in the presence of white women. Their impact, according to one historian, was extremely "discriminatory and severe." In Alabama any freedman caught with a pistol or "deadly weapon" was liable to a $100 fine or forced labor on the public roads. The mayor of Mobile sentenced a group of black women to ten days in the local workhouse for "disturbing the peace" and engaging in a "war of words." Blacks could be fined for damaging a plate or throwing a stone at a sheep.[17]

Along with establishing racially explicit laws, the Black Codes sanctioned racist legal treatment. One Freedmen's Bureau agent in Selma, Sam Gardner, complained to the mayor of the "manifest injustice done the Freedmen in administering justice." Always, he found, blacks were fined "excessively" and treated much more harshly than white people. "In any affray begun and urged on by a white man with a negro," reported Gardner, "the negro is certain to be fined heavily and the white man let go free." Any congregation of freedpeople could provoke a legal crackdown. An indignant agent in Montgomery wrote to his superior that "I am annoyed every morning with colored people coming into my office and complaining that they are arrested while going to and from church. Cannot this be stopped without endangering the peace and order of the city?"[18]

Those arrested for violating the Black Codes were fined and forced to work, in chains, out on the streets. By 1866 the public spectacle of blacks in chains serving a sentence of hard labor for the county sent an unmistakable message: emancipated African Americans had better learn their place. As a white crowd in Selma watched county convicts at work in 1866, journalist John Trowbridge heard them exclaim: "That's the beauty of freedom! That's what free niggers come to!"[19]

The Black Codes created a new class of prisoners known as county convicts: men and women incarcerated for misdemeanors and sentenced to up to two years of hard labor. Unique to Alabama, this dual system of state and county prisoners sent convicted felons to the state penitentiary and left misdemeanants in the hands of county authorities. Their offenses were considered minor, but black county convicts still faced severe penalties. Unlike state prisoners, county convicts were responsible for paying their own court costs, the fees incurred by sheriffs, jurors, and a trial. These fees usually amounted to $50, and cash-poor sharecroppers could rarely pay such a sum. County convicts worked off this cost by serving extra time in prison at a rate of thirty cents per day. Of all incarcerated prisoners, county prisoners suffered the worst conditions. The state failed to supervise their treatment, and local courts blatantly used the system to punish blacks. Journalist Trowbridge noted, "It was a singular fact that no white men were ever sentenced to the chain gang—being, I suppose all virtuous." [20]

Despite passage of the Fourteenth Amendment and the end of the Black Codes in 1866, the law remained a blunt instrument of social control and racial repression. According to W. E. B. Du Bois, white southerners turned to the courts "to do by judicial decision what the legislatures had formerly sought to do by specific law—namely, to reduce the freedmen to serfdom." [21] The most blatant abuses occurred in Birmingham where, as Carl V. Harris has shown, sheriffs arrested blacks en masse so as to garner lucrative fees. Other historians have shown how racist antebellum legal procedures designed to control slaves continued to hound black southerners after emancipation. Mary Frances Berry has argued that Old South prejudices regarding proper sexual conduct were reimposed by New South judges. Historians such as John Dittmer and Howard Rabinowitz have used the term *social control* to describe how sheriffs, fines, and trials kept African Americans in a subordinate position.[22]

White officials and citizens were motivated by racism, but they also prosecuted African Americans for their political and economic activities. During Reconstruction blacks asserted themselves because they felt they had a legal right to; white Democrats, in contrast, sought to limit the meaning of freedom. This situation was quite different from slavery times—when the law considered blacks as property, not as citizens. It also differed from the era of segregation, when a new body of law, culminating in *Plessy v. Ferguson,* made many black claims to equality void. Before segregation took hold, African Americans tested freedom by refusing to show deference, bringing cases to court, and asserting their right to freedom as they understood it. Whites responded to black assertions with violence, of course, but also through the law.

Many observers chronicled the political use of the law, but none did so more earnestly and eloquently than U.S. Attorney John Minnis. His lengthy letters from Alabama to the attorney general in Washington describe his frustration with the local legal system. By the mid-1870s the Ku Klux Klan allegedly had disappeared in Alabama, but Minnis saw the group's influence in the administration of justice. "The spirit of the Ku Klux is constantly manifesting itself in one shape or another," he wrote, "and I am sorry to say too often manifest itself in the courts." [23] Minnis saw how merely being a member of the Republican party or bringing a complaint against the Klan could lead to arrest, criminal charges, and imprisonment. Large black Republican voting majorities in Black Belt counties threatened the power of local elites. In the 1870s African Americans asserted their freedom on the street, on election day, and in their efforts to buy and sell goods, but such actions generated a legal backlash. Whites used the law to intimidate black voters on election day and to harass black Republicans. Reconstruction was halted, in part, by the Klan and its extralegal violence.[24] But the legal repression of the period was equally powerful and lasted even longer.

The example of "deadfalling" illustrates how many black prisoners, far from being hardened criminals, were men arrested for the "crime" of trying to become economically independent from white control. Deadfalls were roadside markets, sometimes operating at night, that catered largely to the needs of black farmers and sharecroppers. Whites condemned them. To rural blacks, however, these vital roadside markets were sources of cloth, molasses, sugar, cheap jewelry, and cottonseed. To a black sharecropper seeking freedom from debt, a woman household worker with wages to spend, or a black renter, deadfalls provided independence from the pressure of white control in the marketplace.

In 1871 these markets were not illegal, but they competed with white merchants in the Black Belt. Democratic party newspapers reported on the trade in corn and cotton occurring at deadfalls. They called for legislation "to protect farm produce." The press insisted that such legislation would be race blind: "Statutes for the protection of property and the punishment of trespass and larceny will bear upon white and black alike." However, the racial impetus was explicit, for the paper urged action against "negro thieves." [25] Before rape" had been identified as the "new Negro crime," the charge of theft and larceny haunted members of the black race. There were many reasons for freedpeople to steal, including penury and revenge; but historians have largely accepted that, justified or not, African Americans were responsible for large numbers of property crimes. The controversy over deadfalling, however, as well as the political conflicts between Republicans and Democrats, illustrates the importance of genuine social conflicts in generating growing numbers of black prisoners.

Despite the coercive use of the law, African Americans developed a complex relationship to the legal system. It would be a mistake to see all legal power bearing down against blacks: Reconstruction also inspired the freedpeople to use the courts on their own behalf. African Americans used the law to press their own cases; they saw their right to do so as a part of freedom. Blacks used the courts against employers who withheld wages.

Black women went to court to prosecute assault or sexual offenses. When their family members were murdered, African Americans wanted redress and sometimes hired their own lawyers to prosecute such cases. Although the practice of bringing whites to court diminished with segregation, some African Americans in the Black Belt continued to see the courts as places where they might see justice done, at least among the members of their own race. By 1890 the lease, the peonage system, paternalism, and patriarchy placed innumerable obstacles in the way of rural freedpeople who went to the courts in search of justice. Nevertheless, the entitlement to bring a court case was an important right established after freedom. Despite the limitations and contradictions of such actions, when they could, rural African Americans continued to use the courts to prosecute crimes committed against them.

Nevertheless, the failure of Reconstruction shaped the fate of black prisoners in late nineteenth-century Alabama. That era established a solid practice of whites turning to the courts to prosecute African Americans for purposes of social control; it also solidified prejudicial legal mechanisms, such as all-white juries. This is not to absolve the Republican party from its role in establishing the lease and a racist legal system. While in power in 1868–70 and 1872–74, the Alabama Republican party was indifferent to prison conditions and actually promoted the use of prisoners to build railroads. However, "redemption" by the Democrats placed government in the hands of men even more determined to reimpose white supremacy. Equally important, the debt they inherited from the Republicans made the Democrats keen to generate new forms of revenue that came without taxes and without offending any politically powerful group. In general, this study argues against a functionalist interpretation of the lease, which might insist that men were imprisoned at the behest of the coal companies to provide them with labor. Although coal companies were pleased to use convict labor, the evidence strongly suggests that leasing was initially the solution to the state's money troubles, not to a labor shortage. Its economic success helped to make the new Democratic regime stable, strong, and respectable. When the political opposition to leasing emerged among free miners, Greenbackers, and Populists, the system was too deeply entrenched and profitable for Democrats to consider its abolition.

The leasing system had widespread social consequences. It affected prisoners, of course, as well as free miners and families left behind. It also became a major concern of black leaders. From its inception black public figures railed against the leasing system. Booker T. Washington, W. E. B. Du Bois, and Mary Church Terrell, for example, complained that the law worked unfairly against black people, and they called for the abolition of the lease. However, many middle-class black leaders remained defensive about black criminality, especially in urban areas. The rise in crime grieved and puzzled black educators and activists, and they often tempered their criticisms of the legal system with calls for the moral reform of black people and the provision of juvenile facilities for young black offenders. Their criticisms of black crime must be understood within the context of late nineteenth-century assumptions about race and criminality. When these leaders talked about black crime, they used the new language of social science, not biological determinism; they insisted upon the basic humanity of black people.

Finally, the experiences of former prisoners in Pratt City challenge stereotypes about blacks, prisoners, and criminality. Here, many ex-prisoners became paid workers, churchgoers, and active political participants. Their behavior, perhaps, indicates the kind of men they were before their incarceration. Sometimes the example of ex-prisoner–turned–miner was held up as an example of the benefits of prison labor. But prison was something people survived; it never occurred to white reformers that men became productive citizens after their incarceration in spite of prison, and not because of it.

Alabama's convict-leasing system left an enduring legacy. In the words of Populist critic William H. Skaggs, the lease was "vile," "pernicious," "execrable," "venal," and "brutal."[26] It perpetuated "despotism" by binding Alabama's mineral interests to its political elite. It held the legal system hostage to the crass self-interest of county sheriffs, who collected fees for every prisoner they arrested, and politicians, who refused to forgo revenue paid for in human suffering. It linked race and criminality in a new and powerful way. It generated peonage by forcing convicted individuals to escape prison by allowing a local white landowner to pay their fine and thus control their labor. The lease shaped Alabama's political economy and contributed to the legalized repression of African Americans during the age of segregation. Government officials and corporations willingly and knowingly traded prisoners' lives for profit and revenue. It was common knowledge that coal mining caused an inordinate number of deaths. "Why then are they kept in the mines!" exclaimed Inspector W. D. Lee, in a private letter to Dawson. "Simply in deference to a vitiated public sentiment which demands all the revenue out of the convicts which can be had. That is the whole truth & you know it."[27] Despite the efforts of Chief Inspector R. H. Dawson, A. T. Henley, and W. D. Lee, Alabama prisoners were not removed from convict mines until 1928.

A racist legal system, an inhumane prison system, disfranchisement, and extremely limited economic opportunities were arrayed so strongly against black people that only the most educated and wealthy, one might suppose, could hope to resist their force, and even these privileged few sometimes became victims. Yet as sociologist William Sewell has observed of human agency, even people with limited material resources and formal education are capable of being agents by "exerting some degree of control over the social relations in which one is enmeshed."[28] Any attempt to include black prisoners into an analysis of prisons or to assert their role as agents is sure to provoke charges that a harsh past is being romanticized. Alex Lichtenstein, in particular, has warned social historians of prisoners to guard against what a Holocaust scholar has called "the persisting myth about the triumph of the spirit that colors the disaster with a rosy tinge."[29] This study offers few consolations. Time and time again, however, black prisoners confounded my expectations. The evidence garnered about how they responded to prison does not make the lease less horrible, but more fathomable.

Social historians often bemoan their lack of sources. If one looks for information for and about prisoners, however, a deluge of evidence emerges. This is especially true of Alabama. The Alabama governors' papers of the late nineteenth century contain correspondence from judges, wardens, contractors, prison inspectors, and prisoners and their family members. Although there are few trial transcripts, pardon records give detailed descriptions of crimes. Biennial published printed reports, newspapers, state legislative investigations, the *Proceedings* of the National Prison Association, federal government reports, and the papers of the Justice Department and the Freedmen's Bureau all provide information about prison life and constructions of criminality. The most valuable sources, however, were those generated by the Alabama Department of Corrections between 1883 and 1895 when Reginald Heber Dawson served as its chief inspector. Dawson's personal correspondence with his two subordinate inspectors, Dr. A. T. Henley and W. D. Lee, as well as his diary, contains candid accounts of daily prison life, politics, and contractors. His papers from the Alabama Department of Corrections also contain letters from prisoners—written accounts of prison life, possibly unique, from incarcerated African Americans.

Black prisoners stood at the center of overlapping institutions. As convicts, they were enmeshed within a racist legal system. As prison laborers, they comprised the seeds of a new working class. As sources of revenue for the state, black prisoners became the topic of controversial political debates. Most significantly, however, as human beings, black prisoners—men and women—were members of newly emancipated African-American communities. As this study shows, the histories of the two groups inevitably intertwined.

I begin with an account of one group of black men from Forkland in Greene County, Alabama, who were arrested in 1874 for the murder of a white political opponent. Their story, like that of thousands of others, began in the rural Black Belt during Reconstruction and ended in the prison mines of Birmingham.

The Legacy of Reconstruction

■ In May 1890 a pardon petition organized by "the colored people of Greensboro" landed on the desk of Alabama governor Thomas Seay. Seay, a Democrat and a native of Greensboro, Hale County, was to leave office soon, and it was common for retiring governors to grant a limited number of pardons to prisoners. However, this petition, which requested the release of two African-American convicts, was special. It had been delivered to Seay by a white intermediary—fellow Greensboro resident W. D. Lee, a state prison inspector. Although prepared by blacks, it was signed only by prominent Greensboro whites. Finally, the petition requested the release of two black prisoners—R. H. Skinner and Woodville Hardy—who had been unsuccessfully defended, long ago, by Seay himself.

In 1876 Skinner and Hardy had been convicted of murder and sentenced to thirty years in prison. "It is alleged," stated the petition, "that they were leaders in the riot on Rowe's farm in Greene County, which resulted in the killing of one white man and the wounding of another. Admitting this to be the fact, in our opinion they have served long enough." Fourteen years after the trial, the governor's "friends and neighbors" in Hale County were urging him to commute the remainder of Skinner and Hardy's sentences, but Seay refused. As of 1892 the two men were still incarcerated; Skinner mined coal at a prison operated by the Tennessee Coal and Iron Company, and Hardy worked at a convict farm. The dates of their deaths remain unknown. They were not scheduled to be released until 1906.[1]

Technically Skinner and Hardy were murderers, but the "colored people of Greensboro," who orchestrated the petition drive, did not consider them as such. They remembered R. H. Skinner and Woodville Hardy as two young men who in 1874 had been arrested and imprisoned after a Republican political meeting in the small township of Forkland, Alabama. In retrospect, the event leading to their arrest was called "the riot on Rowe's farm." At the time, however, this incident was one of innumerable clashes between Republicans and their opponents that took place in the Alabama Black Belt during Reconstruction. Many of those confrontations resulted in the deaths of Republicans, but this dispute was different: here the violence led to the death of a white Democrat. Shortly thereafter, in the election of 1874, the Democratic party would "redeem" the state from the alleged excesses of Reconstruction. Prior to that election, an unofficial civil war raged between Republicans and Democrats in Alabama: Skinner and Hardy were its legal casualties. To the victors went the spoils of political power and racial domination; to the losers, jail.

Memory has become a prominent theme in southern history, and scholars continue to elucidate how white southerners handed down the myth of the "lost cause" from generation to generation.[2] Less explored, however, is how southern blacks recalled and reconstituted their memory of Reconstruction conflicts. The petition on behalf of Skinner and Hardy offers some insight into this issue. Clearly, long after their arrest, these men were remembered by both the white and black communities. But what lessons did blacks derive from their activism? And what of the perspectives of the incarcerated men and women arrested in this era—how did their experiences during Reconstruction shape their response to prison? The story of the clash at Forkland, the trial and prison experiences of Skinner and Hardy, and the petition for their release illuminates some of the complex, even contradictory, ways Reconstruction shaped local race relations and prisoner responses long after its demise.

In the heart of the Alabama Black Belt, close to the Black Warrior River, in Greene County, lies the community of Forkland. A short ferry ride across the river lies Hale County (which, in 1867, had been carved out of Greene) and its county seat of Greensboro. Forkland and Greensboro epitomized two types of Black Belt communities. Rural Forkland, according to the 1880 census, was dominated by black farmers and laborers. Its 780 African-American households grew cotton while supporting two black millers, a carpenter, a preacher, a blacksmith, and two schoolteachers—one male and one female.[3] Greensboro, in contrast, served as a commercial and legal center. In Greensboro farmers from Greene and Hale Counties ginned their cotton, traded with local merchants, and settled legal disputes at the courthouse. Whites worshiped at one of Greensboro's four churches and perhaps sent their children to Methodist-supported Southern University. Although Greensboro was more racially diverse than Forkland, its black and white residents lived in segregated wards. The end of slavery had brought many changes to this locale, but by 1880 old antebellum population patterns continued to prevail: in both Greene and Hale Counties, African Americans outnumbered whites four to one.[4]

In Forkland, on the evening of September 18, 1874, Cato Jackson, an African-American farmer, had just finished conducting a meeting of local Republicans when R. H. Skinner, a Republican from Greensboro, appeared.[5] Skinner warned the assemblage of a plot to assassinate Woodville Hardy (a black Greene County Republican) and two others. He also asked for volunteers to go with him to investigate several murders of blacks rumored to have occurred in Spring Hill, north of Forkland. Cato Jackson adjourned the meeting; Skinner, Hardy, and several others departed. They had gone only a short distance when they met white men on horseback. It was dark. "Woodville?" one asked, "Is that you?" Woodville Hardy replied, "I know you are after me," and then shots were fired. "Woodville says the white folks shot first," according to one account, but the white riders said otherwise. Several blacks were hit, and at least one African-American man died. One of the white men, E. Adrian Robinson, was shot in the left side of his neck and hand. On Tuesday, the next morning, he died.[6]

That same morning Sheriff Cole and 150 armed "deputies" arrived at the Forkland meeting site and demanded an immediate surrender. Several freedmen testified that the blacks had scattered into the woods after they heard the shots; when the sheriff arrived, they remained hidden. "They wanted us to give up and be confined and carried to jail," swore Charles Johnson, but "the men replied that they did not care to be put in jail unless they had done something to be put there for." Cato Jackson concurred: "They wanted the sheriff to let them alone and they would go home. They would not be arrested." Although the majority of the freedmen escaped, Sheriff Cole arrested thirteen others including R. H. Skinner and Woodville Hardy. He charged them all with the murder of Adrian Robinson.[7]

Although the violence at Forkland was hardly unique, the death of a white Democrat was certainly unusual. Hale, Greene, and Sumter Counties in Alabama were notorious for their active Klan chapters and the violent repression of the Republican party. During the crucial 1874 election campaign, in which Democrats hoped to unseat the Republican legislature and reassume control of the state government, violence became especially widespread. Disguised men assassinated W. P. Billings, a white Republican lawyer from Sumter County, and Thomas Ivy, a black Republican leader who worked as a federal mail agent. Democrats believed this election represented a stark choice between "negro domination" and white survival. As many historians have pointed out, Democrats discharged black employees, ostracized white Republicans, and sometimes resorted to violence in order to intimidate Republicans and assure an electoral victory.[8]

The extremely violent "twenty hell week" election campaign reached into Forkland. On October 3, 1874, shortly after the arrest of Skinner and Hardy and the death of Adrian Robinson, black Republicans from Forkland petitioned the U.S. Department of Justice for help. "In the name of the All Mighty God . . . with all of our harts," they asked the government "to make a divideing line between the Republican parties and the Democrat partie. We cannt live together." The petitioners declared: "They kill and kukluks both night and day killing, hassles murder running our wives and children through the woods run your school teachers off and whipping som death." This persecution had continued since emancipation. "For the last Nine years bin cheated out of everything that we have made." Despite these outrages the Forkland petitioners pledged their loyalty to the government and to the Republican party. "We intend to carry this Election coming November." The letter was signed, "Your tryly Republican citizen, Alabama, Greene County, Forkland Beat."[9]

Some historians have concluded that by 1871 the number of Klan outrages in the Alabama Black Belt had decreased significantly because of public pressure from prominent Democrats.[10] The mention of "kukluks" in this 1874 petition, however, indicates the persistence of what Everette Swinney has called "Klanisms": "the attempt by disguised persons, operating at night, to use violence or the threat of violence in order to prevent citizens, usually Negroes, from doing something which they had a legal right to do."[11] White people, too, remarked on this continued organized white violence in the Black Belt. "The Ku Klux are now at Belmont in force," wrote a Republican woman from adjoining Sumter County later in September 1874. Formally the Klan may have been dissolved. However, in practice, as C. Vann Woodward has noted, "their campaign of violence, terror, and intimidation went forward virtually unabated."[12]

The violence culminated in a tumultuous election day. In Barbour County masked white men—including future governor B. B. Comer—shot their way into a voting place, killed Willie Keils, the sixteen-year-old son of Judge E. M. Keils, and stole votes.[13] In Mobile, Butler, and Montgomery Counties, voters were coerced and arrested. A U.S. congressional committee later concluded that violence and intimidation had carried the election for the Democrats; it called the election "an imposition upon popular rights." In some Black Belt contests for the state legislature, Republicans squeaked by, but Democrats gained a new overall majority in the legislature and captured the governorship. Alabama had been "redeemed."[14]

The Forkland prisoners, meanwhile, awaited trial for nearly eight months. Finally, on April 1, 1875, the court charged R. H. Skinner, Woodville Hardy, Winfield Hardy, Sam Hardy, Jim Black, George Williams, and

Kenny Thompson with the murder of Adrian Robinson; all pleaded not guilty. Judge Luther R. Smith, a white Republican circuit court judge, ordered the trial to begin one week later.

Witnesses for the state claimed that when the white riding party approached, the defendants hid on opposite sides of the road. The shot that killed Adrian Robinson came from the left side, where, it was alleged, Woodville Hardy stood. The total amount of handwritten testimony found in Governor Seay's files amounts to four sides of legal paper. One version claimed that the Forkland meeting was part of an illegal Republican plan to trade "government bacon for votes" which the white riders had been trying to stop. The three members of the white riding party who testified admitted they were armed, and that they called out to Woodville Hardy, who, all agreed, told them not to come any closer. The conflict was over who fired first. Witnesses for the state (members of the riding party) insisted they were fired upon. But Henry Tate (race and political persuasion unknown) claimed that the first shot came from a pistol, and that the black men had no pistols. Tate also mentioned Skinner's plea for volunteers to investigate the rumored deaths of several blacks. No defendants other than Hardy and Skinner were named in the official testimony; nevertheless, the jury convicted all the defendants of second-degree murder. R. H. Skinner, Woodville Hardy, and Jim Black were sentenced to the penitentiary for twenty-five years; Winfield Hardy, Sam Hardy, George Williams, and Kenny Thompson each received ten.[15]

Enoch Morgan, the defendants' white lawyer, protested the outcome. "The verdict is contrary to the charge of the court," he said. Furthermore, Morgan argued, Judge Smith had ordered each defendant to receive a list of jurors, but this had never been done.[16] Morgan asked Judge Smith to set aside the jury's decision on the grounds that the jurors had ignored the judge's instructions, that the defendants had never been given a list of jurors, that the verdict contradicted the evidence, and that the case properly belonged in the federal courts. Smith allowed an appeal on the second point alone—that the jury list had not been handed over as he had directed. He set aside the verdict and ordered a new date for an arraignment.

For another nine months, the Forkland prisoners remained incarcerated in the county jail. Finally, Judge Smith ordered a new trial on April 14, 1876. He told the sheriff to summon another one hundred persons for the jury. Eighteen months after the confrontation, a second trial ensued, and the result was nearly the same. Four of the defendants, Winfield Hardy, Sam Hardy, George Williams, and Kenny Thompson, were again convicted of second-degree murder; but this time they were sentenced to even longer terms of twelve years in the penitentiary.[17]

Two of the defendants, however, refused to participate in this second trial. R. H. Skinner and Woodville Hardy requested a severance from the other defendants; they asked for a new trial in a different location. "There is such a spirit of excitement and prejudice existing in Greene County, Alabama," stated their petition to the court, "that they do not believe that they can have a fair and impartial trial in Greene County, Ala., . . . also Sumter, Pickens, and Tuscaloosa counties." Judge Smith granted their request to have their trial moved to adjoining Hale County. At this point Enoch Morgan disappeared from the public record, and Thomas Seay, a young Democrat, suddenly appeared as Skinner and Hardy's new defense attorney. But the move to Hale proved disastrous. Convicted of second-degree murder, Skinner and Hardy received sentences of thirty years in the penitentiary.[18]

Judge Luther Smith had thrown out the first verdict, but he chose to let the case remain in Greene and Hale Counties and had not sent it to the federal courts. Why? His behavior can be better understood by exploring his relationship to the white Democrats in the region. Clearly Smith, a white northern Republican, faced extremely difficult choices. A former Union soldier, Smith moved to western Alabama after the war, became an active Republican, and served in Alabama's Constitutional Convention of 1867. Northern Republicans like Smith were derisively called "carpetbaggers." Yet according to historian Sarah Wiggins, the "scalawags"—native white southerners, sometimes Confederate officers, who turned into southern Republicans—suffered the brunt of white ostracism and Klan violence.[19] Luther Smith at first had enjoyed the support of local whites who from 1868 onwards helped elect him to the post of circuit judge.

By the time of the 1874 elections, however, Democratic newspapers began focusing on Smith's alleged bias in favor of African Americans. When Charles Hays, an Alabama scalawag and member of the U.S. House of Representatives, published the "Hays-Hawley Letter"—a protest describing several political assassinations that had occurred before the 1874 elections— the *Marengo News Journal* warned Smith to take a stand in defense of the white community. "The people of this town and county whose courtesy and hospitality he has enjoyed wish to know if he endorses the slanders that have been heaped upon us . . . the white people of this county . . . have a right to hear from him on this subject and they call on him to speak." But denouncing Hays would have meant undercutting a man he had steadfastly supported since 1867. Smith found it increasingly difficult to be both white and Republican.[20]

Until Smith's retirement in 1880, and throughout the Forkland case, white Democrats criticized his decisions, accused him of favoring black defendants, and threatened him with ostracism. When a freedman indicted for "illegal voting" changed his plea from not guilty to guilty, the *Marengo News Journal* remarked that "from what we can learn he acted unwisely, for if he had been convicted we have no doubt his Honor Luther R. Smith would have granted him a new trial, as he did in nearly, if not every case, when a Negro made the application." Smith took the accusation to heart and in a letter to the editor denied any favoritism. But in a following issue the editors referred to the cases of Joe Rembert, convicted of forgery, Albert Scott, fined $1,000 for "intimidating voters," and Lucinda Lee, indicted for burglary. In all these cases the jury had convicted, but Smith released Scott and Rembert on $200 bail and granted them new trials.[21] According to the paper, such actions proved Smith's racial bias.

Smith's efforts to placate white members in the community and the conviction of the Forkland prisoners went unrecognized. Democratic news-papers and white attorneys continued to heap opprobrium upon him both publicly and privately. "If [only] you could see our carpet bag Judge per-form in a case where a white Democrat is a defendant," wrote W. E. Clarke, a prominent Democratic attorney in a private letter to Governor George S. Houston in 1877. Smith had recommended that a jury convict a white man of assault on the testimony of a black woman. "He is a mild mannered man but for the 'nigger' all the time," wrote a disgusted Clark.[22]

Blacks in Alabama appeared in courtrooms as both defendants and plaintiffs. Often they appeared before Republican judges. Even a judge de-termined to be impartial, however, could not control the outcome of court cases. In the absence of black jurors and black lawyers, the pursuit of justice could be futile. Furthermore, as human beings with families, white Repub-lican judges depended on the company of local white society for social sur-vival. In a manifesto sent from Montgomery, Alabama, to the president in 1874, the Convention of Colored Citizens recognized the political impact of social ostracism. "It is true that the Republican judges have generally presided over the superior courts of this State, and have generally shown a disposition to do us justice," they wrote, "but even these have been, to some extent, warped by local pressure." The authors of the manifesto insisted that only racially integrated juries could assure justice for black citizens in Alabama.[23] R. H. Skinner, Woodville Hardy, and the six other Forkland pris-oners had been tried in front of white jurors, in a hostile political climate; but once they had been convicted, such political questions mattered very little. After they became prisoners, their lives took a new trajectory out of Greene County and into the convict-leasing system.

Meanwhile, in March 1876 (two months before the conclusion of the Fork-land trials) Gaius Whitfield, a large landowner in Marengo County, received an encouraging letter from Alabama's new prison warden, John G. Bass. Bass anticipated that come spring newly convicted black prisoners would be available to be leased. "I hope to be able to furnish you more convicts in 2 or 3 weeks, we are now receiving some, but mostly white men. How many would you like to have in the months of April and May?" As Bass had pre-dicted, when the spring term of the circuit court ended in 1876, a new group of state prisoners became available for leasing. From Greene County, Whitfield received seven African Americans convicted of larceny and the four "Forkland prisoners" beginning their twelve-year terms.[24]

Whitfield paid cash for these prisoners and thus provided the state of Alabama with needed revenue. That money sanctioned horrific treatment. Anxious to preserve good relations with Whitfield, Warden Bass failed to intervene when prisoners at Whitfield's prison farm died from overwork and ill treatment. Conditions were so abysmal that in November 1876, shortly after the Forkland prisoners had arrived, one of Whitfield's neighbors actually wrote to Bass to complain: "The reports are that [Mr. Bush] often [rears] his horse over and against them, that he clubs them with sticks and clubs and clods of dirt and that he allows the guards to do the same . . . that he whips them unmercifully often giving them from 75 to 100 lashes, that he works them in the rain, that he gives little or no attention to the sick; that often their rations are insufficient and badly cooked." Six months after arriving at Whitfield's, two of the Forkland prisoners, Sam Hardy and George Williams, were dead.[25]

In many respects Whitfield's postbellum prison evoked the slave past. Gaineswood, the luxurious but decaying antebellum mansion where Whitfield lived, was famous for its eclectic and extravagant gaudiness. The estate featured "porticos, domes and pavilions" as well as "floor to ceiling mirrors." Outside Whitfield's beautiful home, however, over seventy African-American convicts lived in unspeakable misery. Whitfield worried about escapes. He requested specially trained bloodhounds, but Bass told him to get his own pups: "The best and surest plan is to raise them (yourself) and train them up to run nothing but negroes."[26] Trained dogs, gang labor, an overseer cruelly supervising a black labor force: it might appear that only the absence of slave families distinguished this setting from slavery itself.

Slavery was a multifaceted institution defined by much more than the bad treatment bestowed upon its victims. Nevertheless, southern slavery was a violent institution that undoubtedly bequeathed certain traditions that shaped the treatment of prisoners. To control prisoners southern states copied methods of labor control perfected under slavery, including torture, whipping, patrols, and cash rewards for runaways. Whitfield's utter disregard for the lives of black prisoners stemmed from his slaveholding past, to be sure. Yet to state that Whitfield treated black prisoners like slaves ignores the postemancipation factors that also encouraged the inhumane treatment of prisoners, particularly white anger. Dissatisfied with emancipation, Whitfield turned to the lease to produce crops with a captive workforce. Emancipation precluded treating a free workforce "like slaves," but no such restrictions existed for black prisoners. The state acquiesced in Whitfield's practices because it needed Whitfield's money; Bass never directly ordered anyone to halt the brutal treatment of prisoners.

Another son of a slave-owning family who profited from leasing convicts was J. W. Comer, brother of future governor Braxton Bragg Comer. In the late 1870s Comer operated a prison labor contract company in the Eureka coal mines located in Helena, Shelby County. Comer leased over fifty prisoners from the state and an unknown number from counties and worked them in newly opened coal mines. In a letter to a prison inspector, Ezekiel Archey, a black prisoner who worked in the Eureka mines, described Comer's cruelty. "You know that Comer is a hard man. I have seen men come to him with their shirts a solid scab on their back and beg him to help them and he would say let the hide grow back and take it off again. I have seen him hit men 100 and 160 [times] with a ten prong strap then say they was not whiped he would go off after a escape man come one day with him and dig his grave the same day." The need to control labor cannot explain such sadistic cruelty; it sprang from a deeper source. At a time when slavery had been abolished and free blacks could claim legal rights, Comer, like Whitfield, relished his anomalous role as an agent of total racial control.

In the spring of 1876, a new prisoner arrived at Comer's Eureka mines: R. H. Skinner.[27] Forced labor had not been part of this youth's experience. Skinner had grown up in Greensboro, the only son of David and Mary Skinner. Both of his parents worked in the city; his father was a "jobber," his mother a domestic servant. Skinner had been educated and knew how to read and write. Sentenced to prison in his early twenties, he is not likely to have ever seen a coal mine. No doubt he was ill prepared to face the cruelties of prison mining, which surpassed even the horrors of Whitfield's farm. Of the 120 state prisoners leased to the mines in 1877, 15 died within a year. Most had been convicted of nothing greater than larceny.[28] The mines were replete with dangers: crumbling walls, gas-fueled fires and explosions, thick dust, and waist-high water. But Skinner survived. He learned to use dynamite and detect deadly gasses. He worked without shoes. He suffered terrible whippings. Most importantly, every day he struggled to complete his daily quota, or "task," of coal; if he failed to fulfill this requirement, he was whipped.

The prison stockade offered as many deadly dangers as the mines. Skinner lived in a dark log cabin with no windows or ventilation. The rooms were "filled with filth and vermin." Gunpowder cans were used for slop jars; chained men suffered miserably when the cans "would fill up and runover on bed." On a typical workday prisoners left the camp at three in the morning, in chains, and ran three miles to the mine. They returned at eight o'clock in the evening and stood for hours in the rain or snow to be counted before they could eat. Ezekiel Archey conveyed the feeling of always being drenched, cold, hungry, terrified, and exhausted. "We go to cell wet, go to bed wet and arise wet the following morning and evry guard knocking beating yelling Keep in line Jumping Ditches."[29] Even in death, prisoners at Helena were treated with brutal indifference, often interred in unmarked graves.

Under such circumstances escape often provided the only reprieve. Contractors knew how most men longed for home, and they tracked down escapees by staking out families. Catching an escaped man took time and money, but the symbolic value of a recaptured prisoner made that effort worthwhile. When Wash Williams escaped from a convict farm, Bass wrote to Whitfield and asked him to be on the lookout. "He has a wife and 9 children in Marengo County. Will you please do your best to have him caught." As a reward Bass promised Whitfield that he could keep the escaped man "one year free of charge and perhaps longer." Bass also urged Whitfield to make Williams an example to the other men. "If you catch him put him to work . . . with a heavy spike shackle and ball." Whitfield did capture Williams, but heavy chains could not keep him from his family. When Williams managed to escape yet again, Bass insisted that Whitfield discharge the guard at fault. "It will be demoralizing to the rest of your convicts," he wrote. Yet seeing Wash Williams shed his chains undoubtedly renewed the hope of many and spurred other escape plans.

Because contractors held men overtime with impunity and release was uncertain, escape was often the only means of regaining one's freedom. Great rewards, however, meant great risks. When Bill Johnson escaped from Whitfield's farm, his movements were betrayed after he met his wife Lizzie in Montgomery and left for Houston to set up a shop. Bass promised Whitfield if Johnson was captured, "you may have him the ballance of his life." The promise of labor for nothing proved a great incentive for contractors to hunt down escaped men.[30]

Despite these risks, after a year R. H. Skinner escaped from Helena. The Shelby County paper reported that "F. M. Floyd pursued R. H. Skinner, colored, ex-representative from Greene County, a convict who recently made his escape from the Eureka Company prison, to the swamps near Wetumpka, and shot at him twice, and thinks he put two balls in him, but he made his escape." The *Eutaw Whig and Observer* joined in the pursuit. "Among the penitentiary convicts that escaped from the Eureka Iron Works, on the South and North RR was R. H. Skinner, the leader of the Forkland riot . . . a reward of $150 is offered for his apprehension. He is 25 years of age; 5 feet 8¾ inches in height, black hair, black eyes, complexion black and weighs 165 pounds." No other escaped prisoner was mentioned by name, and both newspaper accounts emphasized Skinner's former political activism rather than the murder for which he was convicted.[31] Skinner remained a fugitive for nearly twelve months. But on

May 24, 1878, he was recaptured and returned to the Helena mines, where he remained for five more years. In 1883 he was transferred to the Pratt mines near Birmingham in Jefferson County.[32]

At the same time Woodville Hardy, another Forkland prisoner, was serving his sentence at prison farms near the state penitentiary at Wetumpka.[33] Hardy, a native of Greene County, appears to have been an agricultural laborer before his imprisonment. The horrors of the mines may make Alabama's prison farms sound salubrious, but even there horrendous conditions killed many prisoners each year. Until 1883 the state never supervised the treatment of any of its convicts, state or county, wherever they worked. Bound by law to forced labor, deprived of daily contact with their families, often held far beyond the date of their sentences, black prisoners in Alabama coal mines and prison farms lived under the mercy of contractors; they were wretched. In 1890 a corrections official acknowledged that during the 1870s prison conditions were so bad that "one year then was equal in punishment to many years now."[34]

In 1883, after nearly ten years of imprisonment, Skinner witnessed the first real reforms in the Alabama state prison system. R. H. Dawson, the new chief inspector, had begun to visit state prisoners, and a recent legislative report had publicized numerous abuses. Alabama's warden, John H. Bankhead, appeared before the legislature and urged comprehensive reforms that included leasing all prisoners to the coal mines. This was a controversial suggestion, however, as other factions favored using convicts as agricultural workers or road builders.

Skinner intervened in this ongoing debate by making a request. He had recently been transferred to the Pratt mines near Birmingham, and he sent a letter to Chief Inspector Dawson supporting prison labor in coal mines. "You know how our families suffer on the outside," Skinner wrote; "therefore at the mines is the best place for us, because we can make a little extra money here after we form our task witch is done in suttain number of hours give us then we can work for ourselves. We who have familes send it to them."[35]

When Skinner wrote his letter, prison mining was expanding at a fast pace. Eureka had been taken over by the Pratt Coal and Coke Company, and Pratt depended upon nearly 500 Alabama prisoners for almost half of its labor force. Prison labor had become so essential to the profitability of the company that Pratt had even begun to pay prisoners for overtime for every ton of coal produced above their quota. For Pratt those extra tons meant increased production and profit. To Skinner, however, the money he earned had a special value. His imprisonment had deprived his parents of a son and his wife of a husband and breadwinner. Earning an extra forty cents per ton, however, enabled him to fulfill those roles. At first, Skinner's request to remain at work in a coal mine might appear perverse. And yet the money Skinner earned in the mines tied him to his family and gave him an identity as well as a reason to live. Unquestionably Pratt's system amounted to the further exploitation of an already abused workforce. Nevertheless, the money the prisoners earned enabled them to feel, to some small degree, like free men.

Although serving a thirty-year sentence, Skinner envisioned a free future. He asked Dawson to sponsor legislation so that "a long time man may get to his dear ones at home."[36] Here, Skinner referred to a statute that rewarded good behavior by deducting two months from every year of a prisoner's sentence. Before 1883 this rule had hardly ever been enforced. High numbers of escapes, however, led Dawson to grant short-time pardons to thousands of Alabama prisoners between 1883 and 1900. Skinner's previous escape attempt had failed; after 1883 he followed a long-term plan by working to acquire a short-time pardon.

Pursuing such a strategy meant embracing hope and rejecting recklessness. As Ned Cobb noted many years later, all prisoners, to a degree, faced a choice. Cobb was a black Alabama sharecropper who had been sentenced to twelve years in the penitentiary for his involvement in the Alabama Sharecroppers Union in the early 1930s. In his memoirs he reflected upon the behavior of a young prisoner who kept disobeying prison authorities until they shot him.

> I had sympathy for him but I seed he was bringing it on hisself. You must first think and realize that you in a bad place, if you guilty of your crime or not guilty. The main thing to do in prison is be good, obey orders to get *out* of prison. If you don't, you aint treatin your own self right. . . . I think of my daddy's words . . . and he always said, "when you in Rome, you got to take Rome's fare." Well, that's very truthful, because you got no way of helpin yourself when you land in prison. You got to obey orders if you think anything of yourself because you got your hands in the wolf's mouth then. . . . If you go by orders, you'll protect yourself. Care and think everything as you should for your own life.[37]

The men who looked at their long-term situation and wished to get out bided their time and accepted the "fare" dished out to them. Dawson's new system of short time, increased state supervision, and the ability to earn money caused Skinner to change his strategy. He remained at work at Pratt for at least another ten years.

The end of Reconstruction has been seen in macroscopic national terms. But the conflicts of Reconstruction were also individual, local, and community struggles. In Greene County, for example, white Democrats contin-

ued to use the Forkland prisoners as symbols of the excesses of Reconstruction and the threat posed by black voting. By 1877 Democrats had regained
the governor's office, won majority rule in the legislature, and rewritten the
state's constitution. Still they felt threatened.[38] The editor of the *Eutaw
Whig and Observer* reminded his readers to stand firm. "Those disposed to
shake hands with Radicalism should recur to the dread scenes of 1874. All
know that Southern Radicalism means hatred to white people; and what
that hatred offers, the fate of poor, brave Adrian Robinson clearly proves."
To prevent "another Forkland" the editor urged unabated vigilance against
black Radicals who ran for office. "Keep the government of State, counties,
and cities in our own hands and all will be well."[39] From a local perspective
compromises made in Washington, D.C., had sent an important signal that
the era of federal support for Reconstruction was over, and yet white Democrats in Greene County still found the challenge of black voting real and
threatening.

African Americans in Forkland continued to support the Republican
party and press for federal action on their behalf. Local elections could still
be won, and the principle of absolute legalized white supremacy had yet to
be fully established. Democrats sought to overcome the overwhelming Republican majority in the Black Belt by perpetuating voting fraud, but blacks
in Forkland refused to accept such practices. In 1880 they joined with others in the Fourth Congressional District to demand a federal investigation
into the most recent election.[40] When U.S. Commissioner John H. Wallace
arrived at Forkland on August 30, 1880, he was greeted by over "600 colored men." They had come to testify that "a great fraud had been perpe-
trated upon them."

But Wallace's authority was challenged by white Democrats from
Greene and Sumter Counties who shoved their way into the crowd. After
being rebuffed, they watched as Wallace took the testimony of 600 freedmen, who all swore they had voted the Republican ticket. The fact that only
349 Republican votes had been returned by the Democrats controlling the
polling place convinced Wallace that something clearly was amiss. Furious
at being "defeated and exposed," local Democrats halted the proceedings.
Wallace watched them in amazement. "I saw men running into the house
after their guns . . . as they had them stacked in there with the guns of the
Greene Co. Greys, a military company with headquarters at Forkland."
Harrison Lassiter, one of the wealthiest and most respected white men in
the county, rebuked Wallace. "Sir," he said, "you ought to be lynched!"[41]
Wallace cautiously attempted to approach his horse, but suddenly he saw
"upon the roadside a body of men armed with rifles and advancing upon
us." He ran for cover. Finally some "friends" persuaded the "greys" to let
Wallace and his companions leave. "We passed on," Wallace stated, "re-
volvers in hand, expecting every moment an attack upon us." When they

reached the plantation of Dr. Alexander Byrd, a white Republican, they found "friendly negroes" who guarded the roads and premises throughout the night. Instead of pushing on to Tishabee, another beat (or precinct), Wallace decided to heed the urging of friends who warned that "Bull Dozers" would be waiting. Wallace returned to Eutaw, Greene's county seat, and then made his way back to Mobile.

Upon his return he described the mob and the case of flagrant voter fraud to the U.S. attorney general. "By intervening providence I escaped with my life," he wrote. "Such lawlessness should be punished," he wrote indignantly. "If not, there will be no protection in this part of our country for citizens of the nation or its officers." Forkland Republicans lived under violence extreme enough to halt the federal government, and yet they continued to insist on their rights as citizens.[42]

Despite such heroic local efforts, however, the hopeful spirit of Reconstruction was giving way to the reality of white power. This was true in the Black Belt, but also in prison. By 1890 Skinner was thirty-five and had been in prison for sixteen years. His right leg, broken at the ankle in a mining accident, had a "joint bone [that] protruded outward like." A crushed ankle and foot made him "a cripple for life." The usual place for disabled men was the state prison at Wetumpka, otherwise known as the Walls, but Skinner had never been transferred. Accidents and abuse had also left their mark on Woodville Hardy, who had a scar near his right eye, a scar over his left eye, and another that circled his body. On the surface, therefore, Skinner and Hardy were scarred, crippled, lonely prisoners whose only homes were the coal mine and the prison farm they had lived in for well over a decade.[43] And yet Skinner and Hardy still communicated with their families. The penitentiary records of 1890 indicate that both men were married. Skinner's wife, mother, and brother-in-law had moved to Jefferson County, home of the Pratt prison mines, where Skinner was imprisoned. Woodville Hardy's wife, three children, brother, sister, and parents still lived in Hale and Greene Counties.

African Americans in Greensboro clearly had given a great deal of thought to the petition they submitted to Governor Seay in 1890. Their strategy reflected the changing political and social circumstances of the era, a time when protest was giving way to white paternalism. Instead of the names of blacks, the petition contained only twelve signatures: five members of the all-white Hale County jury that convicted Hardy and Skinner in 1876, plus seven prominent Hale County whites. Inspector W. D. Lee pointed out that "all of the jury who are now known, have signed the petition, except W. L. Turnstall, who refuses to sign it, and D. L. Stickney Sr. who is dead." Although Lee's letter indicated who really was making the request, the text of the petition contained only a terse summary of the riot. The petitioners then went on to state the well-known fact that serving one year in the prisons of the 1870s was the equivalent of several current years. Because Skinner and Hardy had already served sixteen years, the petitioners "respectfully insist that these men have been sufficiently punished for their crime and we petition your Excellency to commute the remainder of their sentence." Not only had the signatories been carefully chosen; so was the messenger. W. D. Lee, a prison inspector from Hale County and a loyal Democrat, sent an accompanying letter to Seay. He told the governor that "the enclosed application has been gotten up by the colored people of Greensboro who have requested me to forward it to you." His even tone neither defended nor condemned the petition. Skinner had tried escaping long ago, he reminded the governor, and Woodville Hardy's conduct had always been good. The petitioners reminded Seay of the fate of the other Forkland prisoners: two had died in prison, and two had eventually been released; only Skinner and Hardy remained incarcerated. Some of the jurors who had sentenced Skinner and Hardy to prison now urged their release; black Greensboro residents had reason to feel hopeful.

Thomas Seay knew these men, their families, and their communities; as a lawyer he defended them, but as governor he did not pardon them. Seay's refusal showed that Alabama's Democratic leaders clearly understood—more clearly than whites in Hale County—that white supremacy rested upon continuing, not relaxing, the political repression that had sent these men to jail sixteen years earlier.[44]

The petition tells us much about the tenacity of black protest. Yet compared to the overt challenges of 1874 and appeals to federal protection and rights in 1880, the 1890 petition represented a departure from the more assertive forms of challenge associated with Reconstruction. The petitioner's terse wording and their use of former political opponents as intermediaries contrast sharply with the bravura and militancy characteristic of mass Republican gatherings or the open defiance displayed in challenging corrupt elections. What had changed between 1874, 1880, and 1890? And what had remained the same?

Skinner, Hardy, and the black men and women who entered Alabama's convict-leasing system during the 1870s and 1880s were, ironically, freedom's first generation. Consider the youth of the Forkland community on the eve of emancipation. In 1860 nearly one-third of the 2,146 slaves listed in the Forkland beat were under the age of ten; more than one-half were under the age of nineteen. Thus when the Forkland "riot" occurred in 1874, Skinner and Hardy were part of a large cohort of young people in the Black Belt coming into adulthood during Reconstruction. The vigor this generation brought to the political campaigns of the 1870s reflected their youth and optimism. During Reconstruction they experienced hopes, expectations, and struggles unknown to generations before or after. Their parents had struggled with the scourge of slavery, and a later cohort came of age in an era of disfranchisement and segregation. The generation growing up during Reconstruction, in contrast, was steeped in the political culture of Republicanism. They breathed the rhetoric of political parties and felt the suspense of elections. They exhibited hope about justice and equality under the law.[45]

By 1890, however, African Americans in the Black Belt were perhaps thinking differently about social change. How wise was it to protest directly, demand equality, and challenge the white man to his face? As one historian has noted, even before Booker T. Washington's address to the Atlanta Exposition in 1895, many black communities were experimenting with the benefits of appealing to white paternalism.[46] By 1890 blacks in the Alabama Black belt could no longer threaten to withdraw their votes, confront local whites directly, or call in federal officials. When black citizens in Greensboro wanted sympathetic action from Governor Seay, they appealed to local whites to act on their behalf. The tightening of political controls on blacks, which in 1901 led to total disfranchisement, inevitably led to a change in tactics.

Although one of the jurors refused to sign the petition, six of them did, as well as other prominent whites. This compromise is significant, but its meaning is unclear. Was this a softening of attitudes, or perhaps even a local truce of sorts? Agreeing to sign the petition no doubt entitled these white patricians to future favors. Blacks in Greensboro also made a necessary concession by agreeing in the text that Skinner and Hardy were the leaders of a "riot." Nevertheless, whites had to concede that their punishment had been enough. Even though a white man had died, they still asked the governor for Skinner and Hardy's release.

The Forkland story demonstrates in microcosm the consequences of the backlash against black rights. Local jails and privately run prison mines and farms became full of young black prisoners like Skinner and Hardy. And yet the persistence of political challenge in Forkland and the petition drive in Greensboro illustrate the complex legacy of Reconstruction for the South's legal system and its black communities. In 1890 blacks in Greene and Hale Counties were both inspired and constrained by the legacy of Reconstruction. The black citizens in Greensboro who petitioned for the release of Skinner and Hardy remembered the political struggles that had landed these youths in prison during the 1870s, as well as the heady idealism of equal justice under the law. And yet they had to confront the reality of local white power as well as the deadly consequences running afoul of local power brought to black people.

Emancipation and Black Prisoners

■ According to Alabama's chief inspector of the penitentiary, R. H. Dawson, African-American prisoners refused to listen to the moral precepts of white ministers and wardens because of their "inordinate self-esteem." "Is a man of so great consequence to adapt himself to the idea of such humble individuals as prison officials? Is a warden to teach him how he should act, or a chaplain to direct his attention to good morals? Forbid the thought. He feels himself of far too much consequence. . . . In fact, he is enclosed in a shell of self importance through which it is hard to penetrate and which almost absolutely forbids improvement."[1]

Either prisoners obeyed labor contractors, or they suffered cruel whippings. But if Dawson is to be believed, prisoners withheld sycophantic behavior from both contractors and inspectors. Perhaps prison itself cultivated such arrogance. Harsh work, routine punishment, and racist treatment, however, hardly made Alabama prisons a hothouse environment for growing "self-esteem"—a condition, psychologists assert, that results from nurturing and positive surroundings. More likely, black prisoners' "shell of self importance," which led them to reject white efforts at personal control and reform, had its roots in African-American community life after emancipation.

According to historian Peter Kolchin, newly emancipated blacks in Alabama rejected subservience to whites. It was African-American "abhorrence of white control," Kolchin asserts, that defined the Reconstruction experience and proved to be the most salient change in postwar Alabama. "Most blacks did not want to be controlled by anyone, and they were willing to migrate to insure that they were not."[2] Freed men and women left former masters, separated themselves into black-only churches, participated in politics, supported education for their children, and occasionally behaved with perceived impudence toward whites. Even though the Democrats established political dominance in 1874, Kolchin argues, African Americans' "passionate attachment to freedom" and their desire "to live as independently as possible" continued well after Reconstruction ended.[3]

Once blacks became prisoners, what happened to their ethos that valued independence from white control? Many black prisoners indeed suffered a horrific fate. Yet as freedpeople they benefited from schools, legally recognized families, political parties, and churches. Unlike slaves, black prisoners had experienced some of the advantages of freedom. Those benefits inevitably shaped their response to prison.

After freedom, Alabama blacks attended schools and gained new access to literacy. Many black prisoners knew how to read and write and used these skills to communicate with family, friends, and attorneys. In 1883 Chief Inspector Dawson began distributing paper and envelopes to prisoners. "Gradually," Dawson wrote, it became "a sort of system." Every Sunday inspectors collected the letters and mailed them out; the state even paid for postage. "The plan has done very well," Dawson concluded, "and nearly all of the convicts correspond regularly with their family and friends."[4] Unlike slaves, black prisoners of the 1870s and 1880s had grown up with access, albeit limited, to education.

One should not exaggerate the extent of black educational progress. During Radical Reconstruction, Alabama had the lowest number of schools and missionary teachers in the South. Furthermore, some whites in Alabama (not all) continued to be bitterly opposed to any effort to build black schools or fund black education.[5]

But schools did exist. By August 1869 at least 10,000 black children in Alabama attended schools set up by the Freedmen's Bureau, and by 1871 their numbers had swelled to over 55,000. Others went to Sunday schools, and many attended institutions that never reported to the bureau.[6] Adults also attended school, sometimes outnumbering the children.[7] Given the lack of complete documentation, it is easy to underestimate the number of black children in school during Reconstruction.

In addition to learning the mechanics of reading, writing, and grammar, pupils in black schools grappled with the meaning of their own history. *The Freedmen's Book,* a commonly used reader edited by abolitionist Lydia Maria Child, contained speeches by William Lloyd Garrison, a eulogy for the Haitian revolutionary Toussaint L'Overture, a laudatory account of the life of John Brown, and the story of the successful mutiny of African captives on the slave ship *Creole*. According to Horace Mann Bond, the Alabama schools sponsored by the Freedmen's Bureau and the American Missionary Association had "social objectives" and a "political content and purpose."[8] In addition, most teachers considered moral instruction and Bible study as integral to the curriculum.[9]

As new public schools emerged in the 1870s, regular teachers, white and black, began to replace northern missionaries. In 1871 teachers in black schools earned a slightly higher monthly salary than those who taught white children.[10] Only after 1890 did Alabama reduce its per capita expenditures for black children and thus significantly diminish the salaries of those who taught black children.[11] Bond estimated that in 1873 about 24 percent of school-age black children were enrolled in state schools; by 1888 the number of black children attending had risen from 55,000 to 99,000. Far fewer black children than white attended school, yet until 1875 Alabama spent as much per capita on enrolled black students as it did on whites. In 1877 in Greene County 1,142 black pupils were enrolled in thirty-five schools.[12] By 1900, 41 percent of black children between the ages of ten and fourteen attended some form of school, albeit for less than six months a year.[13]

Although many black Alabamians embraced education as a positive symbol of freedom, educated freedmen sometimes ended up in the penitentiary. "Forgery," although not as common a conviction as larceny, frequently appears on lists of crimes for which freedmen were convicted. Mrs. Victoria Clayton, a white Alabamian, claimed in her memoirs that "many young boys that have grown up since the war have been sent to the penitentiary for obtaining money by the means of knowing how to write." An Alabama newspaper derided northern teachers "for coming South to teach the Negroes to lie and steal." A useful scapegoat, education could be blamed when blacks rose above their station, or when they got into trouble with the law. At the turn of the twentieth century, social critics often cited prisoners' illiteracy and poverty as evidence of how a poor environment could lead to a life of crime. Many white southerners, however, argued that education contributed to black criminality and were suspicious of educated blacks.[14]

How changes in school funding, access to education, and curriculum affected the black population, particularly prisoners, is difficult to ascertain. But even in prison, formal schooling and literacy remained part of their lives. Hundreds of black prisoners attended schools funded by the Tennessee Coal and Iron Company and spurred on by Alabama reformer Julia S. Tutwiler. Tutwiler, a close relative of E. M. Tutwiler, manager of the Coalburg mines, was one of Alabama's best-known champions of women's education and social reform. She opposed the lease and decried the number of underage youths imprisoned at the Pratt mines. She proposed that the

Alabama legislature fund a juvenile facility. When it refused, she requested a teacher's salary for a school at the mines and persuaded TCI to build a schoolroom. Tutwiler initially had sought a teacher for the white prisoners only. By 1888, however, a schoolroom at one of the Pratt prison mines accommodated up to fifty men at a time. According to the November 1888 report of the Prison Mission School, 210 black prisoners attended. "The feeling in the school is excellent particularly among the blacks," reported teacher J. A. McGan. "All seem to appreciate their privilege and in study and deportment are perfect." [15]

One year later Julia Tutwiler extolled the achievements of Alabama's prison schools to the National Prison Association. She estimated that forty men attended her prison mission school on a regular basis. "A great many men have learned to read," she reported to the delegates in Cincinnati in 1889. "I have had letters from their mothers and wives saying what a comfort the teacher was to their sons and husbands in prison and how good it was to have someone to sympathize with them." [16] Tutwiler believed the schools made a difference. "One judge wrote the other day that an old man, whose son had been condemned to prison, came up to him and said, "I just want you to look at this letter; my boy has learned to read and write in prison." In her schoolroom prisoners could read magazines, draw, sing, and listen to the Bible being read aloud. Prisoners also found "a table filled with papers and magazines and blackboards where they can draw and some draw right well." [17] This school closed after a few years. But in 1896 a prison school at another TCI prison mine, staffed by a teacher and religious volunteers from Birmingham, soldiered on. Compared to the 1880s, the total enrollment of sixty was poor. Still, an estimated 125 black prisoners participated in intermittent spelling bees and debates "which have excited the greatest interest and enthusiasm." The state never recorded the exact number of literate prisoners. In 1891, however, Dawson's letter-writing system was still intact. Every month he ordered 2,000 sheets of paper and envelopes, enough to supply every state convict with writing materials every two weeks. [18] In 1896 writing classes remained "the most popular study." [19]

By no means did prisoners have access to regular education; and after spending a day at the mines, an evening in a classroom may not have appealed to all. Furthermore, only state prisoners gained the benefits of state-funded stationery. County prisoners, it would seem, never enjoyed these letter-writing privileges. Nevertheless, a significant number of black prisoners wrote to their families and attorneys; they also requested pardons. Well-placed letters of complaint to inspectors or the governor also served as weapons of protest, which occasionally produced results. If a prisoner could not write, access to stationery still allowed him to correspond, as many no doubt employed the services of literate men. This sanctioned communication connected prisoners with the outside world and gave hope to many. Literacy and letter writing were an important part of the black prisoners' world in late nineteenth-century Alabama; they helped many prisoners to endure their incarceration.

The Black Belt region remained tied to the economy of its slaveholding past; in these fertile counties, former slaves continued to grow corn, sugarcane, and the king of all crops, cotton.[20] But extraordinary changes also occurred in the Black Belt and in Mobile during Reconstruction. In these communities blacks were often the numerical majority, and they enthusiastically participated in politics.

In religion, in politics, and in the cotton fields, the freedpeople began to form new organizations, often with individuals they scarcely knew. The confined world of the slave plantation was giving way to a more open society in which African Americans moved and migrated. Kolchin stresses that blacks migrated to affirm their freedom; Freedmen's Bureau agents, in contrast, described indigent black wanderers forced from their homes at the war's end. In either case, although Alabama freedpeople tended to stay within the state, they migrated to the region where blacks comprised the majority, the Alabama Black Belt.[21]

Before emancipation, more than half of the black population in the region (over 150,000 people) lived on plantations consisting of fifty or more slaves.[22] Certainly the experience of living in large slave quarters left many freedpeople hungry for individual privacy and achievement. Prevailing Republican ideology also stressed the ideal of individualism. Countering such beliefs, however, was the legacy of the old "slave quarter community" that had emphasized the importance of racial solidarity.[23]

Even before the formation of Union Leagues and the Republican party, collective action pervaded black life. Freedpeople organized mass religious gatherings and traveled across state lines to attend them. In the summer of 1865, for example, thousands of black Alabamians from Selma and Montgomery, hearing of a great revival in northern Georgia, journeyed hundreds of miles to attend a four-day religious revival. This meeting, sponsored by missionaries from the northern Methodist Church, occurred only months after emancipation, and the multitudes rejoiced in freedom. A "small" crowd of 800 on Friday grew to a throng of 5,000 or 6,000 by the weekend. Rev. J. F. Chalfant, the white minister in charge, was astonished at the gathering. "Such a spectacle had never been witnessed in 'dixie' in the days of slavery," he wrote to his superior. "On Saturday they began to pour in from all the adjoining counties and from Alabama. They came from Atlanta, West Point, Montgomery and some even from Selma. . . . But with this immense multitude there was not the slightest disturbance irregularity or disorder—all was calm, quiet, and beautiful." Although strangers to each other, thousands of freedpeople organized themselves into an orderly congregation of audience and participants. On Saturday they listened to the address of an elderly black male preacher, a former slave. Those who attended Sunday school led the march. Whites stood aloof and watched. Reverend Chalfant described the scene. "The vast multitude on Saturday joined the procession of Sunday School scholars and marched to the stand to hear an address. . . . It was beautiful to see them marching in good order and hear them singing the song with the chorus 'March on, March on, singing as you go. March on, March on, do not fear the foe.'"[24] Religious gatherings soon became intertwined with political and economic organizing as African-American Republicans used their collective might to overcome their political foes.[25]

African-American attitudes toward postwar courts were strongly influenced by the legacy of slavery. But that legacy was complex. Slavery established the legalized racial subordination of black people. Antebellum Alabama courts upheld the "absolute right of correction" of slave owners; even nonslaveholding whites who murdered blacks were rarely imprisoned. In some matters legal authority took precedence over the will of a particular owner. If a slaveholder attempted to free his slaves in his will or pay for their passage "back to Africa," Alabama courts refused to allow it. Regardless of the wishes of the slaveholder, slaves could not inherit wealth or freedom. They "could not be invested with civil rights or legal capacities."[26] The legal history of slavery in Alabama, the ensuing legislation of the Black Codes, and subsequent laws pertaining to larceny, segregation, and disfranchisement warrant a cynical interpretation of southern law as nothing better than "white law." Indeed, the fast-rising number of black prisoners in the 1870s and 1880s and the near absence of incarcerated whites illustrate the racial impact of an increasingly repressive legal system.

As much as they recognized the repressive aspects of southern law, however, black Alabamians also believed in its potential ability to dispense justice. That belief, strangely, also derived, in part, from slavery times. Black slaves in Alabama saw how the courts wielded power, even over white masters. They may also have witnessed the acquittal of slaves accused of crimes. As Eugene Genovese, James Sellers, and other historians have pointed out, antebellum judges who sat in high courts looked at evidence scrupulously; an arrest did not necessarily bring a conviction, even if the defendant was a black slave. This legal structure, in which the courts had the final say in disputes, impressed black people. The South, to be sure, remained a region of dueling and feuding, especially after freedom. However, black people frequently appealed to the Freedmen's Bureau, the federal government, and local legal authorities for justice.

Republican ideals of equality before the law, as expressed in the Fourteenth Amendment, influenced freed men and women to pursue justice by bringing white and black alike into court. As Eric Foner has shown, blacks demanded and expected every right enjoyed by whites including "the rights to vote and to education, the free exercise of religion, access to the courts," and equal economic opportunity. And black religion, according to Foner, "reinforced black Republicanism" by reassuring congregations that the Civil War was "God's instrument of deliverance and Reconstruction as another step in a divinely ordained process."[27]

Thus the residue of legal formalism, abstract political theory, and the faith, developed under slavery, in the power of God's justice all merged to create an ideology of popular justice among blacks in which the courts played a central role. For example, in an anonymous missive signed only "for justis," a group of black workingmen in Montgomery told Governor Seay that all who "do rong" or "violate the laws of the land" should receive "just sentence." Do not, they wrote, "release the white man under the pretense of being crazzie . . . and covic the negro for Life Time[;] no[.] That not just & some one shall atone for it sooner or later."[28] Another letter from Pike County complained that even if a black man brought "a hondred widness," he would still be convicted: "We Can not get no jest ist in these courts."[29] Jane Lightfoot, the mother of a prisoner convicted for life, also invoked the quality of justice in her letter to the governor: "I can not feel that this court have give him jestus so will you please to instruct me in this matter that my child may get justise."[30] Despite witnessing racism in the courts, the freedpeople still firmly believed that, ideally, the legal system should dispense justice.

Because the Freedmen's Bureau represented the federal government, the freedpeople expected its agents to administer justice, even if that meant using force. In November 1865 a group of freedmen in Tuscumbia, Alabama, wrote a letter to the Freedmen's Bureau and listed their community's grievances. They outlined the ways in which white citizens used the law to restrain black life unfairly. "We want a school here and cant get one . . . if we have money we can't buy any thing . . . exsept we get a white man to get it for us . . . if we get sick we cant get 5 cnts worth of whiskey exsept getting a order from a white man . . . they says it is agants the law to sell negroes powder & shot (and even if you) had the amminusion you has not got the land to hunt on . . . if a white man strik you with a rock you are not lowed to lok mad at him." The freedmen were not willing to accept these indignities and restraints on their freedom. And they expressed their desires with one word: justice. "We want Justice we want justice general you can send us one company if you please. We are treated here like dogs."[31] The unwillingness of whites to give up control caused the freedpeople to feel hemmed in, and they strained against the tight rope of white domination. They hoped the Freedmen's Bureau would send troops, come to their aid, and ultimately enforce justice.

Although freedpeople looked to the bureau, the limitations of its officers were painfully obvious. In a gesture designed to make the agency more representative, African Americans in Tuscaloosa elected a black Civil War veteran to act on their behalf and requested that the bureau designate him an official agent. "By a meeting of the colard people of this city we deem it proper to pertission to Gen Swain to grant to us the appointment of some man to the Freedmen Burau and to this end a committee of eleven men and desired that Capt Anderson of the 58 reg." The group expected the bureau to help them rent land and make fair labor contracts. They also wanted the bureau to enforce the Bill of Rights and accused the police, in effect, of violating the Second and Fourth Amendments to the Constitution. "Our police gard serches our houses for arms and takes what little money we have." The freedmen ended their list of complaints with a pointed reference to the Declaration of Independence: "This is not the persuit of happiness." [32] By appealing to the bureau and to the democratic principles it supposedly represented, these Tuscaloosa freedmen signaled that they expected and demanded justice.

Many of these same nondeferential attitudes and a concern for justice appear in the letters of black prisoners. Frank Knox, born in 1864, was forced to work his sentence twice, once for the city and once for the county. "Dear Governor," he asked, "please let me no Is that right Sir I beg you for justus." [33] Prisoners tried to hold those in authority to the letter of the law. In a letter to Governor Seay in 1890, Henry Haden, released from prison and working as a free miner in Bessemer, expressed his outrage at serving over eleven months in prison when his total sentence was nine. "I want to know who is responsible for it. . . . Please tell me whether I am write are wrong Please write me at once Hon. Governor." [34] High expectations of the courts and the law endured among many black prisoners, despite their incarceration.

The African-American community from which black prisoners came was often in conflict. Many divisions existed within it: class, color, gender, and even political persuasion. Black Democrats regularly crossed swords with African-American Republicans. Men and women clashed over political issues and, later, over the proper behavior of women. Black communities also divided over how to behave toward whites: should they continue to battle for their individual rights, or should they rely upon white paternalism for protection? These questions were never fully resolved. In many ways their roots lie in Reconstruction, when African Americans often disagreed about how best to advance.

Yet black communities also exhibited a discipline, a kind of self-regulation, that enabled them to mitigate those differences. In order to promote solidarity, the freedpeople practiced a form of social control not usually recognized by historians and social scientists.[35] Historians have used the term *social control* to describe the negative, repressive effect of white law on black communities. From the perspective of black communities, however, social control meant something more. As David Rothman, the noted historian of the asylum and the penitentiary, has stated, "Those who think of social control as more or less synonymous with repression and coercion may be startled to discover that American sociologists first used the term to capture the very opposite quality, that of cooperation, of voluntary and harmonious cohesion." [36] Rothman warned scholars not to impose upon the societies they studied a simplistic grid consisting only of individuals and a coercive state. He saw how the power of culture and community acted as a cohesive and unifying force. It is doubtful that the freedpeople would have been able to achieve what they did during Reconstruction without employing mechanisms of social control to ensure group solidarity. Another term for it might be *community regulation*.

Such regulation within black communities came into play especially when Democrats tried to lure black voters into their camp. As the party of influential landowning whites, Democrats could promise a freedman employment, money, or land if he rejected Republicanism. The terrorism of the Ku Klux Klan might also dissuade a freedman from voting the Republican ticket. In 1868 a Freedmen's Bureau agent in Greene County noted the rising tension among blacks in the community on account of political differences. The agent reported that whites threatened to fire black carpenters and barbers if they did not vote for the Democrats. Black Republicans, however, answered with their own form of persuasion. The agent reported that "the few [blacks] who are reported to have put their names down as supporters of the [Seymour and Blair Democratic ticket] have incurred the bitter hostility of the colored people who are arrayed in the opposite political organization." [37]

The consequences of breaking Republican solidarity could be severe. Stories abound of black churches excommunicating "traitors" who voted Democratic and of black "whipping clubs" designed to punish black Democrats. When Huff Cheney, a black Republican living in Butler County, informed on his local Republican collective, the group whipped him before allowing him back into the fold. [38] When asked if "Democratic negroes" associated with black Republicans in Montgomery, a twenty-three-year-old black Republican, Robert Ford, tersely responded, "They do not do it." He added, "I do not recognize them as much as I do those who vote the Republican ticket." Even well-protected African-American Democrats feared reprisals. Ceasar Shorter, former slave of ex-governor John Gill Shorter and servant of Democratic governor Robert Lindsay, admitted that he did not stray far from Montgomery: he feared being accosted by blacks hostile to him because of his political ties to the Democrats. [39]

White Democrats sought to attract black voters through rewards and punishments; in comparison, African-American Republicans had little to give in exchange for votes. What they had was idealism and the power of community regulation. Through churches and informal political organizations, rural black communities used the collective force of the group to discourage destructive conduct and reward behavior conducive to group progress. They practiced their own form of social control in the form of community sanctions and public shame. Some of these sanctions were punitive, including social and religious ostracism and even physical coercion. The power of community sanctions helped the freedpeople to resist the entreaties of white Democrats and strengthen the Republican party.[40]

More often group discipline was employed in a positive manner in order to ensure political success. Every political organization needs discipline; black Republicans after emancipation were no different, and successful voting required solidarity. Anxieties on election day, for example, could be eased by walking into town with a group of other black men. In 1868 the *Alabama Beacon* reported that in Greensboro, Hale County, "the freedmen came into town very early in the morning and assembled at the Court House, their place of voting. . . . They were closely banded together, very few of them having a word to say to white men." Gathering in a group served a practical purpose, too. One black organizer described how hundreds of men voted together in 1874: "I would not let the negroes break ranks. . . . I designated the tenth man as the captain of the squad of each nine men, and they went to the polls together, and we voted nearly a thousand." Even if a frightened black voter had been tempted to break ranks and run, his fellow squad members would not have allowed it.[41]

When black Alabamians from the Black Belt went to prison, they left their communities for new institutions of control, where attempts at collective action were often thwarted by brutal treatment and the need for individual survival. They encountered fellow inmates who were strangers and contractors bestowed with absolute power. After Dawson's reforms, however, prisoners began to challenge the authority of contractors. They wrote letters to the inspectors and to the governor complaining of conditions. They insisted on receiving their time cards, which showed the date of their release. They resorted to the courts; Inspector Dawson warned contractors that holding prisoners overtime would lead to "troublesome lawsuits." They also engaged in collective plots to overcome wardens, escape, and strike. Those who did act as informers were singled out by white authorities as "exceptional" prisoners and lauded for their superior character. The majority of black prisoners, however, remained indecipherable to Dawson and his fellow inspectors.

One of the most striking continuities between prisoners and freedpeople was their rejection of sycophantic behavior. Their "shell of self-importance," which so annoyed Inspector Dawson, suggests a skepticism of white pretensions to knowledge and authority. It is this independence, this unwillingness even to appear sycophantic toward whites, that prison inspectors found most outrageous about black convicts. Inspectors assumed all black prisoners were depraved, immoral, and in need of reform. Yet by 1890 Chief Inspector Dawson could only complain about the black prisoners' arrogance and indifference to white authority.

Prison was a jarring, bewildering experience for everyone. But black prisoners also had to confront overt racism. During Reconstruction, blacks often expressed racial pride in public. "As evidence of our superiority as a race," exclaimed one black speaker at a mass rally in Montgomery, "I can tell you that I am a member of the Alabama Legislature, and there are fifty white members who are not as well qualified for the position as we negroes."[42] In prison, however, black convicts were reminded every day of their subordination and subjected to constant racist epithets and racial abuse. How, then, to explain Dawson's observations about "self-esteem"?

Studies of slavery suggest that, paradoxically, slavery fostered feelings of racial superiority among blacks. Having been victimized by the cruelty of the "peculiar institution,' and seeing the pride, laziness, and immorality of the slaveholder, many slaves could only shake their heads in disbelief. They often felt themselves to be superior to whites in their ability to work hard, behave morally, and exercise common sense. According to Thomas Webber, blacks knew that whites possessed power, but they did not confuse that might with right.[43]

Similarly, prisoners recognized their powerless position. Yet they still saw the discrepancy between their importance and their treatment. "We all know that we being Colord Men have not the chanses of the white men and we at the same time know that we are the greatest in Nomber," insisted Ezekiel Archey in 1884. "We ar the men who do the work. . . . Please look at the white men and see how many are cuting 5 or 4 ton coal per day. They are few."[44] The harder Archey worked at mining coal, and the more skilled he and other black prisoners became, the more keenly they felt their superiority. Prisoners recognized their indispensable role as miners. Day after day they completed the most arduous of tasks. Although they knew their race placed them at a disadvantage, African-American prisoners felt they worked harder than their white counterparts. Within the world of the prison mines, prisoners developed a new basis of self-esteem based upon both their experiences during Reconstruction and their newly developed skills as expert miners.[45]

Black women prisoners often showed an even greater tendency toward self-assertion than their male counterparts. They especially resented attempts to force them to wear prison clothing, limit their freedom of movement, and control their sexual activity. Such behavior was not peculiar to women in prison; it was typical of the patterns of resistance exhibited by slave women, and even more typical of newly emancipated black women who wished to reject old patterns of slave deference. Inspector A. T. Henley was particularly appalled by the behavior of female county convicts at Coal-burg. "These female prisoners are certainly the most unruly and disorderly convicts that I have ever had to manage," he wrote to Dawson, "& it will be necessary to enforce discipline at the cost of a good deal of punishment I am afraid." [46] Female prisoners and freedwomen both exhibited a coeval independence of spirit.

Alabama freedwomen asserted themselves both personally and politi-cally. In Alabama black women attended the earliest Republican gather-ings. In May 1867 the *Alabama Beacon* of Hale County reported that "about twenty five hundred males and females of the colored race assembled, with white friends invited, to organize for the purpose of appointing delegates to the Montgomery Convention." In August black women and men walked twenty to thirty miles to attend a political rally and barbecue sponsored by the Republican party. African-American men and women met in churches and at outdoor gatherings to select representatives.[47] Black women also or-ganized themselves into church groups, meeting with other women in dif-ferent cities. Black women lacked the franchise, but as Elsa Barkley Brown has argued, black women in the South sought to "catch the vision of free-dom" through public participation in politics.[48]

Democratic newspapers frequently made freedwomen the butt of ridi-cule. When those women became involved in acts of protest, white rheto-ric turned threatening. After Alex Webb, an African-American voter regis-trar, was murdered in broad daylight on the streets of Greensboro, Hale County, black women and men took to the streets in protest. The behavior of the black women in the crowd drew the opprobrium of the press, which referred to one female as a "tigress." "We shall not be astonished," the paper predicted, "if the first grand jury organized in Hale County should give her case their special attention. We heard of several others, of the same gender, whose deportment and language proved that they were ripe for arson, murder, or any other diabolical crime." [49] Catherine Clinton has argued that during Reconstruction the Democratic press depicted black women as dangerous, aggressive, unrestrained, and criminal.[50] By attempt-ing to exercise political rights that they did not formally possess, black women invited scorn, abuse, and arrest from the Democrats.

Nevertheless, black women in Alabama did participate in politics and even assumed leadership. During the summer of 1874, black and white Re-publicans held meetings in a variety of local spots and businesses in Mont-gomery—Peter Goode's barbershop, Drayman's Hall, and Peacock Track—to prepare for the upcoming elections. One person who spoke at these public places and from her own market stall was a street merchant by the name of Ann Pollard. When Pollard called for female suffrage and con-demned her political opponents, Democratic papers paid special attention. "Ann Pollard performed last night on the subject of colored women's rights and the horrors of the Democratic party," the *Montgomery Advertiser* noted in September 1874. Between 1874 and 1877 newspapers denounced her activities. "That old woman, Ann Pollard, has broke loose again, and performed to a delighted body of ebonies at Drayman's Hall Wed. Night." Pollard directed her speeches to men and women. According to the *Montgomery Advertiser,* she "told the negro men to shoot every colored man who voted the Democratic ticket and advised black women 'to have nothing to do with any black man who voted aginst we 'publicans.'" The paper called for Pollard's arrest. "Of all the nuisances in Montgomery, Ann Pollard is the most intolerable. If there is no law to reach her case, one should be devised. . . . We consider her a fit subject for the handcuffs and chains now so plentiful in this happy land."[51]

African-American women in Marengo County also urged black voters to remain loyal to the Republicans and shamed those who might be tempted toward voting for the Democrats. On election day in 1874, "a lot of negro women collected on the public square here and made all sorts of threats against Democratic 'niggers,'" a Democratic paper reported. The Alabama historian Walter Fleming asserted, rather negatively, that "negro women were a strong support to the Union League, and took a leading part in the prosecution of negro Democrats."[52] In her poem "Deliverance," by contrast, the abolitionist Frances E. W. Harper celebrated the behavior of ordinary black women who withheld food, clothing, and sex from partners who traded their votes for a mess of Democratic pottage.[53]

Even after Alabama had been "redeemed" in 1874, Democratic papers continued to portray black women's involvement in politics, however mild, in a negative light. One article described a speech made by John C. Keffer, a white Republican, to a group of black women at a Colored Methodist Episcopal Church service as an "inflammatory appeal." Keffer had urged the women "to see that their sweethearts, fathers, husbands, brothers voted the Radical ticket in the approaching city election." Women did not enter politics lightly or without risk. Besides being threatened with arrest, Ann Pollard was attacked with a brick. Eventually she was forced to leave her market stall in downtown Montgomery. The *Marengo News Journal* reminded black women in 1876 that "the law against intimidation of voters applies to women as well as men." If African-American women harassed black Democrats as they had done in the past, "they will find themselves in trouble."[54] Although the threat of arrest followed black women in all of these instances, it should be noted that their behavior was not necessarily illegal, though most definitely "unruly."[55]

To white men who demanded sexual subservience and personal deference, the challenges that black women posed in both personal and political realms were bound to upset the legal authorities. Although "unruly" behavior among black female convicts such as talking back and flaunting rules deeply disturbed prison authorities, it ultimately enabled many black women to meet the exigencies of prison.

Not all aspects of freedom found fertile ground in prison. Churches, although a key institution among the freedpeople, could not really exist in convict labor camps, which, in the late nineteenth century, provided prisoners only with an occasional preacher. Although there are reports of individual prisoners praying, there are many more descriptions of them gambling. It was difficult, in other words, to transplant the black church, which was, in essence, a community institution that prided itself on its independence from whites, into a prison setting, where the ministers were chosen by prison authorities. Individual religious faith no doubt sustained many convicts, particularly women, who often mentioned God in their letters to the governor. The institution of the black church, however, represented more than a forum for prayer. It was an expression of racial autonomy and a refuge of racial privacy that had no place in an institution based upon white control.

Compelled to engage in forced labor and subject to brutal mistreatment, black prisoners were in a situation that has been compared, unfavorably, to that of slaves. Yet before their imprisonment Alabama convicts had experienced something slaves never had: freedom. With freedom, blacks took the opportunity to gain education, directly challenge white provocation, form families, create churches, assert themselves, and act in concert. These benefits could not transfer neatly to a prison setting, but neither could they all be entirely quashed. Freedom left black Alabamians vulnerable to new forms of legal repression and control. But freedom also enabled black prisoners to create new challenges against white control and forced prison labor.

Crime and Social Conflict

■ Although the vast majority of Alabama's antebellum prisoners were white, the popular perception was that the South's true criminals were its black slaves. During the 1870s the growing number of black prisoners in the South further buttressed the belief that African Americans were inherently criminal and, in particular, prone to larceny. Newspapers across the Black Belt noted an increase in convictions for petty theft; even the very young were swept up. In Greene County in 1874, three "little negro boys" received twelve months in the county jail for taking oranges and a bottle of wine from a local store.[1] As counties were not required to keep track of their convicts until 1883, the exact number of county convicts at this time is uncertain. But newspapers occasionally indicated the number of people in local jails. In January 1875 the *Eutaw Whig and Observer* noted that "there are now twenty seven prisoners in the jail at this place, all negroes." A month earlier the same paper had tersely noted: "51 prisoners in Dallas Jail, all negroes." In an article entitled "Who Commits Crime in the South," the *Montgomery Advertiser* asserted that for the year 1874 in Montgomery County 2,538 people had been arrested. Of these, 775 were whites, including 13 white women, and 1,763 were black, including 441 black females. Although the vast majority of the arrests were for "disorderly conduct and drunkenness," the paper pointed out that 309 people were arrested for larceny, "all of whom" were freedpeople. The article then went on to condemn "negroes" as people with "low morals."[2]

The number of state prisoners also rose dramatically in this period, tripling to over 700 between 1874 and 1877. According to the annual report on the penitentiary published at the end of 1877, 522 prisoners out of a total of 779, or 67 percent, had been imprisoned for either grand larceny or burglary.[3] What accounted for this startling increase in convictions for theft? One theory asserts that changes in the law turned petty pilfering into felonious larceny. Vernon Wharton has argued that Mississippi whites, frustrated with black thieving, passed draconian legislation: the infamous "Pig Law," which punished the theft of a small animal with five years in the penitentiary. David Oshinsky has similarly argued that Mississippi's 1876 Pig Law pushed that state's prison population from 272 men to over 1,000.[4] Alabama imposed similar changes in its legal code with predictable results. For example, Ann Austin, a freedwoman in Greene County, was convicted of grand larceny and sentenced to two years in the state penitentiary for "killing a shoat." When she appealed, Judge Luther Smith could not reduce her time as the sentence was "the least term of imprisonment allowed by law."[5] Austin's case is a typical example of an individual caught within the web of the South's crackdown on petty theft.

Although Wharton and Oshinsky believed that black pig stealers and other petty criminals received unduly harsh punishment for their behavior, both assert that streams of black convicts—former slaves accustomed to surviving by stealing—had indeed committed theft. This "flood of criminals" caused "enormous strain" on southern prisons after the Civil War, according to Oshinsky, and thus pushed southern states such as Mississippi to adopt a profitable prison system. Edward Ayers, a leading historian of the New South, concurs, concluding that a black "crime wave" swept Dixie after emancipation. This behavior, in turn, produced a legal crackdown. In Ayers's view the depression of the 1870s spurred on a growing number of property crimes by increasing the number of "desperate men," all African-American. According to Ayers, extraordinarily high numbers of black men became prisoners because "southern whites . . . were persuaded that black crime was out of control." He also attributes the rising tide of black crime in the late nineteenth century to tramps and vagrants who transgressed laws designed to curtail black mobility. Blacks known to whites were protected from arrest. But those "with no white boss to speak up for them or pay their bail found themselves at the mercy of local police and courts."[6]

Although sympathetic to the plight of black prisoners and aware of how a racist legal system worked to the detriment of blacks, none of these historians challenges the assumption that freedpeople indeed stole. Ayers, Oshinsky, and Wharton argue, sympathetically, that economic "hard times" led to increased vagrancy and theft among the freedpeople. And yet according to them legitimate white fears, black behavior, and harsh laws led to growing numbers of African-American prisoners. Thus historians, newspapers accounts, and prison statistics all seem to confirm that African Americans committed far more property crimes than did whites.

But criminal charges of theft also concealed deep conflicts between the freedpeople and their political opponents and employers, conflicts that cannot always be seen in the official records. The case of freedman Smith Watley of Coosa County is an example. In the city of Montgomery during the summer of 1871, U.S. Attorney John A. Minnis took Watley's statement swearing that a group of fifteen or twenty disguised members of the Ku Klux Klan had whipped him. Minnis, assigned to the Middle District of Alabama by the Justice Department to investigate the Klan and violations of the Enforcement Act, issued subpoenas and planned to take the case before a grand jury. Watley, scheduled to testify in November, returned home to Coosa County only to find a portion of his crop had been picked and confiscated by his landlord as payment for rent. Determined to leave his employer on good terms, Watley and his family picked the remaining cotton, took it to the gin, and turned over two more bales to the landowner. He then arranged to pick up his one remaining bale of cotton the following week. A few days later, as he was taking his cotton to Montgomery, he was arrested—for stealing. Watley was tried the next day and sent to jail. Minnis intervened and had him released, but in May 1872 a grand jury indicted Watley for grand larceny. "Here is a sample of the beauties of *local law*," an outraged Minnis wrote to his superior in Washington. "I know there is no more pretence to charge him with stealing that bale of cotton than there is to charge you or I. . . . And I tell you this is not an isolated case."[7]

There is no doubt that during Reconstruction, whites complained vociferously about black thieving and employed whatever means they could, including arrests and Klan violence, to halt it.[8] But as the case of Smith Watley shows, theft charges also served as subterfuge for political revenge. After emancipation the courtroom became an ideal place to exact racial retribution.

Certain assumptions about black criminality in this period cry out for reconsideration. The existence of legal formalism obscured the social revolution occurring in southern society, a revolution in which freedpeople challenged traditional expectations of deference. Historians have not appreciated the social and political struggles that underpinned the legal charges brought against the freedmen. As Smith Watley's case shows, criminal charges were used to intimidate assertive blacks.

Local law could also be used to squelch black economic gain. Historians have focused on the legal disputes between landowners and sharecroppers; indeed, it was perhaps inevitable that after slavery's demise freedpeople and landowners would dispute the ownership of cotton grown on one man's land with another family's labor. But an even greater struggle was occurring over access to markets. After 1874 the Alabama legislature targeted "deadfalls"—informal markets catering to the needs of black farmers. Freedmen who bought and sold goods at such markets became vulnerable to charges of larceny.

It would be foolish to assert the innocence of all prisoners, yet the evidence shows that it is equally erroneous to accept the guilt of all blacks charged with larceny, especially during Reconstruction.

Legal disputes between black workers and white employers began with emancipation. Although the Freedmen's Bureau exercised legal authority in Alabama until 1867, it never organized separate Freedmen's Courts, as it did very briefly in Mississippi, for example. Instead, General Wager Swayne, head of the bureau in Alabama, kept local justices of the peace in their posts and swore them in as agents of the bureau. "We had not officers enough to establish more than ten courts," Swayne told a northern observer. "I therefore proposed to educate the civil courts to do the freedmen justice." Swayne required only two conditions of the justices: a sworn oath of loyalty to the Union and a promise to accept black testimony.[9]

In making white southerners and ex-Confederates agents of the bureau, Swayne believed he was taking a practical approach to the problem of Reconstruction. He knew that the bureau was only a temporary agency; it made sense to him to work within existing institutions, using men accustomed to legal administration. If local justices of the peace acknowledged blacks as plaintiffs, witnesses, and defendants, then other whites would come to accept the legality and reality of black freedom.[10] Or so Swayne hoped.

Yet men accustomed to adjudicating the laws of slavery found it hard to fathom the sweeping changes brought by emancipation. As one frustrated but professedly loyal justice of the peace wrote to Swayne in 1865, "I cannot act under the Laws of '61 for the negro is not *now* as he was then. . . . I am constantly applied to by Negroes with complaints of a criminal nature, and know as little how to proceed as if I had never lived in the 19 century, am cursed by your officers, abused by abolitionists, grievously complained at by negroes . . . and generally mixed up as any man must be who knowing not his duty cannot perform it."[11] Right after emancipation blacks appealed to local courts for justice. Yet the vow taken by the justices to accept black testimony could not create color-blind courts or laws. Nor could it counteract the stark reality that no consensus existed, even among bureau agents and the Republican party, as to whether African Americans were to be truly equal to whites under the law.

For example, according to General Swayne, Alabama's strict new vagrancy laws, although written in racially neutral language, applied only to freedpeople. "No reference to color was expressed in terms," he noted, "but in practice the distinction is invariable." The scope of vagrancy was wide. A "stubborn or refractory servant," a servant who "loiters," or simply a servant who refused to comply with "any contract for any term of service without just cause" could all be considered vagrants and hence subject to a minimum fine of $50 or six months' imprisonment. One justice of the peace warned the bureau that arrests for vagrancy and "other offenses of a similar character" were so frequent that his local jail was overflowing with black prisoners unable to pay fines.[12]

Indeed, many economic activities associated with freedom led to arrest and hard labor for the county. When the journalist John Trowbridge visited Selma in 1866 and asked about "a chain-gang of Negroes at work on the street," he was told that "one had sold farm produce within the town limits. . . . For this offence he had been fined twenty dollars, which, being unable to pay, he had been put upon the chain."[13] Even going into business offered legal hazards. Black laundresses, for example, were charged a $5 license fee; those who failed to pay were arrested. Davy Cutler, a black barber in Marengo County, pleaded guilty to "keeping a barber's Shop without a license." He was charged $31 in court costs and a $30 fine. Without the intervention of two white benefactors, he would have gone to the chain gang.[14]

Cash garnered from trials, fines, and fees paid the salaries of local officials and encouraged abuse. Freedpeople who came to the courts as plaintiffs with complaints against other blacks could find themselves the victims of unscrupulous practices. According to Agent Gardner, "It is the practice, whenever colored litigants are brought up, to fine both parties without regard to evidence and exact cash from both." Another agent claimed that freedmen were arrested and tried for vagrancy so that lawyers, sheriffs, and judges could collect payment. "The *case* has lost its interest when the *fees* and *costs* are pocketed by some Justice of the County," he wrote.[15]

Although repealed with the passage of the Fourteenth Amendment, the Black Codes left a legacy. Branded as a criminal class, the freedpeople continued to be victimized by de facto legal discrimination based on their race. Equally important, the fee system begun under the Black Codes remained firmly in place. Forced to pay for their own court costs, which included the fees of lawyers, jurors, judges, and sheriffs, as well as the cost of food, county prisoners had up to eight extra months tacked onto their sentences so as to work off fees amounting to $50 or more.

Undoubtedly, black theft inspired white indignation. But blacks and whites, tenants and landlords, defined theft very differently. For example, although whites often refused to pay blacks for the work they performed, this was never defined as a crime. In Mobile a bureau agent wrote to his superior that "the people here feel indignant that they are obliged to hire the negroes they used to own and will by every possible means endeavor to evade the payment of wages due them." In the fall of 1865, other agents in the Black Belt saw black workers, evicted from farms after the crop had been harvested, wandering the roads "starving and naked." An agent from eastern Mississippi observed empty-handed freedpeople from western Alabama fleeing from cruel treatment: "The plan has been adopted by many [whites] of forcing [freedpeople] off their lands after the crop has been made without any remuneration. . . . Several have appeared badly bruised and showing unmistakable signs of brutal treatments." [16]

Sometimes judges recognized that the freedmen had been robbed of wages, yet the law left them little room to define this as theft. A case involving two black males, employed grinding sugar on a plantation in Lowndes County, is illustrative. B. F. Blow, manager of John Marrast's sugar plantation, brought suit against Jerry and Abram Marrast. Blow accused the two Marrast men of being "absent from labor on a certain day." Both men admitted to taking an afternoon off. Blow wanted to discharge the freedmen, expel them from the plantation, and force both to forfeit all of their pay.

Judge Pruitt looked carefully at the labor contract, which required a working day of nineteen hours. Technically, any absence from work, for whatever reason, constituted a violation of the contract and brought forfeiture of wages. Pruitt ordered the two guilty defendants to pay for all court costs and to leave the plantation. However, he ordered Blow to pay the men for the work they had already performed.[17]

Pruitt knew that most judges would have allowed Blow to dismiss the workers without any pay at all. In a letter to General Swayne, the judge spelled out how existing labor contracts allowed landowners to steal from their workers. "One hand's wages would be worth in money $18 for the three months. The 80 hands wages, in money for three months labor would amount to $1440. Is it right, is it just, is it honorable, that the employer shall receive this large sum of money from the labor of his poor and ignorant freedmen because they have violated their contract by not complying to the very letter of the agreement? Is it right that they should be turned loose to the community without a cent to die by starvation or compelled to steal to satisfy the cravings of hunger?" [18] One could argue that the fault lay with the contract, but in 1865 the freedpeople had little choice but to sign these grossly unfair documents—indeed, the Freedmen's Bureau had encouraged them to do so.[19]

Neither judges nor bureau agents knew how to deal with landowners who refused to pay their employees. The bureau specifically forbade its agents to arrest or pressure landlords who were tardy in their payment of wages. Bureau agents could report, indignantly, when they witnessed freedmen being cheated out of wages, but they could do nothing more.[20] Agents debated among themselves why landowners refused to pay wages—was it simply poverty? One bureau agent thought whites feared losing their status in the county. "The insolvency and financial embarrassments of the planter princes in the neighborhood [Greene County] are a principal cause. It is difficult for them to sustain their present position in society if they deal justly with their colored laborers who make the crops on land heavily encumbered." Freedmen could complain, or leave, or even steal if provoked by hunger. None of these tactics, however, resulted in wages.

One other option remained. In 1868 hundreds of black farmers in Greene County took white landowners to court and sued them. A civil suit brought a landowner's assets, which included land and cotton, into court. By employing this tactic, the freedmen showed they understood the nature of the new legal and economic order. If they could be forced to adhere to contracts, then so could whites. The freedmen's efforts, however, came to naught. According to a bureau agent, the sheriff of Greene County resigned rather than "attach white man's cotton at the suit of 'niggers.' " As the same agent reported in 1868, "When debtors [planters] failed to get the court stopped up at Eutaw by a false telegram . . . they burned up the Court House with records of eighteen hundred suits." [21]

Although they met with little success, freedmen in Alabama continued to challenge nonpayment of wages through the courts. Robert Ford, a black Republican from Montgomery County, told a congressional committee in 1874 that he had been "in court two or three times on account of men owing me money, and I lost the case every time; so I quit." [22] African Americans considered themselves the victims of property crimes as well as violence, but it was whites who complained about a postbellum crime wave.

Undoubtedly nonpayment of wages and general destitution caused freedpeople to commit petty crimes. As one historian has noted, many blacks "either resorted to stealing or starved." [23] By 1868 planters in the Black Belt complained profusely about small-scale crime, particularly the theft of animals. A bureau agent in Greene County observed, "Petit larceny seems to be rapidly increasing. Shoats and poultry seem to be mainly in quest and they are disappearing beyond precedent." The agent then went on to discuss why this was happening. "Planters universally are curtailing their advances to laborers, in many instances they are issuing rations to laborers only, leaving them to supply their families as best they can. This compels them to divide their scanty rations with their families or resort to stealing as the only alternative." To the agent the main problem was the grossly unfair labor contracts the freedpeople signed. "I have discouraged contracts of this tenor," he wrote, "but the laborers being abundant the unmutable laws of supply and demand which regulate all commodities rendered my efforts of little avail." [24]

Undoubtedly the legacy of slavery, not to mention the social chaos spawned by the Civil War, sanctioned certain kinds of stealing, especially if the property owner was white. Historians have documented the deprivations, especially of food, slaves were forced to endure, and they have established that slaves considered the theft of food as justified. Some have argued that slave theft was really a "moral economy" in action, and one could interpret postbellum theft in a similar vein. Yet Eugene Genovese rejects the moral economy argument. He contends that slave theft illustrated the damaging effects that slavery had upon black behavior patterns. By forcing them to steal, Genovese argues, slavery did indeed turn some slaves into thieves, no matter the greater injustice such thefts attempted to alleviate.[25]

Regardless of how such behavior is interpreted, a tit-for-tat retribution for nonpayment of wages or curtailed rations cannot account for the every charge of theft. By 1874 the most controversial economic crime in the Alabama Black Belt involved neither food nor pigs. The most bitter economic conflicts centered around access to markets, particularly informal stores known as "deadfalls." Since 1869 planters had complained about small amounts of cotton being bought and sold informally on the street.[26] By the 1870s such markets had become more formal, and white merchants condemned them as a scourge. Their view is supported by Reconstruction historian Walter Fleming who in 1905 stated that "one of the worst evils that afflicted the Black Belt was the so-called deadfall." According to Fleming,

> A Deadfall was a low shop or store where a white thief encouraged black people to steal all kind of farm produce and exchange it with him for bad whiskey, bad candy, brass jewelry etc. This evil was found all over the state where there were negroes. Whites and industrious blacks lost hogs, poultry, cattle, corn in the fields, cotton in the fields and in the gin. The business of the deadfall was usually done at night. The thirsty negro would go into a cotton field and pick a sack of cotton worth a dollar, or take a bushel of corn from the nearest field and exchange it at a deadfall for a glass of whiskey, a plug of tobacco, or a dime. . . . A bill was introduced into the legislature to prohibit the purchase after dark of farm produce from any one but the producer. The measure was unanimously opposed by the radicals, on the grounds that it was class legislation aimed at the negroes. The debates show that some of them considered it proper for a negro to steal from his employer. After the Democratic victory in 1874, a law was passed abolishing deadfalls.[27]

As Sarah Woolfolk Wiggins has pointed out, Fleming, "a child of his own age," believed in the fundamental inferiority of blacks. "His racial prejudices are so obvious as to be noticeable to even a casual reader, and thereby their danger is minimized."[28] And so while Fleming's racist caricatures of "the thirsty negro" can be rejected, his description of deadfalls as a pervasive threat to white merchants and landlords must be reckoned with.

Other evidence indicates that deadfalls were much more than simply places for black thieves to hawk their stolen wares. On the contrary, these markets served as an important expression of black independence and economic freedom. In order to understand deadfalls and the significance of independent markets in a sharecropping economy, one needs to understand the shifts in labor arrangements that were occurring in the Black Belt, particularly the emergence of African-American renters.

The controversy over deadfalls had its origins in conflicts over black economic independence. Increasingly, freedpeople rejected contracts requiring gang labor, nineteen-hour days, or wages paid at the end of the season. They wanted independence from white supervision, and they wanted to control the pace of work and the marketing of the cotton crop. White landlords, finding it difficult to offer regular wages, began to search for an alternative means of working the land. By 1868 planters in the Black Belt found very often that the best way to keep good black workers was to offer them land to rent. When blacks refused to sign wage-labor contracts, renting emerged as a "practical solution." In the Alabama Black Belt, black farmers rented land from planters such as Henry Watson and Paul Cameron. In Sumter and Macon Counties as well, it became common for black farmers to rent ten to thirty acres of land. White Republicans also rented land to blacks. Michael Fitzgerald has argued that the Union League encouraged blacks to view renting as a viable option and to pursue renting contracts as a means of establishing their independence from whites.[29] In Greene County in 1868, according to a bureau agent, "quite a number of Freedmen are farming on rented land on their own account and are doing well." In 1870 the increasing number of black farmers who had eschewed wage contracts prompted the *Alabama Beacon* to report: "Few planters in this section have been able to procure as many laborers as they wish. Many of the freedmen are renting lands and preparing to farm for themselves."[30]

As Harold Woodman notes, however, during the 1870s tenants and landlords had different definitions of what it meant to rent land. As people who had been cheated under the onerous conditions set forth in many gang-labor contracts, tenants "sought to extend the relative autonomy that tenancy allowed" by controlling what was grown and determining how to dispose of the crop. Some landowners "wanted to continue to exercise close supervision of the work on their lands" and to control the labor process as they had done under the gang-labor system. But others, in accordance with the tenancy laws, "exercised only casual or intermittent supervision of his tenants." Regardless of whether black renters in Greene paid landlords in crops or cash, they exercised more economic autonomy than the gang laborer of 1866 or the future "cropper."[31] Whatever the exact status of their agreements with white landlords, these black renters began to emerge as important agricultural producers and competitors.

When black renters began to grow and sell their own corn, whites initially accepted it, although they accused blacks of charging too much. In 1869 the *Alabama Beacon* chastised freedmen for holding on to their corn and refusing to sell for $1.50 a bushel. "We heard a colored man say a few days ago that the freedmen on the plantation where he worked had corn for sale, but they were not willing to sell now . . . they expected to get $2.50 a bushel for it next Spring. They have been very badly advised." [32] Although the freedmen hoped to turn the surplus corn to their individual advantage, their success depended on united, collective action. To ensure the price of their corn remained high, some freedmen in the Black Belt had established their own corn cartel.

Various means were used to ensure market discipline. At political meetings black Republicans discussed pricing strategies for their corn crop. Charles Daniels described the fateful gathering of the Forkland Republicans in September 1874 as "a political meeting, to nominate our men, and tell them what to do and what not to do as to the selling of their corn, &c." Once a price consensus had been reached, the black church backed it up. In 1875 the *Marengo News Journal* reported that "the colored farm laborers of this section have agreed not to sell their corn below a certain price . . . the penalty for violation of this agreement is dismissal from the church . . . when Brother Jno. Scott pronounces his 'anathema' it is equivalent in effect to condemnation of eternal damnation." For breaking community rules, black church members were threatened with ostracism—a hell on earth, rather than hell in the afterlife. The freedpeople understood the workings of the market and saw how the wealth of individuals could be enhanced through collective, disciplined action.[33]

Whites responded to the black corn cartel with outrage. "It is certainly wise in the colored farm hands to refuse to sell their corn for a song, but on the other hand they should ask no more than a fair price for it. They should need no curse of the church to keep them to this agreement." The invocation of a "fair price" revealed two things: that whites in the area depended upon black farmers for food, and that under a collective strategy black farmers had achieved a measure of economic independence.[34]

The world of African-American markets was much wider than historians have realized. Since slavery times, blacks in Alabama engaged in roadside buying and selling. According to the historian James Sellers, slaves risked imprisonment to trade in cotton, corn, cloth, and alcohol with each other, white neighbors, and merchants.[35] But what happened to those markets after slavery? Roger Ransom and Richard Sutch have argued that racism, poor transportation, and other factors led to a singularly uncompetitive market for capital in the South, which allowed rural merchants to charge exorbitant interest rates and demand that planters and sharecroppers grow a single cash crop—cotton.[36] These merchants became so powerful that it might be reasonable to assume they swallowed up the informal and illicit markets that had once served slaves in the antebellum era.

Such an assumption overlooks other evidence about African-American participation in postbellum commerce, however. On the roadside in Forkland, Greene County, black people bought and sold a variety of items. According to one observer, "Negro drummers are constantly seen on the roads and equestrians . . . met on all sides under whip and spur, we suppose of course engaging a few more pounds [of cotton] to be bought with a trifling number of yards of rotten calico, molasses, sugar—peradventure a set of CHEAP JEWELRY. Let a white man attempt a trade! Ah! Market dull!!! Figures hold out better with the INTELLIGENT negro." Much to the consternation of this letter writer, calling himself "Farmer," black traders excluded whites from their dealings.

"Farmer"'s description of the rural Black Belt economy differs from that painted by historians. The latter have depicted the rural Black Belt as a world controlled by white merchants and landowners. "Farmer," however, shows the nether world of after-hours trading. Historians have emphasized the lack of options for black sharecroppers, showing a direct transition from gang labor to sharecropping and debt peonage. But "Farmer"'s account implies that black cultivators, far from being under the control of white merchants, sold cotton, seed, and luxury goods to each other.[37]

Besides roadside markets and corn cartels, another sign of black independence from white merchants and landowners was deadfalls. Deadfalls were legal, but Democratic merchants tried to discourage them. Whites meeting in Forkland in 1873 deemed the selling of cotton and corn at night "such a great evil" that they agreed to purchase these commodities "from sunrise to sunset only, and to keep a written account from whom, when, and in what quantities we buy the same." They also reserved the right to inspect each other's account books.[38]

Democratic merchants and landowners resented the access to cotton, credit, and seed provided by deadfalls and roadside markets. Throughout the early 1870s the hysteria prompted by these markets grew by leaps and bounds. The author of one letter to the editor insisted that "the man who buys corn or cotton in small quantities at night say to the value of 50 cents ought to be declared guilty of a *felony* and punished accordingly." At stake was the extent to which whites could control black economic behavior. Newspapers complained that the blacks stole small quantities of cotton as well as entire bales. They sought to halt this behavior, however, by targeting all blacks, including renters, with cotton for sale. "We do hope . . . that when negroes profess to offer their own crops for sale the buyers will demand proof that they really own the offered produce."[39] White merchants were determined to outlaw all black trading, not just black "stealing."

The true targets of antideadfalling legislation were successful black renters. "There were no deadfalls before the class of farmers alluded to [renters] became numerous," admitted a Sumter County newspaper in 1874. "And when they [renters] disappear, deadfalls will speedily follow suit." Planters linked the economic independence of black renters with the political independence of black voters. In 1874 a "democrat" in Greene County implored "every white man who is a lover of his country and freedom not to employ or rent land the coming year to any freedman who will not agree to go to the polls on the day of election and vote as his employer does or not at all." [40] One could see the attraction such independent markets held for Republican farmers who wished to be free of the control of Democratic merchants.

Whites complained that blacks brought "stolen" cotton to deadfalls, but this assertion begs the question of how black sharecroppers interpreted ownership. The controversy over theft, in many instances, resulted from a fundamental disagreement over who had first claim to the crop. And this was a question of legitimate legal difference of opinion, not just "moral economy." During the 1870s, as Woodman points out, black tenants and white landowners frequently disagreed as to who owned what cotton at what time in the harvest. Blacks often claimed cotton as their payment in kind, while landowners claimed that all debts had to be paid first. And in the case of renters, the question inevitably arose as to whether the worker or the landowners had the first claim on the crop. As tenancy and renting devolved into "cropper" or lien relations, blacks and whites clashed over rights to property. [41] By criminalizing all informal roadside markets and deadfalls, white merchants hoped to stamp out not only thieves but also legitimate black farmers, whose status as renters gave them a degree of independence. Democrats and Republicans alike understood the political implications of black economic independence. And both sides acted accordingly.

In the Black Belt town of Lowndesboro, planters accused Myer Goldman, a Jewish merchant, of operating a deadfall. Democrats met "to devise some means to put an end, if possible, to an immense traffic in cotton allegedly stolen from plantations and sold to dead-falls." They appointed "two men to watch the store in the evening" and "take down the names of negroes that bought and sold loose cotton, and report them to their employers . . . that they might ascertain whether the produce was stolen or not, and if stolen to institute proper *legal* steps." Whites assumed that any black in possession of cotton and on his way to Goldman's was a thief. [42]

The freedmen in Lowndes County, however, refused to tolerate white encroachment on their trade. One Saturday night in 1874, "two or three hundred" of them gathered at Goldman's store and confronted the merchant "watchers." Another time, black Republicans used Goldman's store as the meeting place for a "grand political pow-wow." Democratic papers, however, remained steadfast in their assertion that any black trading at deadfalls was illegitimate commerce. "The planters are determined to protect themselves from the depredations of the petit thieves." Black farmers, however, insisted on the legitimacy of their markets. They prevailed upon Republican politicians to oppose any "deadfall bills." The Democratic papers represented the efforts of black and Republican politicians as a collusion in crime. "It is an indisputable fact," the *Montgomery Advertiser* wrote, "that the negro vote in the present legislature has, thus far, been cast as a unit in opposition to every measure designed to repress thieving."[43] Yet would true thieves gather in groups of hundreds and make petitions to state legislators? Perhaps white complaints of "Negro thieves" during the 1870s reflected fierce economic competition between black and white farmers as well as clashing interpretations of property rights.

Once Democrats assumed power in 1874, they called for action that would impose a new legal vision of trading, markets, and larceny. The *Marengo News Journal* stated that "there are three very important measures which the Legislature should deal with without delay. We mean, 1. The sale of stolen produce to the deadfalls, 2. The making of bonds of local officials by sureties who live out of the county, and 3. The voting of persons out of their own beats."[44] Sure enough, despite opposition, various bills attacking deadfalls and carrying stiff penalties for larceny made their way through the Democrat-controlled Alabama legislature. In the spring of 1875, agricultural trade was limited to the hours between sunrise and sunset, the penalty for violation being twelve months' hard labor. Section 7506 of the Revised Code defined stealing any part of a corn or cotton crop as grand larceny, a crime which carried a minimum two- to five-year prison sentence. Every year after 1874 new laws were passed designed to thwart black trading.

Laws against larceny and deadfalls affected blacks disproportionately, but up-country white farmers feared this legislation too. One "hill country" editor noted, "Many of our best farmers, for convenience and to save time, arrive at market at a late hour in the day, and . . . do their selling and buying at night, and by sunrise next morning are on their way home."[45] Laws against selling loose cotton also affected poorer white farmers seeking to sell off surplus in amounts less than a bale. In order to allay fears, the legislature made laws against nighttime trading and selling cotton in seed apply only to Black Belt counties. But, as Michael Perman has pointed out, "more stringent and precise regulations were needed. Thus, the Alabama legislature of 1878–9 went so far as to ban the night time transportation of seed cotton, not merely its sale; also, in nine Black Belt counties, selling cotton in the seed at any time and anywhere was to be treated as a felony." Merely to enter a house or garden, take a farm animal, or possess any amount of cotton or corn could attract sentences from two to twenty years in prison.[46]

Nighttime trading was common among both races, but black farmers, however industrious, could not escape the label of thief.[47]

Yet even with such harsh penalties, controlling markets remained difficult. The threat of violence also accompanied these laws. As one newspaper put it, "A man who keeps a 'deadfall' for the purpose of . . . buying produce stolen from his neighbors ought to be hung."[48] The imposed fines of $10 or $25 may seem small, but freedmen could rarely afford to pay such amounts, and they often ended up serving hard labor for the county instead.[49]

The white cry of "crime" in the Black Belt needs to be understood within the context of economic competition between black and white farmers. Ransom and Sutch have argued that the possibility for black economic advancement never existed after emancipation. According to them, few black renters existed because whites believed "that without supervision blacks would be certain to fail as independent farmers."[50] It appears, however, that in the Alabama Black Belt it was the success of black tenants, not their failure, that caused white landowners great concern. To the horror of white Democrats, black renters were growing and selling their corn and even some cotton. And other blacks used deadfalls and roadside markets as a source of cheap credit and goods. The triumph of the Democratic party, however, gave white merchants and planters the political strength to undercut black economic independence, weaken black political power even further, and undermine African-American economic progress through legal action and arrests.

Political conflict also contributed to arrests for economic crimes. In 1882 and 1884 Alabama Republicans brought lawsuits before the Alabama Supreme Court challenging the automatic disfranchisement of men convicted of misdemeanors, such as petit larceny. The plaintiffs argued that such laws fell disproportionately hard upon blacks because white people were rarely convicted for such crimes. The petitioners claimed that "punishment was swifter for the larceny of an ear of corn . . . [than for] miscounting or destroying or refusing to receive the ballots of hundreds of electors."[51] The Alabama Supreme Court dismissed the case, thereby sanctioning the disfranchisement of thousands.

Mass arrests also served as a potent weapon of political repression. The aftermath of the riot at Spring Hill in Barbour County is a case in point. On election day in 1874, Barbour County in eastern Alabama experienced one of the most violent riots of Reconstruction.[52] The Democratic party, or "White League," raised a mob, armed themselves, and drove away over 1,000 unarmed Republicans from the polls at Eufaula, the county's market center. In total, seven or eight African Americans were killed in the Eufaula riot, and at least seventy were wounded. After the voting had ended, the mob then stormed the polling place at Spring Hill, which was being guarded by Judge E. M. Keils and his sixteen-year-old son William. According to Keils's account, the mob burst into the polling place, guns blazing. They destroyed the ballot box and killed William Keils. The death of a white Republican at the hands of local white elites showed the depth of political acrimony and the extent to which Democrats would go to ensure political victory.

But what happened in the aftermath of the violence? According to Judge Keils, white Democrats, "having things in their own hands," refused to count the votes of the Republican majority. (Keils estimated that there were 4,000 Republican voters compared to 1,800 Democrats.) The "White League" forced Republican officeholders to leave, declared themselves the electoral victors, and "seized every county office in Barbour County." In order to prevent any witnesses from coming forward to the federal courts, "indictments were found by democratic grand juries against every Republican who testified, or offered to testify, to the facts as to election frauds, or murder." The witnesses tried on these "trumped up" charges in state court, according to Keils, were all convicted "whether the evidence showed any violation of the law or not." Simply voting for the Republican ticket was enough to get someone indicted. According to Keils, the jurors do not hesitate to say "*in the jury room,* that the defendant *shall not* be acquitted '*because he is a radical.*'" After their conviction, according to Keils, these prisoners were "put upon the block and hired out, *sold,* publicly, at $2 per month, to pay the fine and costs, and bidders intimidated and made afraid to bid more than $2 a month." Keils, writing in June 1875, declared that the election of 1874 had turned local courts in Barbour, Russell, Bullock, Pike, and Henry Counties of the Eastern Black Belt into "simply engines of oppression."[53]

The western Black Belt seemed little better. During the election of 1874, would-be voters were arrested at the polls and at Republican gatherings. One Republican activist recalled that "Tom Saunders, an active politician in the colored ranks," was sent to get some lights. Saunders ended up handcuffed and arrested. "They called him a vagrant. He had worked every day in his life." Republicans asserted that arrests happened "daily without crime in order to break up the party."[54] Young black male voters were easy targets. One disgusted Democrat in Greene County complained of the "smooth-faced negroes" allowed to vote. He noted that the names of twenty-three "colored chaps" would be presented to the next grand jury and charged with illegal voting. "Let us hope that that honorable body will attend to their cases and . . . give them the penalty of the law prescribed for such offenses."[55]

Zealous prosecutions of political activists contributed to the soaring black prison population. In the summer of 1875, two "radical negroes from Black Bluff in Sumter County were sent to the penitentiary for two years for voting illegally. They had voted in Marengo." For registering to vote in what was allegedly the wrong city ward, Tom Battle, a freedman living in the city of Montgomery, was arrested for swearing a "false oath."[56] Republicans who had been legitimately elected to local office were disqualified if they could not find a local property owner to sign for their bond.[57] When black Republicans did score local electoral successes, as in the case of a black man elected to preside over the City Court of Selma as a judge in 1874, the Alabama legislature passed a bill "abolishing this court . . . thus ridding the already oppressed people of Dallas County of this additional and almost unbearable calamity."[58] It was not uncommon to read that Republican representatives in the legislature were under indictment or in prison: "Frank Bradley, late tax collector of Dallas County, died in the penitentiary a few days ago."[59] The Democratic legislature sent a clear message: black Alabamians may be able to vote, but they had no place in the state's legal or political system.

Racism deeply influenced Alabama's criminal justice system, especially after 1873. U.S. Attorney John Minnis wrote at length about how local law was used to suppress black freedom. As U.S. attorney for the Middle District of Alabama, Minnis, a Republican from North Carolina, was given the task of prosecuting the Klan. Although in the early 1870s he met with some success, winning fourteen convictions, by 1874 he was unable to go forward.[60]

Minnis felt frustrated by local efforts to thwart his investigations into the Ku Klux Klan in Alabama, but he expressed greater exasperation at the capricious use of the law against black citizens. His lengthy letters to the Justice Department provide a detailed record of legal actions faced by black farm laborers, sharecroppers, political activists, and ordinary citizens. Minnis knew it was difficult to substantiate charges of racism against judges, sheriffs, and juries. Nevertheless, he firmly believed that "there is an evident combination, not often that you could prove, by parties to deprive negroes of their equal rights."[61] By 1874 the Klan allegedly had disappeared in Alabama, but Minnis saw the group's impact in the courts. "The spirit of the Ku Klux is constantly manifesting itself in one shape or another," he wrote, "and I am sorry to say too often manifest itself in the courts."[62]

Given the violence of Reconstruction, Minnis knew that to many, the legal detainment of black citizens seemed a small matter. Even sympathetic members of the public would not be especially horrified by politically motivated arrests. Yet, he wrote, "in my opinion they represent a greater injury to society, indeed more, than the whipping or killing of one man." Minnis

then told how fifteen black citizens in Birmingham were arrested on their
way home from a political meeting in August 1874. "They were taken before the mayor next morning and without one particle of proof of any violation or intended violation of law, were each fined twenty dollars and sentenced to work it out on the streets." To Minnis such a blatant use of the
legal system for political ends was "more oppressive, more injurious, more
odious and a greater crime than if done in defiance of law" because its
intent was "to oppress, injure and intimidate a whole race . . . and keep
them in an inferior, degraded, dependent and helpless condition." Minnis
knew that the consequences of formal, legal repression were harder to address, in some ways, than the violence of the Klan, for if racist behavior was
legal, how could it be challenged?

Minnis felt himself in a thorny dilemma. As a lawyer, Republican, and
devout believer in the Constitution, he was outraged to see the law used as
a means of political intimidation and repression. But his job as a U.S. attorney was to prosecute Klan activity aimed at violating the civil rights of black
voters, not racism in the courts. The worst situation, he felt, existed in
the Black Belt of west Alabama, where news of half of all Klan outrages
"never reaches the public ear." His letters described the utter indifference
of local authorities to white outrages committed against blacks. Seldom
could he find white witnesses or local law officials willing to cooperate with
him. Minnis stressed that the Klan took its cue from the indifference of the
courts: indeed, the two forces often acted in concert.

As Judge Keils noted in his letters, the white Democrats in Barbour
County responsible for the death of his son and other Republicans were
never indicted, let alone prosecuted.[63] The U.S. attorney for the Southern
District of Alabama, Nick S. McAfee, felt equally helpless. Black citizens in
Sumter County, returning home from church, were ambushed, pursued,
and beaten; on the same night several black homes and two churches were
burned to the ground. Yet the Democratic papers excused such crimes on
the grounds that black citizens had been "plotting." The sheriff arrested
no one. "The spirit of lawlessness is spreading everywhere in this state—
through the rank and file of the Democratic party," McAfee wrote to
the attorney general in Washington. "Democratic leaders and newspapers
often and publicly commend the assassination of their political opponents
as a means justified by the end to be attained by it: White Democratic
Supremacy." McAfee, a federal official, felt impotent: "What shall we do!
What shall we hope for!"[64] McAfee, Minnis, and Keils would have agreed
that Alabama in the 1870s was engulfed in a crime wave, but they would
have been puzzled to hear that the freedpeople were responsible for it.

Who was to blame? Judge Keils held the U.S. government responsible,
in part. At Spring Hill in Barbour County, federal troops were present, but
their commander Captain Daggett had ordered them, by telegraph, to keep

away from the polls on election day. Daggett himself was acting under new General Order No. 75, which expressly forbade federal troops from acting unless protecting federal revenue agents or enforcing writs of the federal courts. When Keils sought their help on that fateful day, the federal troops in the area refused to stop the approaching mob; Daggett also refused to interfere in Eufaula.[65] But Keils also recognized that election-day violence was the culmination of the failure of Republican governor David P. Lewis to keep the peace during his time in office. "We have too many Republicans in this section," he wrote, "who are afraid to do their duty."[66] Local circuit courts were so powerful that they even indicted and arrested U.S. deputy marshals for "kidnapping" and "assault and battery" when, in the course of federal duty, they tried to detain local suspects. If U.S. Attorney Nick McAfee was spending much of his time "issuing out writs of Habeas Corpus" for federal officers, how much time did he have to pursue cases on behalf of lowly freedpeople?[67]

But what was to be done? A group in Montgomery calling itself "a Convention of Colored Citizens" on December 2, 1874, adopted a memorial proposing several specific changes in the law, particularly in regard to juries. The convention demanded that any person of African descent involved in a lawsuit should have the right to a jury "composed of not less than one half of his own race." Second, the convention argued that black citizens involved in any civil or criminal suit should have the right to remove the case to a federal court. Third, victims of people convicted under the Enforcement Acts should have the right to sue for pecuniary damages, and members of the Klan should be banned from all juries. Finally, the convention urged President Grant to remove all federal officers in Alabama who are "incompetent, unfaithful, timid, feeble or unenergetic in the discharge of their duties." They should be replaced with men "who are honest, zealous, competent, and true."[68]

The authors anticipated objections to their suggestions, especially the demand for racially balanced juries. The convention pointed out that the right of a trial by jury—"a bulwark against oppression"—had traditionally meant a jury composed of "neighbors and friends . . . and *by those of his own race.*" When a black defendant faced a jury of "a different and hostile race, having no sympathies with him . . . it is the surest means of accomplishing his ruin and subversion of right and justice." Legal precedents regarding the composition of juries existed in Alabama. The convention quoted from *Clay's Digest* to illustrate, for example, that when a slave was tried for a capital offense, the law required that "at least two thirds of the jury shall be slaveholders." If white slaveholders had, in the past, legally guarded themselves against unfriendly juries of their own race, then, the memorial reasoned, "how much more obvious the necessity of guarding the life, liberty, and property of the former slave, but now freeman, against injustice and from an unfriendly jury of a different and hostile race." [69] If slaveholders could demand that other slaveholders serve on juries so as to protect their slave property, then why could not the freedmen demand an equal number of blacks serve on juries when their interests were at stake?

As the memorial pointed out, severe consequences followed the absence of black jurors. It led to freedpeople being subjected to "the capricious, perilous, and prejudiced judgments of ex-slaveholders who disdain to recognize the colored race as their peers in anything, who look upon us as being *by nature an inferior race*." The legal result, the memorial argued, was that "the colored race of Alabama is denied or deprived of the benefit of 'the equal protection of the laws' both in their political and civil rights. . . . And in judicial procedure they are denied their right to an 'impartial jury' and 'the judgment of their peers.'" [70]

The memorial did not dispute that freedmen committed crimes deserving of punishment, but it asserted that prevailing racial prejudice made fair trials impossible. Ultimately, when blacks appeared before grand and petit juries composed of "white men who are their political opponents," the consequences were severe: "If innocent, he is nevertheless often convicted, and if guilty he is punished beyond measure." [71] Because whites had dominated antebellum Alabama so thoroughly, the question of whether members of "a hostile race" could judge the other race had never entered into the realm of public debate. Now the authors of the memorial were raising that issue and offering practical solutions as a countermeasure. Their commitment to the trial and jury system, despite its flaws, is striking.

As a society enmeshed in a social revolution, the postbellum South experienced changes that made old assumptions obsolete but new ones difficult to articulate. Nowhere is this more apparent than in the uncertainties and conflicts surrounding postwar Alabama's definition of crime. Those who looked to the law as an instrument of order and justice begged the question of whose order and whose justice. Southerners could not agree: many whites, for example, viewed legal equality for the freedmen as an outrage to be resisted by all means, even murder and mayhem. To their minds the higher principle of white supremacy justified behavior they would otherwise label criminal. Complicating matters even further, the South's legal system professed to be color-blind. But jurors, judges, sheriffs, plaintiffs, and defendants acted with great attention to both color and political persuasion.

In the late nineteenth century, southern society experienced social convulsions that challenged the way the law had traditionally been used. In antebellum times the law of slavery was used to keep blacks firmly under control. During Reconstruction, however, there existed a fresh possibility that the law might be used to defend black rights. And yet political conflicts, compounded by disputes over property and markets, led to the courts being used in a political way. At first the targets were those who got out of their assigned "place" or threatened local merchant control, or blacks and whites who subscribed to the Republican party. William Cockrell, for example, a white Republican from a prominent Greene County family, served in the Alabama legislature. In the early 1880s he received an eight-year sentence for "receiving stolen property" and was forced to mine coal alongside R. H. Skinner.[72] Other white Republicans in the Black Belt suffered a range of punishments from murder to social ostracism. It might be said that these exceptions proved the rule, and that whites with the temerity to cross the color line, including white women convicted of miscegenation, gave up the privileges that their race otherwise bestowed. Still, nearly 15 percent of all state prisoners were white males. Their crimes included murder, rape, and theft. If the act was heinous enough, and the perpetrator was unable to pay fines, whites could and did suffer imprisonment in the penitentiary. When it came to the local county system, however, whites were practically immune from prosecution.

Once the mechanism of excluding blacks from juries and of white supremacy had been established, local courts continued to serve as a means for local whites to exercise power over the freedpeople. After their electoral victory in 1874, Democrats implemented new laws and fiscal policies designed to buttress white supremacy; they also, very quietly, began to transform the state's prison system into a profit-making institution.

4

Prisons for Profit, 1871–1883

■ Since emancipation, the cost of prosecuting and detaining county convicts in Alabama had been recompensed by the fee system. Prisoners paid for their own trials; those who lacked the requisite cash served extra time and paid their fees with their labor. The calculations for costs were crude—one day in prison was worth a mere thirty cents—but the system was widely defended as necessary. "When hard labor for the county is done away with," wrote the treasurer of Sumter County, "when there is no longer provision for paying the costs of prosecution . . . we will enter upon an era of *lawlessness*. Men will no longer take an interest in prosecuting offenders when it must be done at their own expense, and the consequence will be a revival of the K.K.K."[1] County officials depended upon the fee system to cover the costs of prosecuting black misdemeanants; they also argued that it controlled whites, by encouraging them to take freedmen to court rather than to the Klan. Plans to abolish the fee system and turn all county prisoners over to the state never succeeded.

Deprived of this labor force, and the income it would garner, Alabama's Redeemer government began to expect its relatively small numbers of state prisoners to produce increasingly large sums of state revenue. Such expectations were something new. Alabama's state prisoners had always worked, but until 1875 the government had not profited from their labor. Prison labor for profit became a cornerstone of the Redeemers' political agenda only after Alabama's debt crisis forced the government to seek new forms of revenue. The counties had perfected the fee system; the state, however, pioneered the practice of leasing out prisoners solely for their labor. Under the Redeemers the lease brought in unprecedented revenue and created a new relationship between the state and the coal industry.

Leasing prisoners to coal mines produced a set of contradictions that neither the state nor the coal companies could anticipate. Unexpectedly, leasing produced a cohort of highly trained black miners. These men worked as free miners after their release and transformed the mining workforce into a racially mixed group. At times, black and white miners found a basis of solidarity in their mutual opposition to convict labor and in their common interests as members of organizations such as the Knights of Labor and the Greenback party. In addition to the challenges they faced from organized labor, Alabama Democrats had to respond to moral charges that leasing was inhumane and rife with fiscal abuse. Black and Republican newspapers protested the terrible conditions endured by prisoners and bellowed for reforms. During the 1870s Democrats looked to leasing as an easy answer to the state's fiscal woes. Yet competition for prison labor among factions of industrialists and landowners caused leasing to snowball into an unexpected political controversy.

By late 1882 Warden John H. Bankhead tried to resolve these tensions by proposing that Alabama lease all of its prisoners to coal mines. The roots of his proposal, however, lay in the debt crisis of the late 1870s when the state first allied itself with the coal industry and became dependent upon a profitable prison industry.

In antebellum Alabama a state-appointed warden worked prisoners at the state penitentiary in Wetumpka and received the profits from their labor.[2] Sometimes the warden paid the state for the use of the prisoners, and sometimes he did not. Most importantly, the warden was expected to run the penitentiary without any state assistance. This minimal requirement led the state to ignore its prisoners and the upkeep of the penitentiary building at Wetumpka; the government did not hope to profit from prisoners but only to be relieved of the financial burden of their maintenance.

In 1866 Robert Patton, Alabama's first elected postwar governor, leased over 200 state convicts to Smith and McMillan, a company of industrialists who proposed to build a railroad through the heart of Alabama's mineral region.[3] In exchange for the prisoners, the company paid Alabama a total of $5. Smith and McMillan also received a $15,000 "loan" from the state legislature which it never repaid. For the next seven years, Smith and McMillan controlled Alabama's state prisoners. It worked the convicts primarily on the South and North Alabama Railroad and the Alabama and Chattanooga Railroad, which—at a cost of $16,000 a mile—the state of Alabama subsidized. The company also illegally subleased prisoners to builders of connecting rail lines.[4]

While they worked on railroads, interred in "rolling cages," Alabama's prisoners suffered a shocking cost in human life. Between 1866 and 1873 prisoners died at an extraordinary rate. In the beginning of 1869, 263 prisoners (whites and African Americans) were listed "on hand" at the state penitentiary. Through the course of the year, while Republicans controlled the governorship and the state legislature, 92 died.[5] A higher percentage of state convicts died in Alabama in 1869 than in any other year .

Both political parties bore responsibility for this reprehensible state of affairs. Governor Patton's two successors, William Smith, a Republican, and Robert Lindsay, a Democrat, continued to sanction the use of state prisoners to build railroads. Relations between the state and the railroads deteriorated, however, when a missed interest payment prompted Governor Lindsay to take control of the Alabama and Chattanooga Railroad in June 1871. By assuming ownership of the railroad, Lindsay added several million dollars to the state's debt and inadvertently precipitated a further financial crisis. Leasing prisoners to Smith and McMillan appeared to have been a reversal of the state's previous prison policy, but it was not. Despite the formality of a "lease," the contractors had never paid for the use of Alabama's prisoners. By the end of Lindsay's term, prisoners and the state's penitentiary building were in a worse condition than ever before.[6]

In 1873 Republican governor Lewis appointed a new warden, Larkin Willis. Without authorization, Willis removed all prisoners from railroad work and returned them to the penitentiary known as the Walls at Wetumpka in Elmore County. The prison building was "an absolute wreck" and unsuitable for any occupants, but Willis justified his decision by stating that "unless they were better cared for they would all soon die."[7] The fact that Governor Lewis was desperately trying to sell the Alabama and Chattanooga Railroad may have also contributed to Willis's decision to remove most of the prisoners.[8] Whether his reasons were altruistic or political, Willis's act caused a crisis, for idle prisoners cost money, which the state did not wish to pay. To alleviate this financial pressure, Willis purchased a farm and put 69 men to work on it. He then leased approximately 50 prisoners to two mining operations near Birmingham and sent 62 convicts to work for private individuals. Fifty-nine of the prisoners remained at the Walls, and others were sent to work on railroads. Despite these changes, 40 state prisoners died between October 1872 and October 1873.[9] The exact financial terms of Willis's contracts remain unclear. The legislature expected Willis to make the penitentiary self-sufficient, not profitable, but instead he spent over $30,000.[10] When Willis died in office, state legislators discovered that he had embezzled thousands of dollars. Once again, a lease system on paper did not amount to revenue in practice. In 1874 the penitentiary was destitute, and it had never made a penny for the state of Alabama.[11]

The problems at the penitentiary, however, paled in comparison to the larger crisis of the state's fiscal insolvency. The Alabama and Chattanooga's default on its interest payments, the state's subsequent takeover of the line, and the legal battles that followed resulted in a financial maelstrom that completely undermined Alabama's credit rating with northern banks. When the state could not afford the legal cost of running a railroad, Alabama's credit rating sank. Lindsay's Republican successor, former Democrat David P. Lewis, failed to resolve the question of what to do with the railroad. Throwing it into the lap of the lowest bidder went against reason; carrying the metal albatross around, however, proved far too costly. At election time in 1874, the Democrats focused on race, the railroads, and fiscal responsibility. During the campaign Democratic candidate George S. Houston blamed Alabama's poor credit rating on two years of Republican rule.[12] Houston pledged to rewrite the state's constitution, pursue a policy of fiscal conservatism, and restore white supremacy. When Houston became governor in 1874, Alabama was in virtual default and ripe for a drastic economic overhaul.

A faction within the Democratic party, best articulated by journalist Robert McKee, argued for a total repudiation of the debt. Like McKee, hill-country Democrats in the legislature, who represented poorer white farmers, remained inspired by the legacy of Jacksonian beliefs in low taxes and laissez-faire. Wary of government alliances with banks and business and suspicious of Houston's allegiance to railroads, they created a new state constitution in 1875 that reduced the number of state offices, cut salaries, barred the state from subsidizing private corporations, banned funding for internal improvements, and, most significantly, restricted taxes.[13]

Houston, however, refused to repudiate the state's debt entirely. His debt commission, which he headed, reduced the state's debt in part, but much to the chagrin of McKee and his supporters, it also recommended paying over $1 million to Alabama and Chattanooga bondholders.[14] Determined to protect the state's bondholders and its railroads, Houston refinanced the debt with new loans. Alabama covered its railroad debt "at the expense of financial support for every other agency of the State government." Alabama's credit rating was "saved," but according to the historian A. J. Going, its "financial structure . . . [after 1875] necessarily developed around the problem of paying interest on the adjusted debt." [15]

Houston's determination to pay off railroad bondholders, coupled with a state constitution that severely limited state taxing authority, placed Alabama in a fiscal squeeze. That crisis led John G. Bass, the state's new prison warden, to come forward with a novel idea: lease individual prison laborers to willing contractors in exchange for cash. In 1879 Bass wrote about the evolution of this new system in a letter to Governor Rufus Cobb. Bass asserted that in March 1875 Governor Houston had proposed that he take over the convicts "free of charge as Lessee if I would guarantee that the

State should be put to no expense on account of the penitentiary." But Bass had rejected this plan. Instead, he recommended that the state pay him a salary. In exchange, Bass took charge of leasing prisoners out to various contractors. Money earned from prison labor was then placed in the state's treasury as revenue. Profits, he proudly stated, soon amounted to "between eleven and twelve thousand dollars . . . over and above all the expenses of the institution." [16] At a time when the state desperately needed new revenue without new taxes, Bass transformed Alabama's penitentiary into a profitable moneymaker.

Profit from the hire of prisoners streamed from the treasury into the banks. In December 1875 Governor Houston asked Bass to assist the state "in paying January interest on State debt." In response, Bass turned to Gaius Whitfield, who had just hired seventy black state convicts, and asked for a six-month advance payment. "I am well aware you are due us nothing til 1st of April next," Bass wrote. "Nevertheless it may suit your convenience to assist us by paying us some $600 on account of Nov. And Dec." Whitfield promised to oblige, and on January 16, 1877, Bass wrote to say that the money had been received.[17] Without raising taxes or making enemies—on the contrary, the lease bridged alliances between the state, with labor to sell, and those who needed labor—Houston and Bass had devised a new and reliable source of state revenue.

Before the cash could really flow, the pipeline required some adjustments. Instead of handing prisoners over to contractors in one group (as had been done with Smith and McMillen), Bass ranked each prisoner according to his ability and charged accordingly. Healthy prisoners cost more than smaller, weaker men and women; eventually, all prisoners were categorized as either first, second, or third class. Bass leased prisoners out on a month-to-month basis and demanded regular payments. Those with cash ready, such as owners of plantations, lumberyards, coal mines, and railroads, held the advantage over those who did not. And those with extra cash to sweeten their bid had the greatest advantage of all. When Colonel Woolf, a landowner from Marengo County, requested a labor contract, Bass told him he required a $500 "appropriation for [his] assistance." Given the amount of graft state legislators demanded from the railroad companies in exchange for favors, such sums may seem small. Ubiquitous deal making, however, lay at the heart of the system, and it soon led to a powerful alliance between the state, the penitentiary warden, and the coal companies.[18]

Counties, also eager to make money without levying taxes, learned from the state's new system. Since the days of the Black Codes, county prisoners had brought in fees when arrested and tried, but no one had realized that labor could produce revenue too. In Hale County, for example, county prisoners worked "building and repairing bridges" under the authority of a hired superintendent. Nobody knew the cash value of the work they

carried out, and the county paid prison supervisors. In August 1875, however, Hale County hired out its convicts for cash. That year's grand jury
reported that county prison labor "contributed much to the revenues of
the county, instead of being an expense, as in some preceding years." Counties put the money from leasing into their Fine and Forfeiture Fund, the
account that paid the fees owed to judges, sheriffs, and witnesses. Anyone
owed a fee in a county court case was paid in scrip, but it could only be
cashed in if there was enough money in the fund. Thus it became common
practice for people to speculate in scrip, or hoard it, until there was enough
in the treasury to pay the amount owed. As a consequence of the new revenue brought in by prisoners, however, the grand jury of Hale County reported that "the fine and forfeiture fund is in much better condition . . .
and claims against that fund have appreciated considerably." Thus revenue
earned from county prison labor spread into many hands and many
pockets.[19]

As competition for the labor of convicted men and women increased,
counties tried fewer prisoners for felonies, preferring to keep them under
local control. In January 1876 Bass bemoaned the imbalance between the
small number of state prisoners and the growing number of county men.
"We have rec'd but very few hands in the last two months," he wrote to
Whitfield. "All convicts are being sent to the county. . . . Pull for the repeal
of the county hard labor and we can fix you up in a short while."[20] State
officials accused county judges of cynically keeping all of their able-bodied
male prisoners and sending "unleasable" prisoners, such as the elderly,
women, and the sick, to the state. In 1881 the state's new warden, John H.
Bankhead, pleaded for understanding from the mining contractor J. W.
Comer. "As to men, I don't see how I can help you. . . . We are receiving no
additions scarcely. It does seem that a deliberate effort is being made to turn
the penitentiary into a poor house and insane Assylum and Orphans home.
All able-bodied convicts go county. . . . I will give you all Birmingham convictions if there is any."[21] After reaching new heights in 1877, the number
of state prisoners continued to drop over the next five years, with the difference going to the counties.[22]

Despite these worries, keen competition for prison labor signaled the
new system's success. By September 30, 1877, there were 557 state prisoners
working in lumber mills, plantations, and coal mines, with the majority
working at agriculture. They also had been returned to railroad work, as
Bass contracted 70 prisoners to build a branch line on the South and North
Railroad connecting Elmore station to the Walls in Wetumpka.[23] Before
Bass's appointment in 1875, the penitentiary brought in no revenue to the
state whatever. By the end of 1877, however, circumstances had changed
dramatically. "It is truly a cause for congratulations," noted an annual inspectors' report, "to know that after having incurred every expense neces-

sary to the comfort and safe keeping of the convicts, the Warden has still been able, from their earnings, to pay over to the State Treasurer fourteen thousand dollars in cash."[24] Democratic newspapers seized upon the financial largesse produced by the penitentiary as proof of Houston's competent financial administration.[25] By the time Warden Bass retired in 1881, Alabama's Department of Corrections had grown into a profitable state agency with growing ties to one of the most important sectors of the economy: the coal industry.

Prisoners were some of the first workers in postbellum coal and iron enterprises. By 1877, 137 state prisoners worked in coal and ore mines spread among Jefferson, Shelby, and Talladega Counties.[26] Their small numbers belied their significance in an industry desperate for labor. Fledgling companies, such as the Newcastle Coal Company and the Red Mountain Iron Works, badly needed the 48 prisoners received in 1873. Other early mining and pig iron enterprises that used prisoners include Alabama Furnace, Alabama Iron, Pratt Coal and Coke, and the Eureka Company.[27] Eventually Sloss-Sheffield, makers of pig iron, and the Tennessee Coal and Iron Company transformed Birmingham into the center of industrial production. Both companies used prison labor extensively. Sloss gained much of its coal from its prison mines at Coalburg and John T. Milner's prison mine at Newcastle. TCI eventually took over the Pratt works, which in turn had grown out of small beginnings at the Eureka mines in Helena, Shelby County.

During the 1870s the Eureka mines, owned first by Daniel Pratt and then by his son-in-law Henry DeBardeleben, became the area's most important source of coal. In addition to employing free labor, Pratt hired J. W. Comer to operate a separate set of prison mines at Eureka. In 1877 Pratt leased fifty-eight state convicts; by 1880 the number had risen to eighty-six. Prisoners made a difference. In 1879 the *Shelby Sentinel* assured visitors that they "will be surprised . . . to see the enlargement of the coal and iron industries, and new improvements being otherwise made since . . . 1875." Three years later the newspaper bragged that "in 1872 only 10,000 tons of coal were mined in Alabama. In 1879 we mined 290,000 tons; in 1880 340,000 tons; in 1881, 400,000 tons. During the year 1882 we find a single company, the Pratt Co at Birmingham, mining 1500 tons a day. The coal goes to Louisville, Vicksburg, Mobile, New Orleans and other points."[28] In their enthusiasm for the economic growth associated with these enterprises, local newspapers ignored the growing number of convict laborers in their midst.

Upbeat descriptions concealed extreme coercion. In 1879 fifty-eight prisoners tended to Eureka's "long line of bee hive [coke] ovens" and twenty-two coal beds. The newspaper chirped that "the Helena Coal mines are being worked with a vim, and coal is being rapidly raised, both day and night." In contrast, prisoner Ezekiel Archey recalled his time at the Eureka mines with horror: "Every Day some one of us were carried to our last resting, the grave. Day after day we looked Death in the face & was afraid to speak. You may say why or How. In reply I say from Falling Coal and slate." When two black prisoners tried to escape from J. W. Comer's Eureka camp, they discovered the awful price of resistance. A local resident witnessed the hunt for the men. One escapee managed to elude his pursuers, but the other "negro convict was on the ground and the dogs were biting him. He begged piteously to have the dogs taken off of him, but Comer refused to allow it." In order to make the man tell on his companion, Comer "took a stirrup strap, doubled it and wet it, stripped him naked, bucked him, and whipped him—unmercifully whipped him, over half an hour. The negro begged them to take a gun and kill him." After this scourging the prisoner was unable to walk back to the camp. "They left him in a negro cabin where . . . he died within a few hours."[29]

Staying in the camps, however, afforded little protection. Ezekiel Archey remembered his time at the Eureka mines in Helena as pure suffering. Prisoners wore chains as they trudged through the rain and snow. "We can go back to 79 and 77 all these years of how we sufered. No humane being can tell . . . yet we hear. Go ahead. Fate seems to curse a convict[.] Death seems to summon us hence."[30] Between 1878 and 1880 twenty-five prisoners at the Eureka mines died.[31] An 1881 state investigation concluded that prisoners "were well and warmly clad and shod, were served with a sufficient amount of wholesome diet and were kindly and humanely treated."[32] The firsthand accounts of prisoners, however, as well as the commission's own evidence, contradict this conclusion.

Guards and contractors testified in detail how they whipped and tortured prisoners. "We whip with a leather strap or stick about an inch broad and two foot long," said one assistant superintendent.[33] Prisoners were also whipped for "disobeying rules." The state code allowed up to thirty-nine lashes but far more were inflicted for fighting, tearing up bedding and clothes, and "sassing" the guards.[34] If whipping did not cause submission, guards inflicted the torture of "water punishment." A prisoner was strapped down on his back; then "water [was] poured in his face on the upper lip, and effectually stops his breathing as long as there is a constant stream."[35] Contractors wanted prisoners to work, and they maintained control through fear and torture.

In 1881 a legislative committee investigated prison conditions and reported on the abysmal life of prisoners at Newcastle, owned by John T. Milner. Milner worked both state and county convicts in his camp, which on the surface epitomized a dynamic economic enterprise. Newcastle boasted its own railroad track, a row of beehive ovens, and improved machinery. Nevertheless, investigators found that prisoners suffered from filth, vermin, and horrible overcrowding.[36] Newcastle was so awful that it made the head-lines of the *New York Times*. An exposé entitled "Southern Convict Camps: A Crying Disgrace to Our American Civilization" reported that Newcastle's death rate was 600 percent higher than that of northern and northwestern prison camps. Twenty-five white convicts lived in a cabin twenty-four feet long, twenty-two feet wide, and eight and one-half feet high. Over 150 black convicts, by contrast, lived in an area barely twice the size of the white cabin. The black cabin had no windows. Bunks, filled with straw, "ragged blan-kets," and "vermin," were in three tiers. Everyone ate cold food with coal-stained hands, bedding was "revoltingly filthy," and 150 black convicts washed in three half-barrel tubs.[37]

At Newcastle "all convicts, white and black, wear shackles," consisting of an "iron hoop fastened around the ankle to which is attached a chain 2 feet long and terminating in a ring." Marching to and from the mines, the men were chained together around the waist. Three years later state prison inspectors were still urging Milner to allow his prisoners to march the three-quarters of a mile to the mine without being chained. He refused, claiming that removing restraints encouraged escapes. If he removed the heavy chains, he protested, "my best and longest mine men will get away & then ruin my business here."[38] By 1883 twenty-nine counties in Alabama leased a portion of their county prisoners to the mines. Pratt mines used a total of 200 prisoners from fourteen counties, and Newcastle worked 225 prisoners from fifteen other counties.[39] Counties evidently relied in-creasingly on coal mines to gain maximum profits from their prisoners.

The extent to which Alabama industrialists depended upon prison-ers, however, is not clear. As Milner's comment suggests, prison laborers performed highly skilled work for very low costs. Quotas, enforced with the whip, made a small number of prisoners equivalent to a greater number of free workers. Also, the prisoners' race added to their attractiveness. Ac-cording to W. David Lewis, industrialists purposefully chose convicts be-cause cheap, chained, and degraded African Americans fit into their vision of what the South's new working classes should be. John T. Milner pro-vides the most extreme case of this mentality. As early as 1859 Milner saw black labor, properly controlled, as essential to the state's industrial growth. Whites, according to Milner, "would always look upon and treat the negro as an inferior being." But he predicted that an industrialist could use blacks to perform industrial tasks "provided he has an *overseer—a southern man, who knows how to manage negroes.*"[40] In a region with rich resources but few workers, let alone skilled miners, black prison labor in theory appears to have been the ideal means for launching the coal-mining industry.

But prison labor had its drawbacks. Difficult to control and obtain and prone to escape, prisoners made coal companies liable to public exposure, scandal, and criticism. Furthermore, their presence antagonized commu-

nities of free miners and deterred experienced white and immigrant workers from moving to the region. As one Alabama newspaper acerbically commented in 1881, "Our present convict system is a blot upon the civilization
of this century and a shame upon the State of Alabama. . . . Humanity demands legislation on this subject. Christianity demands it. The State will
never prosper as long as the infamous system prevails in her borders."[41]
Inhumane treatment needed to end, the editor argued, and so did the competitive threat to free laborers.

Political opposition to the lease came from many quarters. Southern
black newspapers printed the most consistent condemnations, uniformly
denouncing the leasing system as brutal, corrupt, and discriminatory. The
People's Advocate, a Republican paper published in Washington, D.C., wrote
that "in some States the penal laws are so framed as to consign the most
petty criminals to a condition of servitude so exacting that escape there-
from is possible only in extreme cases and after long years of imprisonment." In 1881 a black Georgia newspaper protested that "it is morally
certain that hundreds of innocent men are dragging out lives worse than
that of slavery in the Georgia prisons and on convict farms, and that this
system of reviving African servitude is growing extremely popular in the
South."[42] In Alabama the editor of the black-owned *Huntsville Gazette,*
Charles Hendley, a black Republican, frequently denounced the lease in
general and Alabama's penal system in particular.[43] The *Gazette* reprinted
evidence of outrages occurring in Alabama, Georgia, and Mississippi. It
commented on legislative investigations in detail. It offered commentary
on what should be done with prisoners and reprinted damning reports that
had appeared in the *New York Times.* The *Gazette* consistently condemned
the inhumane treatment prisoners received. But public exposure of abuse
failed to halt the march of prisoners to the mines.

Given the weakness of the Republican party and a diminishing black
vote, the greatest obstacle to the plans of men like Milner came from those
most directly threatened by prison labor: free miners. A labor shortage in
Jefferson, Shelby, and Talladega Counties should have led to high wages,
and coal operators were forced at first to pay more than they wished. Competition between prison miners and free miners hardly seemed an issue,
especially when free miners could afford to hire county prisoners for one
dollar a day to load their coal.[44] But those halcyon days soon ended. As the
coal industry hired more and more prisoners directly from contractors,
prison labor in the mines prompted protests. Mine workers affiliated with
various unions and workingmen's organizations, such as the Greenback
party, vigorously opposed the use of prisoners. Before prison labor in the
mines could be made truly integral to the industrial setting of Alabama,
then, the opposition of free miners, white and black, would need to be
silenced.

Miners comprised the backbone of burgeoning coal communities, and although they formed segregated clubs, black and white miners worked together under the umbrella of the Greenback party.[45] Formed after the nationwide financial panic of 1873, the Greenback party believed that monetary inflation would alleviate the problems of working people. It demanded government ownership of railroads and prohibition of large accumulations of wealth. Greenback supporters included farmers, mechanics, and miners of both races.[46]

Between 1877 and 1879 the Greenback-Labor movement experienced dynamic growth in the mining regions. The party hired black organizers such as W. J. Thomas to work among black miners.[47] Thomas, "a man not afraid to speak what he thinks," organized "Colored Clubs" on behalf of the party. One black grocer in Alabama wrote to the party's paper, the *National Labor Tribune,* to verify Thomas's identity. "He seems to be a good friend to colored and poor people. . . . I hope he is the right kind of a man, but we have been fooled so much, that we can't trust him yet." The author added that Thomas's speech "beat anything we ever heard." Another of Thomas's admirers described to the *Tribune* how the man swept into town, organized a chapter, and left before being caught by local whites. "He had about a hundred newspapers, handing them around, and storming and crying out something about greenbacks, public lands, banks, bonds, convicts, Chinese and poverty and starvation."[48] Now that blacks were wage workers in the mines, their Republican belief in legal equality was broadening into support for economic equality—even socialism.

Thomas, in particular, evoked keen enthusiasm among black mining families. Black women "turned out in force and gave countenance to our young orator," rejecting the suggestion that they "go behind the door"—presumably to give away their seats—until Thomas began his speech. The women remained and listened as Thomas quoted from the Bible. "He spoke of Moses of Joseph and others. He spoke of Christ, and his love for the people, and indeed the meeting looked, for the moment, more like a missionary meeting than a political one." Thomas then read from the *Tribune* and discussed the Greenback party's platform, challenging anyone in the audience to dispute what he said. When no one opposed him, he called out for the men to come forward and join. Warren Kelley, editor of the *National Labor Tribune,* was impressed. "This meeting added ten names to the roll of the Irondale club, thirteen to the Newton club, and eighteen to the Jonesboro Club—a pretty good night's work!" The black men and women implored Thomas to stay. "Go on. Go on!" they shouted. "We'll stay here a week longer to hear you talk the greenback gospel." The deacon of the Baptist church sang a song, the parson led a prayer, and the group dispersed.[49]

In many respects the short-lived Greenback movement in the Alabama mining region echoed the successful organizing style of the Republican party in the Black Belt. The use of a church to hear a political speaker, the participation of women, and the use of public shame to encourage participation were all part of a political culture familiar to blacks. Like the Republicans, the Greenbackers attracted a variety of classes, including small businessmen and miners.

There were differences, however. The Greenback party was socialist-oriented and segregated: blacks had to form separate "clubs" in order to join. The presence of black women at the Greenback gathering where Thomas spoke indicates that women in mining communities expressed interest in politics. Yet whether their participation in a labor-based movement could equal the influence they exerted in the Black Belt during election time remains unclear. In addition, the population of these tiny communities was heterogeneous. Some blacks in the area had worked in the mines since the antebellum period and the Civil War. Other black workers were recent arrivals from the Black Belt.[50] Still others were former prisoners, also from the Black Belt, who had been schooled in labor relations from their time in the prison mines.

As mining memoirs attest, the craft of mining bred a unique form of solidarity among its practitioners.[51] All miners worked under dangerous conditions; all miners, free and convict, white and black, understood the earning potential of mining. In prison mines convicts learned all aspects of the coal business including the lucrative skill of cutting coal. Even the stingy John T. Milner at Newcastle paid prisoners for "extra work done over their task."[52] From the inception of the postbellum coal industry in Alabama, prisons trained miners.

In the late nineteenth century, miners considered themselves self-employed. The company paid them by the ton, not the hour. At the end of the day, their wages depended upon the total weight of their coal. In contrast, day laborers earned $1 to $1.25 a day; they worked for the mining company or for individual miners. They did not cut coal but performed all the other tasks necessary for a skilled miner to work, such as laying track, shoveling and loading coal, and working on top of the mine. In prison, those who performed this day-labor work were known as "dead heads." During the 1890s African Americans comprised the majority of free day laborers, but they were also skilled coal cutters.

Blacks developed those lucrative mining skills early. In the 1880s former prisoners, skilled as coal cutters, worked for themselves and employed day laborers to work for them under the subcontracting plan. The time-keeper and paymaster of the Pratt Coal and Coke Company, Justus Collins, testified in 1883 about his experiences with former convicts. Charles Smith was "an ex-convict, a negro, who was sent here on a sentence for an assault with intent to murder, and he was discharged in due time. That man earned

$414.07 . . . he appears on the rolls as having earned that himself but I suppose he had some laborers employed. . . . Another negro, an ex-convict, Monroe Brown, has one very small boy to help him, and his total earning was $220.40. . . . Another man, by himself, with no laborer to help him earned $72." Their history as prisoners did not bother Collins. "These are good miners," he testified, "who put in good time every day."[53]

According to Collins, many ex-prisoners worked with their families, a practice common among all miners, white and black. "Tom Donaldson, a boy nineteen years old, with two younger brothers, one sixteen and the other thirteen earned $160.18." Having one family member in the coal mines often prompted other family members from the Black Belt to migrate. Tankersley, a white prisoner, testified that "parties were released last week, and I see they are at work now out at the drift mines cutting coal. I think that in the vicinity of Coketown there are about two hundred and fifty ex-convicts. They have got their families there and seem to be at home. . . . Some of them met their families there just prior to the end of their sentences; brought them here with the view of remaining."[54] Coketown later became Pratt City, a significant and highly militant mining community.

Historians have noted that free miners in Alabama cooperated across the lines of race. The extent and the significance of this interracial cooperation, however, remain a matter of debate. Evidence of black and white miners going on strike together, joining the Greenbacks and the Knights of Labor, and even sharing social occasions evokes an atmosphere of interracial cooperation. Nevertheless, in the mining districts the political parties, including the Populists, made antiblack appeals to white voters. Lynching occurred, and job discrimination at the mines prevailed.[55] Such contradictions make it difficult for historians to interpret how black and white miners of the era perceived each other.

The relationship between black and white prisoners evokes a similar uncertainty. It might be argued that racial integration among prisoners laid the ground for interracial cooperation among free men. According to the state penitentiary inspectors' 1882 biennial report, black and white prisoners shared living quarters, much to the dismay of Warden Bankhead.[56] They also worked together at the two prison mines owned by the Pratt Coal and Coke Company and at Newcastle.[57] Furthermore, the demand for labor was such that free black miners in the 1880s worked as skilled coal cutters; free black and white miners were more likely to share a similar status in the workplace.[58]

Yet prison bred racial contempt and mistrust. Most prison camps were segregated, and black convicts suffered in highly crowded conditions. Blacks were berated with racial slurs and, if Ezekiel Archey is correct, tasked more heavily because of their race. Furthermore, the prison itself operated along the lines of a racial hierarchy, which imbued the white convicts with feelings of superiority. Perhaps some characteristics of early prison mines paved the way for interracial cooperation, but prison also reflected the racial customs of the era. Guards, administrators, and white convicts all came from a society that preached and practiced white supremacy.

In the spring of 1878, 600 men employed by the Eureka Company in Helena halted work to protest the use of convicts. The local paper believed that a "good many citizens sympathize with the strikers." But this effort failed. Two years later, when free miners at the Pratt mines struck for higher wages, prison labor saved the day for the company. A mining boss admitted that had it not been for the convicts, "the company would have failed to fulfill their contracts in furnishing coal." [59]

In the meantime John Hollis Bankhead of Jasper, Alabama, took Bass's place as Alabama warden. Bankhead strengthened the state's ties to mining interests, becoming personally indebted to them for cash and favors. "I am busted and want money to pay expenses for two months," he wrote to J. W. Comer in May 1882. "Send me check for $1,000 to be divided between you and C & Mc haven't got a cent. Help Cascius or I perish. Send contract as soon as you can." To H. M. Caldwell, manager of the Newcastle mine, he pleaded for $500 for "expenses." "Please act promptly as I am entirely out of funds." [60] Bankhead helped mining companies by using his influence to direct county prisoners to the coal mines—luring one sheriff to bring county prisoners to the mines by offering a free visit to Birmingham. "If you will deliver [the prisoners] to Mr. Comer at Pratt mines near Birmingham he will pay your expenses both ways. . . . Suppose you would like to visit the mines and Magic City." [61] What sheriff from the rural Black Belt could resist the temptation? Yet despite Bankhead's efforts, mining companies still experienced a labor shortage.

In 1882 over 500 skilled miners and several hundred day laborers at the Pratt mines demanded a halt to falling wages and to prison labor. The two issues were obviously connected. In 1879 skilled miners were paid one dollar a ton, but by 1882 the price paid for a ton of mined coal had dropped to forty-five cents. The company gave the workers an ultimatum: they could either resume work and be paid forty-five cents a ton "or take their tools and materials out of the mines" and work elsewhere. The strikers, confident of finding work, accepted the latter offer and demanded to be paid. But no other company would hire the dismissed workers, and the once-defiant miners had no choice but to leave the area. The newspaper chided the leaders. Because of them, the editor reasoned, "many good men among them . . . suffered." [62] Instead of hiring new, free miners, Pratt leased the empty mines to J. W. Comer, who worked the mines solely with prison labor.

The defeat of the 1882 strike firmly entrenched convict labor in Jefferson County. Free laborers argued that competition from convicts lowered their wages, but prison officials tried to stir public sentiment against free miners. Bankhead called the objections to prison labor in the mines "demagoguery" and "sickly sentimentality": the wages of miners deserved to be lowered. "It seems to me," he wrote in 1882, "that no class of our people can stand competition better than the miner, who can and does earn from $2.50 to $4.00 per day."[63] Throughout his tenure in office, J. W. Bass had maintained close ties with planters.[64] In contrast, Bankhead allied himself firmly with the coal companies. In 1883 he proposed his own plan for reform, one that he hoped would accommodate the labor needs of the coal companies while quieting calls for change.

By 1882 prisoners brought in over $50,000 in state revenue.[65] Alabama "ranked among the lowest of all states in per capita taxation."[66] Although rumors and horror stories about the treatment of prisoners circulated among Democratic party insiders, leasing prisoners simply brought in too much revenue for any sensible Democrat to fight for a complete alternative. Nevertheless, one crucial point divided Democrats: who was entitled to prison labor? Since the state legislature's 1881 report, planters had argued that "prisoners should be worked in the fields, and not at hazardous or unhealthy occupations." Planters also wanted legislation requiring county convicts to be leased within the county of their conviction.[67] The *Huntsville Gazette* joined in the protest for a different reason, insisting that the proper place for youthful offenders was a juvenile facility rather than a coal mine. "God will not look with favor upon the enforced association of the boy guilty of some thoughtless misdemeanor with the hardened criminal of the worst class."[68] Although it applauded some of the reforms plodding their way through the Alabama legislature, the *Gazette* argued the reforms were paper-thin. The bills would punish mistreatment of prisoners and made inspections compulsory, but only "if practicable."[69] Even those who opposed leasing did not demand its complete abolition, as they were unwilling to forgo its financial benefits.

In the early 1880s the calls for reform grew louder, especially outside the South. When George Washington Cable, a white southern author of great distinction, condemned the lease in a speech before the National Conference of Charities and Correction in 1883, people listened.[70] Cable had traveled the nation with Mark Twain reading excerpts from his novels about the South. His horrific accounts of the convict-leasing system were far from fiction, however. His address, later reprinted in a book entitled *The Silent South,* was the first harsh critique of the leasing system by a white southerner. Cable condemned the system for its cruelty and rapacity, calling upon the white South, in the name of Christianity and humanity, to end it. Although it made him a pariah, Cable's speech influenced northern perceptions of southern prisons and also boosted local efforts at reform. Many

Alabamians, notably Robert McKee, former editor of the influential *Selma Argus* and private secretary to Governor Cobb, embraced the need for overhauling the prison system.

Warden Bankhead seemed an unlikely figure to lead the movement for change. A former legislator from Marion County, Bankhead did not alter the lease's operations when he became warden in 1881. Occasionally, he expressed concern about the treatment of convicts.[71] His predecessor, Bass, allied himself with landowners; Bankhead seemed closer to the mining interests. Nevertheless, Bankhead acted in a similar way to Bass: he never revoked a contract, he asked contractors for money to pay "expenses," and he offered only mild rebukes for transgressions of rules, even when they resulted in the deaths of prisoners.

Nevertheless, perhaps sensing the changing public mood, in 1882 Bankhead began a public campaign for prison "reform"; he unsparingly criticized coal contractors. "I found the prisons where convicts were confined in most instances totally unfit for the purpose for which they were intended. . . . They were as filthy as dirt could make them, and both prisons and prisoners were infested with vermin." In his "Warden's Report" he censured the contractors for their selfishness and greed. Prisoners, he said, were excessively punished and thoroughly intimidated. He tried to provoke public alarm about the long-term effects such treatment had upon incarcerated men. Alabama prisons, Bankhead asserted, were "training grounds" for criminals. The state, he declared, had an obligation to do more for convicted men than simply profit from their labor.[72]

What was to be done? Bankhead had a plan—"a complete revolution in our convict system." He proposed building a new prison "with hospital, bath house, female apartments, dining hall, guard quarters, bakery, [and] cook room." Instead of scattering convicts to various locations, all 600 state prisoners would live in a two-story building and benefit from clean water, good ventilation, and segregated quarters. Abuses would end because one prison location would afford the warden real control over treatment. The cost? A mere $18,000; moreover, the Pratt Coal and Coke Company, not taxpayers, would foot the bill. There was one condition. If "the whole force . . . worked together . . . in a coal mine," this vision of cleanliness, thrift, and reform could come true.[73] Bankhead brushed aside his own criticisms of the coal companies; he also ignored the well-known dangers of mining. According to the inspectors' 1882 biennial report, mining camps suffered the worst death rates of all prisons.[74] Put simply, Bankhead's startling proposal gave coal companies a complete monopoly of prison labor.

Landowners and small businesses cried foul at this obvious favoritism, but Pratt had the inside track. The company promised to deliver reform, as well as a new prison. And no other contractor could afford to guarantee to pay the state up to $12 a month for all state prisoners. The legislature, wary of accusations of bias, approved a modified version of Bankhead's master plan. It agreed that a minimum of 200 prisoners should be leased to any one contractor, thus effectively eliminating small enterprises and land-owners from the bidding. No contractor, however, was supposed to receive more than 200 prisoners. The state would retain the penitentiary at Wetumpka and also continue to lease prisoners to Thomas Williams's farm. The position of warden would be replaced by a Board of Inspectors responsible for ensuring that prisoners received decent treatment.

Despite these provisos, Bankhead achieved his goal. In exchange for agreeing to build new prisons, the Pratt Coal and Coke Company received the vast majority of the state prison population. It evaded the 200-man limit by leasing 200 men directly from the state and subleasing another 200 from J. W. Comer. For the next thirty years, Pratt and then TCI worked Alabama's state and county prisoners at two major mining sites, the Shaft and Slope No. 2. Sloss eventually took over all the operations at Newcastle and Coalburg, which worked exclusively county convicts. This legislation signaled a turning point; it was indeed a "revolution," engineered by Bankhead, that made coal mining the major prison industry. Until 1928 the vast majority of Alabama prisoners, regardless of the severity of their offense, became destined to serve out their prison time in coal mines.

Although deeply associated with the politics of the New South, the convict lease in Alabama had its origins in the political conflicts of emancipation and Reconstruction. Beginning with the Black Codes, counties used arrests as a means of controlling the newly emancipated freedpeople. When the political and economic conflicts of Reconstruction heated up, a growing number of state prisoners became enmeshed in Alabama's debt crisis. It was the Redeemer Democrats who made the lease a profitable institution. And it was they who first made prisoners available, wholesale, to the mining industry.

The question of whether prison labor in coal mines represented the old antebellum South or the new industrial South persists. Clearly, elements of both converged. Former slave owners, such as Whitfield, Comer, and Milner, easily embraced their new role as abusive labor contractors. It is alleged that the abuses and punishments heaped upon prisoners made their condition even "worse than slavery"; but we know too little about how these men had run their slave plantations to assume that as slaveholders they had been benevolent paternalists. Instead of emphasizing the disparity between slave owner paternalism and contractor brutality, it may make more sense to investigate the continuities between how slave owners turned contractors treated their black slaves and black prisoners.

The continuity between slavery and the lease is significant if we wish to understand why prisoners were treated so cruelly. Given the labor shortage in the region, among both free miners and prisoners, it does not follow that treating prisoners with such inhumanity to squeeze the most out of their labor was rational. Matthew Mancini strongly implies that a limitless supply of prisoners created a "one dies, get another" mentality among contractors.[75] But prisoners in the 1870s were a valuable commodity, eagerly sought by mining contractors and landowners alike. In Alabama contractors fiercely competed with one another for a limited supply of prison labor. Counties and the state engaged in political squabbling over whether the county system should be abolished. The barbarous treatment may have been meted out to prisoners in the name of economic development, but as John T. Milner's attitude shows, what it reflected was the contempt southern industrialists had toward the poor and unprotected, especially African Americans whom they were accustomed to treating as slaves.

In his recent history of the Sloss Furnaces, David L. Lewis celebrates Sloss's peculiarly southern path to industrialization. According to Lewis, to succeed, Sloss took advantage of what the region had to offer: prison labor and an unskilled, low-paid workforce. Daniel Letwin takes a less sanguine view of Birmingham's industrial story. For him, every step forward down the path of industrialization led two steps backward. Yes, Alabama "progressed," but "beneath this surge of activity remained a shallow foundation."[76] According to Letwin, Birmingham never achieved the industrial greatness it had initially promised, precisely because it followed the tactics outlined by Lewis.

Who is right? On one level, the answer depends on how one defines success. Convict leasing for profit had high costs for Alabama's poor, its free miners, its prisoners, and its black population. Birmingham went on to become as economically polarized as the Black Belt, with a white industrial elite on top and white workers at the bottom, and black workers even further down.[77] From the perspective of political elites and industrialists, however, the lease provided cheap labor, cash revenue, tax relief for white property owners, and social control in the Black Belt. One could also argue that small farmers benefited, as, in accordance with the 1875 constitution, leasing kept taxes low.

And yet, as much as they needed convicts, industrialists could not create them. What Lewis calls a natural resource—prisoners—could not have existed without the state and county legal systems that supplied them. Social conflicts, the paucity of cash available to black laborers, and the fee system created hundreds of county convicts out of men who by all rights should have been able to pay a small fine and walk away from the courtroom. Without the fee system that forced prisoners to work off court costs, industrialists might have been forced to accede to the demands of free laborers, pay higher wages, and thus pursue a different course. The extraordinarily high number of black prisoners does not reflect disproportionate black criminality but a disproportionate effort to control black citizens, as well as the greater inability on the part of black Alabamians to pay their own way out of the system because of severely limited economic opportunity.

Prisoners and Reform, 1883–1885

■ On one level Bankhead's reforms produced chaos. Hundreds of men were transferred from farms to prison mines, and the resulting overcrowding led to even worse working conditions. On another level, however, the change in routine and resulting publicity made prisoners aware that their plight was a matter of political and social significance. Prisoners knew that a new Board of Inspectors had been appointed, and that stricter rules had been issued regarding their treatment. Change was in the air, and prisoners, keen to exploit any opportunity for improvement, felt it.

When Chief Inspector R. H. Dawson and his two subordinates, Lee and Henley, began to visit the Pratt prison mines, black prisoners observed their arrival, behavior, and movements with great interest and high expectations. Ezekiel Archey wrote to tell Dawson that on "Sunday Col. Lee came to mines. Call at Cell No 1 and left the Prison with out Speaking to us. We have bin treated the like once before but looked over it thinking the night caused you to be in hast." The new rules hardly required inspectors to speak individually to each man, but Archey and others assumed that if Dawson and Lee were truly inspectors, then they should speak to convicts.

Prisoners treated the new inspectors as if they existed to supervise wayward contractors. Gus Moore, a prisoner at Pratt, wrote Dawson a letter asking him to "come at once." Even convicts at isolated prison farms expected action from the new state inspectors. J. A. Howard, a county prisoner at work at a remote plantation, wrote to Dawson to say that although Lee and Henley had both visited, neither came "where we could talk to him." But he wanted to tell Dawson that their boss "dont let one hour pass but what he is cursin some convict for a Son of a bitch and sometime the same thing about the inspectors." Howard also complained that sick prisoners received a poor diet and scant medical attention. Other prisoners from a large plantation known as "King's" sent Inspector Lee several letters urging him to do something about their treatment.[1] Nothing in the new legislation indicated that Lee, Dawson, and Henley were supposed to be at the beck and call of prisoners, and yet prisoners behaved as though the inspectors were their protectors and advocates.

The presence of inspectors instilled prisoners with new feelings of hope. Before the arrival of the inspectors, the threat of punishment compelled silence. According to Archey, when prisoners witnessed atrocities there was "no one to say spare the man['s] life but all pass being compell to Smile or be treated the same." But now, Archey wrote, "we appreciate the fact that the greatest change have came about. Since the last Inspectors Board composed of Conl Dawson, Dr. Henley and Mr. Lee and we thank god for this blessing. Before we fell in there hands our punishment was unlimited. but it is not so now." Prisoners took this new opportunity to reveal their horrific treatment. They expected changes, and they sought to make the inspectors feel personally responsible. A trustee had tried to dash Archey's hopes by telling him that Dawson "was not the man we taken you to be." Archey refused to believe it. "I hated to hear that," he wrote to Dawson. "I am yet in hopes to show them better in the future."[2] Prisoners took the authority of the inspectors seriously and expressed disappointment when inspectors failed to deliver on their promises.

As Dawson began to implement changes in prison life, prisoners began to believe that they might gain an early release through "short time." In theory, a prisoner with no marks of bad conduct against him was eligible to have two months deducted from every year of his sentence. This rule had rarely been enforced, but under Dawson's leadership more prisoners began to receive short-time pardons. So that they might know the exact date of their future release, prisoners began to demand their own time cards, which showed the date of their conviction and the dates of their "short-time" and "long-time" releases. In the past, few mechanisms forced contractors to release prisoners at all, let alone on the correct day. With short time and time cards, however, prisoners began to feel that they had more control over their future. This belief, in no small measure, they attributed to Dawson's alleged desire to act on their behalf against their contractors.

It might appear that prisoners had hung their hopes on a thin thread. Bankhead himself did little to indicate he genuinely wished to challenge the power of contractors, so why should Dawson have been any different? Indeed, critics and subsequent historians have emphasized Bankhead's dishonest relations with mining interests. Journalist Robert McKee alleged that Bankhead headed a "penitentiary ring"—a corrupt alliance between Democratic party insiders and industrialists. Bankhead parlayed a two-year stint as warden of the state penitentiary, with a salary of $2,000 a year, into a wealthy political dynasty. In 1888, five years after he left the position of warden, he received a payoff of over $1,200 from TCI so as to ensure that company would continue to receive the lion's share of prison labor. For thirty-three years he served in the U.S. House of Representatives and the U.S. Senate. His son, William, also went to Congress. Bankhead and his family wielded power in the state—and in Washington—well into the twentieth century.[3] It seems clear that Bankhead's reforms were merely a means of getting more prisoners into coal mines and staving off criticism about the lease.

And yet some Alabama Democrats were serious about promoting prison reform. Among them were Robert McKee and R. H. Dawson. An influential editor of the *Selma Argus*, McKee became a Democratic party insider when he became the private secretary to Governor Cobb (Governor Houston's successor) and Governor E. A. O'Neal. In his private correspondence with Alabama senator John Morgan, McKee voiced displeasure at the conditions of the convicts. It is likely that he had some influence in Dawson's appointment to the board.

Reginald Heber Dawson was born in South Carolina in 1838, the son of a lawyer and planter with an illustrious and wealthy family pedigree. He and his older brother, Nathaniel Henry Rhodes Dawson, moved with their parents to Dallas County in the Alabama Black Belt in 1842. In his teens Dawson attended the University of Alabama for three years; he then studied law in Tennessee and returned to Alabama to practice. He served as a lieutenant colonel in an Alabama infantry regiment; he was wounded and returned home from the war in 1864. Presumably he continued his legal practice until his appointment to the board, which paid $2,000 a year. Despite these accomplishments, R. H. Dawson stood in the shadow of his brother, eleven years his senior. N. H. R. Dawson had already embarked on a political career before the war and continued in politics afterward. Eventually he became chairman of the state's Democratic party. He nearly captured the party's nomination for the governorship in 1882, but he was beaten by E. A. O'Neal. Soon after, O'Neal appointed the defeated Dawson's brother to head the Board of Inspectors. Between 1883 and 1885 R. H. Dawson served on Alabama's first Board of Inspectors, along with Albert T. Henley, a physician from Marengo County, and William D. Lee, a lawyer from Perry County. When John H. Bankhead resigned in 1885, the post of warden was eliminated, and Dawson, Lee, and Henley became the Board of Inspectors for the Alabama Department of Corrections, with Dawson in charge as chief inspector.[4]

Dawson, Henley, and Lee were unusual choices to run the penitentiary. Their high level of education and middle-class backgrounds contrasted sharply with Bankhead's humble beginnings and poor schooling. Furthermore, their correspondence shows a devotion to professionalism and a certain sympathy toward the prisoners. Undoubtedly Dawson had political connections, but he turned out to be an atypical political appointment.[5] Of course, Dawson felt a responsibility to make money for the state, and many of his reforms were simply designed to control and discipline prisoners more effectively. And yet for nearly the next twenty years, Dawson fought in his own way to reverse Bankhead's policies by bringing order and a degree of humanity to the Alabama penitentiary. Dawson's concern for the individual welfare of prisoners and his belief that prison mining was wrong contrast sharply with Bankhead's whipping and moneygrubbing. Dawson often provided a moral voice in the midst of an immoral system and tried to bring prisoners out of the mines. In spite of his humanitarian impulses, however, Dawson implemented Bankhead's and the state's policies. Over the next twenty years, he became so tied into the prison system that his own son, Thomas Craig Dawson, also worked as a state inspector. After 1896 both father and son lived at Sloss's Flat Top prison mine, where R. H. Dawson retired and died in 1906. Ironically, the chief inspector's tireless efforts at reform ultimately institutionalized a system he opposed. And yet his reforms did a great deal to instill new hope among prisoners and even encouraged them to challenge the contractors' authority.

When Dawson became chief inspector, he inherited a prison system characterized by chaos, corruption, exploitation, cruelty, and massive attempts at escape. He found prisoners held "overtime" for years, illegally subleased to other contractors, and suffering from abuse and hunger. In 1883 Bankhead was still the official warden of the state, so Dawson took it upon himself to inspect the county system, which the new legislation entitled him to do. He wrote to Governor O'Neal informing him that the "county convict system is in great confusion." Many county convicts were missing or in the hands of illegitimate contractors.[6] He began to keep a diary. At the "Wright place," a county camp, he "found that the negroes were almost on starvation." He took a daily food ration and had it carefully weighed "in a dry good store, the only place except the post office where there is a scale delicate enough for the purpose." It weighed only "128 grains, about one quarter of an ounce allowing one half for loss in cooking." Dawson was outraged and wrote to L. D. Rouse, the owner of the camp. "How you can expect to work people and feed them in this way I cannot comprehend." Dawson felt deceived by Rouse and told him that he should not punish the prisoners for complaining. "Both Mr. Lee and myself spoke pretty roughly to the negroes for not informing us of this state of things, and their not doing so makes me think that they must be badly intimidated."[7] Typically, the prisoners were blamed for their own abuse, but Dawson's frustration indicates that he and the inspectors did come to rely upon prisoners for information.

He visited other county camps including J. W. Comer's prison plantation in Barbour County where he found the prisoners in ragged, filthy clothing as well as "unnecessarily chained and shackled."[8] According to Dawson, one of the best prisons for county convicts was the Pratt Saw Mill, which worked a large number of white state prisoners. But even here, the facilities were overcrowded; prisoners had no privies, and whites and blacks were chained together at night.[9]

By far the worst county prison was Coalburg, formerly owned by John T. Milner. Without informing the board, Milner had sold part of the mine, and the prisoners, to the Georgia Pacific Railroad. Dawson was as shocked by this cavalier disregard for rules as he was by the conditions he found. The prison had no floor or toilet facilities; the food consisted only of bread and meat. Several prisoners complained that their time had expired. Dawson believed them to be "mistaken," but a few months later he realized how common it was to hold men beyond the date of their sentence. Most disturbing were the numbers of dead. Out of 100 prisoners, 8 had died between March 1 and June 21, 1883, "over thirty percent per annum."[10] As Dawson came to realize, however, the number of deaths at the Pratt mines was also high. Dawson wrote to another judge that "there has been very much fatal sickness at all of the mines this year." He believed the causes were overwork and being kept too long underground. Two of Comer and McCurdy's prisons, at Coketon and Slope No. 2, were good, but "those at the drifts have miserable accommodations, unfit for men to be kept in."[11]

As Dawson inspected, he began to oppose Bankhead's plan to lease all state prisoners to the mines. He was distressed to find "so many disabled men." As a result of these initial visits, Dawson felt "stronger than ever in the conviction that the convicts should not be worked in the mines."[12] But once appointed to the Board of Inspectors, Dawson could not overturn the state's contract, which entitled Comer and McCurdy and Pratt to 200 state prisoners each.

Frustrated at his impotence in changing the state system, Dawson turned his attention briefly to stopping the flow of county prisoners to coal mines. As of June 18, 1883, he began writing dozens of letters to county and probate judges urging them to cancel their agreements with mining contractors. When Judge J. B. Tally leased all of his county prisoners to Milner's mine at Newcastle, Dawson asked him to reconsider. "I think you have made a mistake in making an increase of price your object in hiring out your convicts," he wrote. "I am opposed to mines on account of the great mortality from both sickness and accident." To another county judge Dawson explained that "my experience as an Inspector convinces me that the worse possible use you can make of a convict is to work him in a mine. The appalling amt of deaths that have occurred at the mines, both from disease and accidents, the great number of cripples, the men broken down by disease to be found there should convince the public that they should not be forced to incur the augers incident to this sort of work."[13]

But no one in authority paid the slightest attention to Dawson's concerns. County judges rejected his pleas and continued to lease their prisoners to the mines—in even greater numbers. In March 1883 twenty-nine counties in Alabama leased a total of over 400 county convicts to the mines.[14] Even if Dawson had somehow managed to convince the state to change its course and rescind its agreement with Pratt, counties remained eager to lease their prisoners to the mines. By 1883 the lure of cash revenue, combined with the coal industry's eagerness for cheap labor, entrenched the practice of prison mining. Soon after his appointment, Dawson had to face the reality that most of his time would be spent overseeing state and county prisoners in coal mines.

While Dawson traveled and inspected county camps, his subordinates, Inspectors A. T. Henley and W. D. Lee, witnessed firsthand the implementation of Bankhead's plan at the Pratt mines. Bankhead had promised the legislature that Pratt and Comer and McCurdy were in a position to provide clean clothes, good food, hot water, and decent treatment. But by December 1883, six months after Dawson's previous visit, A. T. Henley informed his boss that "Bankhead's promises have not yet been carried out. . . . Most of the negroes have not had a change of clothing in from three to nine weeks and are as lousy as they can be." Henley believed that the horrible conditions were encouraging the prisoners to rebel. "There is a great dissatisfaction among the men. I could hear a good deal of a threatened mutiny but could not get anything definite. . . . there is a good deal of talk among the men to that effect, and . . . it is due to the filthy condition of things. I think you had better come up here and go with me out there and probe it to the bottom."[15]

The dramatic increase in the number of prisoners working at Pratt no doubt contributed to the "filthy condition of things." In 1882 Pratt had leased 92 state prisoners. By December 1883, however, more than 500 prisoners worked daily at the Slope and the Shaft. Suddenly prisoners comprised almost one-half of Pratt's entire labor force. According to Justus Collins, the timekeeper at the Pratt mines, in 1883 the "payroll for the month of October showed six hundred and ninety two free men and . . . five hundred and twenty convicts." To Pratt, prisoners represented much more than merely an extra, albeit captive, labor force. Prison miners produced twice the coal of free laborers. Pratt forced its prison miners to work six days a week, whereas free miners usually worked only fifteen days a month.[16] Without providing any of the facilities it had promised, Pratt exploited prisoners to the utmost. A new prison would not be built until 1888.

Worsening conditions prompted prisoners to complain and not comply. In May 1884 Ezekiel Archey and Ambrose Haskins wrote to Dawson, citing a host of problems. Unjust punishment in the mines, according to Archey, had reached new heights. Prisoners were being whipped for filling their cars with too much rock or for "scant" cars. Even when the mine was only open half a day, Archey said, prisoners were whipped for not completing their entire task. This was too much, and it was up to the inspectors to make things right and punish the contractors. "Conl Dawson our frind we are longing to see the Day when time shall cause evry man to reap what he have sowed." Archey had written of divine justice, but he also threatened mortal consequences if the treatment of prisoners at Pratt did not improve. "We all wanted to Serve our term but the times is geting very hard," he wrote in May 1884.[17]

The letter described other injustices. "We have bin treated very cruel lately by the Board," Ambrose and Archey claimed, "and we wish to find out what we have done to cause such Treatments." Visiting families had been turned away by the guards, and Archey wanted to know why. Inspector Lee had explained that the prisoners were being punished because of the "white mens conduct," but Archey pointed out the injustice of punishing the entire group for the behavior of the few. "They are the men that causes the presant truble & evry State oficer tries to Hold us accountable for there actions by dening us the Previledges of alowing our family& to come to see us." Prison rules should apply to whites and blacks, Archey and Ambrose argued; when white prisoners defied authorities, they should be punished. And when black prisoners behaved, they should be rewarded. "We appreciate good Treatments & we know when we get such."

Archey and Haskins's letter shows that even though they respected the authority of the inspectors, they were equally insistent about their rights as workers and as family members. Such complaints were not always welcome and sometimes were treated with ridicule. On the other hand, when prisoners rebelled in the mines, inspectors knew they had to act. In August of that year, a few months after Archey's warning, Inspector Lee wrote to Dawson about the troubles at Pratt.

> Dont you think that my presence is very much needed at Pratt Mines to get things out of the twist they are in there. When I quit there about the middle of June, every thing was running as smoothly as if greased with refined oil. The greatest complaint that could be trumped up was that the ladies were not allowed promptly on Sabbath admittance to the serene presence of the

Lordly Ezekiel Archey. . . . Now nothing unusual for 50 or so to be
whipped at once. And worse still one Pitt Boss is not sufficient to
bounce a poor devil and beat him, but they must double team on
him & beat and berate him until the subterranean passages of Pratt
Mines resound & reverberate with his cries of murder.[18]

Lee's derisive comment on the "Lordly" Archey shows the distance between
inspectors and prisoners. Clearly he felt annoyed by complaints about family visits. Nevertheless, Lee believed that if contractors were beating and
subduing prisoners underground, then something must be terribly wrong.
When prisoners refused, or were simply unable, to complete the onerous
tasks required, inspectors investigated and even took action. Despite their
skepticism, Dawson, Lee, and Henley soon found themselves responding to
the prisoners' complaints.

Initially there was little Dawson could do about chaotic working conditions, especially since Bankhead, who was still warden, sent him reassur-
ances that conditions would improve. Instead, Dawson threw himself into
the task of turning administrative chaos into order. He sought to implement a more orderly means of keeping track of all prisoners and began with
the county system. Shocked at the ubiquitous dishonesty of the contractors,
he wrote streams of letters to county judges urging them to take notice of
missing prisoners. For example, in November 1883 Dawson found a county
prisoner convicted of burglary in the spring of 1875 and due to be released
in 1885. When Dawson wrote to the Lee County judge, he discovered that
Comer and McCurdy "have never reported him . . . and have never paid a
dollar for him . . . he is a first class man, worth $18 a month. But the beauty
of the thing is that Comer and McCurdy have had him near two years. This
is only one of a number of such cases that I have found out." At the county
mines in Newcastle and Coalburg, Dawson found prisoners from Marengo
County who had never been paid for and never reported. Comer and
McCurdy had also been accustomed to holding prisoners beyond the date
of their scheduled release. "You have no idea how many such cases I have
worked up," Dawson wrote to Judge William Richardson, "and it is a fortunate thing that the last Legislature gave the State Inspectors authority to
inspect county convicts." Dawson advised county judges to demand either
their money or their prisoners. "If you expect any contractors to do their
duty unless you make them, you will be disappointed."[19]

Bringing the county system under control proved difficult as contractors were accustomed to treating convicts as their own personal property.
Dawson was especially appalled at John T. Milner's "transfer" of more than
100 county convicts to the Georgia Pacific Railroad. Whereas Bankhead
had tolerated such transgressions, Dawson appealed to the governor for
help. "Convicts have been hired out and lost sight of, others are in the

possession of contractors and no bond or contract on file. Others have been found in possession of parties different from those to whom hired." Dawson had a great passion for order, and he insisted upon the abeyance of old practices and the implementation of new ones. Under his leadership the Department of Corrections sought to influence, albeit in an indirect way, the treatment of prisoners for the first time.[20]

When Dawson took over, contractors still expected the state to mitigate the cost of sick, dying, and old prisoners by granting them pardons or charging less. Farris and McCurdy, labor contractors who ran a county convict farm, asked Dawson to come and inspect thirteen prisoners who should not, the contractors claimed, cost as much as "full hands." When Dawson arrived, he discovered several boys, one as young as thirteen; the others were about fifteen, sixteen, and seventeen. Dawson described them all as sickly, "feeble," of no account, and "small and poorly developed." In addition to children, Dawson found elderly men of sixty and seventy years of age along with Mary Williams, "a delicate and feeble woman." Here Dawson encountered the ruthless logic of the lease: if prisoners could not work, they were deemed unprofitable and sent back home to die, with the state paying the cost.[21]

Another complication arose from the system of court costs. The money the county received for the work performed by a county prisoner during his sentence belonged in the Fine and Forfeiture Fund. County prisoners had to pay court costs—an amount ranging from $40 to $100—incurred during their arrest, imprisonment, and trial. Judges, calculating a day's labor as worth thirty or forty cents, added extra time onto a prisoner's sentence to pay these costs. For example, $40 in court costs paid off at forty cents a day meant a prisoner served an additional one hundred days in jail. If the lease called for contractors to pay $15 a month for the prisoner's labor, however, the amount the prisoner was working off was more than forty cents a day. Before the time sentenced for costs had expired, a prisoner would have already paid for his actual court costs. Should he then be released early? If so, on whose order? Because the money received from additional time in prison went into county coffers, local judges often overlooked prisoners who had already paid their costs, and contractors never objected to keeping healthy prisoners. When county prisoners or their families contested their assigned date of release, Dawson had to track down inconsistencies and cajole judges and contractors to release county men on time.[22] Dawson expected them to change their ways and begin to keep orderly records. Yet many judges, content to let the money flow, resisted. Many had no idea exactly how much money the county was owed, which account the funds belonged in, and when payments should cease.

The "time" a prisoner spent at labor in the coal mines held differing and conflicting meanings for county judges, the board of inspectors, the attorney general, the labor contractors, and, of course, the prisoners. The contractors wanted as much of a prisoner's time as possible; to them, time spent in prison meant profit from the value of skilled, productive labor. Similarly, county judges had every incentive to prolong a prisoner's sentence. Prison time meant cash income; every day an individual spent in prison represented a financial gain. To the state's attorney general, however, the time of a prisoner's sentence remained an ongoing legal question, and Dawson spent much of his time corresponding with all parties as to the correct way of assessing a prisoner's time. Many questions were raised. Could prisoners be legally forced to pay for the various costs of their incarceration, such as their food and court fees, by serving extra time? When, exactly, did a person's time in prison begin? Did a sentence include only the days a prisoner worked, or the full amount of time spent in a camp? Sometimes the impetus for these questions came from the prisoners themselves as they too began to contest accepted practices of timekeeping.

As contractors could not be trusted to give accurate information, Dawson took it upon himself to overhaul the various methods of determining prisoners' time.[23] In December 1886 Dawson estimated that still "fully ¾ of all reports made to me contain errors."[24] Besides the outright deception on the part of contractors, local judges used wildly different and inaccurate methods to estimate the extra time prisoners would have to serve to pay for court costs. For example, some judges calculated that a sentence did not begin until a prisoner actually arrived at the mining camp.[25] Some did not include Sundays in their estimates, because prisoners did not work on Sunday.[26] Other judges calculated that court costs would be "worked out" at a rate of as little as twenty-five cents a day. All of these methods could substantially increase the length of a prisoner's incarceration. Dawson often had to appeal these cases to the attorney general one by one. Through his efforts and the complaints of prisoners, a somewhat uniform agreement on the meaning of "time" began to emerge among judges, contractors, prisoners, and inspectors. They all had to agree, for example, that a "month" included Sundays!

More than a humane nature spurred Dawson to make these changes. By improving conditions, he hoped to improve prison discipline; he especially wanted to reduce the high numbers of escapes. During the 1870s massive prison breakouts often made the news. Three weeks before R. H. Skinner's capture and return to the Eureka mines in 1878, for example, more than 100 convicts at Eureka launched a breakout attempt one Sunday afternoon. Fourteen succeeded. Contractors dealt with the constant threat of escape by putting chains on men or giving guards shoot-to-kill orders. "If a man attempts to escape, orders are to shoot him—that is if he is running," testified one prison guard. Nothing surprised the contractors. Bankhead wrote to one judge about a convict who wore "double shackles and a waist chain. If however he should escape I will inform you at once." Contractors punished escapes severely because men who successfully escaped inspired others to do so. Prisoners, however, took the risk because they knew that escape was often their only hope of ever being released.[27] Dawson tried to stop the escapes by enforcing new rules that guaranteed prisoners would be released on time.

Dawson tried to reinforce prisoners' faith in the board in other ways. For example, he encouraged more contact between prisoners and their families. Before 1883, prisoners rarely communicated with the outside world. Letters sent from home were not received. One such letter, from a mother to her son, was left in prison farm owner Gaius Whitfield's personal files. It clearly conveys the impact of imprisonment on families in the Black Belt. "My dear Sun," she wrote, "I will try to write you a few lines to let you now that we have not forgoten you. . . . Mandy left one dollar with Margaret to send to you[.] The boyes would send you some money this time but they ar makeing up money for Mr. Glenard. . . . As soon as we can pay him thirty we will send you a letter. The children al sends their love to you. . . . Your friends is but few their is none that is willing to help me but your grandma. . . . You must write to me as soon as you get this[.] Be a good boy and mind what you are told."[28] When they could, family members raised money to gain a pardon or a release. But contractors cared little about fostering those ties, and short of escape, prisoners had little means of entering into contact.

In contrast, Dawson encouraged family ties. In 1883 he implemented a routine system of letter writing between the Pratt mines and families. "In 1883 we found that but little opportunity was afforded the convicts for sending or receiving letters. We found men who had not written home, or heard from them in years." On Dawson's orders paper and envelopes were distributed every Sunday to the state prisoners. When the inspectors came to the mine every two weeks or so, they picked up the unstamped letters, fixed them with postage, and mailed them. Dawson claimed that as a result nearly all of the prisoners communicated with their families regularly.[29] Under Dawson's direction a regular system of letter writing continued throughout the 1890s. Twice a month convicts were furnished with papers, envelopes, and stamps.[30]

Prisoners valued family comfort and became angry and disappointed when they felt their families had been remiss. Incensed at his brother Wade's neglect, Albert McAlpine wrote a letter, in the best family tradition, designed to inflict guilt. Even though Wade had hired a lawyer to secure Albert's release, Albert refused acknowledge Wade's efforts: "Dr Brothr you shoul of written to me sooner you know we is all the boys there is in the world and be cose i am in prisoned it look like to me you all has forgotten me and dont car anything about me a tall . . . plese write plain nx time so i can make it out i cld not read all of your letter." [31] Letters encouraged prisoners to maintain their family ties. They also reveal that prisoners took practical steps to gain their release and plan for their futures.

Prisoners also longed to see their families. One day in 1884 some family members came to visit Ezekiel Archey at the Pratt mines, but they were turned away. Archey wrote to Dawson, telling him how the men felt when families were denied access to the prison. "Conl, Consiter for Instanse. if you were by law or violence be taken from your family. & see them come & go with not speaking one word to them. Sir it is heart-breaking to our familys and to us." Maintaining their humanity in prison was inextricably bound to communication with their families and communities. As Archey put it, "Our family coming is our next Favor to liberty." [32]

As Archey indicated, family members of imprisoned men suffered too. When families did not hear from their sons for long periods of time, they wrote to the Board of Inspectors and to the governor to inquire about them. Jane Childes wrote to R. H. Dawson about her son Walter. "He rote to me that his time would be out in May and then he would come home. I have not heard a word from him since. have ritten to him and cannot get enney anseer. Pleas rite to me if he is alive or dead and when his time is out and how he is geting along." [33] Harry Streety wrote to the governor about his son Sam. He too wanted to know if his son was "dead or not. . . . I have wrote 5 letters and has not got no answer yet." [34] Anderson Lewis's father wanted to pay his son's fine and his court costs, but his son, who was imprisoned at the Pratt mines "in care of Messrs Comer & McCurdy," never answered his letters. [35]

Families envisioned a time in the future when their sons would return home to rejoin the family circle. "We have frequent letters inquiring how much it will cost to buy so & so out," R. Andrews, a probate judge in Hale County, explained to Governor Thomas Seay in 1887. "And often times an old colored Brother will come [and say,] 'Boss how much will it take to buy my sons time.' I turn to my book. the cost is from fifty dollars up. he cant raise that much. goes off & comes back again & again." [36] The exact amount due to pay off court costs mattered a great deal to cash-poor sharecropping families. This judge's story illustrates that once contact with a prisoner was established, family members went out of their way to inquire about him and even saved money to pay off his costs.

Inspectors knew that the greatest reward they could hold out to imprisoned men was the promise of an early release for good behavior. According to the acts of 1878–79, prisoners were entitled to receive "short time"—a two-month reduction from every year of their sentence—if they had no "bad conduct" marks against them. The statute had rarely been enforced. Dawson realized, however, that the promise of short time would reduce escapes and improve behavior. Prisoners sought to obtain short time because it meant an early release from prison; unlike escapes, it guaranteed release with certainty. If the sentences were less than a few years, a short-time pardon substantially reduced a prisoner's sentence. With short time, a prisoner could anticipate returning home to resume a free life.

Prisoners wrote letters to press their individual cases. Sam Black wrote to Governor Seay, the lawyer who had defended him at his trial: "Please sir write to me as soon as you get this please sir about my short time write in care of Mr. HR Gafford to Sam Black your defendant in a case. . . . you promis to do what yu culd for me and i want to go home for i has ben trying to bee a good boy every sence i been here." [37] Albert McAlpine, a prisoner, and his brother Wade discussed various options for his release. "I bin here goin on 13 month and . . . had no trobl atall and it look like I might get parden out of this trobl." [38] Prisoners believed that if they worked hard and obeyed the rules, they might receive the coveted short-time pardon.

In many respects the reforms Dawson ordered—short time, letter writing, family visits, and regular releases—improved the orderliness of the prison mines. Dawson wrote to county judges, urging them to recommend short-time pardons "as an inducement to good behavior. The state convicts get it . . . and it is found to be a great aid in controlling them." [39] Dawson hoped that short-time pardons would decrease the number of escapes, attempted escapes, and general insubordination, particularly in the prison mines.[40] Because the obedience of prisoners was crucial to his vision of how the well-ordered penitentiary should operate, Dawson viewed short time as an effective means of controlling prisoners and enforcing their obedience to prison rules. By exploiting the desire of black prisoners for freedom, inspectors sought to create the public perception of a smooth-running penitentiary, free of corruption and dedicated to reform.

Prisoners frequently looked to Dawson to enforce their new rights. When complainants such as prisoner Robert Wilson approached Dawson about being held overtime, he became annoyed. Wilson, Dawson wrote, "had not mentioned the matter to the Superintendent . . . but waited as they do about everything until I came." Although Wilson had indeed been held past the date of his legal discharge, and although Dawson arranged for his prompt release and payment for the work done overtime, the chief inspector still did not assume contractors to be in the wrong. "It was an oversight," he explained; "there was no intention to violate the law and I feel sure it will not occur again." Dawson usually gave the contractors the benefit of the doubt, but prisoners knew better. At Coalburg they barraged Dawson with complaints of being held overtime. "John Robinson, Moses Croom, and Pleasant Stallworth" told him that their time had expired and demanded their immediate release. Dawson did not believe them, but he still wrote to the county judge to see if they were correct.

These complaints made Dawson realize that prisoners should know when they "should be discharged, so that they can know themselves when their time expires." Soon he began to distribute "time cards" to all prisoners.[41] These cards showed the date of the prisoner's conviction and two possible dates of release—the "short-time" date received for good behavior and the "long-time" date. Without a card a prisoner could be held indefinitely with ease. But with a card a prisoner held tangible proof of when he or she was supposed to be released. When prisoners received a time card, their hope for short time increased even more. Thus, in the prisoners' struggles to gain an early, and legal, release, time cards became important weapons.

No matter where they were, at the mines or at remote county convict camps, all prisoners demanded their individual time cards. A. T. Henley, explicitly acting on behalf of prisoners, wrote the secretary of the Department of Corrections in 1885 to request time cards for the prisoners he recently visited. "The men are anxious to get them," he wrote, "and I write at their solicitation."[42] Contractors had withheld these cards from prisoners in order to keep them ignorant. By withholding proof of the actual date of release, contractors also intimidated prisoners and kept them feeling hopeless. Dawson wrote to the supervisor of a convict camp in Lowndes County to ask why the prisoners there had not received their cards. He had gone there to inspect and discovered that "all of the convicts who had been convicted since last August say they have never received their time cards and applied to me for them. Every card has been sent in your care and I supposed you were distributing them among the convicts. If you still have them on hand please give them to the convicts at once."[43] Time cards continued to be a focus of struggle between contractors and prisoners throughout the 1880s.

In 1885 the new convict law explicitly stated that every prisoner should receive an individual card. Dawson kept tabs on both contractors and judges, reminding them that they were required by law to keep their books accurate and distribute time cards to all prisoners.[44] As long as Dawson remained in charge, the right to possess a time card did not fade away; in 1890, for example, Dawson requested 2,000 of them from the governor for distribution to state convicts.[45]

Despite the law and Dawson's warnings, contractors still tried to withhold time cards. Perhaps they did so because prisoners used the cards to point out discrepancies in their sentences. Albert Ervin, a prisoner, wrote to the Department of Corrections from the Pratt mines demanding that his card be corrected. "I was convicted on the 15th of Oct. 1884 for two years the day was Tuesday. I have got a card of my time saying I was convicted the 18 Oct. 1884 but it is a mistake. I would like for you to please correct it for me."[46] Warren Levett also wanted his card corrected, "as my time expires June the 6/85 according to the record at the court house in Sumter county.

The Judge told me I would have to serve a little over five month when I left home. But this card says my time expires July 28/85."[47] Another letter noted, "The Pen. record shows Ross Peckam to have been convicted April 5, 1884 for 5 years he claims it was only 4 years."[48] Prisoners sometimes challenged discrepancies of as little as three to six days. "Cornelius Thornton & Mose Williams . . . claim to have been convicted Nov. 3, 1883 whereas the Penty Record shows the date to be Nov. 9, 1883."[49] "Melton Pickens, a state convict from Pickens co. claims to have been convicted March 14, 1882. Our record shows it to be May 14, 1882."[50]

Clearly prisoners were not wholly intimidated by authority. If they had legal proof, they pushed their cases forward. Prisoners complained to inspectors about all infringements of prison rules. Aware that the practical meaning of their rights depended on how far inspectors and contractors could be pushed, prisoners regularly complained to inspectors about bad food and coffee. They criticized the system of trusteeship that gave certain prisoners control over others. When Thomas Skinner was brutally whipped 275 times in 1883, he requested short time on grounds that such brutal mistreatment entitled him to a release.[51] Prisoners asked for time cards; once they got them, they used the cards as a basis for further complaints. When some Jefferson County convicts received their time cards in 1885, they insisted that the cards were in error. They had been convicted in March of that year, not in April as the cards said. Dawson wrote to the county judge and reminded him that "to hold any of them overtime even on your report might make the contractors liable to troublesome suits." Dawson was not exaggerating. In fact, several prisoners had already sued the state after they had been held overtime.[52]

Although Dawson saw himself primarily as a corrections officer and administrator, he unquestionably felt sympathy for the prisoners and also believed it was his job to protect them. By 1889–90 Dawson, Lee, and Henley often remarked on the differences their tenure in the Department of Corrections had made in the lives of prisoners. When the inspectors requested the pardon of Sam Thomas, a Montgomery County convict who had been serving time for assault since 1872, they emphasized the horrendous prison conditions before 1883. "Until Acts 82–83, page 134," they wrote to the governor, "there was almost no protection for State Convicts and absolutely none for county Convicts. In most instances their servitude . . . was an earthly hell, and death in its most cruel form was preferable to life."[53] In retrospect, then, Dawson, Henley, and Lee were proud of the changes they had implemented and believed that their actions had drastically improved conditions.

Milner and other contractors, however, were slow to change. In 1885 A. T. Henley wrote to Dawson about the disgusting conditions at Newcastle. "The prison is filthy, the bedding is disgustingly so & the clothing black, dirty, & ragged. . . . I have heard more complaints of whipping yesterday than I have heard in a long time. . . . The stench from privy buckets, seat, and dirty bedding was unbearable." Henley urged action. "We have allowed John T. [Milner] to make fools of us long enough by his pretty, oily talk and fair promises and we must put a stop to it and make him do better with his convicts."[54] Contractors knew they had to gain the trust and confidence of state officials, yet they still sought to subvert the rules, cut corners on treatment, and retain the most able prisoners for as long as possible.

Despite contractors' resistance, the reforms implemented in 1883 and 1885 changed prison conditions, but not always as Dawson, Henley, and Lee had planned. The greatest changes brought about by the reforms were in the attitudes, behavior, and reactions of the prisoners, not the contractors. Prisoners knew the regulations and began to act as individuals who possessed the right to contact with the outside world, limited punishment, a prompt release, and a time card. The bottom line at the Pratt mines was still production and profit. But the reforms implemented in 1883 as a response to contractor abuse and prisoner escapes had an enormous influence on the behavior of prisoners. Armed with the knowledge of their rights under the rules and buoyed by increased contact with their families, prisoners began to challenge the authority of contractors and inspectors alike.

Black and white miners at Shaft No. 3, Pratt mines, c. 1888. (Erskine Ramsey Collection, cat. no. 1.5.10.3.21)

Coke ovens at Pratt mines, Shaft No. 1, 1893. (Erskine Ramsey Collection, cat. no. 1.5.10.3.31)

Armed company guards used during the 1894 strike at the Pratt mines. (Erskine Ramsey Collection, cat. no. 1.5.10.3.35)

Birmingham city convicts, barefoot, in their sleeping quarters. The prisoners were chained together, their shackles never removed. (Thomas Parke Collection, cat. no. 21.8.5.5.22)

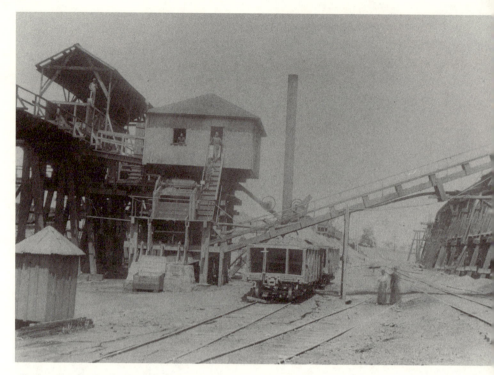

Coal washer at Pratt City, 1901. Notice the two women strolling in the foreground. (Erskine Ramsey Collection, cat. no. 1.5.10.3.36)

Chained prisoners at work on the streets of Birmingham. (Thomas Parke Collection, cat. no. 21.8.6.5.23)

Senator John Hollis Bankhead Sr. with Governor B. B. Comer

(Left) John T. Milner, owner of the Newcastle Prison mine and proponent of industrial convict labor
(Center) Dr. Thomas Dukes Parke, physician hired by the state of Alabama to investigate conditions at the Coalburg prison mine. His lengthy investigation did little to change prison conditions.
(Right) Julia Tutwiler, prison reformer and advocate of prison schools

Banner mines shaft prison complex, 1912. Improved buildings did not necessarily imply improved conditions, as over 100 county convicts died in a fire in the Pratt mines shortly after this photograph was taken. (Pratt City Collection, cat. no. 7.08)

Black women prisoners at work in Alabama. (From an article on convict leasing by W. E. B. Du Bois in the *Missionary Review of the World,* 1903)

6

Working and Surviving in Prison Mines

■ In the late nineteenth century, mining was more than a job and not quite a vocation. Miners were usually born into the profession and schooled by their fathers or other members of the community. And while skill was necessary for economic success and physical survival, no individual miner could last long without the camaraderie of his fellow worker. Men underground depended on each other for knowledge about the mine: where was it weak? where was the gas? where were the best places to work? They also relied on each other to follow a certain code of etiquette. John Brophy, an immigrant from the United Kingdom and future director of the Congress of Industrial Organizations (CIO), began working in a Pennsylvania coal mine during the 1890s at the age of twelve. He learned the mining craft from his father who, he recalled, lectured him on "the care and use of supplies—oil, powder, squibs, and on tools and on proper behavior in the mines, especially matters having to do with safety." Only after Brophy learned these basic conventions did his father show him how to "undercut the face" and "manage other operations involved in breaking the coal loose from the seam." But even this tutelage was no substitute for actual practice, and as Brophy admitted, "there was much for me to learn." Prisoners in Alabama mines could not benefit from such filial instruction. But they learned skills from each other and, ultimately, depended on each other to survive.[1]

Historians have emphasized that the economic success of convict labor depended upon the regular use of excessive coercion. It is logical, to a degree, to attribute the high productivity of Alabama prison mines to the whippings and punishments meted out. There were other prison mines, however, where no amount of coercion could produce a profit. Prison miners in Tennessee, for example, were subjected to unrelenting cruelty, but according to Karin Shapiro their performance was merely "lackluster." In Georgia convict workers, although regularly beaten, never succeeded in making prison mines profitable.[2]

In the Pratt prison mines, contractors certainly coerced prisoners, but other incentives also spurred men to mine coal efficiently. Short time, of course, was one inducement, as was money. Another powerful impetus to production, however, was the pride Alabama prisoners took in mastering their work. When they could, prisoners insisted that contractors and inspectors treat them as valuable workers. They went on strike, disagreed with mine bosses over mining procedures, complained about working conditions, and in the depths of despair threatened suicide so as to deprive contractors of their labor. In all of these actions, they showed that they thought of themselves as highly skilled workers who deserved respect.

After their arrival at the Pratt mines, prisoners were forced to accommodate themselves to a new routine of working underground. A new prisoner would have been classified as a "third-class man." And every day, according to Inspector Henley, a third-class man "shovel[ed] from 8 to 12 thousand pounds of dead weight . . . while he is on his knees."[3] When the work done to help a buddy was taken into account, Henley figured that a new prisoner, on average, lifted 15,000 to 20,000 pounds of rock in a single day. Even young, strong men were completely unprepared for the rigors of mining. Henley tried to convey to a county judge why the coal mines could not suit all new prisoners. "The cramped position that he must assume is entirely new to him, the constant fear of being killed is an obstacle, and the presence of smoke both from the lamps and the powder used in blasting the coal makes him sick."[4] Despite such obstacles, year after year black prisoners sustained a high output at the Pratt mines.

Until the new quarters promised by Pratt were built in 1888, most prisoners lived in primitive barracks and slept on bunks; there were no separate cells. Authorities segregated white and black men, giving white prisoners more space per man than the blacks. The mines operated around the clock in two twelve-hour shifts. Men assigned to the morning shift would awake while it was dark and go to the mess hall for breakfast—coffee, with sugar, and meat. They also received food to take with them into the mine. The company assigned the convicts sleeping clothes and work clothes as well as shoes. It is not clear, however, if prisoners were allowed to bathe regularly or what facilities for washing existed. After breakfast, the men filed off to work.

The amount of coal a prisoner was expected to produce in the mine depended upon his classification. A first-class man was required to mine and load four tons of coal per day, a second-class man three tons, and a third-class man two tons. "Deadheads," men considered too weak to work underground, performed the essential work of clearing the track and performing tasks "on top" of the mine. Contractors received the labor of these prisoners for free. During the 1880s companies paid $18.50 per month for a first-class man. Given the profits at stake, contractors and state inspectors frequently disagreed over a prisoner's classification.[5]

Each mine had only one white pit boss, so prisoners generally worked unsupervised. The company supplied prisoners with dynamite, charges, picks, and shovels. Once underground, the men walked, crawled, or stooped to the section of the mine assigned to them, often known as a "room." (The distance from the mine entrance to room could be as much as a mile.) Rooms were marked off on either side of the track. A skilled prisoner, or a "cutter," would lie down on his back or side and make undercuts three or four feet deep in the bottom of the seam. He then drove a hole into the rock and filled the opening with dynamite. After the explosion the cutter and his buddy used their picks to separate out the rock and then loaded the remaining coal into a tramcar.

The work of a prison miner required keen judgment. As he was undercutting, he easily could be injured by falling coal; thus the miner had to evaluate the condition of the seam. He had to decide where to drill the dynamite hole, as a misplaced charge could result in only a small amount of coal and a lot of wasted effort. Prisoners also had to decide how much powder to use and learn how to set the charge safely. The exploding dynamite shook nearly a ton of coal loose from the rock face. A poorly laid explosive could result in the deaths of many. Prisoners encountered all the dangers that free miners faced but with even greater risks. If prisoners made mistakes, they paid for them by being whipped.

Prisoners worked in teams of two men to a room—an arrangement called the "buddy system." First-class men rarely got to work together. Instead, mine bosses placed new, inexperienced prisoners under the charge of a first-class miner. Under the tutelage of the more seasoned prisoner, the new man had to "try and learn the art of cutting coal." Once underground, white and black prisoners worked together. The amount of coal expected from them exceeded their formal quotas. For example, W. E. Cockrell, a white prisoner, testified before a U.S. Senate hearing that he had been assigned to load ten cars "with a dead head negro," meaning that his partner was barely competent. Cockrell asserted that it took "every bit of the nerve and strength of a man to get it out and I didn't have a particle of spirit after I got done." The buddy system placed both skilled and unskilled men in the same precarious situation. If either partner failed to make his daily quota, both were whipped.[6]

As Alabama's coal industry grew, Alabama prisons became part of a competitive national industry. In 1886 the Tennessee Coal and Iron Company bought the Pratt Coal and Coke Company and took over the running of the prison mines at the two main sites, the Shaft and Slope No. 2. The Shaft really consisted of two working mines, the McArdle Slope and the Rock Slope. The McArdle Slope was about 200 feet below the surface of the earth and was reached by an elevator shaft. Another 120 feet farther down was a mine reached by a sharp drop, or slope, driven through solid sandstone rock, hence the name "Rock Slope."[7]

The Rock Slope was notorious for its lethal gas, but prisoners learned to protect themselves in ingenious ways. One state physician reported that prisoners attached mining lamps to their shoes or ankles: "The lightness or fatality of this gas [causes] it to rise to the highest point in the mines [where it] stagnates in dangerous quantities, and the lamps worn as formerly, on the miners' cap, would bring them indirect contact with the volume of gas, causing explosion." He noted that gas in the mine caused death in other ways. "After combustion, Carbonic Deoxide is produced, the respiration of which is often fatal to life . . . causing death by suffocation."[8] Slope No. 2, located within two miles of the Shaft, also contained gases. Yet many prisoners coped with danger in a matter-of-fact manner. Some even fried their afternoon lunch in the mine over lit gas.

At Slope No. 2 prisoners faced the challenge of constant wet and waist-high water. Prisoners worked pumps night and day to keep the water level down. Even so, convicts often had to work in water up to their necks.[9]

Few prisoners arrived ready to cope with such conditions. After spending months languishing in a county jail, new prisoners often arrived in poor health and frightened. Many, according to a physician, "ought to go to the poor house and not a few to the asylum"—not a mine. Others suffered "the depressing effects of fear which they appear never to get over." As Inspector Henley put it, "No man can go into a mine for the first time without being, as it were, dazed by the new and startling scenes going on around him."[10] Besides coping with noise, darkness, rats, dangerous gases, floods, and brutally hard work, prisoners also feared being crushed by falling rock.

In order to survive, escape the enmity of one's buddy, and avoid a whipping, a new prisoner had to learn quickly. Despite intense pressure to produce, relations between prisoners were not always rancorous. One third-class prisoner paired with a second-class man stressed the cooperative aspects of their working relationship: "If I get through first, I help my partner, and if he gets through first he helps me."[11] Healthy new prisoners sometimes adapted quickly to the mining routine, but many never completely adjusted to prison life underground. A new convict did not have long to adapt.

If a prisoner avoided mine accidents, he still had to be wary of disease. The "cause of death" column in Alabama's biennial reports from the Department of Corrections lists a host of diseases, some familiar, others unfamiliar, to modern ears. Dropsy and erysipelas were common; so were tuberculosis and pneumonia. Lesser known scourges such as "mining itch" affected prisoners around the groin and caused painful, suppurating sores. "The stooping and crawling incident and necessary to the work of mining," Henley explained, "tears open these sores and breaks the scabs, leaving the raw flesh exposed; and into these open sores the coal dust works its way, irritating the flesh still more, and making the pain almost unbearable." [12]

Prisoners bore the responsibility for their own health and safety. Physicians, hired by the mining companies, classified prisoners and determined their fitness for work. They visited the camps every few weeks and were not expected to answer the calls of sick men. Although rarely concerned with healing, physicians did express an interest in the unusual diseases prisoners developed. One physician sought the reason for the "large number of bloated and anasarcous patients" among the men. ("Anasarcous" was the technical term for dropsy, what physicians at the time called the unnatural collection of fluid in the cavities and tissues of the body.) Perhaps it came from inhaling noxious fumes. In 1886 Dr. J. M. Hayes reported that "by a thorough investigation among the old and most experienced miners, I was informed that they avoided the powder smoke, and made it a rule to wait sufficiently long after shooting their coal for the smoke and gasses to escape from the rooms, and the air in them to become perfectly pure, before resuming work." Another advantage of waiting for the room to clear of dynamite smoke before starting to load coal was being able to see. Because any appearance of rock in the trams presented grounds for a whipping, the more experienced prisoners knew the dangers of trying to load up their cart without inspecting the coal. Dr. Hayes, convinced that the convicts had discovered a brilliant means of staying healthy, tried convincing TCI's warden to allow prisoners to shoot powder the last thing in the evening. When the men returned to the mine in the morning, the "clean pure atmosphere" would enable them to see and "thus send out their coal free from rock and slate, thereby saving them much punishment." [13] The warden tried to resist, but Dr. Hayes finally persuaded him. Thus, survival strategies devised by prisoners became accepted daily practice.

Experience often made the difference between life and death, but it could not compensate for dangerous equipment. A faulty elevator at the Shaft mine is a case in point. To get to the rooms at the McArdle Slope in the Shaft, prisoners had to descend nearly 300 feet on an insecurely rigged elevator. In 1885 prisoners at the Shaft complained to the Board of Inspectors. In response, the board required Pratt to "put in a suitable break to the drum and cage at the Shaft," but in March 1887 the new brake on the drum had still not arrived. The board blustered that "unless a suitable break be placed upon the drum at [the Shaft] . . . the convicts will be ordered out of the mines." Pratt knew that such threats were empty.[14]

Free miners, of course, also endured unsafe and unhealthy conditions, but crucial differences distinguished their lot from that of prisoners. Free miners could choose their partners, supply their own equipment, and did not have to worry about brutal punishments. In contrast, prisoners were forced to work every day with unskilled partners under dangerous and at times frantic conditions. If a prisoner became ill or injured, only a physician could keep him out of the mines. In theory, if prisoners obeyed the rules and worked hard, they would survive and be released. In practice, however, they lived under the thumb of capricious guards and wardens. One day in 1884, for example, J. W. Comer forced prisoners to mine extra coal for the personal use of contractors. This violated prison rules, but Ezekiel Archey explained to Dawson why prisoners should not be censured: the fault lay with the contractor. "Dear Sir I wish I could Show you our condition clearly but I am unable but I will try. We are hear all convicts and we have to act the same. Please coompare our cases by your self. When you were a little boy, if you ever had a brier in your hand or foot & your nurce or mother taken your hand in charge to extracate the Brier you would turn your hand the way she mooved it. Yet you knew she would hurt you. But for the brier to remain it would cause great pain. This is our condition. . . . When the lyon once gets hand in his mouth then move as he wished you to move."[15] Contractors, like lions and mothers, had power. If they said something was to be done, simple logic dictated that the prisoners had to comply.

But did contractors exercise absolute power? What distinguished convict labor from slavery? Both leasing and slavery were systems of forced labor for profit that depended upon physical force and the absolute authority of either a white contractor or owner. Prisoners enjoyed none of the privileges of free labor. Like slaves, they had to do as they were told or suffer horrible punishment. Like slaves, their situation appears hopeless: the society at large had little interest in their plight other than to enforce the authority of those holding them in subordination. And both systems depended on the compliance of the state in enforcing the ultimate authority of either the contractor or the slave owner. Such absolute power would seem to leave little room for negotiations. Under the convict lease the bargain seemed to be: work or die.

Such comparisons between slavery and the lease, however, obscure the reality of both systems of forced labor. Historians have long recognized that life and work under slavery often bore little resemblance to the ideal of a master who totally and completely controlled his slaves. Innumerable factors shaped the power equation under slavery, including the individual skills of the slaves themselves, the size of the workforce, the use of overseers and black work leaders, and day-to-day resistance. As James Henry Hammond discovered upon taking charge of his South Carolina plantation, extracting maximum work from slaves was far more complicated than it first appeared. It took Hammond years to stamp out secret black religious services and impose new systems of working the land.[16] One historian of labor relations in industrial slavery has also stressed the role of negotiation over outright coercion. In his study of slave ironworkers, Charles B. Dew concluded that production rested "more on a subtle process of mutual compromise and accommodation than on excessive use of physical force and coercion."[17]

Similarly, prison contractors could not exercise total power at all times, especially in the underground world of work. In situations where prisoners stood to be blamed for a transgression, Archey emphasized their powerlessness. Yet he also made it plain that prisoners expected "favors" in return for extra work. As Archey explained, prisoners mined the illicit coal because of a complex system of reciprocity between prisoners and contractors. "You know we are compell to look to Mr. (R) for evry favor conecting our work & place & if we wish a favor can we denie his frind and Employor. No what would he say (why this) you refused & I will act the same."[18]

It is tempting to use such adjectives as obedient, pliable, cheap, and reliable to describe southern convict labor. The reality, however, is that prisoners, although working under terrible constraints, also engaged the contractors and state inspectors in a system of reciprocal favors.

Indeed, favors passing between guards and prisoners enabled the smooth running of the mine, as well as the survival of the prisoners. Why did prisoners need favors from contractors? In order to survive, according to Archey. "You may say what favor do we want. This many time we send our task & fail to get credit for it & Mr (R) can pass us or punish us just to suite his self & times we fell a little sick and not sick eknuf to stop but to miss a car on our task what then a favor comes next. & where (260) two hundred men work as we do hear Some one of us Daily want a favor."

Hard work alone could not ensure that even the most highly skilled prisoner could get his task and survive. Innumerable obstacles lay in the path of all. Even "good" miners received punishment. "They can put a man in a place where he cannot get a task and whip him every night," Archey revealed. Without the ability to call in a favor, a skilled prisoner might never receive credit for achieving his quota. Clearly many prisoners produced even more coal than their quota dictated. Yet, although exploitative, this system of reciprocity gave prisoners the right to demand favors from contractors.

Archey then launched into a further explanation of why prisoners agreed to the arrangement and mined the extra coal. Using a simile and an image drawn from the Bible, Archey stated that being a prisoner is "like a man drowning who you know will make for a Straw or anything to Save him Self." So desperate are prisoners for friends, Archey wrote, "that if a Dog looks at us & wags his tail we wish to pet the dog." Archey rhetorically asked Dawson, "If a master ask for a present of a servant will the servants refuse. *no-no.*" When the prisoners perceived that the request for extra coal had come from J. W. Comer, then how could they refuse? By comparing prisoners to a drowning man and a servant, Archey stressed the coercive nature of the favor system: given the power that Comer and his warden, William Rogers, possessed, prisoners acquiesced, it seemed, because they had little choice.

And yet Archey also emphasized that prisoners expected good treatment, even rewards, in exchange for their extra work. Archey began one letter by correcting a mistaken impression. J. W. Comer, the chief warden at Pratt, had been presented with a gift from prisoners—"a badg and chain. You and the public think we give that presant for his kind treatment to us. if so you think rite the opposite." Archey then explained what really happened: some "trustees" (favored prisoners with special privileges over other prisoners)—"white men"—convinced other prisoners to contribute extra coal to a collection. Archey complied because he thought prisoners would receive a dinner "and a day to rest on the 9 of Nov 1883." Far from being a gift, prisoners understood this exchange to be a quid pro quo—a bargain between prisoners and contractors. The newspapers, the state, and the contractors had tried to idealize and even paternalize what were essentially brutal, exploitative labor relations. Archey, however, wanted Dawson to know the truth.

Inspectors appeared to be ignorant of these nuances. Even so, this system, one-sided though it was, gave prisoners some feeling of freedom. Archey described to Dawson what happened in the mines one Christmas. "Now look at this point[:] X Mass all those who give a car had a very good Dinner & all that could not eat a little frozen turnips and pice of corn bread & fat meat. Evry man then wished he had give some thing if not for the Dinner for the Honor of X Mass day eating Something Resembling the old times at home." More than food was at stake. By rewarding skill, strength, and expertise with favors, contractors inadvertently encouraged prisoners to take pride in themselves and their work.

Prisoners valued being treated like human beings who had the privilege of celebrating Christmas as free people did. Contractors exploited them, even refusing to give prisoners a decent meal at Christmas unless they had handed over an extra ton of coal. These exchanges could hardly be called equal. The point, however, is that skilled prisoners could capitalize on their proficiency at coal mining to gain status, rest, extra food, and even dignity.

Prisoners knew that granting "favors" to contractors eventually could result in the displeasure of the inspectors—a greater harm. Yet, as Archey explained to Dawson, circumstances decreed that "we have to do many a thing that will do us harm in the future and good at the presant." We can surmise that Archey revealed to Dawson how the system of mining coal really worked because he hoped to engage Dawson into a beneficial relationship at the cost of the contractors.

When they complained, prisoners risked punishment. Despite the existence of Dawson and the Board of Inspectors, contractors used any and every excuse to whip men. Nearly every convict miner who testified before a legislative committee in 1889 reported that he had been whipped or that he had witnessed a whipping. If a prisoner loaded rock in with his coal, failed to get his task, or did not "show interest" in his work, he was whipped. Prisoners who complained about the lack of tramcars were whipped. Even when the mines were open for only half a day, and prisoners could not mine their full quota, they were whipped. If a man was suspected of trying to escape, he was whipped. Once a single prisoner "messed" in the cell, and thirty or forty were whipped for it.[19] Whipping enforced the production of coal, and it kept prisoners in fear. The presence of inspectors and new rules enabled prisoners to complain, but they were still punished by the contractors for doing so.

In general, prisoners wanted to perform their tasks and avoid punishment, but they sometimes took bold action in the face of perceived injustices. In 1885, for example, prisoners at Coalburg went on strike to protest the resignation of a well-liked mining boss. Reporting the discontent, Inspector A. T. Henley explained that "Moore, the Warden, had accepted a situation from the Pratt Co. & resigned his position with the Coalburg Co. on Sunday night. During the day Sunday the convicts heard of it & that Sherling . . . had been employed to succeed him. A good deal of disappointment & regret was expressed during the afternoon by the convicts [and it] . . . grew to such an extent that they imagined that they had been greatly wronged and that they must not stand it." On Monday the prisoners "went into the mine as usual; but a few of the ring-leaders, headed by Henry Carrol from Jefferson County, persuaded them that they had better not work. A good many yielded to their persuasions, and a good many more were forced to yield." The extent of the coercion is difficult to determine. Nevertheless, once on strike, the prisoners at Coalburg entered into the protest with enthusiasm. When Henley arrived, he found the prisoners shouting down the owner and manager of Coalburg, E. M. Tutwiler. They refused to return to work "unless Moore was retained," Henley reported. "They were very insulting to Tutwiler. They were armed with picks and sticks and were very boisterous."

Besides stopping work and making a temporary stand, however, the men could do little else. Half of the hundred or so men involved were persuaded to abandon the protest. The remaining prisoners on strike were returned to the cell in groups of ten. Henley confronted the fifty prisoners who were, as he wrote, "in a considerably inflamed state of mind." He separated the leaders from the group, ordered them into the washroom, and then had each man whipped thirty-nine lashes. Henley spoke to the rest of the men individually and then had each one whipped. Overall, Henley was pleased with the outcome. "By the time I got through I had conquered the whole crowd and had a promise of obedience in the future. . . . I gave them all a good lecture, 'preached a sermon' as you would say and left." [20]

The strike left contractors, particularly John T. Milner, seriously alarmed. "The riot at Coalburg indicates very plainly the turbulent spirit that will rise among convicts when opportunity or occasion may offer," Milner wrote one week after the uprising. He begged Dawson to let him impose tighter controls and greater punishments at Newcastle. "I have been thinking of purchasing a lot of new hand cuffs to bring them back & forth. I hope you will not object to my putting shackles on say 30 more until I can get some safe arrangement to carry them back & forth," Milner noted.[21] Dawson did object; but he had less control over county contractors than over Pratt and TCI.

The implementation of short time failed to stop insubordination entirely, for prisoners could be controlled only so far with pardons and promises. The tensions between contractors and prisoners over work and treatment remained as great as ever. Rules, reforms, and investigations gave a public impression that the Board of Inspectors had the last word on the running of the state's prison. This was not so. Even after the lauded reforms of 1883 and 1885, the mining companies maintained control over the prisoners' pace of work, punishment, and treatment.

Prisoners at the Pratt mines feared for their lives. "Inspectors come hear to see us," stated an anonymous letter written by Shaft prisoners in 1887, "but When they ask us how is we getting along we are compell to say We are doing Well are else We are punished after they are gone." The prisoners wrote of being grievously overworked ("we are jest like old broke down oxens"), of never being able to see the "Gloryous son" ("which God made for man to see"), and of deception ("we are classed one way and task another"). The authors of this letter offered to serve an additional year in prison if they could be taken out of the mines and sent to the Walls. Treatment and working conditions at the Shaft were so bad that prisoners called it "murder in the first degree." As prisoners emphasized, the fear of deadly gas made everyday life terrifying: "We are in danger of loosing hour lives hear by gass. . . . Please dont let us be buried alive in Pratts mine . . . please have mercy on us as We are poor convicts." Somehow the prisoners managed to get this letter of protest out of the mines and delivered to Governor Seay without its being seen by the contractors. "This is a secret letter we write to you," they noted to the governor. They hoped that exposing Pratt's violation of rules to the inspectors would lead to sympathy and corrective action by the state authorities.

The anonymous complainants also made threats. "So if they aint a change made in Pratts mine," they warned, "they will be one of the begest strikes in pratts mine you ever hear of and several cases of suryside committed hear." Prisoners also knew how much the inspectors feared the bad publicity of escapes. The complainants casually remarked that "when a man get a chance to leave hear he always makes good use of it." Dawson's arrival and promises of improved treatment initially had led prisoners to act as if the inspectors existed to protect their interests. By 1887, however, prisoners were threatening suicide, escapes, and strikes if conditions did not improve.[22]

When Governor Seay sent the convicts' letter to Dawson and demanded an explanation, Dawson exploded. "The convicts are not overworked. They are not exposed to danger from gas and no one has ever been punished for any statement made to an inspector," he wrote indignantly. Tellingly, however, he ended his note to the governor by admitting that "if the death rate at this prison was less, I would be entirely satisfied with its condition."[23] Clearly, Dawson felt betrayed by the prisoners and alarmed that such a complaint could make its way directly to the governor.

Shortly afterward, in a private letter to Inspector A. T. Henley, Dawson expressed his horror at the death rates at the Shaft mine. Dawson had begun his tenure at the Department of Corrections as a skeptic about the safety of prison mining. He had opposed using prisoners in the mines, and now, a mere four years later, he headed the state's entire prison mining operation. Previous officials such as Bankhead had tried to convince him of the safety of mining as well as its positive impact on prisoners. Perhaps Dawson had been lulled into complacency. State physicians kept insisting that mining was a "healthy occupation," but Dawson could no longer ignore the numbers. "The reports on file in this office," he wrote, "show that in the last twelve months 21 county convicts and 19 state convicts have died at the Shaft. . . . Now has there not been something the matter?" Dawson compared the Shaft with the state's other prisons. "In the same time Slope No. 2 lost five county convicts, and six state convicts and one state convict at the Walls." The mining prisons for county prisoners had also lost men: "Coalburg with about 200 lost 11 and Milner with about 140 lost 4." Could these deaths be considered normal? "These are the figures," he wrote to Henley, "and against them we have science."[24]

Dawson, Henley, and Lee, skeptical of contractors and doctors, began to listen more carefully to prisoners. When prisoners protested against the use of new mechanized cutting machines in the mines, Dawson wrote to Henley to remind him that "it is as much your duty as mine to protect the men against them if they are injurious . . . because the Pratt co. spent ten thousand dollars for machines . . . it is no reason why convicts should be exposed to unnecessary danger." Increasingly, Dawson began to see himself as an advocate, not merely an administrator imposing order; his adversaries were the contractors, not the prisoners. "Convicts tell me that they are completely used up by running a machine," he emphasized. "If the Pratt co do not want our men to cut coal with a pick there are plenty of other mines that do." [25] Officially, black prisoners had no say in their treatment or conditions. Unofficially, however, they occasionally influenced policy.

Yet these short-lived disputes never seriously threatened the state's public relationship with Pratt, and later TCI. The only contractors Dawson condemned in public were landowners such as Mr. and Mrs. Barton Smith, who ran a county convict camp in Talladega. Every time he went to inspect the Smiths' camp, Dawson saw prisoners who were overworked, underfed, and unduly punished. "I do not believe he [Smith] will ever do right and get out of the old notion of 'fooling the inspectors,'" Dawson reported. As to the food at the camp, he complained that "not a hound . . . would have eaten it." After one unsatisfactory visit Dawson told the Smiths that they had "deceived me basely," and he threatened to remove all their prisoners.[26]

The conditions at the Smiths' farm caused a public outcry in 1886 when Alex Crews, a black prisoner, died at a train depot in Wetumpka shortly after his release. Sentenced to thirty days in prison for some petty act and leased to the Smiths, Crews had been "frequently and cruelly whipped," exposed to extremely cold weather, "insufficiently fed and clothed, and "worked when sick"—all in violation of the state's rules. The day before Crews was due to be released, a guard knocked him down with a shovel and then struck him again while he lay on the ground. The next day Crews was released from the Smiths' camp without food, clothing, shoes, or money. He walked for miles on frostbitten feet. A few days later he died in the Wetumpka train depot.[27]

Crews's death prompted a lengthy published state-run investigation that gathered the testimony of doctors, prisoners, inspectors, and other witnesses. Dawson used the scandal to push for further reform. He wanted the public to know that the Board of Inspectors had no power to limit punishment or change the treatment of county prisoners. In fact, more prisoners were dying in the prison mines than at county camps, but Dawson contrasted the cruelty of the county system with the supposed civility of the Pratt prison mines. Although powerful local interests opposed giving the state more power to inspect county camps, in 1888 Alabama finally passed legislation giving the Board of Inspectors the same authority over county camps as they already had over state camps. As usual, however, the power of inspectors to control life in prisons was more elusive than real. In reality, men like Alex Crews and county convicts in prison mines still worked under the authority of a contractor, not an inspector.

The controversy over granting short time to county convicts illustrates how contractors sought to usurp the power of inspectors. Contractors had the power to issue reports of bad conduct against a prisoner. The names of men on the bad conduct list were sent to the inspectors who then decided if the infraction was great enough to deprive prisoners of their short time. These pardons deducted two months from every year of a prisoner's sentence; county men, all serving terms of less than two years, stood to gain a quick release with a short-time pardon. The inspectors saw short time as an effective means of maintaining prison discipline, but from the county contractors' perspective, short time removed convicts from coal mines just as they were achieving some skill at mining coal. The high number of bad conduct reports given at Coalburg made J. D. Douglass, Dawson's secretary at the Department of Corrections, suspicious. "I think that the problem of short time for county convicts is trying to be solved by the contractors themselves," he wrote to Inspector Lee. "I wish you could see the report of Coalburg for June. The conduct of 62 is reported as Bad, in about half of which cases the offense is not given." Only the board could officially recommend short time, but it depended on the conduct reports from the contractors. Douglass knew that the inspectors would not allow the charge of bad conduct to stand in each and every case. Nevertheless, he acknowledged that the initial charge "has the tendency or rather the effect of staying recommendations."[28] Not all reports of bad conduct indicate prisoners' defiance. There is no doubt that county contractors falsified bad conduct reports to keep good miners in prison.

In fact, prisoners struggled to avoid bad conduct reports so as not to lose their chance of short time. But one slip, one infraction of the rules, one single report of bad conduct from the contractors, and a prisoner lost the possibility of having two months per year removed from his sentence. If a prisoner lost his composure, became angry, and shouted at a guard, he lost his short time. Prisoners did their best to contain their frustrations, but when guards tried to goad men into losing their tempers, the pressure sometimes became too great. Sometimes, holding in emotions was the best form of resistance.

One clear case of a guard who incited a skilled miner involved Ike Berry, a black prisoner at the Pratt mines. In October 1887 A. T. Henley wrote to Dawson about the quarrel between Berry and a pit boss named Smith. Smith had ordered Berry to change rooms in the mine, but Berry had refused. Henley knew that Berry was a highly skilled miner because he was classified as a first-class man and given responsibility for an entire room. Perhaps this is why he listened to Berry's side of the story so closely. According to Henley, "Berry claimed that there was no reason for making him change rooms except a desire on Smith's part to harass and annoy him about a matter which occurred between them in February last. Smith . . . claims that his reason for the order is that he had discovered gas in the room & that it was necessary to cut some openings into the air course before it would be safe. They both say that Berry offered to cut the openings in his own time if Smith would allow him to remain."

Given the dangers of accumulating gas, why would Berry want to stay in his room? Berry had a ready answer. He told Henley that he did not trust Smith. According to Henley, "He [Berry] says that the system of moving convicts form one room to another is frequently resorted to to get good men into trouble; that it is impossible for a man to go into a room with which he is not familiar & do as much work as he could in one the reverse." Henley reported this incident in such detail, perhaps, because Berry's revelations rang true. But if Berry's story was true, then, in Henley's eyes, Pratt was guilty of large-scale perfidy.

Berry was so angered by Smith's order that he took the matter over Smith's head. He asked William Rogers, the warden, if he could remain at work in the room until Rogers looked into the situation. When Rogers agreed, Smith, fuming at being usurped, confronted Berry. "He [Smith] says he spoke in a quiet manner," Henley reported. "Berry says it was in an angry manner. One word brought on another until Berry finally let out on him & told him that he thought that he, Smith, was better fitted for the farm plowing a speckled bull than anything else &C &C." In this exchange Berry released pent-up feelings of rage and contempt against a guard whose knowledge of mining Berry regarded as pitiful. As a highly skilled miner, Berry felt entitled to certain rights, and controlling his own room was one of them.

Berry did more than insult Smith. As Henley explained, "Smith says Berry dared him to fight & talked about killing him &C." When Berry spoke with Henley, he was contrite. "Berry says he was mad and does not remember telling him [Smith] anything of the sort," Henley reported. "Berry expresses himself as being very sorry for his conduct and is willing to do anything to prevent a bad report from being entered against him." It was ultimately Henley's decision whether Berry should be punished and lose his short time. Clearly he took Berry's side of the story seriously. For though he knew that Berry's behavior was "beyond the limit," Henley reasoned that Berry had been sick: "I am not clear in my mind as to extenuating circumstances." [29]

Berry had threatened to kill a white authority figure, yet Henley felt that perhaps his behavior had been understandable. As this case illustrates, black prisoners confronted white authorities in prison and even accused some of lying and deceit. Outside of prison, a similar accusation would never have been taken seriously. The tensions between contractors, inspectors, and prisoners, however, produced distinctive racial interactions. Black prisoners could publicly challenge the veracity of white contractors because inspectors at times trusted convicts more than the contractors.

According to political scientist James Scott, when the weak or oppressed finally take the opportunity to oppose or challenge an oppressor publicly, that challenge emerges from "hidden transcripts"—behavior that had heretofore remained private. Scott has argued that public resistance to authority happens when circumstances or sheer indignity bring to light feelings, speech, and behavior that previously had happened only within the confines of the oppressed group. According to Scott, "hidden transcripts," usually undertaken in private, make public confrontations against authority possible.[30]

Although Alabama prisoners worked under strenuous conditions, the circumstances of prison also gave them ample time and space to speak freely with each other, away from the ears of contractors and inspectors. Letters of protest to contractors and to the governor, for example, surely had been phrased and rephrased in private before being written down. Ike Berry may have lost his chance for short time, but when he confronted his mining boss, he showed what he really thought of his so-called superior.

Henley's reluctance to take away Berry's short time reflected a broader concern among all the inspectors about the mendacity of the Pratt Coal and Coke Company. Dawson knew very well that prisoners were being overworked; furthermore, he believed that the contractors were swindling the state. Once the leases with Pratt and Comer and McCurdy expired in 1888, Dawson was determined to get a better deal. "We are not getting enough for the convicts at the mines," he wrote to W. D. Lee in 1887. "I am pretty well posted now about the cost of mining coal, and I cannot be stuffed anymore about expenses." The mining companies frequently moaned about the high cost of feeding, housing, and guarding prisoners, but as Dawson trenchantly remarked to Lee, "If you and I only had the same amount that is made every month from convict hire at Pratt Mines we could afford . . . to repose under our own fig tree and vine the balance of our days." Dawson believed that prisoners were so overworked that "we will soon have no first class men." He told Lee that he had deliberately reduced the classification of some men "to enable them to have a rest."[31] The more Dawson, Henley, and Lee responded to the complaints of prisoners, the more they came to see their duties differently. By 1887 Dawson had become more than the walking embodiment of the rule book. He was a man convinced that the contractors could not be trusted and that the state would have to demand more.

Although Dawson did care about the treatment of prisoners, his ultimate responsibility was to ensure the profitable running of the prison. He thus found himself on the horns of a dilemma. He wanted the state to get the best return from the labor of prisoners as possible, and he believed that profitability could be reconciled with decent treatment of prisoners. Events, however, would show otherwise.

Since Dawson's appointment in 1883, prisoners had developed higher expectations about fairer treatment in prison. They thought the rules might be enforced. They believed that inspectors would respond to their complaints. They began to assume that if they worked hard and obeyed the rules, they would receive an early release through short time. They thought that time cards proved the limited power of contractors.

But these promises were not fulfilled. Although some prisoners appreciated the difference Dawson's changes made in their lives, men entering the system for the first time still faced its basic horrors. The state's desire for profit cleansed the convicts of any illusions about the inspector's ultimate concern. Even Dawson's humanitarianism could not erase the fact that he was obliged to make sure the state received the maximum amount of revenue from prisoners; this meant tasking men beyond their capacity and punishing them brutally when they fell short. The ease with which contractors could dispense bad conduct reports made the promise of short time lose its luster among the men.

After 1887 prisoners became cynical about the Board of Inspectors and the elusive promise of short time, and they began to take direct action. Prisoners set fires, planned breakouts, committed suicide, and stopped work. Although they continued to push Dawson, Henley, and Lee to protect them from the abuses and excesses of the contractors, their expectations of the board clearly had lessened. Furthermore, extra financial pressures would force the Tennessee Coal and Iron Company to impose a speedup in the prison mines. When the reciprocity with the Tennessee Coal and Iron Company broke down, and increased brutality was used as a means to gain increased production, prisoners engaged in direct protest much more frequently.

In the late nineteenth century, Alabama prison mines would become some of the most productive in the New South. But the consistency of their output cannot be attributed solely to the high quality of the seam or to extreme coercion. In the end, African-American prisoners produced that coal. Through negotiation, mutual exchange of information, and an emerging ethic that valued an individual's pride in the craft of mining, they developed high levels of skill and began to transform themselves into a self-conscious working class.

In 1888 TCI made a new ten-year contract with Alabama which entitled it to the labor of all state prisoners and half of all county prisoners. This takeover of the prison mines coincided with another important change in prison administration: the removal of women prisoners from the common prisons to the Walls in Wetumpka. Alabama was one of the first states to separate women into separate quarters, but this act was not motivated by concern or reform. It was a response to the unruly behavior of the women themselves and the threat to discipline they posed to the prisons at large.

7

Female Prisoners

■ Southern society prided itself on the protection it gave to "ladies," but female prisoners, both white and black, forfeited their right to any special treatment. Because of the acts they committed, their lack of family ties, and the low value placed upon their work, all female prisoners invited mostly indifference or neglect from their communities. Contractors treated them as servants and subordinates and punished them as brutally as they did men.

Though they may not have had husbands, status, or powerful friends, women prisoners did not lack courage or a vision of a free future. They drew sustenance from their children, often incarcerated with them, as well as the occasional assistance of a white lawyer. The women also formed bonds with male prisoners. When they defied prison authorities, they did so in groups, indicating the encouragement they derived from each other. Contributing to their resilience in prison were such intangible yet essential qualities as faith, spirituality, humor, determination, verbal acumen, and the ability to perform hard physical labor. Despite their poverty and incarceration, female prisoners asserted their own unique vision of freedom.

The efforts of African-American women prisoners to defend themselves, free themselves, free others, and survive with dignity echo the behavior of the slave women described by Brenda Stevenson in her work on antebellum Virginia. Stevenson stresses that when black women described their memories of slavery, they "were forthright in their appreciation of self-reliant, self-determined survivalists who had the wherewithal to protect themselves and theirs."[1] Prison inspectors and others saw female prisoners as antifeminine, unruly, and threatening, but their behavior undermined prison discipline, served as an example of resistance to others, and ultimately enabled many to survive.

The female prisoners had all been working women. Of the 111 women incarcerated as state prisoners between 1869 and 1883, 39 gave their occupation as "house servant," and approximately 50 called themselves "laborers." Other occupations included nurse and cook.[2] Paying occupations—nurse, cook, and servant—suggest that female prisoners participated in the underground markets of the Black Belt. Goods for sale mentioned in the letter from "Farmer" included foodstuffs, calico, and jewelry—items certain to tempt women.[3] Domestic workers paid in cash, and female agricultural laborers with access to cotton and seed possessed either the cash or produce necessary to purchase such goods.

As independent markets came under legal attack in the mid-1870s, all buyers and sellers, including women, became vulnerable to prosecution. Larceny and burglary were the charges against nearly half of all black female state prisoners between 1869 and 1883. On the same day in 1877, for example, Nancy Rowe and Moza Ann Connolly, both African-American cooks from the same county, were each sentenced to three years for "receiving stolen goods." Perhaps they were dealing with Caroline Cheatham, a white cook from the same county, sentenced for "grand larceny."[4]

Cheatham's case, however, was exceptional. In 1882 four of the five white female state prisoners had been found guilty of adultery, a crime which implied interracial sex. Three of these white women shared rooms with seven African-American women at the Walls in Wetumpka. Warden John Bankhead used the crimes of these white women and their integration with black women to buttress his arguments about the necessity of reform and shock his white audience. "White women who are sentenced to the penitentiary for living in adultery with negroes, must of necessity occupy the same cell with negro women," he wrote. According to Bankhead the racial integration of women prisoners was an abomination on par with miscegenation. "Do you expect that white woman to be reformed? Will she go out into the world cured of her disease? . . . The State has no moral right to contaminate her citizens; to force them into associations that will demoralize."[5] Bankhead's flourishes about reforming "diseased" white women by separating them from black women, however, remained in the realm of rhetoric. In 1890 ten white women were still working alongside sixty-two black women at the Walls. Of those ten, eight had been convicted of either "felonious adultery" or miscegenation.[6]

As Bankhead's comments illustrate, the image of the fallen woman in the South had everything to do with race. Black women prisoners were seen as inherently immoral, while white women prisoners convicted of sex crimes lost their racial privilege. Prostitution was indeed illegal, but no white prostitutes were ever sentenced to county work camps or the penitentiary. In contrast, the crimes of adultery and miscegenation threatened the racial order. White women who transgressed racial and sexual mores were indeed considered criminal—far more criminal than the functional behavior of a prostitute. Courts cracked down on white women who openly cohabited with black men. In the eyes of the courts, such women were no longer deserved to be treated as white and thus could be placed with black women in prison.[7]

In her study of black and white women in North Carolina, Victoria Bynum observed that "because many poor single women lacked control and protection by a male, it fell upon the courts to monitor their behavior; as for protection, they received little—privately or publicly."[8] This seems true of white women accused of miscegenation and adultery, but it was even more true of single black women, who were incarcerated for a far greater number of offenses. The state and communities turned on certain white women who crossed forbidden racial boundaries and thus flaunted definitions of race. The high number of black women prisoners, however, cannot be attributed to sexual crimes, such as prostitution or adultery. Black women's crimes—larceny, assault, murder—in many ways mirror those of black men.

But appearances can deceive, especially when the charges against black women involved murder. Of the sixty-two black female state convicts in 1890, thirty-six had been convicted of murder, assault to murder, or poisoning.[9] The poisoning charge, such as the one levied against the former slave Isabella in 1866, echoed fears fertilized in slavery. This serious charge brought Isabella twelve years in the penitentiary.[10] Like men, black women undoubtedly had participated in altercations that led to death. Unlike men, however, many black female "murderers" had been involved in the crime of infanticide.

Pardon records show that black women involved, however tangentially, in the death of a infant or fetus were given lengthy prison sentences as murderers. In 1873 Martha Aarons was convicted of murdering her child and sentenced to the penitentiary for seventy-five years. Her pardon petition, however, revealed that "her step-father beat her child to death in her presence." Louisa Stewart, a former slave, told a young girl how to induce a miscarriage. A pardon petition for Stewart stated that "she probably thought she was doing a favor in helping that Girl to save her character."[11] And yet she too was convicted of murder in 1893. In 1892 Julia Ann May of Greene County was accused of murdering her twelve-year-old daughter's illegitimate baby. She was convicted on the testimony of a ten-year-old-child she had taken into her home to raise. Victoria Bynum has documented the rising number of prosecuted infanticide cases among freedwomen in North Carolina.[12] The charges against May and the others in Alabama were no aberration among female prisoners but were typical.

It must be considered that many incarcerated black women, besides being the victims of prejudiced white juries, were prosecuted because their actions offended people in their own community. It is important to understand this legal crackdown on infanticide, especially if, as some historians have suggested, black women under slavery had resorted to it with the support of other blacks.[13] Certainly economic factors propelled many women to take such action. Freedwomen without family or community support or material resources would be likely candidates to choose abortion or infanticide. Changing sexual mores after emancipation contributed to what appears to have been a crackdown on infanticide within the black community. Although living in separate households, free black families were still in proximity to each other. Members of a black woman's household or neighborhood likely knew if a woman had terminated a pregnancy or an infant had inexplicably died.[14]

Historian Anne Butler uncovered an 1894 court case involving a young African-American woman in Austin, Texas, accused of an unlawful abortion. Lizzie Plummer had recently been elected secretary of a black women's church group when rumors of her pregnancy began. A committee formed to investigate the situation barged into her residence and later claimed that they found her in labor. Although the women of the lodge may have been only trying to protect the group's reputation, their actions had serious legal consequences. No evidence of pregnancy or a baby was ever produced, but Lizzie Plummer was convicted of perjury and sentenced to five years in prison.[15] She was known as "a member of one of the best negro families in Travis County."[16] Yet her alleged pregnancy cast doubt upon the character of both her and those around her. From the perspective of the women involved, the real issue appeared to be saving the reputations of black women. Similarly, a letter to the sheriff's office in Greene County, Alabama, asserted that when Julia Ann May killed her daughter's newborn, she was seeking to protect her daughter's reputation. "She was prompted to do the deed to hide the shame, as she belonged to a family of negroes who held their heads pretty high and has tried to raise her daughter to a life of virtue, but with indifferent success."[17] Significantly, the letter writer assumed the twelve-year-old black girl to be guilty of sexual lust. Because whites assumed that black girls, no matter how young, were sexually depraved, the efforts of black mothers such as May to protect their daughters and their reputations take on a heroic dimension.

The connection between a woman's character and her sexual reputation had emerged slowly after emancipation. In slavery black women suffered few community repercussions for having children without a husband, having children with more than one man, or for infanticide. When practiced, infanticide could be legitimized as a vital form of resistance against a hated white master. After emancipation, black men and women certainly valued the marriage contract, but they also felt free to end that obligation, or start a new one, without necessarily abiding by existing law that governed the marriage relationship.[18] Nevertheless, by the 1890s the meaning attributed to certain kinds of sexual behavior was changing.

It appears that a concern for legitimacy left old practices vulnerable to the law. As racist attacks on black people often focused on the allegedly slack sexual reputations of black women, middle-class women and men became more concerned with preserving and creating stable, male-headed family units. Hence the reputations and character of black women took on a new importance.[19] Certain community members had a clear stake in halting and controlling infanticide among black women, even at the cost of sending them to prison.

Economics also played a role in black women's imprisonment. In 1875 the *Montgomery Advertiser* ridiculed Ann Pollard after she had freed herself from imprisonment by paying a $5 fine. "I don't care if the cunvenshun neber gives us cullrd women the right to vote," she allegedly said. "We kin pay de fine and de men de lies in jail." [20] Pollard, a street merchant, apparently had access to cash. Her comment is intriguing, because it indicates that black women, who may have been employed as laundresses or cooks before their arrests, perhaps were better able to extricate themselves from prison because of their cash savings. By observing the relationship between money and freedom, Pollard exposed a basic truth: those able to pay their fines were spared the indignities of the local chain gang or, worse, a sentence as a county prisoner. But women without their own resources had little hope of gaining assistance from others, especially their families.

Poor men had a few more options. Those without cash to pay fines could turn to white employers for assistance. Pardon records contain some instances of black males being released through the intervention of their white employers. The wives of arrested men pleaded with white landowners, with some success, to use influence in order to gain their husbands' pardon. For example, when Larry Greer and Sydney Patterson of Hale County took "some corn out of the field" and "hauled it in open daylight with their own to Demopolis to sell," they were charged with grand larceny and sentenced to the penitentiary. Mrs. Greer and Mrs. Patterson, however, urged their white landowner to intercede with the governor. "They have been faithful workers," the landlord wrote, "and it is very desirable that they should go to farming as early as possible." [21] Sydney Boddie of Marengo County was imprisoned for larceny in 1873 after he gathered corn that had been left for hogs. The owners of the land on which Boddie worked joined with several black legislators in petitioning for his release, claiming that he had been convicted "solely thro malice on the part of the overseer." They added that "the Boy has a large family, entirely dependent on him for support and is a hardworking, sober, honest, and faithful laborer." [22] The wives of Greer, Patterson, and Boddie, in petitioning for the release of their husbands, exploited the perception that men's work was essential to the economic success of white landlords. And clearly many white landlords agreed.

Only access to money or to influence could guarantee release from a fine or court costs. Black women prisoners also had been employed: they were nurses, cooks, servants, field hands, and housekeepers. But they had no leverage to offer in a legal system where blacks could only hope to influence whites by offering their labor power. No employers urged the pardon of invaluable black females. Thus, women without an independent source of income were especially vulnerable to the whim of the courts.

Using the concept of control theory, sociologists have asserted that women in prison lack the resources of family, friends, or employers: "Weakness of ties to family, church, conventional activities and so on increases the probability of committing crimes," according to sociologist Nicole Hahn Rafter. But it is difficult to sort out whether their actual behavior or their poverty caused women's incarceration in the late nineteenth century. It appears, in keeping with the theory, that black women prisoners then did have "looser or more disrupted bonds to the conventional social order." [23] But it may have been the lack of those bonds, rather than their actual behavior, that left them vulnerable to imprisonment. For example, Susan Ross, "a poor freedwoman with several small children," was too poor to pay an attorney and was found guilty of larceny. The weak circumstantial evidence against her prompted the presiding judge to request her pardon. He had been willing to grant Ross a new trial, but because she had no attorney, no application was made, and she went to jail.[24] Money or connections would have spared Ross her ordeal and being branded a criminal.

Prison records did not usually note the marital status of prisoners, but one list of hospital patients does provide a few clues. Between March 28, 1881, and September 30, 1882, ten women prisoners, three white and seven black, received treatment at the prison hospital at the Walls. The women's illnesses included dysentery, fevers, "softening of brain," "suppression of menses," and bronchitis. The black women treated gave their marital status as single. Two of the three white women were sometimes listed as married and other times listed as single.[25] Of course, such a label only designates marriage and not other relations, such as children, but the absence of a marital partner distinguished female prisoners from their male counterparts.[26]

The absence of family ties may have spurred black women into direct contact with lawyers and others who could advocate on their behalf.

Julia Ann May, who had no family of her own, dictated a twenty-six-page letter telling her story to attorney R. B. Smyer, who wrote to the governor requesting May's pardon. Smyer described several other "similar cases" of infanticide in which the women received much shorter sentences. In four other cases, Smyer wrote, the lowest punishment was thirteen months, the highest ten years. He urged leniency for May. "Had this been a white person that was convicted," he wrote, "or anyone else that had friends . . . the jury would not have been so severe on them." [27] Smyer summed up the situation of many black female prisoners: discriminated against by juries because of their race and "friendless" within their communities because of poverty, lack of family, or the sexual nature of their crimes, these women were bereft of economic and social standing and thus lacked protection.

Yet the existence of family was in itself no security against imprisonment. African Americans increasingly used local courts to settle family and personal disputes. Successful plaintiffs included black women who charged men with assault and bastardy. When black women were accused of crimes, however, they often stood trial with other family members. Martha Aarons's baby died because of her stepfather, who was also convicted. Bettie Perkins asserted that her stepfather forced her to steal. Hannah Rembert and Laura King were jointly convicted of poisoning Rembert's husband.[28] Julia Ann May's husband had also been accused of murder, but he had been acquitted. One letter to Governor Seay in 1888, which complained in general of the injustices heaped upon "cullerd people," told the story of "M Millie," whose husband "shot at her becose she wood not stay with him in that way." He "told a ly" about her, the letter stated, and had her arrested.[29] Thus, in contrast to black male prisoners, incarcerated black females either lacked family at the outset, or their crimes involved acting with other family members who were also arrested and thus of little assistance. The fact that women's crimes included acts like infanticide also put them in a bad light within the black community. Family could not protect black women from the law, for it could not completely mitigate the racial and economic inequalities of the legal system; furthermore, black women were still vulnerable to sexual and economic exploitation within it.

When prison officials and labor contractors designed facilities, work, and punishment, they assumed their prisoners would be men. Authorities saw women prisoners, therefore, as aberrations. Besides violating gender norms within prison, female prisoners had transgressed the dominant culture's definition of womanhood. The ideal woman was subordinate to her father or husband, either sexually chaste or a mother, an inhabitant of the home, and not a participant in public life or debate. Because they fitted so poorly into the expectations of both prison and society, women prisoners were often seen as beyond the hope of reform.

Female convicts struggled to have their humanity recognized. Reformers focused their efforts on male prisoners, not women. Prison authorities, concerned that "idle" female convicts would drain the state financially, set them to work on farms and roads and at coal mines. Some gender conventions were respected; for example, women were not sent underground to mine coal. But authorities whipped women prisoners, sexually abused them, made them the personal servants of labor contractors, and subjected them to intense personal surveillance. Women prisoners basically lost whatever privileges being female had given them in the free world and gained further ignominy through their status as prisoners.

Until 1888, female prisoners in Alabama lived among men. Although separate prisons for women began to emerge in the North in 1874,[30] the majority of women prisoners in the nation were incarcerated with men. In her book on women's prison reform, Estelle B. Freedmen observed that in northern gender-mixed prisons, female prisoners almost inevitably became subordinate to men. As one female reformer noted, "It results that women prisoners . . . major in mending, washing, ironing, and sewing for men prisoners."[31] For black women in Alabama, prison indeed duplicated their subordination to whites and to men. Between 1869 and 1888 black women cooked, cleaned, and sewed for male prisoners at mining camps and farms; they also worked as personal servants to male wardens.

Typically, a mining camp or prison farm of fifty to one hundred men housed only a single black woman prisoner. For example, when Nellie Boyd was convicted of second-degree murder in 1878, she went from being a house servant to the only woman in a prison mining camp of eighty-six men. Annie Gilmore, a twenty-year-old "house girl," lived as the only woman prisoner among forty-six men at the prison mine at Newcastle.[32] The state scattered women prisoners among the prison farm in Wetumpka, the Pratt mines, and J. F. B. Jackson's rock quarry and farm. Women prisoners were also forced to live with mining bosses or prison managers, making them vulnerable to rape and sexual abuse. To be a black woman in an Alabama prison camp was a nightmare of hard work, bad treatment, and isolation from other women.[33]

The 1882 biennial report gives a typical snapshot of how the five white female prisoners and thirty-three black women prisoners were scattered throughout the state, regardless of their age, crime, or race. (The fate, or even the number, of county female convicts in these years remains unknown.) The largest concentration of women lived at the Walls, the penitentiary in Wetumpka, which was also the most racially integrated prison. Dying male prisoners and those unable to work were routinely sent to the Walls, which suffered the next highest number of deaths after the coal mines; in 1882 ten of its thirty-eight prisoners died.[34] In that same year ten female convicts lived at the penitentiary. Of the seven black women at the Walls, four were eighteen or younger. They included two girls, Ella and

Mary Edwards, ages twelve and thirteen, sentenced to a year each for burglary. Five had been cooks, including Sarah Bonner, twenty-six, who had been sentenced to five years for burglary; Jane Kendall, seventeen, who had received a life sentence for murder; Dora King, another teenager, who was serving a four-year sentence for grand larceny; and Hattie Wiggins, twenty-three, who also was serving a life sentence for murder. Of the three white women, two had been convicted of adultery, and the other, of murder. The women prisoners at the Walls lived alongside eleven white and seventeen black men.[35] It is unclear what work was required of men and women at the Walls, but helping to take care of the sick was probably part of the women's duties.

In contrast, 7 black women lived among 1 2 3 black males at state prison farm operated by Thomas Williams in Wetumpka. Williams's contract specified black prisoners only, and black women farmed alongside black men. In yet another variation, Nellie Boyd was still the only woman among the men at Comer and McCurdy's camp at the Pratt mines. Two black women, ages sixteen and twenty, had been leased to a rock quarry with forty-four male prisoners. White women prisoners were treated similarly and also sent out to male work camps. Mary Ann Cox, a white "farmer" convicted of adultery, was the sole woman at the Newcastle mine where she lived with seven white and thirty-one black male prisoners. Mary Mixon, another white woman convicted of adultery, was sent to B. B. Comer's prison farm in Barbour County where she worked with three black women, including fifteen-year-old Ann Kennedy, a cook whose crime was "not stated."[36]

No sex-specific rules protected these women prisoners or exempted them from physical punishment. Female prisoners who testified before a state senate investigating committee in 1 888 told of repeated whippings. At one farm a woman had been tied down to a chair and whipped "till whelps were raised on her back." Contractors whipped women for quarreling, fighting, and "sassing." At one county farm a woman who had never picked cotton before was whipped because she could not pick 1 2 5 pounds a day. One warden whipped Flora Adams "for dancing while the preacher was here on a Sunday."[37] Prison authorities sought to make black women obey orders and work, but they also pursued control over their spirit, personal behavior, and sexual activity.

However, women prisoners exercised some personal freedom. Because of their work responsibilities, women convicts moved and walked around. Annie Tucker, convicted in 1 883, spent several years working in the Pratt prison mines. She recalled that she "was not locked up at mines, cooked, washed, and ironed at mines. . . . Was trusty at mines." In contrast to female prisoners in the North, Tucker and other black women did not spend their days in a prison cell. Nevertheless, prison authorities expected black women to proffer personal obedience.

In 1 883 P. J. Rogers, a superintendent for Pratt, punished Annie Tucker so brutally that the Board of Inspectors censured him for "cruel and excessive whipping."[38] R. H. Dawson wrote about the case in his diary. "These are the facts. She ran away from Mr. McCurdy's house—was caught and carried to the prison. Col. Bankhead whipped her himself—not severely—After he left by order of Mr. McCurdy, P. J. Rogers stripped her, had her held down, and inflicted 56 lashes upon her with a heavy strap."[39] Tucker had tried to run away from McCurdy, one of the largest prison contractors in the state, and the highest prison authorities personally took it upon themselves to control and beat her. Such abuse inevitably recalls the days of slavery.

Yet despite this incident of outrageous treatment, Annie Tucker took a larger view of her prison experience at the Pratt mines. She testified that at the mines she had raised two children while carrying on a relationship with their father, who was a black convict.[40] Tucker seemed to prefer the mines to another prison farm where, she testified, she suffered poor treatment and was "locked up at night." Still, that did not prevent her from having a relationship with a freeman, Jack Bozeman. "We got together night and day time. . . . Jack got to me before I went from the house to the stockade." She became pregnant and later gave birth to a child at the Walls.[41] Although women prisoners were clearly vulnerable to rape, cruel punishment, and exploitation, they still had relationships with male prisoners and their children. Those ties would prove vital to their ability to survive prison.

Annie Tucker's case also illustrates the point that black women prisoners participated in what Darlene Clark Hine has called "a culture of dissemblance." R. H. Dawson's diary clearly reveals her subordination to the prison contractor, as well as the severe beating she endured at the hands of several white inspectors and Warden John H. Bankhead himself. But Annie Tucker, who could not resist rape or beatings, chose not to reveal her vulnerability to white authorities. Instead, when she testified before a committee, Tucker stressed her independence, sexual and otherwise. As Hine has noted, "The dynamics of dissemblance involved creating the appearance of disclosure, or openness about themselves and their feelings, while actually remaining an enigma." Secrecy enabled women like Tucker to "harness their resources" and survive.[42]

As Tucker's testimony suggests, male and female prisoners commonly engaged in voluntary sexual relations. Sexual jealousy led to quarreling and insubordination. The inspectors wrote to the governor that men and women "are at the same place, no matter how much care is taken to prevent it, they will sometimes get together; and they are on the look out for opportunities of the sort all the time, which makes it difficult to preserve discipline."[43] To rectify the situation, Inspector Henley recommended a separate state prison for women. Only by placing women beyond the reach of male prisoners could sexual activity be stopped and order preserved.

In the North female reformers campaigned to establish separate facilities for women prisoners. These reformers, convinced that women could be changed through prayer and understanding, sought to emancipate women prisoners from brutal treatment, sexual abuse, and labor exploitation. Male prison wardens, although skeptical, gradually handed the management of women's prisons over to women guards and authorities. Northern female reformers, inspired by Quakers, believed that if women could be made to feel penitent for their behavior, they could change, lead virtuous lives, and not return to prison. Driven by the belief that they were responsible for their less fortunate "sisters," female reformers in the North believed in the potential of all women to lead productive lives.[44]

A separate place for women prisoners in Alabama, however, was established for entirely different reasons. In the 1880s no female reformers in Alabama, including Julia Tutwiler, took up the specific cause of women prisoners. Furthermore, male prison authorities did not believe that women prisoners should, in essence, be treated less leniently. Nor would they admit that women prisoners had been abused or sexually exploited. Prison authorities insisted on separate facilities for women because they believed that putting women with men in prison caused lapses in discipline. Thus in 1888 the Alabama attorney general forbade the leasing out of state women prisoners to private farms and mining camps; he ordered women prisoners sent to the Walls in Wetumpka.

Other factors, related to economics, also contributed to the creation of a separate location for female prisoners. Before 1888 counties leased their prisoners according to a per capita system. They charged contractors a flat rate for each prisoner, regardless of sex, age, or ability. In 1888, however, the state forced counties to switch to a class or tasking system. Before a prisoner could be leased, his or her ability to perform work had to be evaluated and the prisoner classified. Under the new system female prisoners inevitably received a lower classification and thus brought in far less income to the counties. Now unable to ask the same price for men and women prisoners, counties began sending more female and indigent prisoners to the state. As a result, after 1888 an increasing number of women became state prisoners.

Women prisoners living at the Walls worked on a state farm under the direct control of a reluctant inspector. Dawson did not want to take on the responsibility of working the women prisoners, as he found them "hard to manage, insolent, and frequently quarreling and fighting."[45] He put the approximately forty-five to fifty women and fifteen children at the Walls to work at farming. During the growing season of 1889, thirty-five women cultivated 100 bales of cotton, 1,000 bushels of corn, 60,000 pounds of hay, 200 bushels of peas, and 500 bushels of sweet potatoes.[46] Women at the Walls provided labor vital to the profitable continuation of the leasing system. Besides growing food for prisoners to eat, they washed, sewed, and mended prison clothing. At no time did women consist of more than 10 percent of the prison population, but their labor provided food and clothing to all prisoners.

Life at the Walls removed women from their previous isolation, but most felt the loss of some personal freedoms. Now all women prisoners became subject to the gaze of male prison authorities, who routinely asked female prisoners about the "opportunities" for sex at various prison sites. One woman said that there was "no chance for a woman to get pregnant here (at the Walls)." Nevertheless, many of the women prisoners brought to the Walls in 1888 from other prisons had children with them. One woman testified that there were "sixteen babies here. Some born here and some brought here; seven babies born in the Walls this year. Two women will soon have babies; both came lately and were pregnant when they came. The oldest child here is four years old—Annie Tucker's baby." [47] Placing women at the Walls did not remove them from the presence of male prisoners or from male control. Voyeuristic male guards, not caring female reformers, supervised and punished women prisoners at the Walls.

Many women prisoners felt their new situation to be worse than before. Female life at the Walls meant arduous labor, close supervision, brutal whippings, and the burdens of raising children and babies in a prison setting. According to Annie Tucker, they were allowed to bathe twice a week. Living together, working together, and raising children in dirty cramped quarters heightened tensions among women prisoners, and they often fought and quarreled.[48] The only emotional release permitted the women seems to have been preaching and religious services twice a month. The women expressed themselves through church services, talking back to prison guards, and quarreling with each other. The Walls did not remain an exclusive prison for women. Soon it also became a site full of "undesirable" prisoners, including sick youths and the elderly. The state expected female prisoners to care for those too ill to work, thus adding domestic duties to their agricultural chores.

To maintain their dignity and humanity, female prisoners established relationships with other prisoners—men and women—took care of their children, and tried to keep clean. Rarely could women prisoners depend on their families. One woman wrote to the governor that she had "no one to look to but you as my father is dead and my mother cannot help herself. . . . So I am looking to you and the Lord." [49] Julia Ann May told the governor that if he "cut [her] time down to six month I will shout and the good Lord will bless you." [50] Women, like men, sought relief from prison life by appealing to outsiders who could help, such as lawyers. Yet they never mention receiving letters or visits. To keep their spirits up, they relied upon their own boldness, faith, and sense of humor. They also looked to their children and sexual relations with male prisoners to sustain them.

Children, both in prison and at home, clearly played important roles in the lives of female prisoners. One woman appealed to the governor for her release for the sake of her children: "I know the power is in you to parden and parole me or cut my time down, . . . I am the mother of five little children none able to help themselves." [51] The children of Frances Woods were apprenticed out after her conviction, but she sent her own money to enable them to visit her at the Pratt mines. In order to fetch them, her lawyer had to serve papers on the persons who had gained custody of them when Woods was sent to prison.[52] Another prisoner, Bettie Perkins, had left three small children, "each of whom were under six years of age," with their grandmother, an indication of some family support. (Perkins's case, however, illustrates how family ties could cut both ways. Although her grandmother cared for her children, Perkins's stepfather had forced her to associate with "bad company." She was with him when both were arrested for burglary.) [53] Still, the number of children female prisoners brought to prison indicates that no relatives willing or able to care for them existed. And not all women wanted children with them. Thomas Williams, a contractor, testified in 1888 that a woman prisoner died on his farm during an attempt to have an abortion.[54]

Women prisoners worked at remote county camps as well. Before 1888, the majority of county camps were beyond the reach of state inspectors, who limited their visits to mining camps such as Coalburg and Newcastle. And not all of the women in these county camps were prisoners. Even detailed research into the penitentiary and county camps fails to plumb the total effect of prison on rural communities. Farmers bought the labor of men by paying their court costs and even gained the labor of the prisoners' families. Under the county system of hard labor, often entire families remained with the convicted man at the contractor's farm. In 1876 the secretary of the Democratic Executive Committee in Marion, Alabama, wrote to the state chairman to complain about the supposedly lax treatment of black prisoners in his county. "It is *no* punishment to a negro to put him at what is *called* hard labor (i.e., to hire him out to the same planter with whom he was living at the time of his sentence and allow him to live with his friends and family as before the conviction)." What the lawyer objected to was the efforts of black families to stay together despite a prison sentence.

The wish to sustain family ties and the lack of economic options sometimes led women to follow their husbands into prison. The *Eutaw Whig and Observer* noted that "it is too often the case, however, that the planter, who thus hires the convicts, can get the control, not only of the convict's services, but that of his entire family for the term for which he is convicted." [55] In a sharecropping family a father's incarceration could spell economic doom. For some black women the only solution was to take one's family into a prison camp.

Despite the changes in state law, a significant number of female county prisoners still worked at camps with men. At the Coalburg prison mine, for example, women lived and worked under much less onerous conditions than the male prisoners. Women tended to have shorter sentences than men; because women did not mine coal, perhaps coal companies were not so eager to keep them incarcerated indefinitely. For example, the dozen or so women leased to Coalburg prison mine were sentenced for less than one year, including prison costs. Moreover, instead of working in or near the prison mines, "several of them were hired out to different persons about Coalburg as cooks and house servants."[56] Their short sentences, work outside of the prison, and mutual camaraderie shaped a distinctive kind of resistance.

Black women at Coalburg defied many prison rules outright. They refused to wear prison clothing or return to the prison after they finished their work in the community. Their audacity left Inspector Henley infuriated. "These women are not required to stay at the house where they are hired & it is no uncommon thing on Sundays to see them dressed up in their finest clothes & walking about the village."[57] He continued, "My information is that those who do not sleep in the prison are allowed to roam at large at night and can be seen almost every night in the company store and about Coalburg where ever they choose to go." Those inside the prison also refused to wear official garb. "I found several of these women [inside the stockade] yesterday, and in one or two instances they were dressed very elaborately."

The women's refusal to wear uniforms or return to the prison on time had repercussions throughout the prison. "They should be required to wear a uniform at all times," Henley fumed. "There is no reason why the discipline of the prison should not apply to the female convicts as well as the male and any other course is demoralizing."[58] One month later the situation had not improved. "The female convicts at this prison are a very unruly set and give a good deal of trouble. We have had them put in uniform, and try to keep them under control but it is a hard matter."[59] Henley wanted control over their nonworking hours as well as their working hours, but the women would not give in.

Officials at Coalburg also bemoaned the sexual activity of black women prisoners, believing that fraternization with male prisoners undermined prison discipline. F. P. Lewis, the prison physician at Coalburg, wrote that "women should not be confined in the same prison as men nor even admitted in the same enclosure. They are the cause of most of the quarreling between men, besides having a tendency to make them harder to manage." Women at Coalburg could not be sent to the Walls, which was for state prisoners only. Instead, Henley planned to put them "on the mountain above the house of the warden" to keep them away from the men. "These female prisoners are certainly the most unruly and disorderly convicts that I have ever had to manage & it will be necessary to enforce discipline at the cost of a good deal of punishment I am afraid." [60]

Neither the women at the Walls nor the women at Coalburg had female sponsors to "uplift" and reform them. Middle-class black women were busy with other community concerns, and white reformers like Julia Tutwiler focused exclusively on the problems faced by male prisoners. In the North middle-class reformers urged incarcerated women to assume a penitent role and recant their bad and immoral behavior.[61] Yet in Alabama women prisoners at the Walls and at Coalburg never acted the role of a contrite woman prisoner. Perhaps authorities considered female prisoners beyond reform, but strong self-assertion enabled them to survive the hardship of prison.

Negative perceptions of black women made them vulnerable to sexual assaults, and black women prisoners were even more susceptible to such attacks. When they happened, prisoners like Julia Pearson resisted. Pearson, a Jefferson County convict, had just arrived at the prison road camp outside of Birmingham when she had to fight off the sexual advances of a guard named Mooney. According to the inspector's report of the incident, Mooney had entered the women's cell on Saturday night and offered Julia Pearson a dollar to go outside with him. When she declined, "he then presented his pistol and told her he would kill her, but immediately said he was joking." After leaving to get some whiskey, he returned, went to Julia Pearson's bed, and fell asleep. "Julia says that she asked him repeatedly to go out of their cell and let them alone and finally told him that she intended reporting his conduct to Warden Pittman." Mooney finally did leave. When he returned at 4 A.M. to get the women so that they could cook breakfast, "Julia Pearson started towards the gate and said she was going to see Mr. Pittman." He cursed at her. She cursed him back. And then he shot at her twice. The second bullet broke her collarbone.[62]

The fact that Julia Pearson had been in the prison camp only a few days makes her bravery that much more significant.[63] She had been convicted on July 26, 1890, of assault and battery with a knife; one week later Mooney shot her. Pearson, new to prison life, might have assumed Warden Pittman would discipline her, not Mooney, for the incident. Pearson's appeal to prison authorities, however, demonstrates how black women drew on their own preexisting sense of rights in their struggle for decent treatment. Female prisoners in county camps were clearly vulnerable to the sexual aggression of armed guards. For a black woman to charge a white male with rape was unheard of in slavery and rare after emancipation.[64] Nevertheless, Julia Pearson refused to concede that rape was a white man's right, even if she was a prisoner and he a guard. Pearson was lucky to escape with her life. Another woman prisoner, Nellie Anderson, was shot and killed at Coalburg by a guard one year later.[65]

Prisoners were poor people, and they depended on family and friends to hire lawyers to try to get them out; but unless they were fortunate enough to be able to hire a lawyer, these women frequently had no money with which to raise an appeal. Smyer told the governor that he was acting on May's behalf free of charge. But convicted women such as Bettie Perkins, "with no kinsman or friends able to bear the expense of the application" for pardon, were more likely to serve longer time.[66]

Still, female prisoners like Martha Aarons, sentenced to seventy-five years for the death of her child, persevered in the hope of a pardon. After sixteen years in prison, she wrote to her attorney that "I am so hopeful once more to be free." Since 1873 she had picked cotton, grown food, scoured and mended prison uniforms, and performed other arduous work on various Alabama prison farms. Years of exchanging letters with her lawyers (and paying their fees) had given her encouragement but little fruit. "Of late I am very dispondent," she wrote in 1889, "and when I think that I have for sixteen years been a faithful Slave for the State of Ala, the time has come when she might be generous and forgiving to me."[67] In letters to her lawyer Aarons expressed no penitence over the incident. Perhaps in her own mind, she felt her innocence. As someone who had known actual slavery, Aarons retained her moral indignation over working hard for nothing, as well as her belief that freedom was a right derived from hard work. Eventually Martha Aarons prevailed, and in 1890 she gained a pardon.

But she never said goodbye to the penitentiary altogether. After her pardon she visited regularly, for during her time as a prisoner she had fallen "in love with a convick man" by the name of Charley Jemison. She tried numerous times to have Jemison pardoned. She even asked her employer, J. W. McLigill, to intercede on Jemison's behalf. In 1898 McLigill wrote a simple appraisal of Aarons and her situation to the governor: "She is my cook. She has been very true to her prisoner and every thing she makes she give it to Lawers to get Charly out. She paid one lawer 35 dollars in money and 1 bale of cotton weighing over 500 lbs. . . . She will show you the recit and she paid one lawer 40 dollars in money and they have done nothing. . . . she says she loves him and will marry him if she can get him out. She goes to see him evry month. She has ben true to him."[68]

Martha Aarons hoped to secure Jemison's freedom the same way she had procured her own: through the patient application of pressure. Such Herculean attempts to free herself and Jemison echo similar antebellum efforts of free blacks to secure the freedom of enslaved family members.[69]

Martha Aarons's devotion to Jemison over many years shows that women formed significant relationships in prison. Her persistence in seeking a pardon for him is similar to the efforts of male prisoners who helped each other adjust to freedom after being released. The key difference, however, is that Aaron's struggles were motivated by her vision of the relationship between love and freedom. Her monthly visits to Jemison, her appeals to governors and lawyers on his behalf, and her labor in the cotton fields and in the kitchen to earn extra money represent her efforts to create a future on her own terms. Her actions caused confusion. Her employer, for one, thought that the lawyers taking her money would never secure Jemison's release. And Thomas Williams, for whom she worked as a prisoner and to whom she also appealed for assistance in gaining Jemison's release, remarked that Martha Aarons was "a much better convict than a free woman."[70] Apparently when a prisoner, Aarons did as she was told. But when free she went against the advice of white men and pursued her own dreams of companionship and love.

The behavior of other black women in Alabama prisons echoes Martha Aarons's attempts to use her freedom on behalf of love and family. The new control that black people exercised over their family lives and nonworking time emerged as a social fact of enduring significance, particularly for black women. Historians have tended to view emancipation primarily in terms of changing labor relations, but the destruction of slavery affected far more than work. Emancipation meant that black citizens could live open, public, and legitimate family and community lives. Even inside prison, blacks forced white authorities to honor their familial ties. Contact with families sustained prisoners, enabling them to survive and hope for the future. Women in prison sought to return to their children; once released, they tried to reunite their families. Men, such as Ezekiel Archey, could anticipate visits from female family members and a home life upon release.

The small number of women prisoners should not allow us to underestimate their impact on prison life. Despite suffering abuse and prejudice at the hands of white inspectors, black women prisoners valued freedom of movement, freedom of speech, and sexual freedom. The struggles of black women prisoners reveal their intelligence, courage, personal independence, economic fortitude, spirituality, loyalty, and humor. They could also be violent and defend themselves when necessary. Through daily acts of self-assertion that reclaimed personal and social space, women resisted the dehumanizing effects of prison life. The wearing of one's own clothes, personal unruliness, and sexual relations with men undermined discipline for the entire prison and, from the state's point of view, needed to be suppressed. Moreover, the actions of women prisoners show that they entered prison with strong feelings about what constituted captivity, control, and freedom.

Prisoners Confront TCI

■ Despite its financial benefits, leasing remained mired in public controversy. When TCI was awarded the labor of all state and county prisoners in 1888, John T. Milner, owner of Newcastle, alleged corrupt dealings between TCI and the state. Spurred on by the press, the legislature launched an investigation and arrived at a compromise. According to the new contract, TCI gained all male state prisoners and half of all county men. The remaining county prisoners were leased to the Sloss Iron and Steel Company, which had bought Coalburg and Newcastle from Milner. TCI agreed to pay $18.50 a month for a first-class convict, seemingly assuring the state of a steady income for the next ten years.

TCI could well afford the new lease. After the company bought out the Pratt Coal and Coke Company in 1886, it became the largest mining concern in the state. Under the Pratt Mines Division, TCI operated ten mines in Jefferson, Bibb, and Shelby Counties. By 1890 approximately 1,000 state and county prisoners worked at the Shaft and the Slope—now owned by TCI. Approximately 15,000 free miners also worked for TCI.

By 1888 coal production in the region had soared to new heights. In November of that year, according to Pratt official P. J. Rogers, Pratt's daily output was 4,233 tons, with "about 1450 tons mined by the 'boys,'"—the prisoners. This, according to the warden, was "the largest output ever made south of the Ohio River by any one Co."[1] Prison mining had become an enormous source of private and state profit, as well as the primary source of coke for steel. The leasing system reaped enormous profits for the state. In the 1890 fiscal year, Alabama received $113,000 from convict leasing, or about 6 percent of its total revenue.[2] Everything about the lease seemed to be going well, and not just financially. R. H. Dawson had imposed administrative order. The Board of Inspectors—Dawson, Henley, and Lee—met regularly and corresponded with the governor and TCI. Every few weeks prison inspectors and physicians visited the mines. A secretary, J. D. Douglass, kept track of payments, releases, and correspondence. This left Dawson free to attend meetings of the National Prison Association and to see to other duties.

TCI had even begun to spend money on the prison buildings. In 1888 the first of two long-promised new prisons at the Pratt mines finally reached completion. The prison at the Shaft now stood two stories tall. The building was "in the shape of a cross" and was located "on the highest point around Coketon." It had eight rooms, each 125 feet long and 35 feet wide. One room served as a dining hall, and another was partitioned into a segregated classroom. The remaining six rooms housed 500 men who slept on beds suspended from the ceiling by iron rods. Toilets, with "ample flushing arrangements," were outside. The new prison also boasted bathtubs, an innovation. "No two convicts will be allowed to bathe in the same water," the regulations stated. "Every convict will have his number and a peg with a corresponding number upon which to hang his clothes, and thus the same man will wear the same suit all the time." After bathing, prisoners were "hoisted to the top of the shaft and go to the prison through a manway enclosed with plank and covered to prevent exposure to wet and cold weather." Such changes had transformed the old prison into a modern labor barracks. The local paper felt compelled to explain why prisoners lived in such relative comfort—after all, how many citizens in Alabama had hot and cold water and flush toilets? It reassured taxpayers that none of the money for these buildings came from the public, explaining that prisoners paid their way and more. "The gross income from the convicts at Pratt Mines to the State during the month of July was $6,500 and it will probably be more during the month of August. From the income of the convicts the State pays the cost of prosecution in every case, under the late law, which requires the contractor to pay when the convict is delivered to him all the costs, for which he gets a credit on his account with the State monthly."[3]

Even critics of the convict lease system began to see gradual improvements. The reformer Julia Tutwiler instituted night schools at Coalburg, the Slope, and the Shaft. The penitentiary hired an official chaplain who drew a state salary; prisoners were required to attend church services every Sunday.[4] A reformed legal code passed in 1886 gave inspectors the power to regulate the treatment of county prisoners. Female state prisoners ceased to work alongside men and now worked solely at the Walls. By the late

1880s, in the words of one historian, "the organization of the Alabama penal system had been stabilized."[5] Indeed, it is tempting to see institutional order and legal reforms, high production, and lucrative profits as evidence of the system's success.

The appearance of order and reform, however, belied disorder, confusion, and outright conflict between contractors, state inspectors, and prisoners. Behind the scenes, in fact, the entire leasing system had entered a state of physical and financial crisis.

TCI's financial stability was not all it seemed. One year after its contract with Alabama began, the company failed to make its monthly payments on time. A letter from G. B. McCormack, general manager of TCI, gives a glimpse of the financial house of cards upon which TCI stood. In December 1889 the company still owed Alabama for the month of November; that amount, McCormack wrote, "would be sent today." But the $9,000 due for the month of December was another matter. Although Alabama needed that cash to make it through its own financial quarter, TCI could not deliver. Instead, McCormack asked if TCI could pay Alabama in "bills receivable," that is, through the debts other companies owed it: "Ordinarily we would have no hesitancy in promising the money but it seems that everyone who owes us for coal, coke, or pig iron either does not pay at all or pays in paper [and] with the present stringency of the money market it is almost impossible to have even first class paper discounted in Nashville, Louisville, Cincinnati, or New York. If we should fail in getting the money, do you think you could arrange with some Montgomery Bank to discount some first class paper, with our endorsement on it?"[6] Of course the state's governor could persuade the state's bank to accept TCI's discounted, and perhaps worthless, guarantees. In fact, the governor had no choice because Alabama needed such guarantees of payment from TCI to maintain its own solvency.

TCI's periodic penury continued throughout the 1890s. Strikes and the depression of 1893 weakened the company. For the next several years, TCI's monthly payments to Alabama continued to lag. In January 1894 the company's treasurer reassured the governor that "we have thus paid over $11,000 within the past three weeks, and I can assure you that we will continue to pay as fast as possible to catch up." A week later he tried to convince the governor of TCI's financial stability. Treasurer James Bowron reiterated that "we are doing all we can to catch up on accounts which have been thrown into arrears by causes wholly beyond our control during the recent financial panic."[7] Despite TCI's financial weaknesses, it still wielded power and knew that its prison mines would keep running. Even if the company could never pay, Alabama's governor could not remove the prisoners from the Pratt mines: where would they go? No state-owned facilities capable of housing and working over 1,000 men existed. Dispersing prisoners throughout the state would have meant administrative chaos and financial loss. The white public, fueled by the propaganda of the Democrats themselves, expected prisoners to make a profit for the state. Finally, the state needed the high profits of the mines; TCI's assurances of future payments, although doubtful, still amounted to more than small farmers or local industries could afford to pay for prison labor.

Both black prisoners and free labor bore the brunt of TCI's problems. In order to gain more revenue, TCI cut wages for free miners and forced a series of work speedups in the prison mines. The amount of whipping also increased. TCI and the state inspectors crossed swords over how much prisoners should be tasked. A pneumonia epidemic at the Shaft and the Slope and a scandal regarding the horrendous conditions at Coalburg illustrate the brutal manner in which TCI and Sloss sought to squeeze coal production out of prisoners. Nevertheless, the Department of Corrections and the state, fearful of losing revenue, refused to end mining as the major source of prison profit. An increased number of escape attempts, prisoner suicides, arson attempts, insubordination, and work stoppages showed a supposedly stable system to be in a whirling crisis.

The mining companies constantly developed new ways to make prisoners work harder. TCI forced prisoners to do more work than their classification required and then cheated prisoners by refusing to count "scant" cars. Prisoners also suffered more frequent beatings. Slope No. 2 was especially notorious for the "unnecessary amount of punishment" meted out by Willie Rogers in his efforts to increase production. During one of his visits to this mine, Inspector Henley discovered that a team of two prisoners who would ordinarily be expected to mine five tons a day were in fact required to mine six. He wrote to Dawson that "I asked Rogers about it and he said it was so; but that he gave them an extra amount of dynamite and I might add an extra amount of butt paddling." When Henley told Rogers that he had no right to increase the task, "he merely laughed and said it was the custom there." Henley, mortified at Rogers's flippancy, asked Dawson to investigate. "I [am] begin[ning] to think that he thinks he can get along without our Rules." [8]

Angered by the indignity of being ridiculed, Henley also worried that contractors were defrauding the state by—to paraphrase the Shaft prisoners' 1887 letter—classifying prisoners one way and tasking them another. As a result, inspectors tried to anticipate cheating by raising each prisoner's classification. In August 1890 Henley wrote to Dawson that "we were satisfied that a good many men were classed too low and raised them to such a task as we thought right." [9] The motivation behind such a work speedup was clear: by raising the classification, Henley wrote, "I think we increased the revenue at the Shaft and perhaps at the Slope." [10] Later in the summer Inspector Lee increased the tasks of still more men. [11] Given TCI's profits, Willie Rogers's behavior, and the information they received from prisoners about the day-to-day operations of the mine, inspectors had become more confident in their ability to judge how much work a skilled prisoner should do. In raising men's classifications, however, they contributed to the work speedups.

Prisoners at the Shaft and the Slope complained about the speedups and whipping by appealing to the inspectors. Babe Ellis and other convicts at the Shaft wanted to know if "the contractor has a right to require a convict, when an accident happens to the machinery, to make up for lost coal."[12] Gilbert Keenan asked to see Inspector Henley on the grounds that he had been unjustly punished.[13] Prisoners also complained that they failed to get their task completed because of the scarcity of tramcars. "Frequently [we] do not have cars to put coal in," testified a prisoner at New Castle. "Get whipped all the same."[14] Contractors did not care about being reasonable; as long as they could punish prisoners with impunity, they continued to do so.

Not surprisingly, the company spent as little money as possible on prison operations. In July 1889 Dawson ordered TCI to put fifty more tramcars in both the Shaft and the Slope. P. J. Rogers, the general manager at the Pratt mines, told Dawson that he knew such measures amounted to "economy to our company, *but I get the devil for it all.*"[15] TCI's reluctance to invest in basic equipment underscored its indifference to the working conditions of prisoners.

Prisoners also responded to the work speedups, unsafe conditions, and increased whipping in the 1890s by setting fires, escaping, and being generally insubordinate. The promise of short-time pardons and the presence of inspectors, touted as measures that brought stability and order, could not compensate for the speedups and whippings. By 1888 economic pressures had destroyed any reciprocity between prisoners and the contractors. While the company resorted to desperate measures to increase production, prisoners responded with bolder forms of resistance, including arson and digging out of Slope No. 2.

Prisoners continued to complain of long-standing dangers such as the presence of poisonous gas in the Rock Slope of the Shaft mine. Henley reported that "a convict by the name of Jones had been slightly burned in the arm and neck by an explosion of gas in the Rock Slope at the Shaft mines. . . . Because of information received from several convicts, he apprehended danger from Gas in this part of mine."[16] The numerous complaints he received from prisoners led Henley to take it upon himself to go down into the Rock Slope and investigate. He believed the prisoners, not the contractors. He wrote to Dawson and urged him to remove prisoners from the Rock Slope. "We cannot afford to rely on what we are told about the safety of the Shaft any longer," he wrote.[17] In March 1889 the Board of Inspectors seemed poised to act. After an emergency meeting Dawson and the board ordered TCI to sink an air shaft from the surface down 340 feet to the deepest part of the Shaft mine.[18] TCI refused. In May a gas explosion in the Rock Slope injured five prisoners.

Prisoners began to take matters into their own hands. Two months later, in July 1889, a fire at the Rock Slope stopped work for a week. A conflagration that began in the prisoners' bathhouse soon set the entire interior of the mine ablaze. Sixty free miners worked day and night to extinguish the inferno, costing TCI $300 a day. Dawson tried to explain to Governor Seay why it was taking so long to get the mine operating again. "You can understand the difficulty of effecting anything," he observed. "The slope is 10 or 12 feet wide and 6 feet high—imagine the heat and smoke with coal 52 inches thick on fire on each side . . . and the fire in the 'Dog Hole' which is only 5 feet wide. It is a miniature Hell. No one knows who is to blame."[19] The fire occurred on a Sunday, and at first it was thought that sparks thrown from a fan had produced the accident. In his diary, however, Dawson speculated that arson was the cause.

Prisoners at the Shaft refused to reenter the mine. Three weeks after the fire was extinguished, Dawson was still trying to persuade them to return. "The men are demoralized by the fire," he wrote to Governor Seay, "and timid about going into the mines. I shall have to go in enough to let them see that I do not think it dangerous; and I hope to satisfy them."[20] Dawson saw timidity, but prisoners at the Shaft took a stand. They refused to work in the Rock Slope—which still did not have an air shaft—and agreed to work only in the McArdle Slope, which was unaffected by the fire. "Of course," Dawson wrote ruefully, "some do not wish to work anywhere." In the middle of August, "some of them set that part of the mine (the McArdle Slope) on fire . . . so as to stop work again, but it was discovered soon enough to prevent any damage."[21] Prisoners at the Shaft complained of bad air in the McArdle Slope and continued to object to the presence of dangerous gas.

Subsequent accidents vindicated their complaints. In September 1889 William Nest, a free white miner who worked as a gas boss, took Newman Bonner, a black prisoner, into the Rock Slope to check for gas. An explosion killed them both.[22] More explosions and accidents occurred at all three major prison mines during 1889 and 1890. Arson and mass escapes became increasingly common. In July 1890 several prisoners gave a false fire alarm and then attempted to escape; two succeeded.[23] There was also an attempt to burn Slope No. 2.[24] In December 1890 another case of arson occurred at the Shaft. Well-planned escape conspiracies followed. On the heels of an arson attempt later that month, several black prisoners in the Shaft made what Henley called "a bold attempt to escape." Arson and escape attempts succeeded in stopping work at the mines, thereby helping to keep prisoners alive by keeping them out of unsafe conditions.

The inspectors demanded that the state legislature make prison arson a crime "punishable by death." After the arson attempt in December 1890, Henley urged Dawson to contact members of the legislature. "I don't know whether you have heard that another attempt was made a few days ago to fire the Shaft mine," he wrote. "Unless something is done to put a stop to this we will yet have to record a horror there that will raise a howl all over this country."[25] Henley feared a public outcry, but none came, not even when stupidity and carelessness caused a string of fatal accidents. In 1890 two avoidable mine explosions killed twenty prisoners. Twelve men died at the Coalburg mine in March when a spark caused gunpowder to explode as prisoners lined up to receive their charges for the day. Nine more prisoners were killed in an explosion at the Shaft mine in May 1891. Dawson explained the cause of the explosion to the governor: "The gas which caused this explosion was not the carbonic acid gas or 'Choke damp' which was complained of to us before the air shaft was finished; that will not burn nor will a lamp burn in it and it kills by suffocation. The gas which exploded was carburretted hydrogen, known among the miners as 'Fire damp' or 'Fire.' . . . It exists more or less in all deposits of coal. It is exceedingly flammable and a body of it coming in contact with a light emplodes instantly and with fearful violence."[26] The explosion occurred when a mine boss sent prisoners to work in rooms containing pockets of hydrogen or natural gas. Although prisoners had told the mine boss that those rooms had gas, he sent nine men to their deaths anyway.[27]

In a lengthy letter to Governor Thomas G. Jones describing the dire history of explosions and accidents in the mines, Dawson became defensive. At first he blamed careless prisoners ("We believe that convicts are more reckless than others") and the whimsy of fate ("As we said in regard to the explosion of powder at Coalburg last year, by which 12 persons were killed, as long as mines are worked there will be accidents"). But eventually he acknowledged that the economic pressures placed upon the penitentiary forced him to work prisoners in mines, and that such work was inherently dangerous: "As long as our Department is required to pay out the [expected] amount of money . . . at least a portion of the convicts [must be worked] in the coal mines."[28]

Dawson, Henley, and Lee saw much to criticize in the TCI-run prison mines, particularly the high number of whippings meted out to prisoners. Lee wrote to Dawson in March 1890 that he was "beginning to doubt the wisdom of flogging now in vogue" as such brutality did not seem to encourage better behavior. Why not, then, call a halt to it? Lee saw whipping as the prerogative of TCI. Any other kind of punishment, such as isolation, "infringes the right to the labor of the convict, which the contractor has."[29] Henley also concluded that "the present system of managing men by fear of the strap is wrong."[30] Instead of physical punishment, Henley suggested that the Board of Inspectors "withhold all recommendations for short time pardon until this spirit of rebellion is quelled."[31]

Yet even the promise of short time did little to deter men such as John Floyd, who, after receiving twenty-one lashes for defying the authorities, hid away in the mines for over ten days. Eventually, Floyd was forced to wear shackles and a chain while he worked.[32] But his behavior did not change. He was suspected of heading a conspiracy to escape early one morning "when the cooks are let out of the cells." To punish Floyd and others like him, William Rogers, the warden, built a "dark cell." Even so, as Lee noted, contractors expected prisoners to work; little could be done when they refused besides increased whipping.[33]

Arson and escape attempts during 1891 and 1892 caused serious damage, leading to a shutdown of the mines. All work stopped in January 1891 when another fire in the bathhouse at the Shaft spread into the mines. "All the mining clothes are burned and the engine which hauls out of McArdle slope is damaged so that it cannot be used for several days." Some of the mine's roof caved in after the coal caught on fire.[34] After this incident TCI attempted to halt such sabotage through sheer repression. Guards at the Shaft, on constant alert, were ordered to kill anyone caught attempting to torch the bathhouse. In May 1891 a guard named Nelson, acting on an informant's tip, waited outside the bathhouse for Clayton Lloyd, a prisoner. In his sworn testimony Nelson stated that Warden Rogers had told him to lie in wait by the water closet, and "that if an attempt was made to set fire to the building I should kill him." When Nelson saw Lloyd light up some matches in the bathhouse, he shot him dead.[35]

Instead of halting the unrest, this shooting encouraged other plots and escape attempts. In June 1891 prisoners rushed a guard at the Shaft mine entrance, pelting him with billets of wood known as "sprags." Other guards fired at two prisoners, killing them both and causing the rest to halt.[36] The inspectors noted that after these events the level of insubordination increased. "The shooting of Clayton Lloyd & the explosion and the shooting of Harry O'Hara and the killing of Rube Harmon" had left the convicts "surly and insubordinate." They continued to gamble with impunity and argue with inspectors throughout the summer.[37]

In January 1892 prisoners at Slope No. 2 celebrated the new year by escaping through the old works of Slope No. 1. They had tunneled into the newly discovered openings of an old adjoining mine to dig their way out. In June more carefully planned dig-outs were executed. Jim Massey led a group of eight or so prisoners in digging out of Slope No. 2 into the old works. As the inspectors remarked, the only thing that kept more from escaping was the fact that the plan was so well concealed. Such success inspired others, and inspectors warned that "it is evident that many more attempts will be made through the same channel."[38] The Shaft was also plagued by escapes. On May 2, 1892, another fire burned the bathhouse, and it was several days before the convicts returned to their work in that slope.[39] The following day three white prisoners tried to escape through the manway by cutting through some boards in a fence. In September 1892 the inspectors reported "an unusual number of escapes" at the Pratt mines and at Coalburg as well as more mining accidents.[40]

Besides the dangers inherent in their work, prisoners at the Shaft and the Slope faced the invisible dangers of disease. Tuberculosis and pneumonia, easily spread in such close quarters, took the lives of more and more prisoners in the early 1890s. Beginning in March 1893, a pneumonia epidemic spread through all six wards of the Slope No. 2 prison, each of which housed 125 prisoners. Symptoms included a high fever, "diseased lungs," and massive heart clots. Dawson praised Dr. Jones for sterilizing the prison, but sickness continued to kill prisoners. "It would be of great importance to have the cause, not only of this disease but of the frequent occurrence of consumption, typhoid fever, and chronic diarrhea at convict mines." Before the epidemic ended in May, Jones estimated that half of the fifty-six prisoners infected with pneumonia died.[41]

The lure of short-time pardons had worked initially as a means of halting escapes and temporarily disciplining the labor force. But after TCI took over the management of the entire prison in the late 1880s, short time could no longer compensate for the loss of freedom, work speedups, dangerous conditions, and brutal treatment. This "spirit of rebellion" that began in 1888–89 should be seen as a collective, rational response by prisoners to new conditions imposed by TCI. When prisoners engaged in protest, escapes, and arson, they decided that to risk punishment and even death was worth the sacrifice if the only alternative was to accept conditions as they were.

The suicide of Sydney Holman in 1892 provides an important example of one prisoner who chose death over continued exploitation and hopelessness. In 1888 Holman was marginally involved in an attempt to overpower and kill William Rogers, the hated warden at Slope No. 2. Although Holman did not try to kill Rogers, according to Dawson, "by his conduct and his language he incited and encouraged the outbreak." Holman received an official bad conduct report along with seven other convicts, including Ike Berry.[42] When the Board of Inspectors let that report stand, Holman's chance to receive a short-time pardon vanished.

Nevertheless, Holman continued to hope. In December 1891 he wrote a letter to Governor Jones outlining the reasons why he felt he deserved short time. "I am not treated write about my short time," Holman wrote. "I now wish to consult the highest power." He insisted for several reasons that he was being unfairly deprived of short time. Two of the participants in that same mutiny, but not he, had since been granted short time. And, Holman argued, to deprive him of short time was counterproductive: "Sence that time I have tried to do my duty and given no truble Gov to further oppress me under the circumstance of that affair shoes no desire what ever of the Penitentiary for my Reffromation. . . . I have a good reputation here about my work."[43] Holman tried to hold the governor and the inspectors to the explicit promises made to all prisoners about the relationship between short time, working hard, and skill. If those promises were not going to be kept, then Holman was going to take matters into his own hands.

In April 1892 Holman died in a mine explosion at Slope No. 2. On that fatal evening ten other prisoners, supervising the pumps and wishing to earn extra money, were present in the mine. The explosion happened when the room Holman customarily worked in became engulfed with gas. The mine boss had warned all the men about the dangers of keeping the gate closed. "Being an experienced miner, and in full possession of the fact that gas was being given off in that room," explained Henley, "it seems strange that he [Sydney] did not take the necessary precautions to protect himself from danger & the best information I can get leads me to the conclusion that gas could not have accumulated there if the door mentioned had been kept closed."[44] Holman was an experienced miner, a first-class convict who for several years had cut four or five tons of coal daily. But according to his fellow prisoners and mine workers, he had grown despondent and "reckless" in his work because of the inspectors' refusal to grant him his short time. After Holman's death, Inspector Henley recalled their last meeting:

> The last time I was at this prison in the early part of this month, he asked me if we did not intend to let him have his short time. I told him that it was useless for him to think any more about short time as his conduct had been such that the Board would not think of recommending him. He was apparently very much disappointed by my reply. The convicts say that since that time he has been very irritable & reckless. John Rentz says that he told him one night last week that he did not care whether he lived or died; that the Inspectors had refused him short time and he was reckless. Charley Jackson says he heard him repeat the same sentiment on Saturday night last.[45]

Holman was willing to work for short time and willing to work for cash, but the thought of further exploitation drove him to despair and ultimately suicide.

The inspectors concluded that Sydney Holman killed himself because he knew he would never receive short time. However, Holman knew that

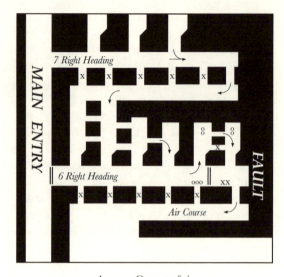

Arrows - Current of air
x - Brattice
‖ - Gate
⚇ - Rooms where the explosion occurred
xx - Location of pump
ooo - Point where Sidney was found

Map of the interior of the coal mine where Sydney
Holman, a prisoner, committed suicide. (Redrawn
from Inspector A. T. Henley's map in Reports of Inspectors and Other Officials, Alabama Department
of Archives and History, Montgomery)

he was depriving contractors of the profits from his skilled labor, and so his
suicide can also be interpreted as a defiant act. Denied short time, Holman
decided not to give any more labor.

Black prisoners also defied prison authorities by gambling, bartering,
and creating informal markets within the prison barracks. Before the 1890s,
prisoners had received cash wages by performing Sunday work or by mining
coal that exceeded their assigned quota, but this money had not disrupted
the prison routine. Instead, prisoners either spent their earnings on small
luxuries or sent it home to the Black Belt. In 1883 R. H. Skinner and
Ezekiel Archey claimed that they sent their extra money home to help their
families. Archey testified before a U.S. Senate committee that he was usually
able to get his task completed by nine or ten o'clock; after that he would, if
he chose, mine an extra five or six tons of coal for himself.[46] He used these
earnings to make himself "as comfortable as possible." For example, he
bought "papers, books, pens, and ink, and so on." In addition, he used the
extra money to help his mother. As he explained, "I have got a mother who

comes from Selma to see me sometimes, and I give her shoes or a couple of dresses sometimes. . . . I always preserve a little for her." [47]

Burgeoning strike activity, however, pushed prisoners' incomes to new heights. In 1889 one prisoner revealed that "when free miners struck, some of the convicts made as much as $25 a month." [48] Often, extra labor was forced upon the men. At wet mines the pumps had to run all the time, regardless of whether prisoners wanted to perform extra work or not. As a prisoner noted, "Men work on Sunday by just calling a man out and making him work; he is then paid." [49] During December 1890, according to Inspector Lee, "about $1,000 in money was paid to the convicts at the Shaft . . . and about $600 and $700 has been paid every month since." During all of 1890 TCI paid over $7,000 to the convicts for all extra work.[50]

This cash, paid directly to the prisoners, circulated throughout the prison and created dissension. Henley complained that "we have had fights, quarrels, and gambling without limit and it is hard to preserve . . . discipline." [51] He wished to limit the amount paid to prisoners to one dollar a week, regardless of how much coal they mined. He argued that extra money caused not only gambling—a vice that spawned fighting, stealing, and rioting—but also a general atmosphere of insubordination.[52]

Much to the chagrin of the state inspectors, however, TCI tolerated prison gambling and even encouraged it. The company depended on prisoners working overtime, and convicts depended on cash to make their prison life tolerable. R. H. Cunningham, the company physician employed by Pratt to oversee the Shaft and Slope No. 2, opposed the prohibition of gambling in prison. "Fortunately," he said, the rules against gambling are "not strictly enforced. Large numbers of them [prisoners] being in a ward, they are allowed to talk, joke, sing, pray, preach, write, and while it is not allowed, they do play 'five-up' a little for fun, tobacco, and nickels." [53] Some of this cash returned to TCI as "thrifty" convicts, according to Cunningham, spent their hard-earned extra dollars buying "cigars, cigarettes, fruits, canned goods" from the company's "convict merchant."

Ironically, these increased labor demands, and the money they generated, created an atmosphere similar to a labor barracks, rather than a prison. No separate cells with bars separated the men. Instead, prisoners slept on swinging bunks close to each other. They also worked together and ate together; when they returned to the barracks they used their free time to entertain each other by telling "terrible tales," according to Julia Tutwiler. On Sunday, their day off, Cunningham saw "some reading, some wrestling, some telling stories, some sleeping, some praying and singing, generally about two to four preaching," and of course a few gambling.[54] In this setting prisoners seemed to pay very little attention to the inspectors or the mine bosses; from sundown to sunup their world was their own.

State inspector Henley constantly grumbled about prison gambling, however, complaining that it undermined discipline. At Slope No. 2 he found prisoners gambling "in full view of the door of the cell."[55] In the summer of 1891 he reported that the prisoners at the Shaft were "very noisy and disorderly. This I believe due to the fact that they had been allowed to play cards during the day." Not everyone engaged in this behavior. Many of the convicts, Henley insisted, "asked him to have the order that allowed card playing and crapshooting rescinded." Gambling also caused thieving among the prisoners. Henley ordered John Walton, a prisoner at the Shaft, to receive twenty-one lashes for stealing $10 from the trunk of another black prisoner.[56] Still, if prisoners were allowed to have dice and cards in their cells, then nothing could stop them from gambling.[57] After years of railing against it, Henley still found gambling to be "no uncommon thing." He wrote that he "found that most of the convicts who are allowed to have Shuckster stands in the cells had cards for sale."[58]

This roaring trade in goods, cards, and other items linked prisoners to men and women living on the outside. The prison was a center of money-making for TCI, to be sure, but it also became a focal point in the community of Pratt City. Ex-prisoners came and went between the prison and their new homes. Prisoners with extra cash to spend attracted men and women from Pratt City with items to sell. By the late 1890s the attitude of prisoners toward money had changed. Instead of sending money home, prisoners used more of their income on themselves. The amount of money generated by prison labor created markets within the prison itself, and gambling provided sport, competition, and resistance to the authority of contractors and inspectors.

Even when inspectors tried to limit the amount of circulating cash, prisoners at Coalburg responded by trading in company scrip.[59] Indeed, it appears that the Sloss Coal Company paid prisoners in company scrip before ever using it with free miners. In the summer of 1891, for example, Henley visited Coalburg to investigate the unusual amount of whipping and marks for bad behavior that the company had meted out. What he discovered was a widespread trade among prisoners in Coalburg company scrip. President Thomas Seddon told Henley that Sloss Company officials had complied with the inspectors' wish that they not pay cash to prisoners for extra work. Instead, the company gave prisoners a choice. They could be paid in cash when their sentences expired, or "they could get the full amount in checks payable in goods at the Commissary."[60] In practice, however, Henley found that the prisoners always received payment in scrip, never in cash. Prisoners received less than free miners for the extra coal they mined: 33⅓ cents per ton as opposed to the 55 cents a ton paid in cash to free labor. After exchanging the checks for goods "at a profit of perhaps fifty percent," prisoners discovered that the actual pay received "is very far below what the work is actually worth."[61] Although Seddon denied that Sloss marked up goods at the company store so extravagantly, Henley reported him to Dawson for grossly exploiting the prisoners.

Prisoners did not complain about the scrip system at Coalburg, however, because they discovered other ways to increase the value of their compensation. The commissary was not the only market available to the men, and scrip checks often were worth more than their face value. Prisoners created their own underground market as sophisticated as that of any alternative economy. "I find," said Henley, "that these checks are being bought at a discount of 25% by several of the convicts from each other & some of the officers of the prison and that a regular system of 'scalping' is being indulged in by them." In addition, these company "checks" fueled gambling, another diversion and a source of income that prisoners wished to continue.[62] Sloss had other practical reasons for paying county prisoners in scrip rather than cash. Paying them in cash would have enabled them to pay their court costs, thus eliminating their remaining time in prison. This would have left Sloss without skilled labor. By depriving men of short-time pardons and by paying prisoners in scrip, the Sloss Company kept alive the goose that laid the golden eggs.

Dawson, Henley, and Lee considered gambling and prison markets as insubordination because such activity directly defied prison rules. In the prisoners' desire to earn money, they created markets that, although exploitative, still provided an arena of choice, pleasure, and contact with the outside world.

The frequency and audacity of black protest in the mines during this period count as more than spontaneous outbursts. Indeed, white contractors and inspectors alike found all black behavior in prison, nearly to a man, appallingly arrogant. Dawson's observations about the prisoners' "inordinate self-esteem" can be seen as the culmination of his frustration: whipping and brutal physical punishment could not stem the insubordination. The "shell of self importance" among black prisoners showed no signs of cracking during the early 1890s.[63]

Although black prisoners resisted increasing work demands, they also accepted the company's offer of extra cash for extra work. Was this contradictory behavior? Or can any form of self-assertion among the oppressed be seen as resistance, even if such acts benefit the oppressor? To historians of black America, the definition of resistance has grown so wide that the distinction between adaptation and resistance merits a fresh look.

Initially, historians such as the white Communist Herbert Aptheker worked alone, outside of the mainstream, to show that black revolts and resistance had been an integral part of slavery in America. In 1943 Aptheker's *Negro American Slave Revolts* rejected scenarios of slavery, perpetuated by Hollywood and the mainstream academy, that asserted black slaves and white masters loved each other. Stripping away that facade meant showing the raw power involved in exercising domination and in opposing it.[64]

In 1942 anthropologists Alice and Raymond Bauer opened up to historians the psychological realm of slave resistance. The Bauers argued that work slowdowns, destruction of property, malingering, and self-mutilation — all common behavior of slaves — could be seen as daily resistance to slavery. The Bauers admitted that tangible evidence proving hostile motives was elusive. But they drew on John Dollard's contemporary study of segregation in Mississippi to illustrate how racially oppressive situations lead to deviousness, lying, and dissimulation.[65] The Bauers urged historians not to take the appearance of accommodation on its face. Like Dollard, they stressed the inner lives of their black subjects. In their study of slavery and daily resistance, the Bauers sought to strip away the image of slave stupidity created by U. B. Phillips and others and replace it with cunning and knowledge. The Bauers argued that "patterns of adjustment" found among slaves should not be confused with acceptance of their subordination.[66]

Writings about slavery influenced thinking about black resistance in freedom, especially when historians began to interpret the responses of freedpeople to newly oppressive institutions such as peonage or the lease. Since the 1960s the majority of scholarly studies of the accommodation and resistance of workers and African Americans have stressed the dual roles the oppressed play, one for authority and one for each other.[67] The consequences for honestly expressing one's opposition to white power, as freedom's first generation found out, were severe. During slavery, and even in Dollard's town in the Mississippi Delta in the 1930s, direct challenges to white people based upon honest confrontation — not trickery or deceit — were met with swift, often violent, punishment. Historians have documented the violent retribution imposed upon direct black resistance on an institutional, legal, and individual level. Those caught trying to escape slavery or challenging the authority of the master were punished. Only by "fooling" the master or practicing their religion and family life in secret could slaves maintain their dignity. Similarly, African Americans living in the segregated South often had to conceal their true feelings from whites. Black institutions and private lives, even in freedom, remained largely hidden from white view.

Dollard recognized that unequal power relations and the threat of racial violence in the Delta precluded honest interaction between blacks and whites. "One informant said that Negroes cannot be trusted, that they will invariably tell a white person what they think he expects them to say. If we postulate that people lie when they are afraid, this is equivalent to saying that dealing with a white man is always viewed by the Negro as a potentially dangerous situation in which he does not feel he can afford to be honest."[68] In slavery blacks certainly could not afford to be honest with many white persons, and neither could black people living in the Mississippi Delta in the 1930s. Racial oppression in slavery and in freedom forced black people into playing a dual role—one for the community and one for whites.

Some of the patterns of behavior associated with slaves can be seen among black prisoners, who did not always behave the same way in front of guards and contractors as they did with each other. In their daily lives and work routines, prisoners were required to obey white authority and achieve work quotas under the pain of brutal punishments. Black prisoners surely had to practice duplicity and cunning to survive.

Yet the daily struggles of prisoners working in Alabama's convict mines also deviated from the image of the Janus-faced African American. Prisoners often expressed their grievances to state inspectors with honesty. Letters from prisoners to inspectors and the inspectors' own accounts of their interactions with prisoners reveal prisoners to be far from submissive and self-deprecating. Prisoners complained about their treatment and working conditions, appealing to justice and fair treatment under the law and prison rules. During the 1880s and 1890s, in a variety of circumstances, prisoners complained to white authority in honest and direct assertions. They complained about excessive punishments and unfair work tasks. They requested time cards. Black women talked back, accused guards of assault, and refused to wear prison clothing. They challenged the veracity of white contractors. They said these things directly to the inspectors and did not couch these complaints in terms other than what they were. These were direct statements of protest, made to white authority figures.

Prisoners also took bold, defiant action. They set fires, plotted escapes, and committed suicide. They also ignored rules about gambling and selling playing cards. Through gambling and prison markets, they carved out their own space away from the prying eyes of inspectors and contractors.

Unlike Dollard, political scientist James Scott emphasizes the private world of the oppressed—what they say and do with each other out of the purview of those in control. Scott hypothesizes that in this private space oppressed groups "rehearse" their feelings and frustrations, so that when the opportunity for confrontation does arrive, those involved are ready to articulate and/or act upon their feelings and beliefs. It is clear that black prisoners, especially males, lived outside the control of guards and inspectors. Both living and working conditions at the Slope and the Shaft bestowed prisoners some privacy and room away from white authority. Prisoners were crowded in with each other, but the amount of personal surveillance they endured, especially at the new TCI mines, appears to have been minimal. That space allowed them to develop critical perspectives on both the contractors and the inspectors.

The large amount of time prisoners spent with each other during their working day, as well as during their limited leisure hours, provided opportunity for private talk. If Scott is correct, and public contestation occurs only after extended private expression of feeling, the improved conditions in the new TCI prisons may indeed have contributed to the increasing challenges to the authority of TCI and the inspectors.

Sociological analysis of labor relations in factories can also be used to gain insight into how prisoners behaved after TCI took over the lease. Before the arrival of inspectors in 1883, prisoners had little choice about how to adapt to the system. They either had to work and endure or escape. When inspectors introduced short time and time cards, however, many prisoners developed a stake in adapting to the prison system. Michael Buroway and other industrial sociologists would call this behavior "game playing"— a tactic familiar to twentieth-century factory workers.[69] By engaging in the "game" of trying to receive short time, prisoners tacitly adapted to prison rules. Game players, whether chess fanatics or workers in a factory, cannot question the rules. By establishing games with implicit rewards such as short time, capitalists, according to Buroway, secure their surplus by obscuring the origins of their profits. In other words, according to the state and TCI, black prisoners in Alabama did not work at forced labor—they were trying to meet their official quotas so they could achieve an early release through short time. Many black prisoners went along with the game of short time and time cards because it made sense to do so in order to achieve their ultimate goal of freedom. However, once the company effectively abandoned the policy, or the game, by refusing to reward good behavior and imposing work speedups, then prisoners also changed their behavior. Outright resistance and defiance became more common in the 1890s partly in response to changes in the prison game as played by contractors and inspectors.

The antagonistic relationships between free miners and coal companies in Birmingham also influenced prisoners' behavior. The prison mines at the Shaft and Slope No. 2 existed in the heart of the free mining capital of the state. Mutual concerns between free miners and prison miners seeped into the prison walls. Prisoners had contact with free people, including free miners, in their work and family visits; this contact and prisoners' private discussions of company policy were all acts that Scott would call "hidden transcripts." Once prisoners were released and became free miners, their "hidden transcripts" were allowed full expression within the militant labor movement.

9

A Mortal Crisis

■ At the end of 1890, R. H. Dawson remained optimistic about the possibility of reforming the Alabama penitentiary from within. In the New Year's Eve entry in his diary, he asked God "for strength" to "make the convict system something of which the people need not be ashamed." During the 1890s Dawson began to plan for a future in which prisoners would no longer work in coal mines. He sought the support of Jefferson County reformers and placed pressure on the governor to force an independent scrutiny of Sloss's prison mine at Coalburg. The ensuing report, issued by Dr. Thomas Parke, blamed Sloss for the appalling rate of death at Coalburg and urged immediate action. Dawson also began a long-term project to remove all state prisoners from the TCI-owned coal mines and put them to work at state-owned farms and mills. He bought land and a cotton mill. He also succeeded in getting legislation passed that created a new Board of Managers with increased powers over the penitentiary. Dawson hoped ultimately to reform the county convict system, to end the lease altogether, and to remove all prisoners from coal mines.

He failed. And the fact of his failure speaks to the limits of reform within the Democratic party. The details of exactly how and why Dawson's plans were thwarted remain unclear. It is plain, however, that prison reform mattered little to politicians or the public, both of whom expected the penitentiary to contribute significant amounts of revenue. Despite Dawson's best efforts, his retirement from the Board of Inspectors in 1897 allowed the system to revert to the private deal making that characterized the Bass and Bankhead years. Prisoners never left the coal mines. Instead, the state took over the mines previously run by TCI and sold the coal that prisoners produced, rather than their labor. County men and state prisoners continued to work in coal mines and also were leased to private enterprises throughout the state. Prisoners still wrote letters to inquire about pardons and short time and complain about conditions, but the new Board of Managers never saw itself as the protectors of prisoners, as did Dawson and his staff.

The abuse and corruption that followed Dawson's departure took their cue from the political climate of the time, particularly the defeat of Populism and the triumph of the wing of the Democratic party most sympathetic to the Sloss Iron and Steel Company. R. H. Dawson had planned to transfer prisoners out of the mines after TCI's contract expired in 1898. For his plan to work, he needed to persuade the state that the lives of prisoners were more valuable than the income the mines provided. Neither Dawson's well-laid plans, however, nor shocking medical evidence could persuade Alabama to abandon prison mining.

Much about the county system struck state inspectors as ironic. They shook their heads at conditions at Coalburg, finding it pathetic that the county prisoners there, convicted of mere misdemeanors and petty crimes, should suffer more than the "hardened" state criminals who lived in comparative luxury at the TCI prison mines. The Newcastle and Coalburg mines became synonymous with disease, death, and harsh treatment. Besides the excessive amounts of punishment, men at Coalburg and Newcastle often worked without shoes. Inspectors frequently chastised Milner and the Sloss Company for filthy conditions, lack of sanitary plumbing, a tainted water supply, and disgusting privies.[1]

To compound their troubles, most county convicts were ineligible for short time. Although many county prisoners insisted that they deserved short-time pardons, in June 1889 Inspector Henley rejected the short-time appeals of seven prisoners at Newcastle because all of the applicants were prisoners sentenced to terms of less than one year. If they were granted short time, who would pay their remaining court costs? Inspectors thus refused to reduce the time of "any man whose aggregate sentence and cost did not amount to a year."[2] Still, prisoners in county convict camps pleaded for their time cards so that they could insist on their release on the correct date. Inspectors did help county convicts obtain their time cards, but they could do very little to mandate how county prisoners were treated.[3]

The brutal conditions of county convicts exceeded those endured by the state-held prisoners for several reasons. County prisoners greatly outnumbered state prisoners in the 1880s, and overcrowding was rife. The camps themselves were old; neither Milner nor Sloss had ever built any new accommodations at their prisons. The state held TCI to its promise to build two new prisons, which it did, but Sloss had never made such a promise to county officials. Like the state prisoners, county men worked harder after TCI and Sloss took over their lease in 1888. Although the inspectors began to monitor conditions at the county camps in 1883, a tradition of unaccountability prevailed. For years Milner had dodged his promises to clean up the prison; when Sloss took the mine over from Milner, it continued his evasive practices. The Sloss Company continued to run the prison as it pleased. It resented the presence of state inspectors.

For example, inspectors continually argued with the wardens at Newcastle over the issue of punishment. Who had the right to whip men and under what circumstances? In February 1889 Lee wrote to Dawson about a sharp argument between Henley and Mr. Roddy, the "whipper" at Newcastle, after Roddy ordered two prisoners to beat up and whip another. William Ross, the man whipped at Roddy's orders, told Inspector Henley the source of the trouble. Ross's "fellow workman" was a new man by the name of John Williams. Ross complained that Williams either could not or would not work in the mines. Instead he would run away and hide out, leaving Ross to load their entire task of eight tons of coal. Inspector Lee suggested that a long chain be put on Williams so that he could not run away. Not surprisingly, this failed to solve the problem. One day Williams was paired with an old experienced convict, Hardy Carlisle, who became so frustrated that he cut Williams in the face with a rock. Henley ordered Carlisle to be given fifteen lashes on his bare skin; Carlisle also received a bad conduct mark. Contractors, intent on maintaining the practice of working experienced men with new ones, refused to listen to men like Carlisle and Ross who insisted that the buddy system required two men to load too much coal.[4]

To a point, the inspectors listened. Henley, who had ordered Carlisle's whipping, nevertheless insisted that it was his duty to have the prisoners "protected." He urged Dawson to ask the attorney general if the Board of Inspectors could be responsible for "fixing" the task for county convicts.[5] They waited months for an answer. In the meantime, contractors continued to force new county prisoners—men who had been farmers a few days before—to mine and load tons of coal or else suffer a whipping. Inspectors tried to change the treatment of county convicts by reasoning with contractors and slowly gaining new powers, but the companies remained intransigent, causing acts of considerable desperation in the early 1890s.

Coalburg, the other mine operated by Sloss for county prisoners, fostered an even greater climate of abuse. In 1889 the inspectors' monthly reports for Coalburg list tragedies, complaints, fights, deaths, and diseases; it was obviously a chaotic and desperate situation. For example, Henley went to Coalburg in January 1889, at the request of one of the wardens, to discipline a prisoner who had attacked the officer with a knife. Henley faced the guilty prisoner down in the women's jail cell where he had been hiding for two days. Gib Lawrence, the prisoner, defied Henley, threatened to kill him, and taunted him: "Shoot and be damned." Henley shot him in his knee. Even then Lawrence fought off the guards with a plank of wood. Henley wrote that shooting the prisoner "was the only way to preserve the discipline of the prison."[6]

Lawrence's act of rebellion reflected the desperation of hundreds of men forced to work in brutal and sickly conditions. Throughout the month of February, both inspectors reported to Dawson that dozens of the men worked in mines without shoes. Even more alarming was the number of convicts in the hospital. On February 11, 1889, there were 22 men in the hospital; two weeks later the number had nearly tripled. By March over 100 men—one-third of the prison—were on the sick list. If not on death's door, men were still forced to work. According to Henley, out of 300 prisoners, "not over 50 are entirely well."[7] These men, weakened from diarrhea, suffered an epidemic of dysentery that lasted all winter and killed scores. In July 1890 Henley reported that the men at Coalburg ate with their hands. There were so many "broken down men & deaths," he felt that the Board of Inspectors must act. Henley also recommended that 50 sick men at Coalburg be pardoned immediately by the governor because they were so weak they could not perform any work. Henley also discovered that prisoners were being "used as helpers by free miners," and he told Warden Sherling that this practice must cease.[8]

The spread of disease placed extra pressure on healthy men to get out their quotas of coal; both Henley and Lee reported cases of prisoners whipping and beating their partners in the mine. Another prisoner, Henry Thomas, was disciplined for striking a female prisoner on the head.[9] The cause of this friction among prisoners could be found in the extraordinary amount of punishment meted out to the men at Coalburg. The extent of the whippings, given daily, alarmed and disgusted the inspectors. "It is beyond the limit of reason and we ought to stop it at once," Henley wrote Dawson.[10] In December 1888, 248 Coalburg prisoners were whipped—nearly every man in the prison. The number decreased to 61 in January but then rose to 114 in February and 129 in March. Henley told the warden that he wanted the whipping stopped, especially of men who were sick, weak, and unable to get their task. Warden Sherling defended himself on the grounds that the men had to get out quotas for the company. Henley suggested giving prisoners lower tasks; he was ignored.

A water supply tainted by the dross from the mine caused deathly diarrhea, exacerbating the sickness and disease at Coalburg. Still, the company and the inspectors moved slowly. In April 1889 E. M. Tutwiler, Sloss's Coalburg manager, still had failed to fix the plumbing at the prison or make other repairs as he had promised. Two prisoners, perhaps too weak to get out of harm's way, were injured by falling slate in the mine. Fifteen prisoners had now died at Coalburg since January 1, 1889. In a personal aside made during one of his reports, Henley confided to Dawson that if conditions at Coalburg did not improve, the contract with Sloss should be canceled. Both sides, however, tried to smooth the conflict over. Major Seddon of Sloss feigned surprise that so many "darkies" had been whipped in his mine and that conditions were so bad. Henley, not convinced of Seddon's sincerity, ordered all time cards for new prisoners at Coalburg and Newcastle sent to the inspectors instead of the contractors. He believed they withheld the cards on purpose. "I am anxious," he wrote, "that the convicts should have a full list of time cards once more." [11]

Despite efforts to push contractors to clean up the prison, the diarrhea epidemic still had not abated by June 1889. Sixteen more men had died, bringing the death rate at Coalburg to 20 percent per annum. Henley continued to note more cases of excessive punishment; 137 men were whipped in June. Prior to 1889, inspectors did not have the power to "class" the county prisoners the same way they did state men. As soon as he could, however, Henley reduced the task for "a number" of convicts; this seemingly simple act was a new power for inspectors. Finally, Henley suggested that the state health officer, Dr. Jerome Cochran, be sent to Coalburg to investigate the diarrhea epidemic that had been going on for over six months.[12]

In the early 1890s the inspectors continued to focus their attention on the conditions of county convicts, particularly those unlucky enough to be sent to the mines at Coalburg. A total of forty counties in Alabama sent their petty criminals, some 553 people in 1893, to Coalburg. These prisoners had two things in common. Besides being convicted of mere misdemeanors, all were African Americans. Sloss complained of being saddled with men too sick to work. Moreover, the diseases contracted in far-flung county jails converged at Coalburg. Coalburg already had gained a grisly reputation for a high death rate and epidemics—a scourge between 1888 and 1890 killed nearly one-third of its prison population.[13]

Conditions at Coalburg worsened in the 1890s. Tutwiler refused to relent on the killing work pace or unreasonable punishment. In April 1891 Henley found that 103 prisoners had been whipped at Coalburg, a figure he called "excessive." [14] He noticed that the vast amount of punishment was inflicted on "new men." When he complained that Coalburg had classed them too high, the company reminded him that most of these prisoners were men with brief sentences; to get the maximum amount of work out of them, it needed to raise their classification "as rapidly as possible." Thus new men were whipped for "not loading," "grumbling," "fighting," and being "disorderly." But as Henley saw it, the majority were whipped for "failure to get task"—the simple inability to perform the arduous work. He felt frustrated with the company's refusal to comply with even the simplest rules. "I have been kicking about things at Coalburg for so many years that I am getting tired of it."[15]

Dawson took a dim view of the conditions at Coalburg, where "there have been many complaints of bad treatment." He suggested two courses of action to Governor Jones. First, Dawson asked that dying men be pardoned so that they could return home. Second, he urged that the state's health investigator, James W. Locke, investigate Coalburg.[16] Until Locke's report came through, Governor Jones ordered counties to stop sending their prisoners to Coalburg—the first time in the history of the Alabama prison system that a governor had prevented prisoners from being sent to a specific site.[17] The inspectors hoped that Locke's report would cause a loud public outcry. Dawson and Henley had contacted Sam Will John, a Birmingham lawyer affiliated with the YWCA and other Christian reform movements, urging him to write to the governor regarding Coalburg, which he did. As a result of these combined efforts, the "manway," or the three-quarter-mile-long underground path leading to the entry of the mine, was enlarged so that men did not have to crawl and stoop the entire distance underground.[18] Public concern over the fee system and the leasing system was growing; Dawson hoped to ride that wave, or at least use it to push the governor toward reforming Coalburg.

The Sloss Iron and Steel Company, the corporation that managed Coalburg, reacted indignantly to the governor's measures. H. W. Perry, the manager of Sloss's coal mines, blamed Coalburg's high rate of sickness on the counties who sent "all their paupers and their sick and dying." He insisted that if the inspectors prevented the ill from being leased out, "our sick list will be very light, as also our death list."[19] In April 1893 Henley recommended that the ban on counties sending prisoners to Coalburg be lifted. He also urged that the county prisoners waiting to be sent to Coalburg, including one hundred convicts in the Jefferson County Jail, be medically examined as "we desire to keep all sick men away for sometime to come."[20] Henley ended on a sanguine note, noting that during April only one man out of 475 had died at Coalburg. Thomas Seddon, the president of Sloss, wrote to the governor thanking him for letting county prisoners back into Coalburg. He too urged that sick county men be sent to the Walls.[21] It seemed, apparently, that the situation at Coalburg had been explained. Once sick prisoners were prevented from entering the prison, the death rate was bound to improve.

Optimism of sorts also characterized the weekly reports of James Locke, the state investigating agent. Locke began issuing reports on Coalburg in April 1893. His letters observe that the prisoners were well dressed, shod, and fed, and that the officers had treated him with courtesy and consideration. He remarked that the number of prisoners at Coalburg changed constantly; new men and women prisoners arrived and others were discharged all in the same day. Who were these "county convicts" Locke observed entering the prison, often forty to fifty at a time? One was a woman about to give birth; one man lacked a hand, the other an eye; one man had syphilis; another was deaf. Locke's reports demonstrate beyond doubt that counties continued sending prisoners to coal mines who could barely walk, let alone work.[22]

The working prisoners on hand were not much healthier. Out of 600 prisoners, over 30 were in the hospital with broken legs, diarrhea, and consumption. Locke reported that men continued to suffer whippings for not working—the same pattern of conditions Henley observed in 1889. The mine bosses said that these prisoners produced short weights of coal at the end of the day; hence they were punished. Locke's next letter noted that 22 men were whipped for not working and that the broken leg of a young boy had been amputated. However, he noted the progress being made on the underground manway, the sufficient diet, and the "very good coffin" used to bury a prisoner who had been ill with diarrhea. Sometimes he said that only the idle were punished. Locke's letters inferred improvement and progress; in May 1893 he wrote his last report.[23] Accustomed to the routine of prisoners escaping and being whipped, Locke showed no special concern for the prisoners' health or safety when several feet of water suddenly appeared in the mine.[24] After Locke left, Henley and Jones reclassified the convicts at Coalburg and gave them more work.

Later in May 1893, however, Governor Jones received a letter from the Department of Corrections listing seventeen Coalburg prisoners with no record of convictions or sentences. J. D. Douglass, Dawson's secretary, wrote that "no one in authority seems to know why those above named were sent to the mines or for how long." [25] For several months Sloss worked these men in the mines and paid Dallas County for them; given the lack of record keeping, the prisoners could have been kept indefinitely. The remedy, as Douglass pointed out, lay with the county keeping better track; but that such blatant incompetence happened in 1893, a full ten years after the counties were required to maintain records, hardly inspired confidence. As long as county men went to prison, county officials would receive fees commensurate with those numbers. Sending people to prison garnered remuneration for county officials; sending them to an almshouse would constitute a cost. The correct choice was obvious.

Not all transgressions were the fault of the county; when it came to keeping track of prisoners, no one could beat the Sloss Company's game of cat and mouse. After holding court, counties sent prisoners to Sloss where they were then worked to the limit of their endurance. Sloss then urged the governor to pardon sick convicts, thereby relieving the company of the expense of caring for them. H. W. Perry, the manager at Sloss, insisted that the county prisoners arrived diseased and with "physical disabilities." They were "averse to work, and consequently get into trouble. This class of convicts keep our Hospital crowded and in many cases gradually succumb to their diseases and die." [26] Perry insisted that if sick prisoners were filtered out to the state hospital, as they were at the Pratt prison mines, the death rate at Coalburg would automatically decrease. That summer, a pneumonia epidemic swept through the state prison at Slope No. 2, prompting Dr. Cochran, the state health officer, to implement the unprecedented step of having prison bedding disinfected. This seemed to do the trick, and Dr. Cochran was sure the epidemic was finished. [27]

But Coalburg still concerned Dawson, and when he received reports of an "unprecedented amount of whipping" during January and February 1894, he wrote to the governor and urged him to send the state's mine inspector to determine if the seam at Coalburg and the tools available enabled prisoners to mine their required task. [28] Finally, Dr. Thomas Parke, health officer of Jefferson County, was asked to make an independent investigation into Coalburg. His assignment was to determine the reasons behind the punishments, the large number of men in hospitals, and the persistently high death rate. Parke asked Sloss to provide him with the name of every man who died in Coalburg between February 1, 1883, and February 1, 1895, as well as information about daily working conditions, diet, time spent in prison, medical records, and the location of the prison.

Parke studied Coalburg's history carefully, and in 1895 he published a damning report. Parke laid the blame for sickness, disease, and death squarely at the door of the mining companies. Unlike the physicians employed by the state, who regarded the deaths of county prisoners as natural, Parke pointed to actual living and working conditions at Coalburg. The prison buildings, made of logs, had no windows or other means of ventilation. He described how men walked to the mine opening underground, and how they were never allowed outside for recreation, even on Sunday. He laid great stress on the lack of sun and ventilation, the crowded living conditions of the men, and the lack of cleanliness. Most deaths, however, Parke attributed to erysipelas, an infection that began in the legs and feet and then spread.

> A miner [receives] an abrasion of the skin around the knees or ankle from his awkwardness in the mines, or some slight wound which scarcely attracts his attention. In a day or two inflammation begins to spread from this abrasion or wound, manifested by pain . . . and redness. It may stop and not pass beyond this, constituting what might be termed the first degree of trouble. In another it may pass on to deeper infiltration . . . puss in the areolar tissue, high septic fever. . . . These cases sometimes go on for months,

occasionally killing patients or debilitating them to the degree that
their systems [provide] a most favorable soil for the development
of the bacisilli tubercular patients in adjoining beds furnish them
in abundance.[29]

Parke suggested that leg scratches and wounds be treated at once "with a
hichloride of mercury solution from a two ounce spray." Seddon agreed to
this, but only on a trial basis.

Parke then discussed the enormous number of prisoners suffering from
tuberculosis, "the disease that causes the largest sick and death rate in the
prison," and the conditions in Coalburg that facilitated its spread. Here,
Parke agreed with Dr. Lewis, a physician employed by the state, that black
prisoners were "naturally susceptible to the disease." He also noted that
prisoners tended to be depressed, to be "shut out from sunlight from nine
to eleven hours daily and working six days a week. From the poor ventilation of the mines, the men enter a poorly ventilated and crowded prison,
where they were also forced to spend their Sundays and Holidays. . . . In a
word, they never get into the sunlight."

Parke made his strongest point when he discussed the death rate of
prisoners in Alabama. He calculated that the death rate at Coalburg between 1893 and 1895 was 90 per 1,000. This figure included men who died
in mining accidents, men who were sick when they arrived at Coalburg, and
healthy men who developed sickness and disease over time. Parke anticipated that the coal companies would object to these figures: after all, mining was a dangerous profession—were owners responsible for all accidents?
The companies also argued that the sickly men they received from the
counties, already weak, were bound to die anyway. Surely, they should not
be held responsible for these deaths. Parke then calculated another death
rate that included only men who were healthy when they arrived and who
died from illness, not accidents. This rate of 64 persons per 1,000, "among
men in the prime of life and in such physical condition as to work in the
mines," Parke called "simply frightful." [30]

Compared to the death rates in other prisons throughout the nation,
Alabama came in first, or last, depending on perspective. The Missouri
penitentiary's rate was 16 per 1,000; Ohio's was 9 per 1,000; Maryland's was
27 per 1,000. The only state coming close to Alabama was Mississippi,
whose death rate was 40 per 1,000 in 1894. Parke's most telling evidence
was a comparison between death rates in Alabama's prisons and Georgia
prisons, which also worked prisoners in coal mines. After conceding the
factors of poor health upon arrival and mining accidents, the mortality at
Coalburg still remained, Parke stated, "very great."

What needed to change? Parke condemned the fee system that allowed
county sheriffs to charge thirty cents a day to feed prisoners the paltry,

unhealthy, but steady "diet of fat meat and corn bread," while pocketing the difference. He also suggested improved ventilation in the prisons and immediate treatment for scrapes and cuts.

The Sloss Company received Parke's report coldly. "It is a fact," stated Dr. Judson Davies, the physician inspector of convicts employed by Sloss, "that the negro race is inferior to the white race physically as well as mentally and morally—their powers of resistance so far as a great many diseases are concerned, notably tuberculosis, does not compare at all favorably with those of the white race." The death rate of black prisoners was "two and three times as great" as that of the white prisoners even though these two groups shared the "same environment." [31] Davies failed to explain, however, that prisoners were segregated. White prisoners lived at a different site; black prisoners were all housed together. The greater number of deaths from tuberculosis no doubt came from the overcrowding of the black prisons. White prisoners shared a room with only twenty or thirty other men, black prisoners with several hundred.

The irony of attributing to black prisoners a weaker immune system can hardly be overlooked. For generations the prevailing attitude of white plantation owners was that black slaves were stronger than whites and were immune from disease. But when faced with the overwhelming numbers of deaths from disease in prison, doctors created new racial differences to account for deaths. How convenient, then, not to have to compare Coalburg's death and disease rates with northern prisons "whose convicts are nearly all white and none of them in coal mines." Reformers who did so created statistics "unjust and worthless," according to Davies.[32]

An alternative explanation used by Dr. F. P. Lewis, another physician employed by Sloss, was that the physical nature of county convicts differed dramatically from state prisoners, who largely consisted of "murderers, burglars and such." "Everyone knows," he wrote to the governor, that "to commit these bolder crimes it takes a certain amount of brute courage, and such courage is always connected with bodily strength and activity." County convicts, on the other hand, were "the sneak thieves and minor criminals," and as such were undoubtedly "sickly and badly developed." [33] For years Dr. Lewis had been using such rationales to explain the weak physical conditions of county prisoners when they arrived at Coalburg; this faulty reasoning continued to be used when Sloss's physicians made their biennial report in 1896. The doctors did admit that the system was at fault for sending all county prisoners, regardless of age, strength, or sex, to the coal mines. But this was no great concession, as Sloss had resorted to this explanation many times in the past. Doctors in the employ of the company attributed deaths to fickle and imprecise causes such as race or "character" and resisted implementing the minimal sanitary measures recommended by Dr. Parke.

Between 1894 and 1896 approximately 420 prisoners died. In the spring of 1895, a diarrhea epidemic took hold at the Pratt mines, "one of the worst epidemics experienced in convict history," according to Dr. Davies. By pointing his finger at the convict deaths at TCI, however, Davies hoped to divert attention away from Coalburg. All death rates over a short period would be high, he stated, if they included the results of an epidemic. Thus, just as the Pratt mines should not be judged on the basis of one epidemic, so should Coalburg be excused. Davies insisted that morbidity at the prison would be less if more of the men on the verge of death were pardoned.[34]

Prisoners obviously knew of the policy of pardoning those too ill to work: did they therefore hurt themselves purposefully in order to receive a pardon? Dr. Lewis, the physician at Coalburg, thought so. He reported that "the convicts try not to get well; some eat soap; some rub poisonous things into their sores or cuts."[35] To call these injuries "faked," however, is misleading. Throughout the 1880s and 1890s, physicians and inspectors alike remarked upon the mental state of prisoners. After telling of patients who refused to get well, Lewis claimed that "by far the greater obstacle to their making quick and good recoveries is the mental depression of the new men, and their sudden and radical change in the manner of living."[36] Not all these acts were the result of despair. Men undoubtedly used sickness, and perhaps even exacerbated their own, to escape death in the mines.

The physicians hired by Sloss published a rebuttal pamphlet entitled *Facts about Coalburg Prison: Dr. Parke's Report Reviewed.* They used statistics published by the Medical Association of Alabama to buttress their claim that black prisoners died at a higher rate than white prisoners, the exact ratio being 3.69 to 1. Given these "inherent" and "natural" statistics among members of the "negro race," how could the company be held responsible? Other statistics comparing black and white mortality rates in the Union army and in prisons in New York, Pennsylvania, Ohio, and New Jersey also reflected large racial differences. During the Civil War the annual death rate among white troops was 53.4 per 1,000, "of colored troops 143.04 per 1,000 or 1 to 2.68—almost as much as the difference in the Alabama penitentiary." The implications of these statistics, retorted Sloss's doctors, were crystal clear. "Given the same environment the white man will have much the longer life."[37] Sloss's reply attributed Coalburg's problems to the weak condition of county prisoners, and not to company neglect.

Parke responded to these criticisms in a letter to the Board of Inspectors in December 1895. He agreed, in essence, that the normal amount of mortality among blacks was always higher than among whites. But he stuck to his basic position that deaths in Alabama far outstripped those in Georgia, and that Coalburg suffered from an unchecked epidemic of erysipelas. "For ten dreary years erysipelas has been allowed to attack men in this prison . . . enough suffering and pain has already been unnecessarily endured to warrant the most energetic measures." He ended his letter with a call for immediate action: "Is it putting too low an estimate on the humanity and civilization of the people of Alabama to believe that . . . they will allow county prisoners who have committed only minor offenses to be subjected to conditions of prison life, either at Coalburg or Pratt Mines, that destroy the health and lives of such a relatively large proportion?" Until the time of a great public outcry, it was up to the board, Parke wrote, to alleviate the suffering of prisoners.[38] Parke had done his best to erase the notion that the deaths at Coalburg were natural, normal, or caused merely by the presence of weak men or the inherently poor constitutions of "sneak thieves." He had shown that the large number of deaths was caused by the lack of attention paid to the wounds of healthy men and the subsequent spread of infectious diseases such as tuberculosis. But Sloss never admitted these facts to be true, and Dr. Parke's report had little impact on either public opinion or treatment.

What about the state penitentiary? Long before Dr. Parke had made his official report, R. H. Dawson had sought alternatives to prison mining. In 1883 Dawson confided to his diary the unsuitability of putting prisoners in coal mines; by 1890 he had expressed those thoughts to Inspector Lee. Lee, appalled by the conditions at TCI, even after the implementation of the new prisons, agreed with Dawson that signing a ten-year lease with TCI had been a horrible mistake. No matter what the physicians claimed, Lee agreed with Dawson that mining was inherently unhealthy and harmful. "When I see such men as Joe Morse and Joe Jackson, strong and healthy men worked in the mines only a few months, and then after a short spell of sickness, sent to the Walls to recuperate and probably to die, I begin to think there is something wrong in the whole system," Lee wrote. He rejected as "horrible" an alternative plan of working prisoners in small squads again, but he favored putting large numbers of men on farms and at sawmills.[39]

As long as the contracts with TCI and Sloss existed, however, the majority of prisoners remained in the mines, and Dawson did his best to bring order to those conditions. Yet during the last years of Dawson's tenure as president of the board, he forecast the day when only "physically able" men would work in the mines; the rest would be sent to farms, lumber camps, and turpentine works or to the new state-run brick manufacturers and cotton mill. In 1893, hoping to lay the foundation for the abolition of leasing, Dawson managed to win legislation that eventually would lead to the dispersal of prisoners to contractors outside of Jefferson County, away from the coal mines. The 1893 law, as well as the establishment of a new Board of Managers, "at last puts the state upon the road of progress in prison management and promises the abandonment of the lease system."[40] TCI's lease, which entitled it to the labor of all the state and half the county prisoners, expired in 1898. Dawson wanted to be ready for that day.

In addition to the state farm at Wetumpka, Dawson had set about providing other alternatives to mine work. He continued his contract with a farm owned by Thomas Williams in Montgomery County. He also made a contract with Williams to take over land in Fort Jackson, in Tallapoosa County. The state worked this land free of rent, and its contract with Williams lasted until 1897.[41] Eventually, Dawson encouraged the governor to buy the land so that the state could expand its prison farms permanently.

Dawson worked the farm at Fort Jackson with 40 to 50 of the 287 men assigned to the Walls. Their job was to clear land, supply the penitentiary with corn, and grow cotton for the profit of the state. In one year they cleared 100 acres of land, grew 4,000 bushels of corn, and raised 22 bales of cotton. At Thomas Williams's farm, prisoners grew oats, millet, peas, and potatoes. Dawson wanted to improve the conditions at the Walls by enlarging the "colored" prison and building a proper sewage system to replace the dry earth method. Dawson praised the health of the prisoners who worked on the state farm. And in one of his reports to Governor Jones, he contrasted the salubrious conditions on the farms with the disease-ridden Pratt mines, which experienced "frequent occurrence of consumption, typhoid fever, chronic diarrhea," and pneumonia. He also took it upon himself to transfer 50 men to the Walls from the mines.[42] Although TCI continued to account for nearly 90 percent of the monthly revenue accrued by the prison system in 1893, Dawson clearly preferred farming and lumber work to mining as occupations for the prisoners; he strove to make the prison profitable, but he also cared about the health of the convicts.

In 1896, when Dawson handed over his office to S. B. Trapp, the system seemed poised to be both profitable (although not to the extent of the previous ten years) and independent of the mining companies. Fort Jackson continued to be worked. The state had purchased a farm on the Tallapoosa River, and a cotton mill had been established at Speigner to "give employment largely to women and children." Speigner, a sturdy brick structure, was built entirely with prison labor. The inspectors cautioned the governor in their 1896 report that "to put [prisoners] at public work that brings in no revenue also necessarily means a tax upon the people." But they added, "There is no work that a convict can do that has to be turned into money which is not in direct competition with free labor. We know the people of Alabama to be patriotic and just and believe when they think of this matter carefully they will say we are right." [43] The board hoped to build a new woman's prison at Speigner and to remove all females from the Walls. They also hoped to build a new "Boys' Reformatory" at Speigner.

These were great plans; in making them sound positive, the inspectors tried to cushion the blow that the state and the public would take from the loss of revenue. Dawson knew the proposed changes would cost money, "probably $25,000 to $50,000 a year for several years." But he reminded the state that since 1885, when he took office, the Department of Corrections had paid into the state's treasury, "net, over $300,000 and that all the money spent by the managers in buying the lands and making the improvements thereon was earned by the convicts . . . not one dollar paid for this large and valuable property was raised by taxation." Given this history, Dawson thought his new plan reasonable; indeed, just.[44] Only when these changes were made, Dawson insisted, "will the death rate of our convict system be reduced to the average death rate in the outside world."

Dawson's reference to the death rate was no accident; indeed, the papers and much of the 1896 biennial report focused on the numerous deaths at both the Pratt mines and Coalburg. The state had 1,710 prisoners on hand in August 1896; in the previous two years, 233 men had died. The 745 county prisoners on hand in 1896 were a smaller number than in previous years; in the past two years, 181 county prisoners had died, all of them black.[45] Because prisoners were still dying in such high numbers, Dawson felt confident that when TCI's contract expired, the public and the legislature would consent to prisoners being put to work at labor outside of the mines.

Dawson's plans for the future of the state's prisoners were thwarted, however, by his successor as head of the penitentiary, S. B. Trapp, and Governors William Oates and Joseph F. Johnston. Trapp patently abused his role and made decisions unilaterally. He used prisoners as private servants in his own home in Montgomery and bestowed the title of trusty on scores of hardened criminals, giving them authority over other men. He hired scores of useless guards and workers, creating positions "to discharge some political obligation of the past or to secure some political service for the future."[46] He allowed the mill at Speigner to go to ruin and even went so far as to have it dismantled, ordering prisoners to haul away the brick. Trapp failed to file monthly or quarterly reports; he abandoned the Tallapoosa River Farm; he allowed his inspectors to accept gratis coal and lumber from the companies working prisoners. The men and women at the Walls were allowed to remain idle.[47] A legislative committee later condemned Trapp's entire administration and implied that he was guilty of massive fraud. Record keeping at each prison was so poor that "it has been virtually impossible for [the] Committee to ascertain with any degree of accuracy the results of working convicts directly by the State during the last four years."[48]

Before Trapp's administration, prisoners had been leased for up to $18.50 a month to the mines and $11 a month outside. Trapp, however, made new five-year leasing arrangements with Sloss and TCI for fees between $7 and $14 a month. He also let prisoners to other contractors, such as the Hand Lumber Company, for as little as $5 a month. He never advertised for bids but simply handed over men to whomever he chose. Contractors made bids and then broke them. Trapp allowed Milner, Caldwell, and Flowers, a lumber company, to keep prisoners "four months after the expiration of the contract."[49]

What of Dawson's plans to build new facilities for women, boys, and the sick? In 1901 a legislative committee found boys "side by side with hardened criminals" throughout the state. The number of consumptives at the Walls was so great, the committee recommended their isolation at Speigner. This report barely mentioned female prisoners, except to comment on their "idleness" at the Walls.

Detailed information about prisoners dries up after 1896; no more biennial reports specifying the particulars of their work, health, and crimes appeared. Prisoners still worked at the Pratt mines, Coalburg, and two other mining camps, but they were also leased to other businesses. Inspectors never saw prisoners in person, nor did they write reports; hence, their visits cannot truly be called investigations. In fact, the committee found "some instances of brutal treatment, but it is exceedingly difficult to get any satisfactory evidence on this point." Not only did the inspectors fail to write reports, but they also ceased to respond to complaints. A free miner who worked at one mine wrote to President Trapp, "For God's sake," that "a negro and a Hebrew" had been beaten and flogged unmercifully. But Trapp did not respond. Instead, "he contented himself with writing to the contractor and the warden in regard to the matter."[50]

Prisoners continued to work for TCI and Sloss, and Trapp acted as a labor broker for other concerns as well. In the summer of 1900, G. W. Sherling, the warden at Coalburg, requested "forty or fifty convicts" at once. He asked Trapp not to send men from Montgomery County, as these were "inferior convicts." Other companies were not so choosy; their desperation for labor led them to swap convicts among themselves. J. D. Hand, president of the Hand Lumber Company of Mobile, informed Trapp that a local landowner in a "tight need for plow boys" would keep some prisoners until July. When the prisoners finished their crops, Hand would take them to work for him. It is difficult to imagine previous contractors addressing Dawson, Henley, or Lee in such a matter-of-fact manner. Contractors saw Trapp as their friend, and he, in turn, saw it as his duty to supply them with labor, not protect prisoners.[51]

Businesses from Nashville, Tennessee, and Pensacola, Florida, wrote to Governor Johnston and to Trapp to inquire about leasing Alabama's prisoners. A hosiery mill that used Tennessee prisoners assured the board that their factories were suitable for women, the young, and prisoners with missing limbs who "would be of little service elsewhere." A turpentine company in Pensacola requested 50 or 100 state convicts and guaranteed Johnston the prisoners would be worked in Alabama.[52] Private arrangements replaced administrative order. The Horse Shoe Lumber Company wanted Trapp's permission to keep a one-armed boy prisoner free of charge. Coalburg wrote to Trapp that it was ready to receive more prisoners.[53] The system had changed, certainly, but it embodied every aspect Dawson had sought to stamp out: cronyism, corruption, abuse, and an overreliance on mining.

Prisoners at the Shaft and the Slope continued to complain by sending letters to the Board of Managers. In 1900 "a lot of convicts at Shaft No. 1" sent letters to Trapp complaining they were "cheated out of their checks" for the extra work they performed in the mine. Prisoners also protested that they were forced to trade with the "convict merchant" who, it appears, worked directly for TCI. P. J. Rogers, the superintendent at the Shaft mines in Pratt City, made light of the matter but promised to investigate. He later assured Trapp that checks were made out to each individual prisoner "just as they would be if they were free people." And prisoners, he said, traded with whomever they pleased and were not forced to buy anything from anyone. (Rogers's comments imply that the Shaft prisoners bought goods from merchants in the surrounding community. Just how they converted their checks into cash or bought items, however, remains unclear.) Dawson's departure did not discourage complaints or letter writing; prisoners continued to request transfers, and family members of prisoners continued to inquire about them.[54] But with his departure the entire tone of the relationship between inspectors, contractors, and the prisoners had changed.

Certainly, the beatings and whippings prisoners suffered at the mines became worse. The committee remarked that prisoners at the mines often engaged in fighting, which the company did little to discourage. The old practice of placing new men with experienced miners and then requiring a high quota of coal from both was practiced with new vigor. The old prisoner, the report says, "takes advantage of his opportunity to abuse the men under him in the mines."[55] But it failed to mention the quota system imposed upon the experienced and inexperienced alike, or that the penalty for not reaching one's task was a severe beating. Indeed, the systematic mistreatment of prisoners and the practice of whipping them for their failure to "get task" was not mentioned at all. "Instances of brutality," the report says, "are due to the character of a guard now and then and not to the system."

The committee that reviewed Trapp's administration did not address the issue of treatment; it focused instead on Trapp's poor prison management. It recommended that the state retain the farms, the brickyard, and the cotton mill, and that these facilities be made profitable. It also recommended the continued leasing of prisoners to private industries, such as the coal mines and lumberyards. The only change the committee proposed—one that harkened back nearly twenty years—was that "no contract be made for less than one hundred convicts." Ostensibly, this was to ensure better treatment; in practice it favored large contractors over smaller ones.[56]

The committee recommended further changes. A Parole Board should be formed and all perquisites for board members abandoned. Inspectors should be required actually to see prisoners. Accounts of all purchases and sales of prison-made goods should be kept. Doctors should visit the sick. Contracts for all services should be given over to public bidding. The committee pointed out what Trapp had done:

> Some years ago . . . a policy was mapped out looking to the ultimate abandonment of the lease system. All convicts were to be gradually withdrawn from contractors and employed in industries under State control. In line with this policy farms were purchased and the cotton mill started. . . . But on the accession of the administration four years ago, the lease system seems to have been regarded with great favor, the mill was run only about one half the time and the farms were half manned and poorly managed. The plan seems to have been to put nearly every available man out on contract in order to make as large a financial showing as possible. . . . The inauguration of a far sighted policy by one administration and the total abandonment of it by the next cannot but result in harm to the State.[57]

Dawson's best efforts over nearly twenty years had been destroyed. But how, and why?

Dawson's inability to implement his reforms reflected the general failure of reform in Alabama after the defeat of Populism. Dawson himself appears to have been a staunch Democrat, but there were Democrats who supported aspects of reform championed by the Farmers' Alliance, such as cooperatives that cut out the merchant middleman, prison reform, and higher wages. Although the Alabama Farmers' Alliance participated in the organization's national convention in St. Louis, its members wished to remain within the state's Democratic party.[58] In 1890 Reuben F. Kolb and his supporters attempted to dominate the party convention and win the Democratic nomination for governor. They failed. The Alabama Alliance did command a good deal of support within the Democratic party, but only to a point. In a private letter written in 1890, Inspector Lee explained to Dawson why he would ultimately reject the alliance: "I am an Alliance man and believe its objects good, at the same time, I am a Democrat. When the two conflict, and it becomes necessary for me to give up the Alliance, or Democracy, then the former must go. Because I believe to give up the latter in this country means negro supremacy. These are my sentiments and I expect to live & die by them." [59] Thus, even Democrats devoted to reform, as were Dawson and Lee, would never be persuaded to leave the party in favor of a coalition that solicited black votes.

In tracing the pro-alliance beliefs of influential Democrat Robert McKee, historian Sam Webb has argued that McKee attempted to transcend the issue of race by focusing on the economic complaints of the farmers who comprised the majority of Democrats.[60] And it is true that Dawson and W. D. Lee, in the tradition of Robert McKee, supported reform in education, suffrage, prohibition, and prisons. They opposed the system of putting prisoners in coal mines and making profit the primary concern of the state. They believed prisoners should be treated humanely. In this respect, they were reformers, even alliance men. But as Lee's letter illustrates, he would not reject white supremacy or the political party they believed to be that ideology's greatest defender.

In 1892 Kolb still refused to split from the conservative, Bourbon "machine democrats" and called himself a "Jeffersonian democrat." To counter his challenge, Governor Jones condemned the "nigger rights section" of Kolb's platform.[61] Jones won, but only through fraud. Kolb clearly had the majority of white votes throughout the state, but black votes in the Black Belt were manipulated to give Jones the needed edge.[62] In 1894 the Democrats nominated the conservative William C. Oates, who hated the alliance and everything it stood for. Kolb and his supporters closed ranks with the Populists, and both groups reached out to labor, particularly black coal miners in Jefferson County. Pratt City and other mining communities supported Kolb, but once again fraud in the Black Belt gave the election to the Democratic party and to Oates.[63]

During the next election in 1896, the Alabama Democrats, conscious of the need to capture growing white support for the opposition, nominated Joseph F. Johnston to secede Oates. Johnston styled himself as a reformer and co-opted the free silver platform from the Populists. Such tactics mirrored national events. Although both William Jennings Bryan and Johnston were anathema to conservative Democrats, the Democratic party was determined to squelch the Populist appeal by reaching out to the white voters they had lost. Populists appealed to the black vote, but calls for racial unity alienated potential white support and could not halt fraud in the Black Belt. In 1896 William Jennings Bryan lost, but in Alabama, Johnston beat his Populist opponent with strong support from the white-majority northern counties.

Johnston talked reform, but when it came to prisons, his administration set improvement back thirty years. As a native of Birmingham and the previous president of the Sloss Iron and Steel Company, Johnston had expanded Sloss's use of prison labor at Coalburg. His continued business alliances with Sloss while governor led him to value prisoners for the profit they brought to both the company and the state.[64] He appointed as the new head of the Convict Board of Managers his old business partner S. B. Trapp, who favored leasing prisoners to industry and using them to accrue even more revenue. No wonder Sloss officials felt comfortable sending Trapp friendly requests for more prisoners. Dawson's proposals were discarded.

It is tempting to see a lack of continuity between Dawson and his successors. Dawson did try to eliminate the lease by prescribing productive, state-owned enterprises such as the mill at Speigner and the prison farm, which he intended to be both profitable and safe. Yet Dawson's best efforts, although commendable, demonstrated the futility of reform in the context of Alabama's dual commitment to white supremacy and prison profitability. The Democrats had made profitable prisons its cornerstone. Although Governors Cobb and Seay had supported Dawson's efforts, the system had remained lucrative and the contract with TCI ironclad, thus protecting them from making difficult choices. In 1895 Oates cited a deficit in the state budget and refused to end the lease with TCI. Johnston gave some indication he wished to end the lease gradually, but his actions spoke louder than his words.[65] His appointee Trapp renewed the lease with TCI and Sloss and actively recruited prison labor contracts with other small businesses.

Despite Dr. Parke's damning report, Sloss continued to depend upon the convict mines at Coalburg. But in 1902 a new scandal erupted: thirty-two prisoners died in the first three months of that year. Once again an Alabama governor ordered an investigation. This time Sloss officials foresaw the futility of keeping prisoners at Coalburg and began to look for a new location for its prison mines. It found the ideal location at a rich coal vein at Flat Top, and by the end of 1902, all Coalburg prisoners had been transferred to this new location. Optimistic officials predicted that Flat Top would produce enough coal and coke to supply all of Sloss's pig iron furnaces. Conditions for prisoners remained wretched. Sloss continued to control all county convicts, and state inspectors supervised the state men at the mine. T. C. Dawson, R. H. Dawson's son, was in charge; the senior Dawson lived there, too, and died at Flat Top in 1906.[66]

Prisoners at Flat Top continued to be used as strikebreakers. Miners, incensed at wage cuts, embarked on a two-year strike supported by the United Mine Workers of America. But Sloss weathered the storm, supported by its formidable prison labor force. Once again, in 1908, a wage cut prompted another walkout among free miners, but that strike failed too. Convict labor, and the opposition of Governor B. B. Comer, who ordered National Guard troops to tear down a "Tent City" erected by the strikers, effectively ended Alabama's long history of union activism among its miners.[67]

David Lewis summarizes his detailed study on the Sloss pig iron mills with an ironic tribute to the "effective entrepreneurial decision making" that led southern industrialists to pursue a path that capitalized on the "resources" Alabama had to offer: convict labor, low wages, and racial divisions.[68] Lewis recognizes that the tactics used by Sloss, especially the use of prison labor, lowered wages of free miners, depressed the markets for consumer goods, and sanctioned ruthless treatment of black and white workers. In his view, though, Sloss adapted to the natural and human resources Alabama had to offer and, in so doing, succeeded against its competitors. However, Sloss did more than just adapt to conditions; it created them by actively thwarting the demands of free miners to put an end to convict labor. By treating prisoners with racist brutality, and by using its political influence to rein captive prisoners back into the workforce, Sloss created the very conditions it exploited.

Lewis contrasts Sloss's prison policy with TCI's, but even the latter firm's commitment to company paternalism did not lead it away from the path of prison labor. After 1904, a new contract with TCI stipulated that the state would feed and house prisoners as they worked in the mines. TCI, in return, guaranteed that it would buy all the coal prisoners produced at a specific price per ton. This system proved to be the most profitable of all, but it also spawned unprecedented corruption. The new president of the Board of Convict Inspectors, James Oakley, removed prisoners from turpentine and lumber camps and redeployed nearly all in coal mines. Thus began a new series of mishaps and mismanagement: thousands of dollars disappeared; the accountant absconded; and Oakley was eventually removed from office, arrested, and charged with embezzlement. He was never convicted, however.[69]

In 1911 an accident at the decrepit Banner mines killed 123 black county prisoners. Even after this horrendous event, progressive reformers failed to pass legislation outlawing the lease. In 1912 TCI announced that it would give up leasing prisoners and work its mines solely with free workers. The state of Alabama then took over the Banner mine completely and supervised the work of prison miners until 1928. By selling the coal that prisoners produced to TCI, however, both Alabama and the company profited.[70] Despite such mismanagement and tragedy, prison mining garnered greater profits than ever. In 1912 Alabama prisoners brought in as revenue a whopping annual sum of over $1 million.[71]

From the perspective of prisoners, the leasing system regressed, becoming, perhaps, even more cruel and brutal between Dawson's retirement and 1928 than it had been in the late nineteenth century. Guards such as Jack Saunders, who worked at one early twentieth-century Alabama prison mine, recalled brutalizing prisoners on a regular basis.

We done some things that wasn't right, I know. . . . We useta keep a big barr'l out back of a shed at the mines, an when I think back on it now, I know we whooped niggers jes to have fun. We'd pull their britches off an strop em across the Barr'l by their hands an feet so they couldn't move, an then we's lay it on em with a leather strop. I've seen niggers with their rumps lookin like a piece of raw beef. Some of 'em would pass out like a light but they'd all put up a awful howl, beggin us to stop. It wasn't right fer us to do that. The company had lots of ways to make a bad convict work but us guards didn't follow em much. Didn't nobody want to put a convict in the sweat box, or feed him on bread an water, fer they wasn't no fun in watchin that.[72]

Between 1910 and 1914 Alabama earned over $2 million from convict labor, more revenue than ever before; state supervision of the coal mines certainly had increased profitability, but it did not appear to have led to any improvements in the treatment of prisoners.

In 1924, when James Knox, a white prisoner serving a short sentence for forging a $30 check, died at Flat Top, Sloss officials claimed that he had committed suicide. But this single incident sparked off an explosion in public outrage that finally dealt a death blow to the system. A closer investigation proved that Knox had been tortured and lowered into a vat of hot water. A grand jury heard convicts testify that they had been beaten with clubs and rubber tubes. The alleged state supervision of the system seemed a cruel illusion. Sloss still vigorously fought to keep its prison labor force intact. Governor Bibb Graves responded slowly but firmly. He had pledged in his campaign to eliminate convict labor, and the time was opportune. Four years after Knox's death, in 1928, Sloss's convict workers were removed from Flat Top. County and state prisoners were finally removed from other Alabama prison mines and put to work at road camps, prison farms, and a state-run textile mill.[73]

The years of Dawson's tenure as head of Alabama's Department of Corrections produced contradictory results. Although he pressed for reform, by himself he could not overcome Sloss's desire for the continuation of the lease, and he could not undo the state government's dependency on the revenue prisoners produced. But Dawson did what he could, considering both the limitations and positive attributes of his character. Prisoners did benefit from some of these changes. Drawing upon their own resources, such as family, literacy, mining skills, racial pride, endurance, and self-reliance, thousands managed to gain release from prison. Some returned as cripples to their families, and some to their homes. Others, however, sought to make new lives working as coal miners in Pratt City and Birmingham.

Black Leadership Responds

■ By the turn of the century, the growing black prison population in the South confirmed white stereotypes concerning the inherent criminality and immorality of black people. The dominant culture—from highbrow scientists and educators to lowbrow magazines—all agreed that without the social control of slavery, blacks had regressed to a criminal state. In an 1890 report Alabama prison authorities supported the conclusions drawn in a pamphlet by a "distinguished Alabamian" who urged "the continued union of white people to avoid the evils that are threatened by black supremacy." Officials cited the "rapid increase in the number annually convicted in our State" as proof of the "debased moral condition of the negro." Prison officials in Alabama insisted that "the negro is retrograding physically as fast as morally" because of the "loathsome diseases incident to the unrestrained indulgence of lust." According to prison officials, "negroes . . . deprived of the control and care of a master" could only look forward to an "appalling future."[1]

As C. Vann Woodward has pointed out, the lack of coherent political opposition contributed to the virulent white supremacy of this period. With the advent of disfranchisement in the South and the waning of credible critics, white politicians felt free to scapegoat black southerners and accuse them of possessing "race traits and tendencies" that fostered sex crimes, immorality, and criminality. "The New Negro Crime," according to *Harper's Weekly,* was rape.[2] In 1912 former Populist leader Tom Watson of Georgia declared that the "negro" had "no comprehension of virtue, honesty, truth, gratitude or principle." Northern scientists, historians, and university presidents also accepted and promoted the "fact" of black inferiority and immorality. Scientific proof of the allegedly inherent criminal nature of blacks was used to justify racial hatred.

Black leadership, therefore, battled social scientists, the assumptions of white public opinion, and politicians. It was not enough for African-American reformers to point to the needs of poor black communities; they also had to convince whites that blacks, as a group, deserved to be thought of as human beings. As Thomas Gossett has observed, "What was most needed at this time was a direct challenge to the intellectual bankruptcy of racist theory." [3]

Black intellectuals and activists of the late nineteenth and early twentieth century attempted to provide that challenge. W. E. B. Du Bois, Booker T. Washington, Kelly Miller, and Mary Church Terrell, among others, wrote of the progress black people had made despite the deprivations of slavery and racism. They spoke of the accomplishments and respectability of the black middle classes and dared to criticize white racism. Along with extolling the virtues of black communities, however, black leaders also had to answer white charges that blacks constituted an inherently criminal race.

The overwhelmingly black prison population posed an intellectual and personal problem for the black middle classes. To illustrate the gross unfairness of the southern legal system, they focused on the brutal conditions of convict camps and the racist treatment meted out by prejudiced courts. Nevertheless, the growing number of black prisoners troubled black middle-class reformers and intellectuals. They felt obliged to explain that black crime had risen because of social conditions such as poverty, discrimination, and lack of hope. At the same time it fell to them to refute the racist beliefs of a general public. This difficult challenge—to convince the nation of the lease's inhumanity—was further compounded by the widely held belief that all prisoners should work at productive labor. Reformers failed to dislodge the assumption shared by penologists, politicians, and the public that prisons should be profitable. A U.S. Supreme Court ruling against peonage offered some hope of change. Yet the far more profitable system of convict leasing remained strong in Alabama.

Criminologists in the North and South discussed prison policy within the two larger contexts: shared racism and the belief that prison labor should be profitable. The latter problem concerned northern administrators more deeply. During the 1880s wardens, politicians, and unions in northern cities debated the merits of prison labor. Solitary confinement, silence, reflection, and repetitive labor—the tenets of the Albany system—sought to produce moral reform among prisoners. In theory, solitude and the notorious treadmill gave a prisoner time to reflect upon his moral transgressions. Such intense isolation, however, had led to insanity and rebellion, not to mention high costs. As the prison population in the North increased after the Civil War, a call arose for productive labor instead of meaningless toil. By the 1880s two systems of prison labor prevailed in northern penitentiaries: the piece-price system (in which companies employed prisoners to work inside the penitentiary under the direction of state-employed wardens) and the contract system (which allowed capitalists directly into factories).

Politicians and public officials led the movement to link prisons to production and profit. In this "enlightened age," said a delegate before the New York State Assembly, "the employment of convicts at unproductive labor, like the crank or the treadmill cannot . . . be for a moment favorably considered."[4] According to the same politician, the piece-price plan and the contract system helped the state impose "the real purposes of labor in prisons, viz: income, discipline, and the rehabilitation of the prisoner."[5] Even prisons not seeking great profit forced prisoners to learn trades such as barrel making or shoemaking.[6] Imposing productive labor upon prisoners caused unions to protest, but prison officials promoted the efficacy of productive prison labor. Charles Felton, the assistant superintendent of the Illinois penitentiary, spoke for the majority when he addressed the National Prison Association (NPA) in 1886 and said, "We are here today as scientists, and reformers, and as business men."[7]

Although devoted to profitable prison labor, northern prisons never employed the leasing system. Their officials viewed leasing as emblematic of a backward South. George W. Cable's descriptions of horrific southern prisons confirmed the belief of many northern penologists, wardens, and prison superintendents that the leasing system ought to be abolished. When the National Prison Association held its annual meeting in Atlanta in 1886, however, those negative feelings changed.

Carroll D. Wright, a lawyer who later became the U.S. commissioner of labor, attended the Atlanta conference—the first time the NPA had met in the South. Prison officials from Georgia invited northern delegates to tour a nearby convict camp, and Wright went. Prior to this conference, Wright later recalled, any northerner with an interest in penology "would condemn in the most unmitigated terms the lease system of the South." Yet after his visit to the Georgia camp, Wright wrote: "Going out on the train one could hear only general condemnation of the southern system. Coming back to the city the remark was frequently made, and by some of the most distinguished penologists of the country, that they had seen a great light; that the employment of the class of prisoners which prevailed most generally in the south must for a time be under the odious lease system, for it furnished them with outdoor work and at the same time helped the treasury." As early as 1886, white prison administrators from the North and South began to agree about the suitability of convict leasing for southern black prisoners.

Why couldn't southern black prisoners be housed as northern ones were? Why was it suitable for them alone to be shackled and worked outside on a chain gang? To Wright, the answer was obvious: their race. "It would have been insane on the part of the southern authorities to have placed the Negro convicts especially, in such prison constructions as we have in the north." The northern delegates were convinced that putting black prisoners indoors would lead to an "enormous death rate." It made Wright and his colleagues feel better to know that southern officials "regretted the necessity of the lease system." However, "after the war, when the southern states were obliged to take care of a large class of criminals . . . they were compelled to resort to the most primitive methods of employing them." By the end of his visit to Atlanta, Wright's opinions had been transformed, and he regarded the lease system as "really a valuable suggestion at the time."[8]

As men of the Gilded Age, northern wardens and penologists were impressed by profit, and the leasing system produced far more revenue than any other arrangement. In speaking with southern corrections officers and wardens, Wright and his northern colleagues became convinced that southern penal work practices, however extreme-sounding, nevertheless were based on the same underlying principles as the piece-price and contract systems practiced in the North. By 1886 both northern and southern officials believed prison work should be productive labor. The financial success of the southern lease acted as powerful evidence in the system's defense.

Ultimately, however, northern administrators accepted the necessity of the southern leasing system because of their own racism. Southern officials insisted that because their prison population consisted of "Negroes," their prison discipline had to be harsher and the work more demanding. Northern officials, sharing the racist assumptions about black "laziness," criminality, and the need for increased supervision of black people, agreed. When Illinois delegate Charles Felton addressed the 1886 Atlanta NPA meeting, he assured the southern corrections officers present (R. H. Dawson and W. D. Lee among them) that he understood the particular problems posed by a largely black prison population: "Riding through this southern country, one sees hundreds of ragged, shiftless, indolent, and ignorant people, lying on the grass or perched upon the rail fence—members of a race lately freed and who have not as yet adapted themselves to their new political condition—who live without work, unless it be enforced work and who have not a thought of the morrow as a duty of the present day. From this class comes largely the prison class." To Felton it was obvious why black prisoners could not be used in factories. "They are not suited to avocations requiring Brain work," he stated. "Their muscles only cautilized; and at what else, pray, can these prisoners be employed?"[9] Northern officials approved the lease as an antidote to the excesses of emancipation.

Even as the leasing system continued in the South throughout the 1890s, northern reformers continued to reassure their southern brethren. During an NPA meeting in 1890, all of the delegates present, including a large Alabama contingent, agreed that leasing was "bad," but none condemned the southern states outright. In his keynote address, "Twenty Years Growth of the American Prison System," Frederick H. Wines, son of the association's founder E. C. Wines, talked at length about his father and prisons in the United States. Of the South he said: "When the war closed, the Negroes were free. Unaccustomed to liberty, many of them construed it to mean license. The states had been impoverished with their treasuries empty, and they had no means with which to build prisons, or to maintain prisoners at public expense. Where they tried the experiment it soon became evident that they could not furnish remunerative employment for ignorant and unskilled Negroes."[10]

Not only did northern delegates agree that blacks were lazy and criminal, they also thought them to be biologically inferior beings. For example, when R. H. Dawson came before the convention in 1888 and admitted that black prisoners in Alabama suffered from a disproportionately high mortality rate, his northern audience was neither surprised nor alarmed. Dawson bared his soul to the convention: "One great cause of distress to me and to all of us, is our mortality among [Negro] convicts. I come here to tell you facts. I do not want to hide anything, because I want help." His audience sympathized. "Might not the cause for the great mortality among Negro prisoners be found in the smaller viscera of the colored people?" suggested Dr. Crawford, a delegate from Massachusetts. "Colored people are inclined to lung disease," stated Mrs. C. H. Dall, a Washington delegate. "That is due not merely to lack of vitality, but to the manner in which the race ran down during and after the war. . . . Besides that, they have not the mental power of resistance. . . . The blood of educated people can resist a great deal more than the blood of the uneducated classes, because there is in them a moral and mental motive which does not act in the colored people." Dawson, agreeing with these assertions, reiterated that black and white prisoners were treated exactly the same. But Dawson's statements were false. Black prisoners were more likely to die because they were worked harder; they succumbed to tuberculosis because they were kept in more crowded conditions than white prisoners. Dawson never discussed overcrowded prison cells, work demands, or punishment as factors in the mortality rates of black prisoners.[11]

Still another factor contributing to northern acquiescence in the leasing system was a strong desire for sectional reconciliation between North and South. No regional animosity erupted during the proceedings of the NPA. Far from it. R. H. Dawson served as one of the National Prison Association's directors until 1896. Although he attended annual meetings infrequently, for many years he carried on friendly correspondence with Frederick H. Wines and other association members. Common grievances and common interests bonded these delegates together. While serving on the Warden's Committee in 1891, Dawson suggested a minor change in the committee's title that other members mildly opposed. He immediately, and graciously, withdrew his proposal by saying, "As there seems to be some objection, [from] my old friend from Massachusetts . . . and as I never wish to part from my old friend—for I hope when he and I part here, it will be to meet in a better land, and I do not know anyone in whom I have more confidence than I have in him whom we call the 'lone star of Massachusetts'—out of respect to him I will withdraw my amendment." [12] Unquestionably the association was northern-dominated. But every year one southern state usually attended. When a southern delegate did not attend, the NPA did not discuss southern prisons. Belief in white supremacy, a keen interest in profit, personal friendships, and perhaps the realization that northern prisons also lacked direction and purpose all contributed to the general acquiescence of northern delegates on the leasing question.

Only Julia Tutwiler, an occasional participant in NPA meetings, directly addressed the issue of the black male prisoner's humanity as she made a plea for prison schools. After seeing young boys at work in the Pratt mines, she proposed a juvenile facility; when the state legislature refused funds for the project, she requested merely a teacher's salary for a school at the mines. By 1888, with the assistance of TCI, she had established a prison school that could accommodate approximately forty prisoners. Like other reformers, she felt the black population to be sorely lacking in morality. Unlike the other delegates, however, she saw black prisoners as more than the sum of their labor. "We are trying to show first that these men are human beings. It seemed to me that they were not treated different from the animals. They are sheltered and fed, and so are the animals. Even the legislative committee that reported on their condition did not by a word show that they recognized any difference between them and the mules in the mines. . . . They did not say a word to show that these men had souls and minds; but they have." Tutwiler played a prominent role in Alabama progressive movements, including prison reform and education. But her opinions on prisoners were merely tolerated by Dawson and other members of Alabama's Board of Corrections. Thus by the late 1880s the denunciations of the lease by George W. Cable and black newspapers no longer persuaded northern officials. It would appear, ironically, that the southern leasing system held the higher moral, as well as financial, ground.

Black teachers, writers, and critics, however, always contested white assumptions about the criminality of black people, particularly youth. The *Huntsville Gazette*, for example, protested when young black people were branded with the label of "criminal" and sentenced to a lengthy prison term. The Alabama State Teachers' Association (ASTA), founded by Booker T. Washington, condemned the leasing system because of its effect on youth. Meeting in Selma in 1888, ASTA called for the creation of a juvenile reformatory. The organization put on the record a "protest against such inhuman and barbarous treatment, and we urge that the practice of thrusting young boys and girls of tender age into the same prisoners with old and hardened prisoners, is one to be severely condemned." [13] A "Colored Convention" that met in Montgomery in 1891 "to discuss subjects which would benefit the negro race in Alabama" repeated the call for a reformatory.[14] Jesse Duke, a black newspaper editor in Montgomery, bravely denounced convict leasing as "the curse of the present age." He condemned the racism of "prejudiced grand and petit juries" who "fill up the coal mines and public works" with black citizens. Duke asserted that black people were prosecuted "more for spite and revenge than anything else." [15]

Booker T. Washington influenced black teachers' organizations in the South, but he also inspired northern black intellectuals such as D. E. Tobias to debunk white myths surrounding black criminality that he felt the leasing system perpetuated. A black graduate of Yale University, Tobias wrote extensively on crime and racism in America during the 1890s. According to him, the leasing system was "responsible for the large number of colored prisoners being found in the United States. Abolish this huge evil and the mischief will be abated." [16] He urged Washington to remember that racist "tractates," which sought to prove that "the Negro is a criminal by nature," were written "to show that freedom has been a curse rather than a blessing to the Coloured Race." By showing the underlying aims of white propaganda, Tobias hoped to show that the behavior of black people in the United States did not differ significantly from that of other groups. Using the census figures from 1890 and other statistics, Tobias reminded Washington "that crime is increasing in the U. S. A. among all classes and Races & I think the same is true the world over, not the colored alone." [17] Tobias also emphasized the economic motivations behind black imprisonment. He called the convict lease system the "means of which, prisoners are manufactured for the market." [18]

In the late 1890s, fitting with the era of progressivism, other black sociologists and intellectuals offered critiques of the leasing system rooted in the new discipline of social science. From the pens of Booker T. Washington, W. E. B. Du Bois, Kelly Miller, Mary Church Terrell, and others came critical speeches and essays that placed the system within the context of slavery, racism, and the southern need for cheap labor. Like Tobias, these writers contested the growing body of "evidence" compiled by white social scientists that purported to prove the biological basis of black criminality.

At the turn of the century, Du Bois addressed a number of issues of concern to blacks, including housing, savings, crime, education, and work, from a social science perspective. Much of his writing appeared in newspapers and periodicals, and much of it competed directly with overtly racist pieces. For example, Du Bois's article "The Negro and Crime," printed in the *Independent* in May 1899, appeared juxtaposed to another piece whose author claimed that the "negro is the mongrel of civilization. He has married its vices and he is incapable of imitating its virtues."[19] Du Bois anticipated his audience's assumptions, therefore, when he wrote, "The development of a Negro criminal class after emancipation was to be expected." This opening sentence, however, quickly gave way to his main point: the completely unexpected fact of black achievement and the existence of "so many striving law abiding citizens." Even though some blacks have "sunk into vagrancy, poverty and crime," black criminals were the exception, not the rule. According to Du Bois, "The Negro criminal in no southern community represents the mass of the race."[20]

Having disposed of the stereotype of rampant black criminality, Du Bois then addressed four principal causes behind black crime in the South: the convict lease system, the attitude of the courts, mob rule, and segregation. Because southern prisons were profitable, the state indiscriminately lumped the hardened criminal together with youthful offenders and women in order to produce a gang-labor force. Clearly, Du Bois argued, the unlucky persons who entered the prison system would emerge from its cruelty and debasement as criminals. The courts also participated in producing an inordinate amount of black prisoners, according to Du Bois, when they routinely ignored the crimes of whites and unduly punished the merest transgressions of blacks. This double standard of justice Du Bois poignantly illustrated with a clipping from the *Atlanta Constitution*. In one afternoon a judge sentenced a thirteen-year-old black youth to ten months on a chain gang for larceny, but a white man convicted of murder was sentenced to only two years in the penitentiary. Du Bois warned of the inevitable consequences of "treating the crime of whites so leniently": both whites and blacks would lose faith "in the methods of justice." Whites knew of their relative impunity from punishment, and blacks felt too keenly the injustices of the law.

This observation gave way to Du Bois's next point: the toleration of lynching and mob rule in the South could only lead black citizens "to shield criminals" and "transform horror at crime into sympathy for the tortured victim." What good did it do, Du Bois asked, to preach patience and honest endeavor if the legal system tolerated "increasing lawlessness and barbarity of mobs." No black person could be expected to respect "a civilization which is not civilized."

Finally, Du Bois pointed to the evil of segregation in erasing any possible honest communication or "ties of sympathy" between the two races. Segregation, which spawned ignorance, made it possible for whites to misinterpret "condemnation of lynch-law for sympathy with crime" and for blacks to believe that all whites gained joy by "taunting" and "crucifying" black people. Du Bois hoped that interracial understanding, a legal system that treated the races equally, and the abolition of prisons for profit would lead to the disappearance of lynch law and the abatement of crime.

In 1901 Du Bois specifically addressed the evils of the convict-leasing system. According to Du Bois, the leasing system owed its existence, in part, to the breakdown of the South's legal structure caused by the crisis of emancipation. Just as whites sought control over blacks during slavery, Du Bois argued that after emancipation whites aimed to control black behavior through imprisonment and the lease.[21] Du Bois also viewed leasing as part and parcel of the legacy of forced labor left to the South by slavery. In addition to being techniques of social control, leasing and the crop lien were "two systems of controlling human labor which still flourish in the South."[22] The southern court system ruthlessly pursued blacks, the guilty and innocent alike, resulting in a sprawling prison system with too many men. Because the state did not want the responsibility for so many prisoners, it passed the cost on to the highest bidder who willingly bought the labor of these men and kept them under control. Like many historians after him, Du Bois interpreted the leasing system primarily as a carryover from slavery, an attack against the freedom of all black people, and an insidious means of exploiting labor from the freedpeople.

Nevertheless, Du Bois condemned the existence of crime in black communities. In the same 1901 article, he accepted stereotypes about black prisoners: when it came to morals, they had none; prison was a hotbed for recidivism. "Worse then, the chain-gangs became schools of crime which hastened the appearance of the confirmed Negro criminal upon the scene." According to Du Bois, prisons had produced a new, undesirable element among the black lower classes. "There has arisen in the South since the war a class of black criminals, loafers, and ne'er-do-wells, who are a menace to their fellows, both black and white."[23] Still, he stressed that "crime is not normal; that the appearance of crime among Southern Negroes is a symptom of wrong social conditions—of a stress of life greater than a large part of the community can bear." Du Bois reminded his audience that the vast majority of black people were "patient and law abiding."

Du Bois above all emphasized the blatant racial discrimination of the leasing system and the unfairness of the courts that fed black prisoners into it. Racism in the courts caused blacks to "lose faith in the integrity of the courts and the fairness of juries." The negative result of an unfair prison system, in his mind, was that the criminal "gained pity instead of disdain" within the black community.

After 1900 Du Bois continued to address the issue of black crime, particularly in northern cities. His riposte to those who accused blacks of being disproportionately responsible for crime, however, began to take on an edge of exasperation, if not defensiveness. In 1905 he addressed the impact that growing numbers of black migrants had upon northern cities.

> It is untrue to suppose that the jails full of black folk throughout the South represent *only* prejudiced courts. That Negroes are punished where white men go free; that no Negro's testimony weighs as much as a white man's; that an elective judiciary militates against the Negro—all this is true. It is also true that the Negroes, as a mass, are guilty of stealing, brawling, and fighting, burglary and gambling. . . . And yet is it strange? Is there any set of human beings on earth who, if enslaved, and then proscribed and discouraged and persistently hemmed in like the Southern Negro, would not find an outlet for its animal energy in crime?

Du Bois ended his article with a warning that the problems of racial inequality in the South would inevitably appear in the North.[24]

White racists looked upon black criminality as a genetic trait. Du Bois, in contrast, used the existence of black criminality to emphasize the humanity of black people. Most blacks suffered prejudice and discrimination patiently, he reminded his white readers. The growing number of black criminals, he argued, was a direct result of the degrading social conditions that black people were forced to endure, especially in urban areas. Like Washington, the Alabama Teachers' Association, and other black reformers, Du Bois proposed juvenile reformatories to separate youths from hardened criminals. The leasing system itself, according to Du Bois, contributed to black crime because small-time offenders learned all about depravity and vice in prison; white criminals, on the other hand, seldom went to the chain gang.

The few remaining white critics of southern prisons, most of them Christian reformers, no doubt influenced by Du Bois, also used sociological analysis to illustrate the point that black criminal behavior did not differ from that of other racial groups. Clarissa Olds Keeler, for example, used statistics to make her case against the leasing system, an institution which she called "the Crime of Crimes."[25] Her pamphlet contained a detailed overview of prison conditions throughout the entire South. Using health statistics and accounts printed in official state reports, Keeler used officialdom's own words to condemn the officials and the system. In Alabama she pointed to the atrocious rates of pneumonia and tuberculosis, as well as the horrors of punishment and treatment. She used the exact words of the president of the Convict Board to denounce the fee system and the practice of sending "thoughtless boys" and the innocent to their deaths. Furthermore, Keeler's exposé condemned the entire nation, not just the South. She asserted that "there is not such Thing as Justice in the United States in the Punishment of Crime." Such arguments, even from whites, however, did little to undermine racial myths or change policy.

Mary Church Terrell, one of the founders of both the National Association of Colored Women and the National Association for the Advancement of Colored People, also condemned southern lease systems and chain gangs. Terrell had gained a national reputation as a public speaker who lectured white and black audiences throughout the nation on issues pertaining to race relations. In her estimation the lease camps of the South placed men, women, and children into a "bondage . . . more cruel and more crushing than that from which their parents were emancipated forty years ago."[26] She cited white legal authorities such as Judge Emory Speer of Savannah, Georgia, a well-known critic. "Judge Speer attacked the chain gangs because men, women and children by the hundreds are forced into involuntary servitude . . . accused of some petty offense such as walking on the grass, expectorating upon the side walk, going to sleep in a depot, loitering on the streets, or some similar misdemeanors which could not by any stretch of the imagination be called a crime."[27] Terrell expressed amazement that despite shocking evidence of atrocities "perpetuated . . . with the connivance of those who administer the law," intelligent people refused to protest or even to acknowledge how the southern leasing system infected the entire legal system and perpetuated peonage.

In 1894 peon William D. West sent a letter to Alabama governor Thomas G. Jones describing his situation. Back in 1892 he had been convicted of carrying a concealed weapon and ordered to pay a $50 fine and $96 in court costs. But West did not go to a county convict camp. Instead, contractors Milliken and Meigs came forward in court and offered to pay West's fine and court costs if he agreed to work for them at a rate of $8 a month. West had to sign a contract that read, "I bind myself to labor &c for the said Miliken and Meigs." Until his fine was paid and until he repaid with interest any additional amount the two men spent on him, West was obliged to work at the camp.

Nearly two years later West wrote the governor in outrage: "I will write you a few lines to inform you of my mistreatment." West claimed that he had been promised $16 a month in wages; half was supposed to be applied to the fine, and the rest saved for him. But since his arrival, he had not heard anything about his money. In addition, he wrote, "I work all time from 3 and 4 oclock in the morning up till 10 and 11 o'clock at night." His wife and two small children were at the camp with him; they also went hungry and worked half naked. West accused the contractors of being liars. "He promist the judge and solister boath that he would treat me as one of his own children and he has treated me as if I had of bin a dog." West counted 173 other workers at this camp; he reckoned himself as one of the "best hands." He worked in the "rain, heat, and cold," but he was tired of being cheated and overworked. "I wish you Gov. to repreave me if it in your power and if you aint the write man pleas state to me what man to apply to. . . . I wish to be a free man again."

Jones's secretary passed the letter to R. H. Dawson, who quickly pressed the judge in the case for more information. Exactly one week after West first wrote, Judge Dan Gordon replied to Dawson that West's fines amounted to $146 while the amount he had earned while at Milliken's, at $8 a month, was $176: West had earned enough to pay the fine and costs "and could not be prosecuted if he should now quit," but no one had bothered to have him released. The judge ended his letter with a tribute to the character of Milliken and Meigs. "I . . . know them to be kind, honorable, and upright men and feel certain that they have not in anyway mistreated West."[28]

Milliken and Meigs operated with the blessing of county judges who clearly acted in concert with such schemes. They worked hundreds of men, women, and children and yet, unlike the official county and state prisons, were not subject to any supervision. Using the language of paternalism, Milliken and Meigs paid the fines of convicted men and forced them to work on their farms while promising to treat their black charges like their own "children." In reality, however, Milliken and Meigs exploited the county cost system to gain the cheap labor of convicted black men and their families.

As she traveled through the nation, Mary Church Terrell linked peonage to the lease and decried both as brutal reincarnations of slavery, two tornadoes that even swept up unfortunate whites. In Terrell's view leasing and peonage used the courts as a means of gaining cheap labor. "Coloured men are convicted in magistrates' courts of trivial offenses . . . and are given purposefully heavy sentences with alternate fines. Plantation owners . . . are promptly notified . . . and immediately appear to pay the fine and release the convict from jail only to make him a slave."[29] In her newspaper articles and speeches, Terrell publicized peonage charges against white landowners in Alabama in 1903, a case that ultimately led to the U.S. Supreme Court ruling against peonage.

Instead of worrying about the alleged crimes of black prisoners such as William D. West, Terrell pointed her finger to the "nest of illegality" created by peonage. "Every man employing misdemeanor convicts for private gain," she argued, "is a law-breaker." White legal officials and landowners felt free to take advantage of poor black laborers, however, because of the example of disfranchisement. "The planter sees the negro robbed of his suffrage with impunity, with the silent consent of the whole country . . . he is encouraged, therefore, to apply the same principle for profit's sake to his business affairs."[30] Terrell described southern planters and politicians as "tyrants" who justify their actions by reasoning that "the negro is unfit for citizenship," or that "the negro is lazy." Terrell's speeches sought to demonstrate to "intelligent" whites that when they failed to question the racist assumptions of powerful southerners, the latter felt licensed to exploit and destroy blacks.

Like Du Bois, Terrell indeed knew how despair and poverty led to crime. She was also determined, as was Du Bois, to uphold the respectability of the majority of black people, especially black women. Indeed, when a white newspaper editor asserted in 1895 that "the Negroes of this country are wholly devoid of morality, the women are prostitutes and are natural thieves and liars," Terrell and other black clubwomen launched a nationwide campaign as a challenge. The black women's club movement, however, focused most of its energy addressing the problems faced by poor black women. Convention sessions addressed the questions of sanitation, education, temperance, "mothers and children," "women in the home," and the needs of working wives and mothers. Like Du Bois, Terrell represented part of the black elite. Unlike Du Bois, however, she and other black women squarely placed themselves "in closer touch with the masses of our women" in order to "uplift and claim them." Terrell addressed the issue of alleged low moral standards among black women head-on. White women who made these charges, Terrell said, need only look to their own husbands to find the truly culpable and immoral party. As activists, intellectuals, and public critics, both Du Bois and Terrell sought to address the real problems of poor blacks while simultaneously attacking the racist behavior and assumptions of whites.

Kelly Miller, professor of sociology at Howard University, looked at race, region, and incarceration from the perspective of white prisoners. How can it be, he asked, that Massachusetts in 1914 had a total of 5,477 whites in prison, and Mississippi only 114? Did this mean that Massachusetts whites were less upright than those in the South? Or did it mean something more insidious, that "in the South the number of white prisoners falls immensely below the number of white offenders against the law." Like his peers Miller did not excuse black criminality, but he insisted that "crime is a question of condition, not of color." He urged black Americans "with light and learning" to do what they could to reduce the black crime rate. But again, he also averred that it was the responsibility of lawmakers to pass legislation that black people could obey without compromising their dignity and self-respect.[31]

By the teens and 1920s, black social scientists studying southern prisons began accumulating and comparing more systematic evidence about African Americans and crime. Monroe N. Work, a black sociologist at Tuskegee Institute, found that statistics about crime in the North and South showed the drastic increase in the prison population in the South between 1870 and 1890, when it tripled from 6,031 to over 19,000 inmates.[32] To explain, he, like the northern reformers, began with the South's poor economic position after the Civil War and its lack of "resources from which to make appropriations for the support of prisons." Like so many others, he then offered a functionalist description of events. Inside the prisons lived "thousands of able bodied Negroes." Outside was "a great demand for labor. . . . And so it was discovered that what had been an expense could be converted to a means of revenue and furnish a source for which the depleted state treasuries could be replenished."[33]

Yet Work did not stop there. Instead of seeing the growing prison population and the demand for labor as a meeting of two coincidences, he asserted a causal relationship between the two. Instead of condemning black people as loafers or criminals, he pointed to the obvious point: that the lease system itself caused crime because "each state [had] a financial interest in increasing the number of convicts."

A legal system that gave "the severest punishments for the most trivial offenses" also contributed to the high number of black prisoners, according to Work. He quoted two Alabama judges who admitted that white defendants committing similar acts never received similar punishments, and that black defendants, especially those living in overwhelmingly white counties, always unjustly received lengthy sentences. Work did not absolve black behavior; he cited the negative effects of ignorance, drink, and lack of respect for the law. Yet he believed it was the treatment blacks received in the courts that undermined their respect for the law. The courts had become places "where punishment is meted out rather than where justice is dispensed"; black people saw "the law" as something to be avoided rather than a means of protection. Work's views echoed the reasoned interpretation of Du Bois, Terrell, and Miller, and they were backed with statistics.

Work argued that leasing should be abolished in favor of the contract system and that the South should adopt "modern principles of prison reform."[34] R. H. Dawson had agreed with this stance at the turn of the century, but his efforts at reform had been completely thwarted by the state.

Changing the leasing and peonage system in Alabama proved beyond the reach of Dawson, Booker T. Washington, and other critics. Yet black and white reformers did succeed in abolishing peonage in Alabama. Washing-

ton and his followers held strong opinions about peonage, and he is now
known for his behind-the-scenes activities in the Alonzo Bailey peonage
case. The comparison between the successful effort to eliminate peonage and the unsuccessful campaign to rid the South of prison labor is
instructive.

Under the widespread system of peonage, black farmers were forced to
work to pay off alleged debts. Peonage fed from the trough of leasing because white landowners, on the lookout for cheap labor, volunteered to pay
the court costs of those blacks unlucky enough to fall into the clutches of
the law over a minor matter. The debt to the landowner, however, could
only be paid back by work, and black defendants who signed into these arrangements often found themselves in perpetual servitude. As Pete Daniel
has noted, such camps often contained a mix of forced laborers, including
both convicted prisoners serving out their sentences and individuals whose
court costs had been paid but who were now bound to the white landlord
for debt.[35]

Despite this overlap, the larger differences between leasing and peonage are important. Landowners—not corporations and not the state—
profited from peons being held for debt. Thus, when Booker T. Washington
joined forces with white attorneys in Alabama to stamp out peonage, they
waged war against a particularly brutal form of personal corruption, not
against a corporation. Moreover, the successful peonage case brought by
Alonzo Bailey in Alabama was decided by the U.S. Supreme Court, not by a
locally elected state judge.[36] The Thirteenth Amendment explicitly out-
lawed involuntary servitude, but until this case it had never been used to
outlaw peonage. Ending peonage, even in theory, did not touch the larger
system that required county prisoners to pay off incurred court costs
through prison labor. Furthermore, the Thirteenth Amendment still sanctioned forced labor in prison. Although the defeat of peonage was an important victory, plenty of other means of coercing black prisoners continued to exist. Abolishing peonage dented but did not destroy the complex
system of laws that controlled the debt and movement of sharecroppers.

The black intellectual community of the late nineteenth century, varied
as it was, agreed on certain basic middle-class assumptions that took a dim
view of black working-class culture and pleasures.[37] Its members also agreed,
for the most part, that the black urban population was responsible for negative, antisocial behavior that inexorably led to arrest. Nevertheless, they did
not divorce themselves from the despair of either the growing urban poor
or unschooled sharecroppers. They employed sociology to explain black
behavior in human terms, to fight for the extended legal rights of all black
people, and to urge an end to racial hatred in America.

Paternalism, the Lease, and the Law

■ Black sharecroppers in rural Alabama had little reason to be sanguine about a legal system that sanctioned peon camps and leasing. White claims to paternalistic benevolence in Alabama were further undermined by the widespread practice of lynching. During the 1890s Alabama whites lynched more blacks than in any other state in the nation. Between 1889 and 1899 lynch mobs murdered 177 blacks in Alabama.[1] Just why the 1890s signaled the height of violence directed against blacks remains unclear. Alabamians suffered a severe economic depression between 1893 and 1898. One theory posits that heightened economic competition coupled with the political threat blacks posed as voters made lynching appealing to those who wished to see blacks keep to their subordinate place. This might explain the high number of lynchings in industrial Jefferson County and in Mobile where blacks and whites competed for jobs.

Race relations in the rural Black Belt, however, still await a closer investigation.[2] Most of the mob violence directed against blacks in the 1890s occurred in the Black Belt, where African Americans comprised a vast majority. As Glenn Feldman has shown, a wide regional variation of violence makes it difficult to state the cause of lynching and violence directed against blacks. For example, in eastern Alabama between 1889 and 1921, thirty-one lynchings occurred in Montgomery, Bullock, and Elmore Counties, but adjacent Macon County experienced two. In western Alabama whites in Dallas, Marengo, and Choctaw Counties lynched thirty people, but close-by

Hale and Perry Counties did not experience a single lynching; in Greene County one African American suffered a lynching. Allegations against the victims of lynching were seldom made public, making patterns difficult to determine.[3]

Regardless of where they lived, however, all African Americans were affected by such widespread violence. Winfield Henry Mixon, a presiding elder of the AME Church, reflected on lynching in his diary entry of January 22, 1895, written in Selma, Dallas County. "The world moves gently and quietly on. Every now and then the wicked, ill-gotten, squinty-eyed, blood suckers hang, lynch, shoot, burn or flay their superiors—the ebony, pure and most God like in the heart—Negro. My pen shall never stand, my voice shall never stop, my tongue shall never cease."[4] Reverend Mixon tried to make sense of white atrocities by attributing to blacks Christ-like qualities of endurance and moral superiority. Their opponents had the power of law and popular opinion in their favor. But "their superiors"—black and pure—had God's favor. Mixon vowed to fight lynching through the power of his words and moral influence.

Recognition of white injustice did not mean that violent revenge or lawlessness among blacks became widely sanctioned. Because whites were hardly ever punished for crime, and black people were overpunished, blacks saw themselves as heroes facing down a terrible enemy.[5] However, as Lawrence Levine explains, black folklore did not idolize prisoners, outlaws, or criminals. Despite popular songs that told the story of "Stagolee" and other "bad men," according to Levine, "black folk refused to romantically embellish or sentimentalize" such characters. As he points out, black folklore lacks a criminal hero such as Robin Hood or Jesse James, bad men who nevertheless were chivalrous to women and gave riches to the poor. No "noble" outlaws exist in black folk culture. Instead, these "negro bad men" preyed on everyone: rich, poor, male, and female. They were to be feared, and their acts resulted in prison or death—decidedly undesirable, antisocial outcomes. As Levine trenchantly observed, "The situation of Negroes in the United States was too complex for nostalgia."[6] This was especially true in the Alabama Black Belt, where black people suffered criminal acts at the hands of both whites and blacks.

Even if they never became prisoners, black sharecroppers in rural Alabama had contact with the law. They brought lawsuits, signed legal contracts and petitions, saw prisoners at work, and witnessed the arrests of family members. And to paraphrase Ned Cobb, not "all of God's dangers" came in the form of whites. African-American men and women also became the victims of theft, murder, or assault, and sometimes the perpetrator was a black neighbor or spouse. Although they knew the law worked in the favor of whites, African Americans saw the power of judges and juries. By the 1890s it was unrealistic for a black person to haul a white offender into court. But when it came to resolving disputes among blacks themselves, appealing to the local courts remained a viable option. This paradox of a people subjected to extralegal violence who chose legal and peaceful methods for pursuing social change would find its full fruition in the civil rights movement. But the roots of the blacks' belief in justice and their enthusiasm for making appeals to the courts reach back into the nineteenth century.

As two cases from Hale County suggest, ordinary male and female share-croppers used the court system to prosecute black offenders. One case began with a quarrel over a broken gun, and the other was a domestic dispute. In both cases, however, the plaintiffs eventually were murdered by the defendants, and members of the wider black community inserted themselves into the legal proceedings, both as witnesses and as petitioners. These cases reveal conflicts concerning gender, race, and class in a sharecropping community that included a working black majority, a somewhat influential black middle class, and a white elite. These cases show how paternalism and patriarchy were part of the social fabric of these African-American communities. Both cases show the best possibilities and the limitations of what ordinary black sharecroppers could expect from the legal system.

In 1890 over 22,000 blacks in Hale County lived alongside just over 5,000 whites.[7] Politically, Hale County, like the rest of the Black Belt, was dominated by a landowning elite who ran elections, controlled the state legislators, and made sure the Democratic party received the bulk of the black vote on election day. Reverend Mixon's diary, however, gives a nuanced picture of daily life. Mixon, who lived in Greensboro, Hale County, between 1892 and 1895, was ecstatic to discover that some blacks in his religious jurisdiction of Dallas, Marengo, Perry, Hale, and Greene Counties had become landowners. He traveled throughout the western Alabama Black Belt frequently. "Within these counties," he wrote, "thousands and thousands of acres of land are owned by colored people. Many of them have comfortable and beautiful homes . . . a great many of them have money in banks." Owning land epitomized the essence of black success; the sight of thrifty, hardworking middle-class blacks made Mixon proud. As the statistics on lynching show, the 1890s represented the worst of times for many African Americans in the Alabama Black Belt. But for some it was the best of times, too. As powerful as whites were, African-American life there still revolved within largely black communities.

Not all conditions in the Black Belt conformed to Reverend Mixon's standards. In his opinion, poor African-American sharecroppers still had a lot to learn, especially in matters of financial thrift. "We have lectured upon the importance of not mortgaging crops before even they are planted. We have been in opposition to excursions and law suits in pettie things. . . . Our people are improving in morals."[8] Mixon's concerns reflect what Kevin Gaines has recently criticized as "uplift ideology."[9] Mixon echoed the beliefs of many middle-class African Americans, most especially Booker T. Washington, who promoted hard work, religion, and thrift as the bedrock of black life. Black newspapers such as the *Huntsville Gazette* constantly criticized blacks for spending money on such frivolities as organized day trips to neighboring towns. In 1888 the *Gazette* told its readers that these "excursions must cease; people need to prepare for the winter, and going on Sunday is awful!"[10] Instead, Mixon and other members of the black middle class in Alabama urged the poor to give up drink, work harder, and buy homes. Sharecroppers should put pleasure aside and money in the bank. Debt and frivolity would keep blacks down. Hard work would lift them up.

Mixon also despaired because he saw poor black people bringing each other to court for "law suits in pettie things." The presence of a large prison farm in the heart of the Black Belt, such as the one run by Milliken and Meigs, depressed him. "To our shame, to our disgrace in the centre of my district is a convict farm. Man and woman are they, They are the sons and daughters of Ham, sent there by colored people. We have tried to check the seemingly increasing spirit of our people from rushing into law."[11] Two reasons underpinned Mixon's concerns. As a consequence of petty suits, black prisoners ended up within the clutches of local white landowners or even in coal mines. Furthermore, Mixon feared that black prisoners at work on a convict farm made all black people look immoral. Reverend Mixon and other members of the black middle class wanted the image of black criminality suppressed. To poorer black sharecroppers, however, the value in gaining justice through the legal system outweighed any concern of how their behavior might appear to whites.

In particular, historians have debated the extent to which freedwomen used the courts. Although black women had brought suits against whites during Reconstruction, according to Catherine Clinton they were reluctant to prosecute black men for domestic violence. "Most freedwomen resisted bringing [Bureau] agents into domestic matters" and appealed to the Freedmen's Bureau for assistance only under the direst circumstances.[12] Clinton says that black women appealed to white authority "reluctantly" because they understood the double bind of applying to whites for justice within the black household. For the good of the community, Clinton implies, black women endured abuse. She states that black women supported "a strengthening of gender roles and conventional, if not puritanical, sexual morality within the black community."[13]

Other historians, however, have emphasized how black women used the law to redefine gender roles or assert a new meaning of marriage. Laura Edwards has shown that freedwoman emphasized their right to quit their husbands if they chose. Leslie Schwalm demonstrates convincingly that domestic violence and property disputes spurred freedwomen in South Carolina to complain to the Freedmen's Bureau or the provost courts. Clearly conflict did occur within black households after emancipation, with men trying to assert greater dominance over women.[14] Now that marriage was legal, it was revered among blacks as "the basis of all our rights," and yet no shared consensus emerged among black men and women about proper gender roles.

By the 1890s class divisions within the black community had created competing visions of the proper behavior of black woman. Studies of black female organizations in that decade have traced the efforts of black women to rise above sexist and racist stereotypes portraying them as lascivious Jezebels who disobeyed their husbands and slept with white and black men indiscriminately. Hazel Carby, for example, has argued that "black women intellectuals reconstructed the sexual ideologies of the nineteenth century to produce an alternative discourse of black womanhood."[15] Black female teachers, writers, and activists emphasized racial uplift, sexual propriety, and adherence to the values and behavior of the "best thinking" black men and women. These women supported female suffrage, education, and uplift. They valued marriage and defended black women's sexual virtue, but they saw themselves as paving the way for female advancement, not subordination.

We know less about the views of poorer black women. Tera Hunter emphasizes that in the Atlanta of the New South, urban female workers strove for independence and freedom on their own terms. Although employed in the most menial tasks of laundresses and servants, they nevertheless fought for better wages and respect; they also participated in the lively urban culture of the city.[16] Did working rural women have fewer options and more constraints? Susan Mann has argued that although black men and women in sharecropping families depended on each other and worked together, rural black women were still subject to male authority. The law buttressed this domestic inequality by recognizing males as the head of households. Mann argues that women in sharecropping households often performed double duty in the fields and in domestic work. In addition, sharecropping women were subject to domestic violence. Although black men and women in sharecropping families may have had complementary roles, Mann contends that they were not equal.[17]

Despite their subordinate position in the black household, some poor black women sharecroppers in rural Alabama prosecuted their husbands for assault. In 1898 Rebecca Hall, an African-American sharecropper from Hale County, took her husband Charley to court and charged him with beating her. Her suit succeeded. The judge placed Charley Hall under a restraining order which prohibited him from going near Rebecca. In addition, Hall was fined and ordered to work off the amount of his debt on a nearby plantation.

One Sunday, shortly after the conviction, Rebecca Hall visited friends who lived on a plantation close to where Charley was being held. As she walked with three other women back to her home, Charley Hall saw Rebecca and chased her. Although pregnant, she managed to outrun him until she tripped on the hem of her dress and fell down in the middle of a field. Charley approached her, and in plain view of Rebecca's three friends and other witnesses, he pulled up Rebecca's head and cut her throat "from ear to ear."

Despite her brutal murder, some blacks in the neighborhood did not have much sympathy for Rebecca Hall. After she was dead some witnesses painted her as "an overbearing and unfaithful wife" who had enraged her husband by making him jealous. On that fateful day, according to her detractors, Rebecca had gone to the plantation not to visit her friends but to stir Charley up, "to arouse him and in fact to defy him." Other witnesses alleged that Rebecca had told Charley that if he "could not furnish her with all she wanted, she would let other men sleep with her, who would give her what she wanted." Rebecca had brought suit against Charley, it was claimed, not because she was an abused women, but because she was determined to "send Charley to the mines." These witnesses implied that Rebecca herself was to blame for Charlie Hall's behavior. It was she who had provoked him with her unfaithfulness and she who had caused his imprisonment. By flaunting her pregnancy, she had driven Charlie Hall insane with jealousy, causing him to beat her, and eventually kill her.

Despite overwhelming black popular prejudice against the victim, a white jury sentenced Hall to hang. Chasing after a pregnant women and murdering her in full daylight without provocation evoked little sympathy from jurors or the judge. Clearly Hall was a violent man who should be made to pay for his crime. The death sentence, however, caused a clamor within black church congregations in both eastern and western Hale County. Tellingly, Hall's sentence did not provoke disagreements about capital punishment or murder, but about women.

Reverend Mixon had commented on the number of middle-class blacks in the Alabama Black Belt; when a crisis emerged in the community, these men stepped forward to influence events. African-American men of property and standing in Hale County did not think the death sentence against Hall should stand, and they circulated petitions demanding that his sentence be commuted to life in prison. The black men leading the petition drive included a minister in charge of two large Baptist churches in the county, a landowner, and two merchants.

E. D. Wimbs, who leased 2,600 acres from a former governor and who owned land in his own right, explained to Governor Johnston the reasons behind the petitions. "To be plain, Charley's hanging will license the women to defy their husband's and to set him absolutely free would be to encourage men to kill their unfaithful wives, while taking the middle course by sending him to the Penitentiary for life will do good." Wimbs acknowledged, however, that others in the black community disagreed with this "middle course." "There was a clamor on the part of the rabble women of my race that Charley be hung," he wrote, but he assured the governor that the "best" black women disagreed with the "rabble." The "best thinking" black men and women, Wimbs told the governor, believed the sentence should be commuted.[18]

It is clear that the "best thinking" blacks, including men like Reverend Mixon and Wimbs, wanted to encourage behavior among poor people befitting the image of a sober, thrifty, and stable working class. Because controlling the sexual behavior of women within the family had clearly emerged as integral to this ideal, hanging Charley Hall for killing Rebecca would be counterproductive. Her behavior and her challenges to Hall's authority were excuse enough for her death. For the good of the black community, Wimbs pleaded for Charley Hall's life. "I think I know my people, and I boldly say that no greater injury could be done to them than by allowing Charley to be hung about that overbearing, unfaithful wife and one half-witted as he was he did not have sense enough to quit and let her go her own way."[19]

What about the "best thinking" black women? Why would they not also join with the "rabble women" in demanding justice for Rebecca Hall? Wimbs's assertion that the "best thinking" women of Hale County disagreed with the "rabble women" confirms a picture of educated black women who wished to uplift their race through respect, education, propriety, and reform. Reverend Mixon's journal also confirms the existence of black female reformers in Hale County and the surrounding Black Belt.[20] He wrote approvingly of the black ministers' wives who diligently helped their husbands and attended black female club meetings. For middle-class black women concerned with erasing negative stereotypes of sexual promiscuity, joining their middle-class brothers and husbands in urging a lesser penalty for Charley Hall made sense. They surely shrank from Rebecca Hall's alleged behavior—which included defying her husband, taking him to court, and becoming pregnant while estranged from him—because whites had long used the image of Rebecca Hall and women like her to justify the sexual exploitation and derision of all black women. Undoubtedly, middle-class black women did not want Charley Hall to be completely exonerated, yet they may indeed have urged that his death sentence be revoked. But because no women's names appear on the petition, it is difficult to know exactly what these "best thinking" black women truly felt.

Petitions such as these give a perspective on the way the murder trial of Charley Hall brought out divisions over women's behavior, class, and sexuality within the black community in Hale County. People with no firsthand knowledge of Charley or Rebecca Hall, people who did not even live in the same vicinity, became determined that Hall should escape the death sentence. At stake were the proper roles of married black women, the rights of their husbands, and the importance of community stability over the individual rights of certain females. For black women such as Rebecca Hall and her friends, however, other issues were more important. They were determined to assert their right to be protected from domestic violence, as well as their right to quit their husbands when they chose to do so. As Laura Edwards has shown, newly emancipated women in North Carolina exhibited similar concerns.[21] By 1898 conflicts over the proper behavior of black women in sharecropping households were still contested and unresolved.

Middle-class blacks saw Charley Hall as the victim of his wife, an example of the breakdown of patriarchy. But they also lamented how a paternalistic legal system fell short in such cases. Although white paternalism often worked to the benefit of wealthier blacks, it did not reach poor men like Charley Hall, whose lack of funds guaranteed an all too speedy trial. "It is very hard," E. D. Wimbs wrote, "that a white man or a rich negro can have his case continued from term to term in our courts in order for him to get his witnesses and prepare his case." But in the absence of such a delay, Charley Hall "could not get a first-class white citizen to be present to testify in his behalf." Without such character witnesses, Hall's fate was sealed. And yet through their petition Wimbs and other middle-class blacks expressed what they felt to be the will of the community to the governor. The petitions had the desired effect: Governor Johnston commuted Hall's death sentence to life in prison.

During Reconstruction the Alabama Black Belt had been home to interracial Republicanism, in which African-American men and women had both participated. The "unruliness" and self-assertion that black women displayed during Reconstruction and their resistance to white social control in prison had served their individual and group interests. In the 1890s, however, such behavior appeared to threaten the aspirations middle-class blacks had for themselves and their race. By the late 1890s class status, white paternalism, and a concern over the "proper" behavior of black women had redefined race and gender relations in the Black Belt. Although many rural uneducated black women shared these views of sexual propriety, not everyone did. Poorer black women did not heed the advice of Mixon and others, either in their sexual behavior or in their attitude toward bringing legal actions against black men. Since emancipation, independent black women had been seen as defiant of white and black authority. Some black women in the rural Black Belt, however, did bring black men into court; although the number of such cases is not large, they are significant. Court cases brought by black women provide some clues about the power, as well as the limits, of patriarchy within rural black communities.

Millie Hudson, a twenty-three-year-old unmarried woman who lived in

Perry County, brought action against James Crooms, claiming that he was the father of one of her three children. She charged him with bastardy and succeeded in having him sentenced to the state penitentiary. Those petitioning for Crooms's pardon made the same arguments that Wimbs and others did on the behalf of Charley Hall. His petition states that Hudson "was commonly known as a common lewd woman" and that she admitted all three of her children had different fathers.[22] Crooms denied he fathered any of her children. The petition for Crooms's pardon is full of the names of white lawyers, merchants, farmers, and schoolteachers. Why should these men care if James Crooms was released? The answer must remain speculative. Perhaps Crooms's employer wanted him out of prison and induced his friends to sign the petition. Perhaps these men sympathized with Crooms's predicament. Still, the fact remains that Millie Hudson did bring a paternity suit against Crooms and that she was successful, to the chagrin of many. Perhaps because she was unmarried and known as "lewd" she was not deemed worthy of other community sanctions that would have encouraged Crooms to take responsibility for the child. The actions of Millie Hudson and Rebecca Hall show that when black women used the legal system to take action against black men, they did so at risk to their lives and with the disapproval of many in the community. And it must also be acknowledged that these prosecutions, like any that involved a black defendant, pulled more men into either the local prison farm or a county convict camp, a consequence not to the dislike of local judges and landowners.

White paternalism had emerged as the mediating force in legal conflicts involving blacks. A good word from a white landowner could result in a trial continuance or a paid fine. White intervention was also key to the pardon process. But such pardons did not always represent the popular will in the black community. As Neil McMillen has shown for Mississippi, "The gravity of any crime was determined . . . by its impact on white interests." When "black-on-black" crime aroused white racial fears or involved a favored black worker of an influential white, then the penalties for such acts could be severe. However, when such interests were not involved, then whites tended to ignore crimes in which the victim and the perpetrator were African-American. The paternalistic system had its winners and losers based upon black sycophancy to white stereotypes. A defendant with a white man of influence to back him could expect to be let off, but those with no one to speak for them could expect much harsher treatment.[23]

White paternalism distorted the legal system, yet some African Americans in the Alabama Black Belt still sought justice on their own terms. The murder of William Cottrell, a black sharecropper in Greensboro, and the subsequent efforts of his brothers to prosecute his killer illustrate this point. In 1890 Cottrell worked with another black hand, Tom Walker, on a plantation near Greensboro. One day they argued. Cottrell had loaned his gun to Walker and accused Walker of breaking it. When Walker refused to have the broken gun fixed, Cottrell went to the local justice of the peace and had an arrest warrant issued against Walker. Although Walker was arrested, he convinced the constable to release him temporarily. Walker then proceeded to the store of Ivy Cottrell, the plaintiff's brother, where he saw William Cottrell in the doorway. Walker allegedly spoke of his plan to go to Louisiana and stuck out his hand for Cottrell to shake. When Cottrell extended his own right hand, Walker grabbed it with his left, pulled a gun with his right, and then shot and killed William Cottrell.[24] Tom Walker ran off to Louisiana but was eventually brought back to stand trial for murder.

The brothers of the murdered man did not seek personal revenge through a vendetta, lynching, or private assassination. Instead, they hired a lawyer, Charles Waller, to prosecute the case. In 1891 Tom Walker was tried in the Circuit Court of Hale County, convicted of murder, and sentenced to die. He appealed his conviction to the Alabama Supreme Court. His appeal was based on a technicality (a juror's name had been misspelled) and the claim that he had been drunk at the time of the murder. More significantly, however, Walker claimed that the circuit court judge had excluded important evidence about his character. Walker wanted to introduce testimony to the effect that "the white people all liked him and considered him the white man's friend," but the judge in the case had refused to allow such testimony. The appeals court concurred that allowing such testimony was inappropriate; it affirmed Walker's conviction and his death sentence.

Despite this setback, Tom Walker refused to give up. When his appeal failed, he sought to win his release by gaining a pardon from the governor. Over the years he accumulated a voluminous pardon file, thick with letters from whites in Hale County requesting his release. Among them is one from his former employer, Thomas Morrisett, who praised Tom as "a splendid hand" with "many good qualities." Another letter of support came from Charles Waller, the lawyer who prosecuted Walker, who argued that Walker had been drinking when he shot Cottrell and therefore deserved a pardon. Even though the appeals court had expressly rejected Walker's appeal on those grounds, this logic somehow made sense to the prosecuting attorney. He assured the governor that "Tom Walker stood unusually well in our community for a negro" and "ought to be absolutely pardoned." These personal testimonies reveal the gulf that existed between the law and actual practice when it came to admitting white evidence of black character. The Alabama Supreme Court indicated that such testimony was inappropriate, yet E. D. Wimbs's letter to the governor in the Charley Hall case and Waller's letter illustrate that such testimony indeed was common.

In addition to letters from influential whites in Hale County, Tom Walker also received the hearty commendations of prison officials. While a prisoner, Tom "assisted the officials in preventing several escapes and aided in arresting parties through information which he gave to the officials at the mines." [25] William Rogers lauded Walker as "a negro with a good deal of character" who had on "several occasions assisted the prison officers in preventing escapes." J. H. Edwards, a doctor at the mines, wrote that "I cannot believe that he is a murderer at heart, but on the contrary, a worthy man in every respect." Walker's willingness to be of service to the prison authorities prompted the physician to assure the governor that Walker was "one of the most trustworthy, kind, polite and industrious negroes that I have ever met: in fact he is the only negro that I have personally known possessing a white man's principles." [26] This was precisely the kind of testimony the court had prevented jurors from hearing, but it could not ban it from the ears of the governor.

The black community in Hale County adamantly opposed Walker's pardon. Walker's defense attorney, however, undermined their concerns by telling the governor that "the witnesses for the state, all negroes, were deeply prejudiced against Walker because he was popular with the white men of the county and was their superior in many respects." Walker's attorney never disputed Walker's guilt, but he insinuated that black popular prejudice against Walker had led him to be unjustly convicted. William Cottrell's brothers never received the justice they sought. Tom Walker was not executed; instead, he succeeded in getting his sentence commuted to life imprisonment. Eventually, Walker received a full pardon from Governor Johnston and was discharged on December 24, 1899. He had served only eight years in prison.

The black community in Hale County no doubt agreed with the prison physician that Walker possessed "a white man's principles," but their definition of what those principles entailed differed vastly from that of whites. The behavior one group saw as utter sycophancy and betrayal of the race, whites viewed as the epitome of integrity and superiority. Cottrell's brothers and the black community had tried to make Tom Walker pay for his crime, and the circuit court had concurred by excluding the kind of testimony that later swayed the governor. Ultimately, however, their efforts were to no avail. The force of paternalism could even overcome the legal formalism that technically forbade it.

How are we to view Tom Walker? No one can dispute his ingenuity in getting so many different white men, all in positions of authority, to write letters for him. It was common for landowners to write pleading letters to get an employee pardoned. But Walker's file is highly unusual in that it also contained letters from his own lawyer, the prosecutor, his employer, several physicians at the prison, and even William Rogers, the prison superintendent. Their letters to the governor show how whites, in and out of prison, judged the character of black individuals by the way they behaved and responded to white authority. What was important to these men was not Tom Walker's crime but whether he conformed to white expectations of black behavior. Men like Tom Walker knew this and undoubtedly used sycophancy to their advantage both in and outside of prison.

But not all freedpeople, prisoners or not, agreed with this tactic. Walker's exaggerated obsequiousness as a free man and in prison was the exception, not the rule. The letters from Rogers and the prison physicians all emphasize that no other black man they had ever met possessed Walker's high degree of character. Ironically, their remarks reveal that the vast majority of blacks they encountered did not behave like Walker. Even with the pressures of prison and the double binds placed upon them by white paternalism in rural communities, African Americans rejected sycophancy when they could. They valued loyalty to their race and proper punishment for murder. Even paternalism had its limits. The fact that Walker was disliked and mistrusted in the black community illustrates the distinction black people made between sycophantism and proper behavior. The yawning gap separating black and white perceptions of Walker's behavior also shows the exact opposite values by which blacks and whites defined good and bad behavior. Most black prisoners, particularly those whose escapes he betrayed, certainly did not share the view of Walker's character held by the white prison authorities. And the Cottrell brothers did not see Walker as "trustworthy, kind, polite and industrious." Indeed, Walker's behavior in prison vindicates the black community's perception of him as a sycophant. Tom Walker dealt with white authority as a prisoner the same way he did as a free man. As badly as all black prisoners wanted to survive and go home, the majority still did not behave like Tom Walker.

Growing class divisions within some black communities led wealthier blacks, such as merchants and clergymen, to encourage respect for the authority of the law. Even in these few cases, it is clear that blacks used the law to prosecute infanticide, murder, assault, the damage of goods, and paternity suits. However much the criminal justice system oppressed black people, blacks of all classes seized upon the contradictions posed by a government that mouthed equality before the law while practicing discrimination. Many blacks still hoped that the law would protect them from criminals.

Despite the controversies caused by both of these cases, African Americans of both genders and all classes in rural Alabama looked to the courts to make decisions that would reflect community sentiments and values. Local judicial decisions could buttress or undercut community authority. Blacks placed importance upon court decisions because they believed that in spite of racial abuse, courts were ideally a place where justice should be dispensed. Occasionally, it was. But as the case of Charley Hall illustrates, the black community did not always agree as to what constituted justice.

And in Tom Walker's case, even the will of the local courts was thwarted by the higher power of the governor and white paternalism. It was ordinary black people, not the "better class" of blacks, who insisted that the courts be the place where wrongs inflicted upon them be punished. But black people took each other to court because they believed it to be the proper forum for gaining justice and settling disputes.

12

Prisoners and Ex-Prisoners

■ Prison mines destroyed the lives of thousands of men. William Johnson, an African American from Talladega County, lived through his incarceration, but he undoubtedly wondered how. In the early 1890s, after being convicted of petit larceny, Johnson began serving a sentence at the Pratt mines. Shortly after he arrived, he fell through a manhole and hurt his leg. Never treated, it soon became infected, and eventually the leg was amputated. But even prisoners with missing legs mined coal. Johnson continued to work in the Pratt mines. All day long, lying on his side, he drove fissures into the coal face until his stump and side became a bloody mess. When he was no longer able to work, TCI sent Johnson to a charity hospital in Birmingham where a doctor removed two of his ribs. Johnson was released with a raw, open wound in his side. He had no money but managed to return to Talladega to live with an elderly aunt, a cook, who supported him.

It was she who managed to convince a white lawyer to take some interest in Johnson's plight. C. C. Whitson, a Talladega attorney, pitied Johnson and his aunt and told their story to Governor Jones. "I know this woman well and she is an excellent cook, far better than the majority of her race, and it was by accident that I found out the condition of this negro and on her account I went to see him." TCI became known for its company-run schools and health care; its paternalism, however, did not extend to its prisoners. William Johnson, still in his twenties, was completely disabled; he would never be able to earn a living again. Whitson asked the governor if

TCI could not be forced to pay reparations. "Certainly his punishment and the injuries resulting from his punishment far exceeds his offense." [1]

Like many other former convicts, William Johnson's life was destroyed by the Pratt prison mines. Unable to recover from prison and thrown back upon their families, this population inspired some pity but no movement for reparations or medical care. The Pratt prison mines sucked in labor and spat out cripples, the dead, and the fortunate who survived. Prison officials and corporate heads ignored the fate of men like William Johnson and instead emphasized the men who survived and stayed to work as free miners.

Nevertheless, coal officials did not celebrate former prisoners who took up residence in Pratt City. Occasionally, they cited these ex-convicts as examples of the benefits derived from forced labor. More often, they blamed ex-prisoners for the soaring crime rate in Jefferson County. But the men released from the TCI's prison mines defied such stereotypes.

Many former prisoners living in Pratt City joined eager immigrants from Europe, Pennsylvania, and the Black Belt who had flocked to the region throughout the late nineteenth century to work in its coal mines and iron mills. African-American miners in Birmingham joined the Knights of Labor and the United Mine Workers, giving the region a unique history of interracial solidarity, as well as labor militancy. Nevertheless, as Paul Worthman has noted, "Little is known about Birmingham Negroes who encouraged black workers to join unions—or about the men who joined. The particular experiences which drew them to the labor movement are unknown." In order to explain with greater precision why black workers joined unions, Worthman has urged historians to explore the backgrounds of black miners. Their activities during Reconstruction, their experience with slavery, and the amount of time they spent in the district, he suggests, "could illuminate much of Alabama's labor history during this period." [2]

"The ex-convicts are the most blatant about the rights of free labor," an inspector noted in 1886, "forgetting that had they never been convicts, they would never have been miners." [3] Regardless of whether coal companies deserved the gratitude of ex-prisoners, it is difficult to imagine that they ever forgot how prison taught them brutal relations of power or the various ways in which a miner could be cheated. As prisoners they could do little to improve their situation. Once free, however, the could use their knowledge to demand better pay and respect.

The question is not whether, but how, the presence of ex-prisoners contributed to the Birmingham mining region's distinctive character. One mining community whose history provides some clues is Pratt City, a town of several thousand black and white miners located near the Pratt mines that became a favored place for ex-prisoners to settle and to live. An 1889 legislative investigation worried that Jefferson County was becoming another Botany Bay, and that ex-prisoners were forming "a nucleus around which assembles the criminal classes from this and adjoining states."[4] Whether ex-prisoners who settled in Pratt City caused rampant criminality, however, needs to be explored, not assumed. Although blamed for Birmingham's high crime rate and its reputation as a city of ill repute, former prisoners contributed to Pratt City's labor activism and rich political life.

As Pratt and TCI leased more and more prisoners, the number of prisoners working in the Pratt mines reached nearly 1,000 by 1890. Between 1888 and 1890 over 900 prisoners were released from the Coalburg prison mine, and over 700 state and county prisoners were released from the Pratt prison mines run by TCI.[5] "Coketown," located near the Shaft and Slope No. 2 of the Pratt mines, soon became known as Pratt City. Ex-prisoners and their families comprised some of the town's first residents. By the early 1890s former prisoners merged with free miners in growing numbers. Despite stereotypes of indifference and laziness, ex-prisoners were eager to work, and work hard, for a wage. John Tankersley, a prisoner at the Pratt mines, testified in 1883 that "when [a man] is released he will generally get employment immediately. He generally goes to Mr. Johns [a Pratt Company superintendent] here and he will give him a job of some kind."[6]

During the 1880s and 1890s, as former prisoners settled in Pratt City, they became involved in politics and even became active in the Republican party. Although it was against the law for convicted felons to vote, newspaper articles in the *Weekly Iron Age,* a Democratic paper published in Birmingham, indicate the significant risks that Pratt City blacks took in order to cast ballots. One article, "Startling Discoveries Made by an Investigation of the Convict Records," sounded an alarm to its white readers about the growing number of registered black Republicans who allegedly were ex-convicts. Fergus McCarthy, a county clerk, compared the Coalburg convict records "with his registration books for Beat 37." He found that in one beat "about 100 ex-convicts had registered [to vote], and it is known that quite a number have also registered under assumed names." This clustering of former prisoners indicates that released men lived close together. Clerk McCarthy, determined to prevent all ex-prisoners from voting, hired prison wardens and guards in order to identify ex-convicts at the polls. "All who make an attempt to cast a vote will be arrested and prosecuted." Even if they stayed away from the polls, registered ex-prisoners were threatened with arrest for perjury. The discovery of former prisoners as registered voters gave the Democrats a new rallying cry: "Jefferson county might submit to Republican rule, but to ex-convict rule, never."[7] The political activities of black miners, fresh from the prison mines, showed that former prisoners were not discouraged but organized, not ignorant but politicized.

Ex-prisoners seemed to be especially active in party politics in precincts near the Pratt mines. Another *Weekly Iron Age* article stated that the "demo-

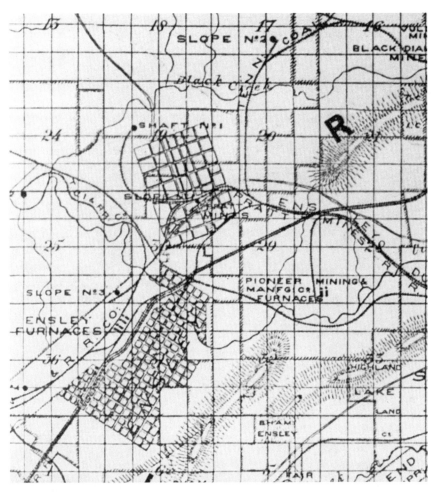

Map of Pratt mines community and surrounding prison mines. (By E. Grieg, C.E., 1889, Birmingham Public Library, Map Room)

crats of Coketon are . . . making strenuous efforts to carry this box in the next election for the Democracy. It has heretofore been carried by the Republicans, but the good Democrats here are tired of this kind of thing. . . . They realize the fact that the result of the coming election will determine whether Jefferson county shall be ruled by the negroes or the whites." In order to win more votes, Democrats appealed to white racism. "The color line has been drawn, and the battle has got to be fought out on that line and the white man who fails to do his duty should be forever pointed at with scorn and loathing by the true white men of the country." Although Democratic politicians knew that by supporting prison labor they weakened their position among white miners, they urged white workers to set that issue aside and think like men of their race. "The convict question and every other question sinks into insignificance when compared with the main issue, i.e., shall the whites or the blacks rule the country?" The Democratic party in Coketon hoped to have 300 white "working Democrats" ready to "insure this box for democracy" on election day. Ironically, the same paper that condemned the Republican votes of former black prisoners cheered the political support shown by white prisoners. As the *Weekly Iron Age,* referring to the Democratic candidate for president, Grover Cleveland, noted, "Even the white convicts have caught the spirit of the canvas, and have flung to the breeze a flag upon which is tacked a huge bandanna and inscribed with these words: 'Ah, there, Grover, stay there.'"

The paper captured the contradictory nature of race relations in the mines and in Pratt City. Democrats had made leasing the cornerstone of their economic platform, yet the existence of the system threatened to undermine white working-class loyalty. White workingmen resented how the Democrats crushed mining strikes during the 1880s and expanded prison mining into a competitive, profitable system. Like black miners, white miners wished to see the leasing system destroyed. During the 1890s Democrats tried to regain white working-class support by convincing them that prison work in the mines would end very soon. But the Democrats failed to act. As a result, white workers in Jefferson County voted for the Populists, a party solidly against the leasing system.[8]

Populism forged interracial political coalitions in Pratt City. In 1890 Pratt City miners supported anti–convict lease candidate R. J. Lower for U.S. representative, but his opponent, John H. Bankhead, the architect of the modern lease system, defeated him.[9] In 1892 a "Kolb-Republican element" in Pratt City, "composed chiefly of negroes" (but not solely), elected two of their candidates as the justice of the peace. An appalled local Democrat wrote to Governor Jones implying that the contest was won through fraud. However, a local probate judge upheld the election; the two Republicans paid their bonds and took the oath of office.[10]

But mutual support of political candidates did not necessarily indicate that race relations in Jefferson County were good. In 1888 the *Weekly Iron Age* reported the lynching of Frank Stone, a black man, who was hanged from a tree in nearby Seddon and shot full of bullets from at least a hundred guns. What was Stone accused of? "Molesting" a white woman: Mrs. Orr, the wife of a section foreman on the Georgia Pacific Railroad, claimed to have been seized and choked by a "rough" black man. Bloodhounds and 100 mounted "citizens" pursued possible "suspects" and finally settled on a man found hiding in a nearby swamp.[11] Undoubtedly lynching was part of the white response to blacks moving to the city in search of work. Yet blacks and whites in Pratt City lived together, worked with each other, supported the same candidates for office, and even went on strike together.

The relationships of former prisoners, black and white, were similarly complex. In 1984 an African American and a long-term resident of Pratt City was interviewed as part of a series on "Working Lives" in the Birmingham region. Alex Bryant began his story about two prisoners, one released and one waiting to be released, with the word *If*. But his narrative then lapsed into a tense which implied that the tale had actually happened. Bryant told his interviewer that Pratt City streets were "funny and crooked" because they were built by "ex-miners, prisoners come out of the mines." Bryant explained how newly freed prisoners assisted soon-to-be-released men in acquiring homes. "If I was in the mine and he was in the mine and I got out of prison before he did . . . and I worked and earned a little money owed to me while I was in the [prison] mine and when they turn me loose they give me that money and I go back to see you . . . and I say when you get out you come back stay with me. . . . He came back and built a house beside of me." Pratt City was racially mixed. According to Bryant, "White folks and the colored folks [lived] down here in Pratt City a long time. And they got along fine." [12]

One might think that after their release ex-prisoners would never have wanted to see the inside of a mine or a fellow prisoner again. Undoubtedly many did return to the Black Belt or leave the region. But many also remained. And, if Bryant is to be believed, they settled among each other. Why?

To African Americans, a group that had known the humiliation of slavery, forced labor in postbellum prison mines was especially mortifying. Ezekiel Archey addressed this issue when he explained to R. H. Dawson why more ex-prisoners did not come forward to complain about their ill treatment. To do so would have drawn unwanted attention to their pasts. "If he tells a man the man will take the advantage of him in company and tell the ladies that [he] have bin a convict & is marked from the lash. Have worked when he was not able, have looked Death in the face, have worked hungry, thirsty, half-clothed & sore." [13] Archey, and many other prisoners, thought highly of their ability to endure unthinkable hardship. But black prisoners also felt ashamed. In an age that had supposedly abolished slavery, they had been whipped and abused by whites. They feared the ridicule of black women and their communities. They dreaded being known as free men turned back into slaves.

In order to maintain the dignity that freedom warranted, an appearance they associated with manliness, the black community demanded silence or even denial from ex-prisoners. "We all know evry body dislikes a convict," Archey wrote. "After a man once get Free he know or think evry body look on him as an out cast and points that finger of scorn at him so he wished evry man near him to keep silent. So he will not tell any body of the pass." [14] Prison officials sometimes asserted that black prisoners felt no disgrace about their imprisonment, and that this lack of shame seriously impeded reform. [15] But they were wrong. Ex-prisoners felt pain and embarrassment over the indignities of their prison ordeal. By becoming miners and settling in Pratt City, however, they hoped to gain a new status as free workers. And living among former prisoners in a community like that described by Bryant would have ensured privacy as well as support.

Pratt City had a reputation as a rough mining community, but to many black Alabamians, Pratt City also represented black accomplishments. The "Colored Chaplain's Report" from the Pratt mines in 1896 attests to this fact. Rev. L. J. Washington preached sermons, distributed literature, and visited sick convicts at the prison hospital. He wrote of their desire for Bibles and hymnbooks and of his attempt to reach prisoners through personal contact. He felt that his efforts achieved some good. "I am glad to say that I meet them often after they have come out of the prison, and many of them are at work and say they never intend to be prisoners again." Black citizens throughout the state, including Booker T. Washington, expressed positive images of Pratt City during the 1890s. In Pratt City, Washington's students from Tuskegee worked in coal mines and earned $45 to $50 a month. [16]

Pratt City offered monetary and spiritual riches. Between 1895 and 1897 Reverend Mixon recorded in his diary meetings with reform-minded and educated black women in Pratt City; he also noticed a fair number of black churchgoers. The churches in Pratt City were "well attended"; he noted that "they treated me grandly." In 1897 he called Birmingham "one of the greatest cities in the union," and he felt awed to witness "pay-day" in Pratt City, "the greatest mines in the United States." Mixon proudly noted that the AME church in Pratt City had 112 members. "We have 9 churches in and around B'ham," Reverend Mixon recorded, and "4 missions." In his travels to Pratt City and Birmingham in 1897, Mixon thrilled to the preaching of the African-American bishop Henry McNeal Turner: "His lion-like get up ness and rough disposition acquaint a man with him without words. He walks about 10 miles Every time he lectures or preach." [17] Mixon found Pratt City and the black workers within it inspiring, not degrading.

Besides noting the building of a new church, the vigor of the mines, and the pleasantries of his companions, Reverend Mixon also described black "community regulation" in action. In May 1897 he wrote about a dispute raging within a Pratt City congregation. Mrs. Mettie Meelows's character had been investigated; she was found guilty and expelled from her church. "She has many friends. Brockett has many friends—hence the great noise. . . . Rev. JNO Goodloe and Rev. WB Johnson present. Church almost full." Churches in Pratt City dealt with potentially divisive differences of opinion and runaway personalities much like the black churches during Reconstruction in the Black Belt. Whatever prompted the disciplinary action against Mrs. Meelows, her dismissal illustrates the quiet growth and influence of black institutions in the area fueled by paychecks drawn from coal mines.

In addition to its churches, political activism, and large working-class population, Pratt City also was identified with labor militancy. According to Daniel Letwin, Pratt City was "the heart of miners' unionism" during the 1890s and the "bellwether of trends in the district."[18] In the summer of 1890 it hosted the first meeting of the Birmingham branch of the United Mine Workers of America. Fifty-one white and twenty-one black delegates attended and adopted the UMW's national wage scale. TCI refused their offer of negotiations, but instead of striking, the miners waited until the fall to call for a wage increase. When refused, nearly 6,000 men went out on strike in November. According to Letwin, this was the largest strike the TCI-owned coalfields had yet experienced.[19]

Convict labor thwarted the strikers. In December 1890 the superintendent of the Shaft mine, P. J. Rogers, reported to Dawson that "there is some talk of the miners trying to extricate the convicts so as to carry their point . . . if they should attempt such a thing, I will give them a warm reception."[20] The inspectors agreed that the state should do what it could to help TCI during the strike, even if that meant moving prisoners out of the designated prison mines and into the mines formerly worked by free miners. "These strikers do not deserve the protection of the state," wrote A. T. Henley, "and my judgment is that the company ought to be allowed to use the convict as may be best suited to their interests."[21] (It is interesting to note that these threats against Pratt occurred one year before Tennessee miners succeeded in temporarily removing prisoners from their coal mines in 1891.)[22] Besides using convict labor, coal operators boldly brought in black strikebreakers. The strategy worked. One month later the strike ended, and miners went back to work.[23]

For the next few years, the dormant labor movement did little to challenge Sloss or TCI. But the panic of 1893 hit the mineral district hard, and miners began to organize in anticipation of reductions in their wages. They formed a new organization, the United Mine Workers of Alabama.[24] According to Letwin, black and white miners held separate meetings and councils, but "union leaders urged white and black miners to reject the color line."[25] In the spring of 1894, the union voted down a proposal for a drastic wage cut. The United Mine Workers of Alabama declared a work stoppage that eventually spread throughout the entire Birmingham district. By the end of April 1894, 9,000 black and white miners were out on strike.

In Pratt City 2,000 black and white strikers demonstrated their solidarity by organizing a parade to Birmingham.[26] When black and white miners socialized at J. H. Wilson's saloon in Pratt City in the middle of the 1894 strike, they spoke with "TNV," an anonymous Pinkerton agent hired by the governor of Alabama. TNV toured the mines, bars, and streets of Pratt City in order to gain information on the likelihood of violence among the strikers. He visited Wilson's saloon and struck up a conversation with some striking black miners. He reported: "There are a great many negro strikers living at Pratt City and most of them stand by the white strikers and will not go to work for 35 cents per ton for mining coal. While in Wilson's saloon I met [several white miners with families.] . . . I also met several negro strikers, but did not hear any of them make any threats. . . . My opinion is the strikers at Pratt City are too mixed up, Scotch, Irish, Welch, German, and Americans, and they will not trust one another. This is what the negro miners told me in Wilson's saloon." [27] Although the use of "Negro strike-breakers" and convict labor effectively undermined the 1894 strike, black and white miners in Pratt City both saw the need for class unity and practiced interracial cooperation. [28]

Of course, Pratt City was not the only place where black and white miners cooperated. In June 1894 strikers of both races became considerably worked up when TCI used black strikebreakers at the No. 4 slope. But, as Daniel Letwin has shown, the enmity demonstrated toward these men had more to do with their defiance of the strike than with their race. The black strikebreakers were "green" men brought in from Tennessee, not local miners from the area. Agent TNV reported that among the striking black miners at the No. 4 slope, "there has been no break in their ranks at all." Another Pinkerton agent noted that black miners were "well posted on all the movements of the strikers." Although "a great many of them had to beg for something to eat, they would not work for less than 45 cents a ton for mining coal." [29] Despite such sacrifice, these strikes failed. The miners' defeat testified to the power of TCI, the state, and convict labor, not to disunity within their own ranks. [30] The combination of a seasonal market for coal (an element that undermined the strikes of miners everywhere), company intransigence, convict labor, and the force brought to bear by the state made the struggles of Alabama miners during this period especially bitter.

Although blacks joined unions with whites, they still suffered racial discrimination. Historians such as Herbert Gutman, Herbert Hill, Paul Worthman, and Daniel Letwin have tried to unravel this paradox. [31] Their studies have challenged the stereotypical image of black workers as strike-breakers uninterested in unions or working-class alliances. Throughout the late nineteenth and early twentieth century, black miners belonged to the Knights of Labor, the United Mine Workers of Alabama, and the American Mine Workers Union. Most black miners enthusiastically supported the era's numerous strikes, regardless of their official union affiliation. [32] Nevertheless, free black miners did suffer racial discrimination, both on and off the job. According to Worthman, most of the 6,000 black coal miners in the region "were employed as sub-contractors or as laborers by white and occasionally black miners. This subcontracting system divided miners and mine laborers along occupational as well as racial lines." [33]

Although free miners disliked the system of convict labor intensely, it is unclear if they directed those feelings toward ex-prisoners who joined their ranks. As miners, the two groups shared many things. Both, for example, had to conquer fear. Earl Brown remembered the first day he went down into a coal mine in 1939 with two seasoned miners, much in the same way a new prisoner would have been sent down in the late nineteenth century. "Never will forget it," he said. The two older men put him to work on a pillar of coal in a room. They worked on a wall until it fell, and when it did, Earl Brown ran. It was "the awfullest sound I'd ever heard in my life and I just took off and went to running," he recalled. "If they hadn't caught me, I guess I'd have run myself to death. . . . And I would have quit the mine if it had not been for a mine foreman." That foreman put him at easier, so-called green work that he probably did for less than one dollar a day.[34] New prisoners were undoubtedly as frightened as Brown. Although some may have been put to work as "deadheads" temporarily, fear alone would never have excused an able-bodied man from work underground.

Prison schooled men in the various ways that coal companies cheated workers. Like free miners, convicts knew the importance of receiving credit for the entire tonnage of coal mined. Coal companies used false scales and underweighed coal as it came out of the mine. A handwritten scrawled letter from free miners in Walker County, sent to Governor Seay on the eve of the 1890 strikes, gets right to the point. "We would like to know," the miners wrote, "if there is standard weights in this State that we can get to have those scales tested. . . . the coal we dig is weigh[ed] on scales that is not correct."[35] Free miners of the period fought with mineowners over who was to hold the position of checker, the man at the exit who credited each miner with the coal he mined as it rolled out.[36] In 1894 miners were willing to take a pay cut if TCI agreed that they could choose their own check-weighman on the tipple and if TCI weighed all coal before it was dumped. TCI refused both conditions.[37]

Convict miners also complained about the size of the tramcars they were forced to use, and they resented the power of the company to determine if their cars were "scant." If the guard at the tipple, or entrance, of the mine decided that a car was scant or holding too much "slack" or rock, then the prisoner would be whipped. Prisoners contended these arbitrary decisions led to unfair punishment and overwork. They complained so often that in 1894 the state mine inspectors and convict inspectors launched a joint investigation into the practice of "forfeiting scant cars" and whether TCI's new tramcars held more than the allotted ton.[38] Until the inquiry was completed, the Board of Inspectors directed that no prisoner be whipped for "failure to get task." This inquiry had important implications for both the prisoners and the company. In 1894 over 1,000 men worked at the Shaft and the Slope, and the new tramcars, if slightly larger, would make a significant difference in daily output. Eventually the committee found in favor of TCI. The power to determine punishment and scant cars reverted back to the company.

Despite the differences between free miners and prison miners, both groups shared similar worries. Both prisoners and free miners complained about unsafe conditions, being forced to remain in the mine after their work for the day was accomplished, being paid in scrip instead of cash, and the lack of tramcars. When ex-prisoners went to work as free miners, they confronted not only the same company but also many of the same working conditions that they had faced as prisoners.

The major difference between the two groups lay in their respective abilities to protest and organize against their oppression. Earl Brown could run and not be punished, but a prisoner who ran or refused to work was beaten. During the spate of arson and escapes in the early 1890s, Inspector Dawson grimly noted, "Punishment by whipping seems not to deter them and I suggest that the Inspectors adopt some other mode of punishment." Dark cells, starvation, and handcuffing to the side of a wall were considered. Such punishments had their drawbacks, however, for "the contractor is deprived of the labor of the convict." Inspector Lee suggested a punishment popular in the military: hanging by the thumbs.[39] Free miners could retaliate by organizing, striking, and forming militia units of their own. When prisoners resisted labor demands through arson, escape, insubordination, or striking, they faced swift physical punishment, even torture.

Experiences in the prison mines educated men not only in mining but also in power relations. Ex-prisoners, cheated and mistreated by the mining companies while in prison, brought their hard-earned wisdom with them to the free mines. Prisoners had gone on strike within the prison mines and complained about unsafe conditions. The demands of free laborers included respect, decent pay per tonnage, the right to choose personnel, fair weights, and plenty of tramcars—very similar to the complaints prison miners had.

By 1896 the number of state convicts had increased to 1,710. And the urban area of Jefferson County, with 249, had by far the largest number of both state and county convicts. The total number of county convicts had fallen to 745, with the largest number, 181, convicted in Jefferson County.[40] If more young men from Jefferson County were being imprisoned, these were likely to be youths who grew up in cities or recent arrivals, with minimal schooling and perhaps none of the history of community solidarity and political experience the previous generation had when they entered prison. Two criminal populations were overlapping in Pratt City and in Jefferson County. Freedom's first generation was giving way to a more youthful, urban population with very new and much lower expectations of southern society.

Newspapers of the time traduced ex-prisoners by blaming them for the increased crime in Birmingham.[41] It is true that Birmingham had an enormous prison population. Between 1888 and 1908 three persons out of every ten—30 percent of the population each year—were arrested. Newspapers attributed the city's murders, drunken sprees, and robberies to the plethora of mining camps, the high number of black migrants, and the growing presence of ex-prisoners within the city. How does the image of ex-prisoners as hardworking, churchgoing residents of Pratt City jibe with the image of the ex-prisoner as an unreformed criminal, who, when released, plied his trade?

Statistics that seem to indicate widespread criminal activity in Birmingham, however, are slightly deceiving. They record the numbers of people arrested, not convicted. Those arrests were undoubtedly spurred on by the fee system—that is, the means by which judges, clerks, and sheriffs were paid for their work. Instead of salaries, the law enforcement officers of Jefferson County, such as the sheriff, the clerk of court, and the justices of the peace, received individual fees for arrests made, legal notices served, and court cases held. The sheriff, for example, received $4 or $5 in fees for every arrest made in the county.[42] The money for these fees came from Jefferson County's Fine and Forfeiture Fund, which contained the revenue received from leasing county prisoners to the coal mines. The system in Jefferson County worked as it did in counties throughout the state: when a man or woman was convicted in a county court, the judge charged the defendant with all court costs, including the money paid to witnesses, officers, and lawyers. If the prisoner could not pay these costs in cash, an amount ranging from $50 to $75, he or she was sentenced to extra days in prison, at a rate of thirty cents a day, to pay the fees. These extra days to pay for court costs were not to exceed eight months; nevertheless, time spent to pay for fees often exceeded the sentence given for the actual offense. The fee system positively encouraged arrests and convictions for petty crimes in the city, especially drinking, loitering, and gambling, particularly if those participating in these activities had jobs and thus cash to pay the required fees.

The fee system gave sheriffs many opportunities to profit from the misfortunes of prisoners. For example, as prisoners toiled away, contractors paid monthly fees into the county's Fine and Forfeiture Fund. Because sheriffs and witnesses could not immediately claim full payment for their services, they were paid in scrip that they redeemed in the future. But instead of waiting to cash in their scrip, they often sold it to buyers around the courthouse who purchased it for twenty-five to sixty cents on the dollar. This trade in the future of a county's Fine and Forfeiture Fund kept many in the business of speculating when arrests, and thus the fund, would rise. Sheriffs often kept their scrip for years and cashed it in when they needed money.[43]

In addition to profiting from fees and scrip, sheriffs also skimmed money from the state fund set aside to feed prisoners awaiting trial. By law, sheriffs were given thirty cents per prisoner per day. However, they fed prisoners only fatback and cornmeal mush and pocketed the difference. In 1891 it cost the state $18,000 a year to feed the prisoners in Jefferson County. And yet, according to George L. Thomas of the commissioner's court, "two thirds of this is clear profit to the Sheriff." He went on to delineate the reasons behind the waste and high costs. There was, he wrote, "too great a temptation to sheriffs to imprison men for frivolous causes and keep them in prison as long as possible." Williams recommended reducing the payment for feeding county prisoners from thirty to twenty cents a day. The diet of bread, meat, and peas would allow this amount to "still give them [sheriffs] a good profit and save the state treasury a large sum of money annually—$6,000 from Jefferson County alone."[44] Williams stressed the financial rewards of reform over the moral ones, but not a single piece of reform legislation regarding county convicts passed the Alabama legislature until 1916. Even the Commissioners Court of Jefferson County could not break the power of sheriffs.

Sheriffs and deputies in Jefferson County gained an infamous reputation for raiding crap games and gambling houses, where they could arrest scores of workingmen at once. Often sheriffs hired black "spotters" to spy out crap games; this job paid fifty cents for every man the deputies arrested. Decoys led sheriffs to small mining camps where black workers, engaged at craps or games of dice on Sundays, would be hauled into court and fined $25 or $50.[45] Sometimes coal companies paid "protection money" to the local constable to ensure that the black men who worked for them would be able to gamble in peace. Such payoffs precluded arrests and thus, according to TCI officials, kept the men from becoming "demoralized."[46] Still, the average black coal worker in Birmingham was at the mercy of the local sheriffs. By the turn of the century, arrests filled the labor and monetary needs of the local sheriffs and city officials rather than the needs of TCI. As one contemporary critic put it, "Unless people are abnormally criminal in this county . . . something in the system must bring persons to court who would be arrested nowhere else."[47]

Ironically, TCI came to resent the random arrests of black men in Birmingham because they inconvenienced its workforce and created a labor shortage. The Sheriff Department's arbitrary arrests and financial fraud began to irritate the company. In 1912 TCI's chief attorney, Walker Percy, lambasted Jefferson County officials: "When the newspapers announce that the ever alert Sheriff and his trusted deputies rounded up some twenty or thirty negroes in the woods, wounded two or three and landed the balance in the county jail for crap shooting, does anybody believe that the peace of the county is being conserved, or does every man know that the syndicate is trying to reimburse itself for its campaign expenditures?"[48] By assiduously arresting black citizens for gambling, vagrancy, and drinking, the sheriff and his ring racked up nearly $50,000 every year in fees.

Despite this reputation of criminality, black miners regulated their behavior informally, rather than relying on the law. Ideas about proper behavior persisted but changed with new circumstances of industrialization. Black churches, such as those observed by Mixon, tried to enforce law-abiding behavior by sanctioning unacceptable behavior. For example, a physician at a black mining camp in Birmingham in 1907 commented on how the black fraternal organizations and their female adjuncts disciplined their members. "Members of these orders," he wrote, "are more certain to be punished for disorderly and criminal conduct by their lodges than by the State authorities." He added that "the female departments are noted for . . . the instruction of the girls which has for its object the prevention of further amalgamation of the races thru the young negro women."[49] Mining camps were notorious for gambling, drinking, and other forms of rowdiness. Yet cultural forms of organization and community discipline had been adapted to suit the new environment of life in coal-mining communities.

Arrests can indicate high levels of both crime and state repression. In Jefferson County in the late nineteenth century, however, arrests paid the salaries of its deputies and sheriffs and provided a captive workforce to clean its streets, perform municipal tasks, and work coal mines. White citizens in Birmingham grew accustomed to sheriffs, counties, and businesses turning a profit on black prison labor; they grew used to seeing men in chains. "City" convicts, men convicted of offenses so trivial that their fine amounted to a single dollar, could spend up to forty or fifty days in leg-irons cleaning the city streets. Birmingham depended on local prisoners for their labor; 140 were kept at work year-round cleaning the city's residential and business districts at a fraction of the cost of free labor. Boys of sixteen and elderly men wore leg-irons and shackles while they worked and slept. Were they truly more dangerous than the convicts in the coal mines, who worked without chains and lived in barracks with flush toilets, a company store, and schoolrooms?[50]

Even men and women who were accused of crimes but not convicted suffered worse housing conditions than the prisoners at work in the mines, for the city jail in Birmingham was unsanitary, overcrowded, vermin-ridden, and poorly ventilated. All those awaiting trial festered in a single central cell block where a "bare strap iron bed" was preferred over filthy blankets.[51] In 1912 Shelby Harrison, the author of a widely cited exposé of the Jefferson County jails, asserted that young boys sent to jail or the mines for trivial offenses often became the victims of sexual abuse.[52] After a month of such conditions, prisoners were in no shape to begin any physical labor, let alone mine coal.

It is questionable to conclude that the presence of prisons necessarily led to exorbitant criminal behavior in Birmingham. One final piece of evidence supports the conclusion that the fee system caused arrests, and thus crime statistics, to burgeon. After a massive political campaign leading to changes in Alabama's constitution, the fee system in Jefferson County was finally abolished in 1919—and the number of county prisoners dropped dramatically. Prisoners still had to work out their court costs, but sheriffs and deputies received flat salaries. In the 1890s Jefferson County had several hundred men imprisoned, but after 1919 the number of county prisoners dwindled to less than a hundred.[53]

Epilogue

The convict-leasing system no longer exists, but it hardly remains a comfortable relic of the past. In 1995 the state of Alabama decided to resurrect the chain gang on its public roads. The spectacle of hundreds of prisoners, shackled in leg chains, working outside in twelve-hour shifts, caused motorists to stop and schoolchildren to gawk. International media attention and complaints from the American Civil Liberties Union and the Southern Poverty Law Center made Alabama's prison practices once again notorious. For over a year, however, Alabama authorities remained unmoved. Officials claimed that chained prisoners saved money (because they required fewer guards) and that public humiliation led to deterrence. Not surprisingly, prisoners disagreed. "They wouldn't allow you to chain five dogs together like this," said one. "We're moving backwards, not forwards."[1] Thanks to a court ruling and a public backlash against the idea of chaining women prisoners, Alabama was finally forced to stop the practice.[2]

Alabama's temporary resurrection of the chain gang notwithstanding, contemporary prisons and the nineteenth-century lease share other even more troubling similarities. Prisoners are no longer leased out, but private companies still see convicts as a source of profit. The profit motive, the recent sharp increase in the prison population, and the disproportionate number of incarcerated African Americans link current practice to the past. If the United States is truly concerned that barbaric prison conditions remain in the past, it needs to examine how these three factors shape and corrupt prison operations today.

Burgeoning prison construction is a prime example of how the profit motive has become central to modern corrections. Today the United States incarcerates 2 million prisoners, the largest prison population in the world.[3] Simply to build enough facilities to warehouse these men and women requires an unprecedented expenditure of state, federal, and public funds. In order to meet this extraordinary need for secure, labor-efficient prisons, governments look to the private sector to provide everything from the construction and design of prison buildings to electric fences and restraints. The reasons are clear: undoubtedly, private firms build prisons more quickly and cheaply than construction supervised by government can be completed.[4] Private contractors lobby states hard for their prison business, and the financial stakes are high. Texas alone spent over $2 billion on prison construction in the early 1990s, and other states, such as California, need to build at least one prison a year merely to keep their overflowing prisons at double capacity. Not only contractors benefit. Bond issues to finance new prisons produce interest for investors, and new prisons bring fresh jobs into economically depressed communities.[5]

Usually, only the demands of war caused such vast sums to flow from public coffers into private hands with such little protest. During the Cold War and the atomic age, American military spending reached unprecedented heights. But in 1961 departing President Eisenhower warned the nation not to let its political decisions be dictated by the self-interest of the growing "military industrial complex." Even if the nation wished to retreat from spending millions on defense, Eisenhower implied that "special interests" would not let it eschew that commitment. The overwhelming growth of the prison population in the United States has caused the development of another similar complex. According to journalist Eric Schlosser, "The prison industrial complex is not a conspiracy, guiding criminal justice policy behind closed doors. It is a confluence of special interests that has given prison construction in the United States a seemingly unstoppable momentum."[6] It may be alarmist to compare the mammoth political influence of defense contractors with the much smaller prison industry. And yet, constructing prisons for thousands of new prisoners fulfills the overlapping needs of politicians, industry, and the public. A growing prison population is said to prove that crime is under control; it also provides profits for burgeoning sectors of the economy.

Private prison companies have a financial stake in the rising numbers of incarcerated men and women. In the 1980s they promoted their services to state legislatures with claims of being cheaper than state-run institutions. Today twenty-seven states use private prisons to house approximately 90,000 illegal aliens, minimum-security inmates, and felons from overflowing state prisons. Two giants dominate the private prison industry: the Wackenhut Corporation and the Corrections Corporation of America

(CCA), which is the nation's largest private prison company. Wackenhut, based in Florida, operates in thirteen states and seven foreign countries. CCA is a major corporation; its shares are publicly traded on the New York Stock Exchange, and over the last ten years, its returns have consistently performed in the top 20 percent of the stock market.[7]

CCA was cofounded in 1983 by Thomas Beasley, former chairman of the Tennessee Republican party, and Dr. R. Crantz, a Nashville businessman. The corporation made headlines in 1985 when it proposed to buy Tennessee's prison population for $250 million. It claimed that Tennessee would save millions of dollars if it would only place its prisoners in private hands. Governor Lamar Alexander supported the idea, but the Tennessee legislature narrowly defeated the proposal. Despite this setback, over the next ten years CCA became the sixth largest prison system in the United States. It currently controls over 40,000 inmates.[8]

Unlike the Tennessee Coal and Iron Company and the Sloss Iron and Steel Company, CCA does not want prisoners for their labor. Instead of paying the state, as did TCI and Sloss, the state pays CCA. Despite this salient difference, however, Alabama's nineteenth-century lease and today's private prisons have much in common. In both cases the main priority was and is profit.

In the late nineteenth century, counties had an economic stake in arrests. So do today's private prisons. The economics of private prisons are similar to the hotel industry: the longer an inmate stays, the more lucrative the business. To remain profitable, companies like CCA need to keep their facilities full. Empty beds are not cost-effective. When local supplies of men and women prisoners run short, private prison corporations turn to "bed brokers," middlemen who recruit prisoners from outside the state. Bed brokers search for prisons with available beds for the right price; in exchange, they earn a commission of $2.50 to $5.50 per man-day. (Fewer available beds allow them to charge more.) Counties also skim off a fee of $1.50 a night for each prisoner who enters a private prison in their locale. When private prisons in Texas had overbuilt, bed brokers brought in thousands of out-of-state prisoners. In 1996 the Newton County Correctional Center, located in the small town of Newton, Texas, became the state of Hawaii's third largest prison.[9]

In the late nineteenth century, coal companies wished to keep their skilled prison laborers for as long as they could, leading to denials of "short time." Today, a slightly different economic incentive can lead to similar consequences. CCA is paid per prisoner. If the supply dries up, or too many are released too early, their profits are affected. CCA guards can discipline prisoners for minor infractions and place them in segregation, or "seg." Such prisoners lose their credit for "good time" and an early release; they may even have thirty days added on to their sentences. This economic incentive gives guards an additional reason to dole out disciplinary action and prolong prison sentences. Longer prison terms mean greater profits, but the larger point is that the profit motive promotes the expansion of imprisonment.[10]

Because of the expense involved, TCI was reluctant to ensure the minimum safety of prisoners. Faulty elevators, lack of tramcars, and inadequate treatment for wounds were the result of racist indifference as well as cost-cutting. Private prisons of today also skimp on facilities, staff, and safety and put the public at risk. Critics point to the poor food and lack of rehabilitative facilities at private prisons. A state judge in New Orleans recently removed several juveniles from a Wackenhut prison after finding they had been brutalized by guards and deprived of shoes, blankets, education, and food.[11]

Sloss and TCI commonly worked prisoners over and above their quotas. Private prison companies of today have been accused of illegally forcing inmates to perform a variety of profitable jobs. In Kentucky the U.S. Corrections Corporation (later taken over by CCA) used prisoners to renovate employees' churches, businesses, a country club, and a private school. Eventually, the chairman of U.S. Corrections pleaded guilty to fraud, admitting that he paid $200,000 to a corrections official in Kentucky who in return funneled prisoners to U.S. Corrections.[12]

As this case shows, cozy relationships between public officials and companies that benefit from prisoners are hardly a distant remnant of the New South. One aspect of the lease universally recognized was its corruption. "Penitentiary Rings" assured that prison laborers ended up in the hands of the most favored bidders. John Hollis Bankhead's relationship with TCI serves as one of the most flagrant examples of such unethical dealings. Yet today, monetary relationships between prison companies and those involved in federal and state government are both more pervasive and widely accepted. The Wackenhut Corporation, for example, routinely hires former top-level federal corrections employees, the most prominent being the former head of the Federal Bureau of Prisons.[13] Similarly, the Bobby Ross Group, a private prison with headquarters in Austin, Texas, paid an inspector from the Texas Commission on Jail Standards $42,000 a year to act as a consultant. That same inspector gave one of Ross's prisons "the highest possible rating." Bobby Ross, a former Texas sheriff, also has employed William Sessions, former director of the FBI, as a special adviser to the company.[14] Such ties to government help private prisons obtain the inmates they need.

Even though most prisons remain in public hands, many private companies still benefit from prison labor in the United States. Convicts are paid subminimum wages to make shirts, office chairs, and computer circuit boards and to "telemarket" for AT&T. Private industry is absolved from paying health care, sick pay, or other benefits to this captive labor force. Free labor protests against this unfair competition, as did Alabama miners. Sometimes they succeed, but companies still have the right to lay off free workers and shift those jobs to prisons, where they pay one-tenth the wages and none of the benefits.[15]

Convicts in U.S. prisons today share other characteristics with Alabama prisoners of the late nineteenth century. In Alabama county convicts included the disabled, juveniles, and the mentally ill. And in Jefferson County in particular, the "fee factor" led to the imprisonment of people who in other cities never would have been incarcerated. Similarly, the United States today imprisons people who in other societies would be treated for drug addiction, not arrested. Politicians, both liberal and conservative, have seized on the crime issue to gain votes, and a public unwilling to be taxed more for schools or health care seems resigned to spending billions on incarceration. Unquestionably, sex offenders, murderers, and armed robbers comprise a large part of the today's prison population. But in 1995 less than a third of people entering state prisons had been convicted of a violent crime. Mandatory sentences for drug offenses and other "get tough" measures have led to the incarceration of drug addicts, parole violators, and those convicted of nonviolent crimes. In the United States, when politicians look to solve social ills, the answer is almost always prison. In the last twenty years, states and the federal government have increased the prison population by imposing mandatory prison sentences, abolishing parole, and using the death penalty more often.[16]

One could argue that today's prisons are even more highly commodified than was the lease. Currently, some prisoners are put to work building their own bunks and cells, just as Alabama prisoners grew their own food and constructed prison brickyards. But at least in Alabama the state paid for the cost of the letters they wrote. Today, private phone companies earn over a billion dollars a year from inmate calls. MCI has cornered the market on prisoner communications in California; it installed its services at no charge to the state but adds a $3 surcharge to every call made by a prisoner.[17]

In late nineteenth-century Alabama, African Americans comprised over 95 percent of county prisoners and 85 percent of state convicts. Today poor black prisoners are still grossly overrepresented in prison; in every section of the country, African Americans are far more likely than whites to be arrested and imprisoned. In 1926 African Americans comprised 23 percent of the state prison population. Today they make up nearly half of all prisoners despite still comprising only 12 percent of the population. As a result of their incarceration, a disproportionately high number of black males are also kept from voting.[18] Blacks are more likely than whites to become prisoners for similar acts, especially those involving illegal drugs. As in the late nineteenth century, social scientists today are engaged in a fierce debate on the relationship between race and crime. One side argues that more blacks are in prison because "blacks commit a disproportionate number of imprisonable crimes." Another side, however, questions whether arrests alone are an accurate measure of criminal behavior. This latter view also emphasizes the effect of racism upon law enforcement as well as the relationship between unemployment, poverty, and imprisonment.[19] Regardless of the reasons behind their incarceration, the disproportionate number of African Americans in prison is undoubtedly the strongest parallel between the late nineteenth-century South and today.

Supporters of private prisons point to many factors that seem to favor the growing involvement of the private sector in incarceration. CCA is run by seasoned corrections professionals; its record is largely untarnished by systematic cases of inmate abuse or corruption. Furthermore, federal courts can and do intervene in prison operations, making systematic abuse vulnerable to correction.[20] Even those who acknowledge the advantages of private prisons such as CCA, however, point to the broader moral question: is it right for a private for-profit company to possess the authority to deprive individuals of their liberty and exercise coercion over them? Traditionally, with the important exception of the lease, this power has been exercised by the state in the name of the public good. Now, however, individuals wearing patches reading "Corrections Corporation of America" exercise that power. The question originally posed by the lease system still looms: does relinquishing public authority to private hands undermine the moral authority of the law?[21]

The modern developments of today's prison industry, particularly its emphasis on profit and its overrepresentation of black prisoners, makes the furor over Alabama's temporary reversion to low-weight chains in 1995 seem somehow misplaced. Although Alabama was singled out for this barbaric prison practice, the clanging of chains drummed out the larger issues of overcrowding, private profit, an industry that financially feeds on the growing number of prisoners, and the disproportionate number of African Americans in prison. These are issues that infect the nation, not just Alabama. Ironically, abolishing chains in Alabama prisons gave the nation a false sense of security. It made the public believe that certain practices from the past could never happen again. But the profit motive that spurred the convict-leasing system still thrives in our current prison system. In light of its past experiences with the lease, the nation needs to reexamine once again whether profiting from prisoners is ethical; whether a highly disproportionate number of African Americans in prison indicates deep social inequities; and whether prison, and the social control it disproportionately exercises over minorities, is worth its social cost.

Notes

ABBREVIATIONS

ADAH Alabama Department of Archives and History
BRFAL Records of the Assistant Commissioner of the State of Alabama, Bureau of Refugees, Freedmen, and Abandoned Lands, 1865–1870, Record Group 105, M809, National Archives
Justice Department Letters Letters received by the Department of Justice from the State of Alabama, 1871–1884, Record Group 60, M1356, National Archives
NYPL New York Public Library
TCI Tennessee Coal and Iron Company

INTRODUCTION

1. Herbert G. Gutman, "The Negro and the United Mine Workers of America: The Career and Letters of Richard L. Davis and Something of Their Meaning, 1890–1900," in *Work, Culture, and Society in Industrializing America* (1966; rept. New York, 1977), 121–208; Herbert Hill, "The Problem of Race in American Labor History," *Reviews in American History* 24 (1996): 189–208, and "Myth-Making as Labor History: Herbert Gutman and the United Mine Workers of America," *International Journal of Politics, Culture, and Society* 2 (Winter 1988): 132–200; Alex Lichtenstein, "Racial Conflict and Racial Solidarity in the Alabama Coal Strike of 1894: New Evidence for the Gutman-Hill Debate," *Labor History* 36:1 (Winter 1995): 63–76; Paul Worthman, "Black Workers and Labor Unions in Birmingham, Alabama, 1897–1904," ibid., 10:3 (Summer 1969): 375–407, and "Working Class Mobility in Birmingham, Alabama, 1880–1914," in *Anonymous Americans: Explorations in Nineteenth-Century Social History*, ed. Tamara Hareven (Englewood Cliffs, N.J., 1971), 172–213; Daniel Letwin, *The Challenge of Interracial Unionism: Alabama Coal Miners, 1878–1921* (Chapel Hill, N.C., 1998); Henry M. McKiven, *Iron and Steel: Class, Race, and Community in Birmingham, Alabama, 1875–1920* (Chapel Hill, N.C., 1995); Herbert R. Northrup, "The Negro and the United Mine Workers of America," *Southern Economic Journal* 9:1 (1942–43): 313–26.

2. U.S. Immigration Commission, *Immigrants in Industries: Bituminous Coal Mining in the South* 6 (Washington, D.C., 1911): 218; Alex Lichtenstein, "Through the Iron Gates of the Penitentiary: Convict Labor and Southern Coal," in *Race and Class in the American*

South Since 1890, ed. Rick Halpern and Melvyn Stokes (Oxford, 1994), 20–21; Mary Ellen Curtin, "Legacies of Struggle: Black Prisoners and the Convict Leasing System in Alabama, 1865–1900" (Ph.D. diss., Duke University, 1992).

3. For the amount paid by the TCI, see *Second Biennial Report of the Inspectors of Convicts to the Governor, from October 1, 1886, to September 30, 1888* (Montgomery, Ala., 1888), 2–3. For a copy of TCI's 1888 contract with the state outlining its terms, see *Report of the Joint Committee of the General Assembly Appointed to Examine into the Convict System of Alabama, Session of 1888–9* (Montgomery, Ala., 1889), 37–41. According to this contract, TCI paid $18.50 per month for a "first class man," $13.50 for a "second class man," $9 per month for a "third class man," and nothing for a "fourth class man."

4. In 1895 the average death rate over a five-month period at the Pratt prison mines, which held state prisoners, was eighty-six men per one thousand. At the Coalburg mines, which used county prisoners, the average was seventy men per thousand. In Georgia, which also worked convicts in coal mines, the death rate in 1892 was fifteen men per thousand ("Report of State Health Officer to the Governor on Coalburg," *First Biennial Report of the Board of Inspectors of Convicts to the Governor, from September 1, 1894, to August 31, 1896* [Montgomery, Ala., 1896], xvii–xxiv). For prison finances, see A. J. Going, *Bourbon Democracy in Alabama* (University, Ala., 1951), 179–81.

5. A. T. Henley to J. L. Dean, Aug. 9, 1891, attached to letter from A. T. Henley to Gov. Thomas G. Jones, Aug. 12, 1891, Papers of Governor Thomas G. Jones, box 27, folder C, ADAH. For the amount paid by TCI, see *Second Biennial Report of the Inspectors of Convicts, 1886–88,* 2–3.

6. Edward L. Ayers, *Vengeance and Justice: Crime and Punishment in the Nineteenth-Century American South* (New York, 1984), 295 n.57. Out of 904 county convicts "on hand" in 1886, only 34, or 3.3 percent, were white (*First Biennial Report of the Inspectors of Convicts to the Governor, from October 1, 1884, to October 1, 1886* [Montgomery, Ala., 1886]), 186–228; In 1870 whites represented less than one-quarter of all state prisoners. By the late 1880s they comprised approximately 15 percent of the penitentiary inmates (*Annual Report of the Inspectors of the Alabama Penitentiary, from October 1, 1869, to October 1, 1870* [Montgomery, Ala., 1870], 20; *Third Biennial Report of the Inspectors of Convicts to the Governor, from Oct. 1, 1888, to Sept. 30, 1890* [Montgomery, Ala., 1890], 198–220).

7. Dawson's comments are in the *Proceedings of the Annual Congress of the National Prison Association of the United States Held at Cincinnati, 1890* (Chicago, 1891), 210;

8. Testimony of Ezekiel Archey, in U.S. Congress, Senate Committee on Education and Labor, 49th Cong., 2d sess., *Testimony before the Committee to Investigate the Relations between Capital and Labor* (Washington, D.C., 1885), 4:434; U.S. Immigration Commission, *Immigrants in Industries: Bituminous Coal Mining in the South* 6:218; *Report of the Joint Committee of the General Assembly Appointed to Examine into the Convict System of Alabama, 1888–89,* 26; *First Biennial Report of the Inspectors of Convicts, 1884–86,* 21.

9. Armstead Robinson, "Plans Dat Comed from God: Institution Building and the Emergence of Black Leadership in Reconstruction Memphis," in *Toward a New South?: Studies in Post-Civil War Southern Communities,* ed. Orville Vernon Burton and Robert C. McMath Jr. (Westport, Conn., 1982), 71–102, quote on 72–73. See also Robinson, "Beyond the Realm of Social Consensus: New Meanings of Reconstruction for American History," *Journal of American History* 68:2 (Sept. 1981): 276–97. For their approach to working-class history, see the interviews with E. P. Thompson and Herbert Gutman in *Visions of History,* ed. MARHO (New York, 1983), 27–46, 186–216.

10. Tera Hunter, *"To 'Joy My Freedom": Southern Black Women's Lives and Labors after the*

Civil War (Cambridge, Mass., 1997); Peter Rachleff, *Black Labor in Richmond, 1865–1890* (1984; rept. Urbana, Ill., 1989); Julie Saville, *The Work of Reconstruction: From Slave to Wage Laborer in South Carolina, 1860–1870* (Cambridge, Eng., 1994).

11. C. Vann Woodward, *Origins of the New South, 1877–1913* (Baton Rouge, La., 1951), 215. For more recent treatments of southern prisons, see David Oshinsky, *Worse than Slavery: Parchman Farm and the Ordeal of Jim Crow Justice* (New York, 1996); Milfred C. Fierce, *Slavery Revisited: Blacks and the Southern Convict Lease System, 1865–1933* (Brooklyn, 1994); Matthew J. Mancini, *One Dies, Get Another: Convict Leasing in the American South, 1866–1928* (Columbia, S.C., 1996); Karin A. Shapiro, *A New South Rebellion: The Battle against Convict Labor in the Tennessee Coalfields, 1871–1896* (Chapel Hill, N.C., 1998); Mark Carleton, *Politics and Punishment: The History of the Louisiana State Penal System* (Baton Rouge, La., 1971); Donald R. Walker, *Penology for Profit: A History of the Texas Prison System, 1867–1912* (College Station, Tex., 1988); Vernon Lane Wharton, *The Negro in Mississippi, 1865–1890* (1947; rept. New York, 1965), chap. 16; A. J. Going, *Bourbon Democracy in Alabama, 1874–1890* (University, Ala., 1951), chap. 11; Robert David Ward and William Warren Rogers, *Convicts, Coal, and the Banner Mine Tragedy* (Tuscaloosa, Ala., 1987); Robert Perkinson, "'Between the Worst of the Past and the Worst of the Future': Reconsidering Convict Leasing in the South," *Radical History Review* 71 (Spring 1998): 207–16; Christopher R. Adamson, "Punishment after Slavery: Southern State Penal Systems, 1865–1890," *Social Problems* 30:5 (June 1983): 555–69, and "Toward a Marxian Penology: Captive Criminal Populations as Economic Threats and Resources," ibid., 31:4 (April 1984): 435–58; Martha Myers, *Race, Labor, and Punishment in the New South* (Columbus, Ohio, 1998); Blake McKelvey, *American Prisons: A History of Good Intentions* (Montclair, N.J., 1977).

12. Alex Lichtenstein, *Twice the Work of Free Labor: The Political Economy of Convict Labor in the New South* (London, 1996), xvii.

13. For recent work on women in nineteenth-century prisons, see Anne M. Butler, "Still in Chains: Black Women in Western Prisons," in *"We Specialize in the Wholly Impossible": A Reader in Black Women's History*, ed. Darlene Clark Hine, Wilma King, and Linda Reed (Brooklyn, N.Y., 1995), 321–35, and *Gendered Justice in the American West: Women Prisoners in Men's Penitentiaries* (Urbana, Ill., 1997); Nicole Hahn Rafter, *Partial Justice: Women, Prisons, and Social Control* (New Brunswick, N.J., 1990).

14. Going, *Bourbon Democracy in Alabama*, 174–75.

15. Two exceptions are Ayers, *Vengeance and Justice*, and Butler, *Gendered Justice in the American West*.

16. Ayers, *Vengeance and Justice*, 295 n.57.

17. John B. Myers, "The Freedmen and the Law in Post-Bellum Alabama, 1865–67," *Alabama Review* 23 (Jan. 1970): 56–69; Theodore Brantner Wilson, *The Black Codes* (University, Ala., 1965), 76–77.

18. *Mobile Daily Advertiser and Register*, Jan. 3, 1866, *Montgomery Daily Mail*, Oct. 13, 1866, quoted in Myers, "The Freedmen and the Law," 65; Sam S. Gardner to Col. Cadle, Nov. 1, 1865, C. H. Buckley, Ass't Supt. Freedmen, to Captain Charles Scott, Sept. 6, 1865, Letters Received, 1865 A-J, reel 5, BRFAL.

19. The ordinance "prohibits market men from selling so much as an egg before they have reached the market and the market bell has rung" (John T. Trowbridge, *The South: A Tour of Its Battlefields and Ruined Cities* [Hartford, 1866], 435–36; "Laws in Relation to Freedmen" and "An Act concerning Vagrants and Vagrancy," sections 1–7 approved Dec. 15, 1865, reprinted in *Letter of the Secretary of War, Communicating in Compliance with a Resolution of the Senate of December 17, 1866, Reports of the Assistant Commissioners*

of Freedmen and a Synopsis of Laws respecting Persons of Color in the Late Slave States, 39th Cong., 2d sess., Senate Exec. Doc. 6, 170–71).

20. Trowbridge, *South,* 435–36. Alabama was the only state in the nation with this dual state and county system whereby counties also profited from prison labor. See U.S. Department of the Interior, Secretary of the Interior, *Report of the Commissioner of Labor, 2d Report* (Washington, D.C., 1887).

21. W. E. B. Du Bois, "The Spawn of Slavery: The Convict Lease System in the South," *Writings by W. E. B. Du Bois in Periodicals Edited by Others,* ed. Herbert Aptheker, vol. 1, *1891–1909* (Millwood, N.Y., 1982), 111.

22. Howard Rabinowitz, "Epilogue: Race Relations and Social Control," in *Race Relations in the Urban South, 1865–1890* (Urbana, Ill., 1980); Mary Frances Berry, *Black Resistance, White Law: A History of Constitutional Racism in America* (1971; rept. New York, 1994); John Dittmer, *Black Georgia in the Progressive Era, 1900–1920* (Urbana, Ill., 1977), 72–110; Carl Harris, "Reforms of Government Control of Negroes in Birmingham, Alabama, 1890–1920," *Journal of Southern History* 38 (1972): 567–600; Pete Daniel, *The Shadow of Slavery: Peonage in the South, 1901–1969* (1972; rept. Urbana, Ill., 1990), x, uses the term *labor control* to describe the purpose of southern law. For an excellent introduction to current sociological usage of the term *social control,* see Martha A. Myers and George S. Bridges, eds., *Inequality, Crime, and Social Control* (Boulder, Colo., 1994), and Rafter, *Partial Justice;* Richard H. Haunton, "Law and Order in Savannah, 1850–1860," *Georgia Historical Quarterly* 56 (Spring 1972): 1–24; James T. Currie, "From Slavery to Freedom in Mississippi's Legal System," *Journal of Negro History* 65 (Spring 1980): 112–25; Albert C. Smith, " 'Southern Violence' Reconsidered: Arson as Protest in Black-Belt Georgia, 1865–1910," *Journal of Southern History* 51 (Nov. 1985): 527–64; Mary Frances Berry, "Judging Morality: Sexual Behavior and Legal Consequences in the Late Nineteenth-Century South," *Journal of American History* 78 (Dec. 1991): 835–56.

23. John A. Minnis to George Williams, Dec. 26, Oct. 16, 1873, Justice Department Letters, Middle District.

24. Allen W. Trelease, *White Terror: The Ku Klux Klan Conspiracy and Southern Reconstruction* (New York, 1971), 81–88, 246–74, 302–10.

25. *Marengo News Journal,* Nov. 28, 1874.

26. William Skaggs, *The Southern Oligarchy* (1924; rept. New York, 1969), 242–44.

27. W. D. Lee to R. H. Dawson, March 19, 1890, Reports of Inspectors and Other Officials, Department of Corrections, ADAH.

28. William H. Sewell Jr., "A Theory of Structure: Duality, Agency, and Transformation," *American Journal of Sociology* 98:1 (July 1992): 1–29, quote on 20.

29. Lichtenstein, *Twice the Work of Free Labor,* xvii.

1. THE LEGACY OF RECONSTRUCTION

1. W. D. Lee to Gov. Thomas Seay, May 7, 1890, and "Application for the Pardon of Ryan Skinner and Woodville Hardy" (clipped together), Correspondence, Papers of Governor Thomas Seay, ADAH.

2. Gaines M. Foster, *Ghosts of the Confederacy: Defeat, the Lost Cause, and the Emergence of the New South* (New York, 1987); Charles Reagan Wilson, *Baptized in Blood: The Religion of the Lost Cause* (Athens, Ga., 1980).

3. U.S. Bureau of the Census, *Tenth Census of the United States, 1880,* Greene County, Ala., Forkland Beat.

4. Thomas G. Owens, *History of Alabama and Dictionary of Alabama Biography*, 4 vols. (Chicago, 1921), 1:680, 670. Information on Greensboro is taken from the entry "Greensboro," ibid., 672. In 1870 Hale County had a population of 4,802 whites and 16,990 African Americans. Greene County had 3,858 whites and 14,541 blacks.

5. According to the 1880 census Cato Jackson lived with his wife Caroline, their five daughters, his seventy-two-year-old mother Julia, and his eighty-year-old Aunt Gracie who worked as a midwife. His two eldest daughters attended school along with eighty-two other black children. The census listed him as a "farmer" instead of a farm laborer (*Tenth Census of the United States, 1880*, Greene County, Ala., Forkland Beat).

6. U.S. Congress, House Select Committee of Affairs in Alabama, 43d Cong., 2d sess., House Report 262, *Affairs in Alabama* (Washington, D.C., 1875), testimony of Cato Jackson, 709–10, and Charles Daniels, 706–7.

7. Testimony of Cato Jackson and Charles Daniels, ibid., 710, 707.

8. Loren Schweninger, *James T. Rapier and Reconstruction* (Chicago, 1978), 136 and chap. 11.

9. Petition dated Oct. 3, 1874, Justice Department Letters, Southern District.

10. For violence in Greene County directed against the Republican party, see Melinda Meek Hennessey, "Political Terrorism in the Black Belt: The Eutaw Riot," *Alabama Review* 33 (Jan. 1980): 35–48. According to Allen Trelease, Greene and Sumter Counties were "the heartland of Klan activity in western Alabama"; Trelease describes violence in the western Alabama Black Belt and Greene County as well as accounts of its alleged decline (*White Terror*, 246–60, 302, 307–10).

11. Everette Swinney, *Suppressing the Ku Klux Klan: The Enforcement of the Reconstruction Amendments, 1870–1877* (New York, 1987), 47.

12. S. A. Wayne to President Grant, Sept. 18, 1874, Justice Department Letters, Middle District; C. Vann Woodward, "Seeds of Failure in Radical Race Policy," in *American Counterpoint: Slavery and Racism in North-South Dialogue* (New York, 1964), 181; Everette Swinney, "Enforcing the Fifteenth Amendment: 1870–1877," *Journal of Southern History* 28:2 (May 1962): 202–18.

13. For this particular riot and Comer's involvement, see Dan Carter, *The Politics of Rage: George Wallace, the Origins of the New Conservatism, and the Transformation of the American Politics* (New York, 1995), 36–37; Melissa M. Hennessey, "Reconstruction Politics and the Military: The Eufaula Riot of 1874," *Alabama Historical Quarterly* 38 (Summer 1976): 112–25, and "Political Terrorism in the Black Belt: The Eutaw Riot," *Alabama Review* 33 (Jan. 1980): 35–48.

14. Schweninger, *James T. Rapier and Reconstruction*, 147. For accounts of the 1874 elections, see *Affairs in Alabama*; William Warren Rogers Jr., *Black Belt Scalawag: Charles Hays and the Southern Republicans in the Era of Reconstruction* (Athens, Ga., 1993); Schweninger, *James T. Rapier and Reconstruction*, chap. 11; Walter L. Fleming, *Civil War and Reconstruction in Alabama* (1905; rept. Spartanburg, S.C., 1978). For the murder of Willie Keils, see Hennessey, "Reconstruction Politics and the Military," 112–25.

15. Going, *Bourbon Democracy in Alabama*, 16; *Marengo News Journal*, Sept. 19, 20, 1874; handwritten testimony found in Gov. Seay's files.

16. In April, Smith had ordered the sheriff to summon one hundred persons for the jury and to give to each defendant "a copy of said list of persons." One week later the trial began (April 1, 1875, Minutes of the Circuit Court, Greene County, Ala., Book B, p. 458, located in warehouse behind the Greene County jail, Eutaw, Ala.).

17. April 9, 14, 1875, ibid., pp. 498–99, 535, 586.

18. Minutes of the Circuit Court, Hale County, Ala., Spring Term, 1876, located in the county courthouse, Greensboro, Hale County, Ala. Jim Black mysteriously disappeared from the trial record.

19. Sarah Woolfolk Wiggins, "Ostracism of White Republicans in Alabama during Reconstruction," *Alabama Review* 27 (Jan. 1974): 52–64, and *The Scalawag in Alabama Politics, 1865–1881* (University, Ala., 1977).

20. *Marengo News Journal*, Sept. 19, 1874. For information on Luther Smith, see Owens, *History of Alabama* 4:1588; Wiggins, "Ostracism of White Republicans in Alabama during Reconstruction," 52–64; William Warren Rogers, "'Politics Is Mighty Uncertain': Charles Hays Goes to Congress," *Alabama Review* 30:3 (July 1977): 163–90. For the Democratic response to the Hays-Hawley letter, see Rogers, *Black Belt Scalawag*, 111–15.

21. *Marengo News Journal*, May 27, June 10, 1875.

22. W. E. Clarke to Gov. George S. Houston, May 25, 1877, Pardon and Clemency Records, 1866–1915, Marengo County, Ala., ADAH.

23. "Memorial. To his excellency the President of the United States and the Honorable Congress of the United States," Dec. 2, 1874, *Affairs in Alabama*, 1077.

24. J. W. Bass to Gaius Whitfield Jr., March 25, 1876, and handwritten list of "Prisoners Received," Correspondence, Papers of Gaius Whitfield, ADAH.

25. Bass to Whitfield, Nov. 30, 1876, and Dec. 8, 1875, ibid.

26. For Gaineswood, see Ralph Hammond, *Antebellum Mansions of Alabama* (New York, 1951), 114–26; Virginia Van der Veer Hamilton, *Alabama: A History* (1977; rept. New York, 1984), 108–9; Bass to Whitfield, June 22, 1876, Correspondence, Papers of Gaius Whitfield, ADAH.

27. By 1882 Comer controlled hundreds of black prisoners in Alabama coal mines (Ezekiel Archey to R. H. Dawson, Pratt Mines, Jan. 18, 1884, Correspondence of the Inspectors of the Penitentiary, 1883–85, Department of Correction, ADAH).

28. Ibid.; *Annual Report of the Inspectors of the Alabama Penitentiary for the Year Ending Sept. 30, 1877* (Montgomery, Ala., 1878), 4–5.

29. Ezekiel Archey to R. H. Dawson, Jan. 18, 1884, Correspondence of the Inspectors of the Penitentiary, 1883–85, Department of Correction, ADAH.

30. "That is after paying me $60 for him which we charge on the escape" (J. G. Bass to Gaius Whitfield, Nov. 20, 1875, June 3, 1876, March 2, 1877, Correspondence, Papers of Gaius Whitfield, ibid.).

31. *Shelby Sentinel*, June 14, 1877; *Eutaw Whig and Observer*, June 21, 1877.

32. Entries listing dates of escape and recapture can be found in bound volumes entitled "State Prisoners of Alabama," 172:86, Department of Corrections, ADAH.

33. *First Biennial Report of the Inspectors of Convicts, 1884–86*, List 6, "State Convicts Employed by L. D. Rouse on Farms around Wetumpka, Alabama," 124.

34. Ezekiel Archey to R. H. Dawson, Jan. 18, 1884, Correspondence of the Inspectors of the Penitentiary, 1883–85, Department of Correction, ADAH; conversation with Ken Penfold, Helena, Summer 1995; W. D. Lee to Gov. Thomas Seay, May 7, 1890, and "Application for the Pardon of Ryan Skinner and Woodville Hardy" (clipped together), Correspondence, Papers of Governor Seay, ibid. An unmarked prison graveyard exists near the former mine works in Helena, Shelby County.

35. R. H. Skinner to R. H. Dawson, Dec. 1883, Reports from Inspectors and Other Officials, Department of Corrections, ibid.

36. Ibid.

37. Theodore Rosengarten, *All God's Dangers: The Life of Nate Shaw* (New York, 1974), 352–53.

38. As George Rable has put it, "At stake in the South in 1876–77 was what had been at stake for the South since the end of the war: the restoration of white racial hegemony and home rule" ("Southern Interests and the Election of 1876: A Reappraisal," *Civil War History* 26 [1980]: 347).

39. *Eutaw Whig and Observer,* Aug. 30, 1877.

40. Jimmie Frank Gross, "Alabama Politics and the Negro, 1874–1901" (Ph.D. diss., University of Georgia, 1969), 92; "Memorial of Jere Haralson," *House Miscellaneous Documents,* no. 19, 46th Cong., 2d sess. (Washington, D.C., 1880). Wallace later wrote that he traveled to Forkland "for the purpose of taking affidavits of voters of that county who cast their ballots at the election held on the 2d of August 1880." Wallace began and ended his investigation in the Forkland Beat; he never made it any further (interview with John Wallace published in *Mobile Gazette,* Sept. 6, 1880).

41. *Mobile Gazette,* Sept. 6, 1880; John Wallace to the U.S. Attorney General, Sept. 6, 1880, Justice Department Letters, Southern District.

42. Ibid. See also J. Morgan Kousser, *The Shaping of Southern Politics: Suffrage Restriction and the Establishment of the One-Party South, 1880–1910* (New Haven, 1974), 13–18.

43. State Prisoners of Alabama, vol. 1, no. 172, p. 86, no. 80, p. 40, Department of Corrections, ADAH; W. D. Lee to Gov. Thomas Seay, May 7, 1890, Correspondence, Papers of Governor Seay, ibid.

44. W. D. Lee to Gov. Seay, May 7, 1890, and "Application for the Pardon of Ryan Skinner and Woodville Hardy" (clipped together), Correspondence, Papers of Governor Seay, ibid.

45. U.S. Bureau of the Census, Eighth Census of the United States: 1860 Slave Census, Greene County, Ala., Forkland Beat; *Tenth Census of the United States, 1880,* Greene County, Ala., Forkland Beat.

46. John H. Haley, *Charles N. Hunter and Race Relations in North Carolina* (Chapel Hill, N.C., 1987), xiii.

2. EMANCIPATION AND BLACK PRISONERS

1. *Third Biennial Report of the Inspectors of Convicts, 1888–90,* 28–29.

2. Peter Kolchin, *First Freedom: The Responses of Alabama Blacks to Emancipation and Reconstruction* (Westport, Conn., 1972), 23.

3. Ibid., chap. 8 and 189.

4. *First Biennial Report of the Inspectors of Convicts, 1884–86,* 6–7.

5. Loren Schweninger, "James Rapier and the Negro Labor Movement, 1869–1872," *Alabama Review* 28:3 (July 1975): 185–201. This article contains interesting information on black schools during Reconstruction. See also Horace Mann Bond, *Negro Education in Alabama: A Study in Cotton and Steel* (1939; rept. New York, 1969), 96–99.

6. Kolchin, *First Freedom,* 98.

7. Ibid., 86.

8. Bond, *Negro Education in Alabama,* 115–16.

9. Kolchin, *First Freedom,* 84.

10. Ibid., 97.

11. Bond, *Negro Education in Alabama,* 260, 100, 136, 101–5.

12. *Eutaw Whig and Observer,* Oct. 11, 1877.

13. Bond, *Negro Education in Alabama,* 256; James D. Anderson, *The Education of Blacks in the South, 1865–1935* (Chapel Hill, N.C., 1988), 150–51.

14. Victoria V. Clayton, *White and Black under the Old Regime* (Milwaukee, 1899), cited

in Bond, *Negro Education in Alabama,* 114; *Tuscaloosa Observer,* cited in John B. Myers, "The Education of Alabama Freedmen during Presidential Reconstruction, 1865–1867," *Journal of Negro Education* 40 (Spring 1971): 169.

15. "Report of the Prison Mission School Slope No. 2," separate reports for the months ending Sept. 30, Oct. 30, and Nov. 30, 1888, quote from September report, Reports of Inspectors and Other Officials, Department of Corrections, ADAH. The school was located at Slope No. 2. The number of black prisoners enrolled increased steadily. In Sept. 1888, 160 attended, and in October 1888, 195 attended. Julia Tutwiler's father was E. M. Tutwiler's first cousin. See W. David Lewis, *Sloss Furnace and the Rise of the Birmingham District* (Tuscaloosa, Ala., 1994), 120, 248. See also Ann G. Pannell and Dorothea E. Wyatt, *Julia S. Tutwiler and Social Progress in Alabama* (Tuscaloosa, Ala., 1961).

16. Julia S. Tutwiler, "Prison Schools in Alabama," in *Proceedings of the Annual Congress of the National Prison Association of the United States, Held at Nashville, November 16–20, 1889* (Chicago, 1890), 215–19, quote on 218.

17. Ibid., 215.

18. Dawson to Jones, Jan. 6, 1891, Papers of Governor Jones, box 66, ADAH.

19. *First Biennial Report of the Board of Inspectors of Convicts, , 1894–96,* 51.

20. For the Black Belt counties, see Bond, *Negro Education in Alabama,* 3.

21. Kolchin, *First Freedom,* 22–23.

22. Charles S. Johnson, *Shadow of the Plantation* (1934; rept., Chicago, 1966), 8; Kolchin, *First Freedom,* 14–18 and chap. 1.

23. As Herbert Gutman has observed, emancipation "allowed ex-slave men and women to act on a variety of class beliefs that had developed but been constrained during several generations of enslavement" (quoted in Anderson, *Education of Blacks in the South,* 5–6). On the ethos of group solidarity fostered by slavery, see Thomas Webber, *Deep like the Rivers: Education in the Slave Quarter Community* (New York, 1978), 224–43.

24. J. F. Chalfant to J. H. Caldwell, Sept. 1865, Freedmen's Aid Society Papers for Western Georgia and Alabama of the Methodist Episcopal Church, Atlanta University Archives, Special Collections, microfilm, reel 1.

25. John T. O'Brien, "Factory, Church, and Community: Blacks in Antebellum Richmond," *Journal of Southern History* 44 (Nov. 1978): 509–36. For other works that focus on the relationship between the slave and free communities, see Willie Lee Rose, *Rehearsal for Reconstruction: The Port Royal Experiment* (New York, 1964); Joel Williamson, *After Slavery: The Negro in South Carolina during Reconstruction, 1861–1877* (Chapel Hill, N.C., 1965); John W. Blassingame, *Black New Orleans, 1860–1880* (Chicago, 1973); Edward Magdol, *A Right to the Land: Essays on the Freedmen's Community* (Westport, Conn., 1977); Herbert Gutman, *The Black Family in Slavery and Freedom, 1750–1925* (New York, 1976).

26. James Benson Sellers, *Slavery in Alabama* (1950; rept. Tuscaloosa, Ala., 1994), 226, 240–41.

27. Eric Foner, "Black Reconstruction Leaders at the Grass Roots," in *Black Leaders of the Nineteenth Century,* ed. Leon Litwack and August Meier (Urbana, Ill., 1988), 224–26.

28. Anonymous letter to Governor Seay, Aug. 1887, Correspondence, Papers of Governor Seay, ADAH.

29. Letter from Troy, Ala., Pike County, 1888, Pardon and Parole Records, Gov. Thomas Seay, ibid.

30. Jane Lightfoot, Montgomery, Ala., to Gov. Thomas Seay, Nov. 8, 1889, ibid.

31. Letter signed by fifty black petitioners in Tuscumbia to the Freedmen's Bureau, Nov. 29, 1865, Letters Received, A-J, reel 5, BRAFL.

32. They also expressed uncertainty about their rights as workers. "Our men in the country needs someone to assist them in the contracts like the same in the city also the legislature had pass a bill to prevent the freedmen from renting land are houses." They ended their letter by signing their names: "Therefre we hope you will help us out Comitee Prince Marell, Edward Foster, G Barnes L Childers Wm Magee, Gl Logans, G. Woods, Wm Lerish, Wm Short Like Lowery Chairman, AA Williams cty" (Letter from black citizens, Tuscaloosa, Ala., ibid.

33. Frank Knox to Seay, Nov. 23, 1889, Pardon Files, Papers of Governor Seay, ADAH.

34. Henry Haden to Seay, Jan. 11, 1890, Correspondence, ibid.

35. Traditionally the concept of social control connotes, in a negative fashion, society's need to regulate its unworthy or unmanageable citizens. Historians who have stressed the use of southern law as a means of social control over blacks. In the Jim Crow courtroom, according to Neil R. McMillen, "the tensions between social justice and social control was nearly always resolved in the interests of the dominant race" (*Dark Journey: Black Mississippians in the Age of Jim Crow* [Urbana, Ill., and Chicago, 1989

36. David J. Rothman, "Social Control: The Uses and Abuses of the Concept in the History of Incarceration," in *Social Control and the State*, ed. Stanley Cohen and Andrew Scull (New York, 1983), 107.

37. Sydney Nathans, "The Long Emancipation," paper in author's possession; R. Arnilson to Maj. Shorkley, July 31, 1868, Subregional Reports, BRFAL. Nathans has uncovered the case of the freedman Sandy Cameron who bought land from his master after he publicly renounced the Union League in Hale County. I would like to thank Professor Nathans for sharing this material with me.

38. Fleming, *Civil War and Reconstruction in Alabama*, 778; Gross, "Alabama Politics and the Negro," 36; William Warren Rogers and Robert David Ward, *August Reckoning: Jack Turner and Racism in Post–Civil War Alabama* (Baton Rouge, La., 1973), 26–27.

39. Testimony of Robert Ford, *Affairs in Alabama*, 338; Kolchin, *First Freedom*, 132.

40. Loren Schweninger, "Black Citizenship and the Republican Party in Reconstruction Alabama," *Alabama Review* 29:2 (April 1976): 83–103. Yet Alabama Republicans, like the national party, were deeply divided on the issue of racial equality.

41. *Alabama Beacon*, Nov. 7, 1868; Gross, "Alabama Politics and the Negro," 52–53; testimony of Charles Pelham, *Affairs in Alabama*, 1203–4.

42. Webber, *Deep like the River*, 80–91; *Alabama Beacon*, Jan. 9, 1869. The rally celebrated the end of the first legislative session in Montgomery.

43. Webber, *Deep like the River*, 80–91.

44. Ezekiel Archey to R. H. Dawson, Jan. 18, 1884, Correspondence of the Inspectors of the Penitentiary, 1883–85, Department of Corrections, ADAH.

45. Similarly, as Joe William Trotter has shown, when free black miners in West Virginia improved their productivity and worked harder than white miners, they also bragged of their race's superiority (*Coal, Class, and Color: Blacks in Southern West Virginia, 1915–1932* [Urbana, Ill., 1992], 108–9).

46. A. T. Henley to R. H. Dawson, Oct. 1, 1891, Reports of Inspectors and Other Officials, Department of Corrections, ADAH.

47. *Alabama Beacon*, May 25, Aug. 17, 1867. See also Eric Foner, *Reconstruction: American's Unfinished Revolution, 1863–1877* (New York, 1988), 875; Loren Schweninger, "Alabama Blacks and the Congressional Reconstruction Acts of 1867," *Alabama Review* 31 (July 1978): 183, 186–87. Schweninger cites a gathering of 150 former slaves in Florence, Ala., to hear James T. Rapier, who later became one of the first black representatives in Congress. Mobile blacks organized a political society. Former slaves orga-

nized meetings in Madison and Morgan Counties. Tuskegee boasted a Union League with 400 members. In Montgomery, Selma, and Hayneville, whites and blacks met as political equals to choose voter registrars.

48. Elsa Barkley Brown, "Negotiating and Transforming the Public Sphere: African American Political Life in the Transition from Slavery to Freedom," *Public Culture* 7 (Fall 1994): 107–26, and "To Catch the Vision of Freedom: Reconstructing Southern Black Women's Political History, 1865–1885" (paper, Jan. 1990).

49. *Marengo News Journal,* June 15, 22, 1867.

50. Catherine Clinton, "Freedwomen, Sexuality, and Violence during Reconstruction," in *Half Sisters of History: Southern Women and the American Past,* ed. Catherine Clinton (Durham, N.C., 1994), 136–53, quote on 145.

51. *Montgomery Advertiser,* July 7, 10, Sept. 8, Oct. 23, 9, 1874.

52. Ibid., Aug. 29, 1874; *Marengo News-Journal,* Aug. 24, 1876; Fleming, *Civil War and Reconstruction in Alabama,* 763, 768.

53. Frances E. W. Harper, the African-American suffragist and author, described the actions of southern black women during election time in her poem "Deliverance": "You'd laughed to seen Lucinda Grange/Upon her husband's track/When he sold his vote for rations/she made him take 'em back/Day after day did Milly Green/Just follow after Joe,/And told him if he voted wrong/To take his rags and go/I think that curnel Johnson said/His side had won the day,/Had not we women radicals/Just got right in the way" (from *Sketches of Southern Life* [1891], quoted in Gerda Lerner, ed., *Black Women in White America: A Documentary History* [New York, 1973], 249. Some authors have seen this poem as evidence of the desire of black women to prove their loyalty to the race through politics. What the poem also illustrates, however, is that even without the vote, black women exercised political power in their communities (Paula Giddings, *When and Where I Enter: The Impact of Black Women on Race and Sex in America* [New York, 1984], 122).

54. *Montgomery Advertiser and Mail,* April 10, 1875; *Marengo News-Journal,* Aug. 24, 1876.

55. Victoria Bynum, *Unruly Women: The Politics of Sexual and Social Control in the Old South* (Chapel Hill, N.C., 1992).

3. Crime and Social Conflict

1. *Eutaw Whig and Observer,* Dec. 10, 1874.

2. Ibid., Jan. 28, 1875, Dec. 24, 1874; *Montgomery Advertiser and Mail,* Jan. 28, 1875.

3. *Annual Report of the Inspectors of the Alabama Penitentiary for Year Ending Sept. 30, 1877,* 55. Although a total of 831 state prisoners was given, crimes were only listed for 779. For increased numbers of state black prisoners over time, see Going, *Bourbon Democracy in Alabama,* 176, 180.

4. Wharton, *Negro in Mississippi,* 234–39; Oshinsky, *Worse than Slavery,* 34–35.

5. Petition for pardon of Ann Austin, 1877, Greene County, Pardon and Parole Records, ADAH.

6. Edward L. Ayers, *The Promise of the New South: Life after Reconstruction* (New York, 1992), 154. Ayers makes a similar argument about "sharp upswings in prison populations in the wake of national economic depressions" in *Vengeance and Justice,* 170–71, 176–77. The vagrancy theory is plausible—to a point. William Cohen has shown that, in contrast to the years of the Black Codes, relatively few men and women were arrested for "vagrancy" in the late nineteenth century (*At Freedom's Edge: Black Mobility and the Southern White Quest for Racial Control, 1861–1915* [Baton Rouge, La., 1991], 243, 290).

7. The landowner and gin owner involved were "men of property, and good character, all Democrats but not regarded as extreme" (Minnis to G. H. Williams, Attorney General, Jan. 21, 1873, Justice Department Letters, Middle District).

8. Michael Fitzgerald, "The Ku Klux Klan: Property Crime and the Plantation System in Reconstruction Alabama," *Agricultural History* 71 (Spring 1997): 186–206.

9. Wharton, *Negro in Mississippi*, 76–77; Trowbridge, *South*, 446.

10. Myers, "The Freedmen and the Law"; William Warren Rogers et al., *Alabama: The History of a Deep South State* (Tuscaloosa, Ala., 1994), 235.

11. Robert A. Flimmy, Justice of the Peace, Union Springs, to General Swayne, Jan. 4, 1865, Records of the Assistant Commissioner for the State of Alabama, Letters Received, A-J, reel 5, BRFAL.

12. According to General Swayne, the state imposed the vagrancy laws because the freedmen had refused to make contracts before Christmas 1865. Fear that blacks would never work again caused the legislature to issue a "series of bills referring exclusively to freedmen" that in Swayne's words "restored all of slavery that was oppressive." When the federal government told the freedmen not to wait for land, they did make contracts and go to work. According to Swayne much of the racially specific language was repealed, but blacks were the targets (Report of Major General Wager Swayne, Assistant Commissioner of Alabama, Oct. 31, 1866, *Letter of the Secretary of War*, 7; "Laws in Relation to Freedmen," ibid., 170–74. See also H. M. Crowder, Justice of the Peace, Russell County, to Wager Swayne, Aug. 15, 1865, Letters Received, BRAFL. The Alabama Code also demanded a minimum sentence of five years' imprisonment for grand larceny, arson, or burglary (Theodore Brantner Wilson, *The Black Codes of the South* [University, Ala., 1965], 76–77).

13. Trowbridge, *South*, 435–36. The ordinance "prohibits market men from selling so much as an egg before they have reached the market and the market bell has rung" ("An Act concerning Vagrants and Vagrancy," sections 1–7 approved Dec. 15, 1865, *Letter of the Secretary of War*, 170–71).

14. Samuel Gardner to George Sharkley, July 3, 1868, Letters Sent, reel 1, BRFAL.

15. Ibid.; A. M. Prince, Demopolis, Ala., to Gen. Swayne, April 27, 1866, Letters Received, 1866, BRFAL. Other agents also remarked on the fees freedmen in court paid; see Captain Giddes to Col. Cadle, Sept. 13, 1865, Letters Received, 1865, reel 5, ibid.; Agent Hammond to Col. Cadle, Nov. 24, 1865, Letters Received, 1865, ibid.

16. E. A. Hammond, Ass't. Supt. of Freedmen, Mobile, Ala., to Swayne, July 21, 1865, J. W. Cogarrell, Capt., Columbiana, Ala., and Edmund A. May, Sept. 25, 1865, General Gallian, Capt. and Sub Com Freedmen, Prt. Winchester, Miss., to Office Sub Com Freedmen, Aug. 19, 1865, Letters Received, 1865, BRFAL.

17. Lowndes County, Hayneville Beat No. 7, "Action for violation of written contract. Decision of J. A. Pruitt, a Justice of the Peace, acting as Agent of the Freedmen's Bureau, September 12, 1865," ibid.

18. J. A. Pruitt to General Swayne, Sept. 13, 1865, ibid.

19. George A. Hammond to Col. Cadle, March 20, 1866, containing the decision of Justice of the Peace Cook in Lowndes County, and decision of A. L. Loomis, JP, Montgomery County, Sept. 28, 1865, containing the contract of the Perrick plantation, ibid.

20. Hammond to Swayne, July 21, 1865, ibid.; Agent Godry to Major Pierce, Eutaw, Ala., May 22, 1868, Letters Sent, Monthly Report of May 1868, ibid.

21. Report of Agent R. A. Wilson, Aug. 3, 1868, , Letters Sent, ibid.

22. Testimony of Robert Ford, *Affairs in Alabama*, 339.

23. Wilson, *Black Codes*, 49; Kenneth Stampp, *The Peculiar Institution* (New York, 1956), 126–27; Eugene Genovese, *Roll, Jordan, Roll: The World the Slaves Made* (New

York, 1976), 599–609; Alex Lichtenstein, "'That Disposition to Theft, with Which They Have Been Branded': Moral Economy, Slave Management, and the Law," *Journal of Social History* 21 (Spring 1988): 413–40.

24. Monthly report of May 1868, Agent Gordy of Eutaw, Ala., to Major Pierce, Sub Assistant Commissioner at Demopolis, Ala., May 22, 1868, Letters Received, BRFAL; Fitzgerald, "The Ku Klux Klan," 190–91.

25. Lichtenstein, "That Disposition to Theft, with Which They Have Been Branded"; Genovese, *Roll, Jordan Roll,* 599–609.

26. In Marengo County, the *Southern Republican,* Sept. 20, 1869, urged tighter market controls: "What we want is better regulations regarding the sale and ownership of cotton. We want a regular market. We want an end put to 'Street cotton' and an end of irresponsible parties hawking a bale of cotton up and down the streets and becoming alternatively the victims and victimizers.".

27. Fleming, *Civil War and Reconstruction in Alabama,* 769–70.

28. Ibid., viii.

29. Michael Fitzgerald, *The Union League Movement in the Deep South* (Baton Rouge, La., 1989), 147, 150–52, 159, 162, 204.

30. J. A. Gordy, Agent, Eutaw, Ala., to Major Pierce, May 22, 1868, Letters Received, BRFAL; *Alabama Beacon,* Jan. 22, 1870. For varying definitions of sharecropping and renting, see Harold Woodman, *New South—New Law: The Legal Foundations of Credit and Labor Relations in the Postbellum Agriculture South* (Baton Rouge, La., 1995), "Sequel to Slavery: The New History Views the Post Bellum South," *Journal of Southern History* 43 (Nov. 1977): 523–54, and "Post–Civil War Southern Agriculture and the Law," *Agricultural History* 53 : 1 (Jan. 1979): 317–37; Gerald Jaynes, *Branches without Roots: Genesis of the Black Working Class, 1862–1882* (New York, 1986); Roger L. Ransom and Richard Sutch, *One Kind of Freedom: The Economic Consequences of Emancipation* (Cambridge, Eng., 1977).

31. Woodman, *New South—New Law,* 75.

32. *Alabama Beacon,* Nov. 27, 1869.

33. Testimony of Charles Daniels, *Affairs in Alabama,* 706; *Marengo News-Journal,* Sept. 20, 1875.

34. *Marengo News-Journal,* Sept. 20, 1875.

35. This illegal traffic in goods caused public condemnation and fines. Nevertheless, Alabama legal records show slaves persisted in trading (James Sellers, *Slavery in Alabama* [1950; rept. Tuscaloosa, Ala., 1994], 233–34). Sellers found whites receiving fines for trading with slaves, letters in newspapers condemning merchants who paid slaves cash for goods, and evidence of a robust trade in alcohol. For other accounts of trading by slaves, see Loren Schweninger, "The Underside of Slavery: The Internal Economy, Self-Hire, and Quasi Freedom in Virginia, 1780–1865," *Slavery and Abolition* 12 (Sept. 1991): 1–22; Barry Gaspar, "Slavery, Amelioration, and Sunday Markets in Antigua, 1823–1831," ibid., 9 (May 1988): 1–28; Betty Wood, *Women's Work, Men's Work: The Informal Slave Economies of Lowcountry Georgia* (Athens, Ga., 1995); Larry Hudson, "'All That Cash': Work and Status in the Slave Quarters," in *Working toward Freedom: Slave Society and Domestic Economy in the American South,* ed. Larry Hudson (Rochester, N.Y., 1994), and *To Have and to Hold: Slave Work and Family Life in Antebellum South Carolina* (Athens, Ga., 1997).

36. Ransom and Sutch, *One Kind of Freedom,* chap. 6 (106–25), discusses how local merchants became heirs to the antebellum factors as the dispensers of credit to landowners; chap. 7 (126–48) explains how "merchant landowners and landowner merchants" came to gain a monopoly on credit. Although historians have tended to focus on the politics of Reconstruction and changes in the southern labor system, Ransom and

Sutch emphasize that the "financial reconstruction" of the South, and the new power of local merchants, had the most "far-reaching repercussions" (106).

37. *Eutaw Whig and Observer,* Oct. 28, 1875.

38. *Alabama Beacon,* Sept. 23, 1871; *Marengo News-Journal,* Sept. 6, 1873.

39. *Eutaw Whig and Observer,* Dec. 31, 1874.

40. *Livingston Journal* quoted in the *Eutaw Whig and Observer,* Dec. 24, 1874; *Eutaw Whig and Observer,* Dec. 3, 1874. The paper went on to say: "To effectually squelch the illicit traffic mentioned, the root must be destroyed. This is a work the legislature cannot perform. It cannot prohibit the renting of lands to whomsoever the owner may choose to rent."

41. Woodman, *New South—New Law,* 76–77.

42. *Montgomery Advertiser and Mail,* Sept. 15, Dec. 4, 1874. One Democrat proposed a law that would have indicted the store owner along with any "person seen entering a store . . . in the night time carrying a bag or basket, full or partly full of something, and leaving it with said bag or basket empty" (letter to the editor from Greensboro, Hale County, ibid., Nov. 28, 1874).

43. Ibid., Sept. 15, 17, 1874 Jan. 28, 1875.

44. *Marengo News-Journal,* Nov. 28, 1874.

45. Quoted in Michael Hyman, *The Anti-Redeemers: Hill Country Political Dissenters in the Lower South from Redemption to Populism* (Baton Rouge, La., 1990), 179.

46. The text of the initial 1874 bills can be found in the *Eutaw Whig and Observer,* Feb. 25, March 4, 1875. Subsequent legislation is described in Michael Perman, *The Road to Redemption* (Chapel Hill, N.C., 1984), 245, 259–60; Gross, "Alabama Politics and the Negro," 66.

47. Undoubtedly, as Michael Hyman argues, white elites in the Alabama hill country, as well as those in the Black Belt, benefited from the restrictions on buying and selling that applied to farmers of all races (*Anti-Redeemers,* 180).

48. *Eutaw Whig and Observer,* Sept. 9, 1875.

49. Ibid., Oct. 28, 1875.

50. Ransom and Sutch, *One Kind of Freedom,* 94.

51. *Anderson v. State,* 72 Alabama 187 (1882), and *Washington v. State,* 75 Alabama 582 (1884), cited in Gross, "Alabama Politics and the Negro," 93. The law is described in *Eutaw Whig and Observer,* June 1, 1876.

52. Hennessey, "Reconstruction Politics and the Military."

53. E. M. Keils to Judge Pierrepont, Attorney General, Washington, D.C., June 9, 1875, Justice Department Letters, Southern District.

54. Testimony of Joshua McNeil, *Affairs in Alabama,* 954–55.

55. *Eutaw Whig and Observer,* Nov. 19, 1874.

56. Ibid., Jan. 28 1875; *Marengo News-Journal,* Nov. 28, 1874.

57. Sheriff Nicolson, a Republican elected in Greene County, could not find a Democrat in his county to post his bond and would likely be forced to vacate his seat. "Any man with a small modicum of self respect would resign a position which he holds only by virtue of negro votes" (*Eutaw Whig and Observer,* Dec. 17, 31, 1874). Similar cases of an elected tax assessor and a "colored clerk" of the circuit court are detailed in ibid., Dec. 10, 1874, May 11, 1876.

58. *Montgomery Advertiser,* Dec. 6, 1874.

59. *Eutaw Whig and Observer,* March 18, 1875. "Both representatives in the legislature from Macon are under indictments for crime. G. Patterson, for adultery, and G. Johnston for grand larceny" (ibid., Nov. 9, 1876).

60. For a summary of Minnis's efforts in Alabama, see Swinney, *Suppressing the Ku Klux Klan*, 298–306.

61. John A. Minnis to George Williams, Attorney General of the U.S., Oct. 16, 1873, Justice Department Letters, Middle District.

62. Ibid., Dec. 26, 1873, Oct. 16, 1873.

63. Keils to Pierrepont, June 9, 1875, Justice Department Letters, Southern District. U.S. Attorney Nick S. McAfee wrote that he would be unable to sustain any indictments against the White League in Barbour County for its role in the election day murders. "By the machinery of State and County courts, witnesses for United States against parties in Barbour Co are being driven out" (McAfee to Hon. George H. Williams, Attorney General, Jan. 13, 1875, ibid.).

64. John A. Minnis to G. H. Williams, Sept. 2, 1874, and McAfee to Williams, Aug. 31, 1874, ibid.

65. Hennessey, "Reconstruction Politics and the Military," 119–20.

66. Keils to Attorney General Williams, Nov. 11, 1874, Justice Department Letters, Southern District.

67. McAfee to George H. Williams, Attorney Gen., Jan. 13, 1875, ibid.

68. "Memorial. To his excellency the President of the United States and the Honorable Congress of the United States," Dec. 2, 1874, *Affairs in Alabama*, 1079. This memorial addressed to President Grant reads like a lawyer's brief. Clearly it was written by men knowledgeable of all aspects of federal, state, and local legal procedures.

69. Ibid., 1079.

70. Ibid., 1077. As the memorial indicates, a lack of black jurors contributed to the disproportionate number of blacks convicted for crimes. This was not true everywhere in the South. Donald G. Nieman has shown that African Americans served on both grand and petit juries in Washington County, Texas, even after 1876 ("Black Political Power and Criminal Justice: Washington County, Texas, 1868–1884," *Journal of Southern History* 55 [Aug. 1989]: 391–420). In Alabama, however, the complete absence of black jurors moved even Booker T. Washington, who remarked, "So far as concerns the Gulf states, the Negro is completely at the mercy of the white man in the state courts. . . . in the whole of Georgia & Alabama not a negro juror is allowed to sit in the jury box in state courts" ("A Speech Delivered before the Women's New England Club," Boston, Jan. 27, 1889, in Louis Harlan, ed., *The Booker T. Washington Papers*, 14 vols. [Urbana, Ill., 1979], 3:29).

71. "Memorial," 1077.

72. Testimony of William E. Cockrell, *Affairs in Alabama*, 232–36. The *Eutaw Whig and Observer*, July 19, Aug. 17, 1876, mentions Cockrell's affiliation with black Republicans, his sponsorship of a public meeting in Greene, and his victory in the legislature, from which he eventually resigned (ibid., July 12, 1877). Cockrell also testified as a prisoner. See U.S. Congress, Senate, Committee on Education and Labor, 49th Cong., 2d sess., *Testimony before the Committee to Investigate the Relations between Capital and Labor* 4:430.

4. PRISONS FOR PROFIT, 1871–1883

1. Herr, Treasurer of Sumter County, to Robert McKee, March 29, 1882, Letters, 1882, box 2, folder 5, Robert McKee Papers, ADAH.

2. Mancini, *One Dies, Get Another*, 100–101; Ayers, *Vengeance and Justice*, 68; R. H. Dawson, "The Convict System of Alabama—As It Was and Is," in *Handbook Of Alabama*, ed. Saffold Berney (1892; rept. Spartanburg, S.C., 1975), 254–58.

3. Alabama's first postwar governor was Lewis E. Parsons, appointed by President

Andrew Johnson in 1865. Parsons, Patton, and Smith had all opposed secession but supported the war. They could not be called Unionists (Rogers et al., *Alabama*, 230–33).

4. Mancini, *One Dies, Get Another*, 100–101; Robert Cvornyk, "Convict Labor in the Alabama Coal Mines, 1874–1928" (Ph.D. diss., Columbia University, 1993), 21–22.

5. Governor Cobb, "History of the Penitentiary," contained in *First Biennial Report of the Inspectors of Convicts, 1884–86*, 348–66, 351–52; Mancini, *One Dies, Get Another*, 100; Going, *Bourbon Democracy in Alabama*, 170–71, 180, gives the racial composition of prisoners. The composition of state prisoners, men convicted of felonies, was more of a racial mix. Still, whites never comprised more than approximately 15 percent of the state prison population. The overwhelming majority of all state prisoners remained black throughout the late nineteenth century.

6. Taking over such a valuable asset seemed like a good idea, until it was discovered that Alabama could not afford to run a railroad. According to Mark W. Summers, Lindsay's refusal to extend aid until the railroad turned a profit indicated either naiveté or stupidity. Despite these difficulties, Summers has argued that the project was a success: ultimately, the railroad was completed on time, and it connected Alabama coal mines to valuable markets in Tennessee and beyond (*Railroads, Reconstruction, and the Gospel of Prosperity: Aid under the Radical Republicans, 1865–1877* [Princeton, N.J., 1984], 213–36).

7. *Annual Report of the Inspectors of the Alabama Penitentiary from March 1 to Sept. 30, 1873* (Montgomery, Ala., 1873), 3, 20.

8. Summers, *Railroads, Reconstruction, and the Gospel of Prosperity*, 234.

9. *Annual Report of the Inspectors of the Alabama Penitentiary from March 1 to Sept. 30, 1873*, 6.

10. Mancini, *One Dies, Get Another*, 101.

11. Ibid., 100–101; *Annual Report of the Inspectors of the Alabama Penitentiary from March 1 to Sept. 30, 1873*, 20; *Annual Report of the Inspectors of the Alabama Penitentiary from October 1, 1873, to Sept. 30, 1874* (Montgomery, Ala., 1874), 4–5 and Exhibit A.

12. Woodward, *Origins of the New South*, 9–11. Woodward writes, "Houston was a close associate of Sloss and the L & N, for one of whose affiliated lines he was a director."

13. For the divisions within the Democratic party on the debt and spending issue and the Jacksonian roots of Alabama's 1875 constitution, see Samuel Webb, "A Jacksonian Democrat in Postbellum Alabama: The Ideology and Influence of Journalist Robert McKee, 1869–1896," *Journal of Southern History* 62 (May 1996): 259–65.

14. According to Summers, "The state's Debt commission of 1875–76 abandoned all hope of Alabama's recovering its losses. Just to be freed from further expense, it surrendered every state claim to the road to . . . bondholders and paid back interest as well as an additional $1 million" (*Railroads, Reconstruction and the Gospel of Prosperity*, 213–36, quote on 236).

15. Ralph B. Draughton, "Some Aspects of the History of Alabama Bond Issues," *Alabama Review* 6 (July 1953): 25–27; Going, *Bourbon Democracy in Alabama*, 91. Governor Houston was a good friend to the railroads. He appointed an independent commission "which was believed by many to be the result of a deliberate effort by Houston's administration to salvage much of the state's indebtedness to the railroads" (Gross, "Alabama Politics and the Negro," 74).

16. J. G. Bass to Governor Cobb, May 31, 1879, Governor Rufus Cobb, Administrative Files, Jan. 1–June 2, 1879, box 1, folder 1, ADAH.

17. Ibid.; J. G. Bass to Gaius Whitfield Jr., Dec. 6, 1876, Jan. 16, 1877, Correspondence, Papers of Gaius Whitfield, ibid.

18. J. G. Bass to Governor Cobb, May 31, 1879, Administrative Files, Jan. 1–June 2,

1879, box 1, folder 1, ibid.; J. G. Bass to Col. H. A. Woolf, Linden, Ala., June 25, 1875, Correspondence, Papers of Gaius Whitfield, ibid. .

19. Oct. 30, 1877, Minutes of the County Commissioners Court, Hale County, Adjourned term, ibid.

20. J. G. Bass to Gaius Whitfield, Jan. 19, 1876, Correspondence, Papers of Gaius Whitfield, ibid.

21. J. H. Bankhead to J. W. Comer, May 23, 1882, Letter Book, July 23, 1881–May 1, 1885, Department of Corrections, ibid.

22. The county system took in more men. Between 1884 and 1886, 2,017 county prisoners and 209 state prisoners were released (*First Biennial Report of the Inspectors of Convicts, 1884-86*, 228).

23. *Annual Report of the Inspectors of the Alabama Penitentiary for Year Ending Sept. 30, 1877*, 3–7.

24. Ibid., 4, 7.

25. *Eutaw Whig and Observer,* June 15, 1876.

26. *Annual Report of the Inspectors of the Alabama Penitentiary for Year Ending Sept. 30, 1877.*

27. McKiven, *Iron and Steel,* 7–13. The early owners of these enterprises were "Birmingham's Founding Fathers." They included Daniel Pratt and John T. Milner, but also newcomers who arrived on stage after the Civil War. Henry F. DeBardeleben, for example, was Pratt's son-in-law and the owner of the Eureka mines. McKiven tells a little about these "boosters," but he fails to mention their use of convict labor in these early enterprises. See also Lewis, *Sloss Furnaces and the Rise of the Birmingham District,* 61–69.

28. *Shelby Sentinel,* Nov. 6, 1879, May 18, 1882.

29. Testimony of Jno. D. Goode of Jefferson County, *Testimony Taken by the Joint Special Committee of the Session of 1880–81 to Enquire into the Condition and Treatment of Convicts of the State* (Montgomery, Ala., 1881), 6; Ezekiel Archey to R. H. Dawson, Pratt Mines, Jan. 18, 1884, Correspondence of the Inspectors of the Penitentiary, 1883–85, ADAH.

30. Archey to Dawson, Jan. 18, 1884, Correspondence of the Inspectors of the Penitentiary, 1883–85, ADAH.

31. The total number of men at work in Eureka in Helena under the authority of J. W. Comer was 86 (*Biennial Report of the Inspectors of the Alabama Penitentiary from Sept. 30, 1878, to Sept. 30, 1880* (Montgomery, Ala., 1880), 34–37, 72–74.

32. *Report of the Joint Committee to Enquire into the Treatment of Convicts* (Montgomery, Ala., 1881), 4.

33. Testimony of Captain James O'Rourke, *Testimony Taken by the Joint Special Committee,* 17.

34. Testimony of J. W. Comer and J. C. Hunter, Superintendent of Convicts at Alabama Furnace, ibid., 11, 18–19.

35. Testimony of F. H. Gafford, ibid., 7.

36. *Shelby Sentinel,* Nov. 6, 1879; *Biennial Report of the Inspectors of the Alabama Penitentiary from September 30, 1880, to September 30, 1882* (Montgomery, Ala., 1882), 3–4.

37. "Our Convicts: Horrors of Their Treatment," excerpt of article from *New York Times,* reprinted in *Huntsville Gazette,* Dec. 23, 1882.

38. *New York Times,* Dec. 17, 1882; John T. Milner to R. H. Dawson, June 10, 1885, Correspondence of the Department of Corrections, March–Dec. 1885, Department of Corrections, ADAH.

39. Approximately half of all county prisoners were being leased to the mines as of

March 1883. See *Convicts at Hard Labor for the County in the State of Alabama on the First Day of March, 1883,* microfiche, ibid.

40. Lewis, *Sloss Furnaces and the Rise of the Birmingham District,* 34. See Alex Lichtenstein's review of Lewis's book in *Alabama Review* 51 (April 1998): 106–13.

41. *Huntsville Gazette,* Sept. 3, 1881, reprinted from the *Jackson Republican.*

42. William Cohen, "Negro Involuntary Servitude, 1865–1940: A Preliminary Analysis," *Journal of Southern History* 42 (1976): 49. In 1879 the *People's Advocate* in Washington, D.C., denounced the racism of the South's entire legal system. Two years after the Compromise of 1877, in a piece entitled "Southern Deviltry," the paper stated that white southerners were "bent on reducing the colored laborer to a condition for worse than that of chattel slavery. . . . Excessive fines are put on the most trivial offenses, the effect of which is to deprive men of their liberty for years. In this way, men are being practically enslaved" (*People's Advocate,* July 12, 1879).

43. Hendley was born in 1855 and grew up in Huntsville where he attended Rust Normal Institute. He was a teacher, grade school principal, Mason, and receiver of public moneys, a position to which he was appointed by President Harrison. In 1879 when the Huntsville Newspaper Company was organized for the purpose of publishing a newspaper, it chose Hendley as its editor and manager. The paper was published from 1880 to 1895 (Leilafred Ballard, "The American Negro as Portrayed in the *Huntsville Gazette*" (M.A. thesis, Howard University, 1952), 21–22.

44. Judge Richardson in Jackson County leased prisoners to free miners who paid the county $1 a day to use prisoners to load coal. Patrick McArdle, a mine boss in charge of twenty-two prisoners at Newcastle, testified in 1881 that "the convict and free labor work together" (*Testimony Taken by the Joint Special Committee,* 9; *Shelby Sentinel,* Feb. 8, 1877).

45. Daniel Letwin, "Interracial Unionism, Gender, and 'Social Equality' in the Alabama Coalfields, 1878–1908," *Journal of Southern History* 61 (Aug. 1995): 519–54.

46. Philip S. Foner and Ronald L. Lewis, eds., *The Black Worker during the Era of the National Labor Union* (Philadelphia, 1978), 2:243–70. One of the Greenback party's most prominent spokespeople was Peter W. Clark, a dedicated socialist from Cincinnati and the African-American grandson of the explorer William Clark.

47. For more on Thomas and black participation in the Greenback movement, see Letwin, *Challenge of Interracial Unionism,* 55–63.

48. Henry Hospun, Colored Club No. 3, to the *National Labor Tribune,* July 9, 1878, B. Jones, Oxmoor, Ala., to the *National Labor Tribune,* July 10, 1878, in Foner and Lewis, *Black Worker during the Era of the National Labor Union* 2:254–55. It was more than Thomas's speechmaking that impressed Henry Hospun, the grocer: "I like this paper called the *Tribune,*" he wrote. He wondered if the editor would accept half-price flour in exchange for a six-month subscription.

49. Warren Kelley to the *National Labor Tribune,* July 30, 1878, printed in the *Tribune* Aug. 17, 1878, ibid., 2:253–54.

50. McKiven, *Iron and Steel,* 43–44, describes recruiting trips made to the Black Belt in search of labor.

51. John Brophy, *A Miner's Life* (Madison and Milwaukee, 1964), 38–46.

52. Testimony of F. H. Gafford, *Testimony Taken by the Joint Special Committee,* 8.

53. Testimony of Justus Collins, U.S. Congress, Senate, Committee on Education and Labor, 49th Cong., 2d sess., *Testimony before the Committee to Investigate the Relations between Capital and Labor* 4:440.

54. Ibid., 434.

55. Dan Letwin has tried to decipher the meaning of interracial cooperation among black and white miners in Alabama in *Challenge of Interracial Unionism.*

56. *Biennial Report of the Inspectors of the Alabama Penitentiary, Sept. 30, 1880, to Sept. 30, 1882,* 20–21.

57. Official figures exist for leased state prisoners only. Out of the ninety-two prison miners at work at the two Pratt mines in 1882, twenty-four were white. Of the thirty-nine prisoners mining coal at Newcastle, seven were white (ibid., 82–89, 98–101).

58. By the 1890s, however, most of the black coal miners in the region worked as day laborers for white, and occasionally black, miners. Subcontractors were paid by the day, not the ton. According to Paul Worthman, "The subcontracting system divided miners along occupational as well as racial lines" ("Black Workers and Labor Unions in Birmingham," 388–89).

59. Testimony of Sampson Allsop, *Testimony Taken by the Joint Special Committee,* 14–15.

60. J. H. Bankhead to J. W. Comer, May 23, 1882, to Col. H. M. Caldwell, May 23, 1882, Letter Book, July 23, 1881–May 1, 1885, Department of Corrections, ADAH.

61. J. H. Bankhead to B. P. Harrison, Sheriff of Athens, Ala., May 30, 1882, ibid.

62. *Shelby Sentinel,* March 28, 1878, May 11, 25, 1882.

63. *Biennial Report of the Inspectors of the Alabama Penitentiary from Sept. 30, 1880, to Sept. 30, 1882,* 17.

64. Warden Bass to Governor Cobb, May 31, 1879, Governor Cobb, Administrative Files, Jan. 1–June 2, 1879, box 1, folder 1, ADAH. Bass offered to take over the lease as the sole warden to keep prisoners away from mines. His backers were planters.

65. *Biennial Report of the Inspectors of the Alabama Penitentiary from Sept. 30, 1880, to Sept. 30, 1882,* 5.

66. Going, *Bourbon Democracy in Alabama,* 91.

67. "Alabama Politics—The Penitentiary," correspondence from the *Selma Argus* reprinted in the *Shelby Sentinel,* Dec. 8, 1881.

68. *Huntsville Gazette,* Sept. 3, 1881, reprinted from the *Jackson Republican.*

69. "The agitation of the convict question has not been without its fruits. Already a bill with regard to the hiring of convicts has passed the Senate. . . . If passed, it will be some improvement over the present law which unquestionably exposes convicts to hard and inhuman treatment" (*Huntsville Gazette,* Dec. 16, 1882).

70. Arlin Turner, *George W. Cable: A Biography* (1956; rept. Baton Rouge, La., 1966), 143.

71. During his first year in office, Bankhead wrote one letter to Comer and another to Milner questioning their truthfulness about the amount of punishment inflicted on prisoners, and he corresponded with Robert McKee, the governor's influential private secretary, on the issue of prison conditions (Bankhead to Comer and McCurdy, July 25, 1881, and to Milner and Caldwell, at Newcastle, Aug. 9, 1881, Letter Book, July 23, 1881–May 1, 1885, Department of Corrections, ADAH; Bankhead to Mckee, Sept. 16, 1882, box 2, folder 5, Robert McKee Papers, ibid.).

72. *Biennial Report of the Inspectors of the Alabama Penitentiary from Sept. 30, 1880, to Sept. 30, 1882,* "Warden's Report," 11–24.

73. Ibid., 21.

74. Ibid., table Z; testimony of J. H. Bankhead, U.S. Congress, Senate, Committee on Education and Labor, 49th Cong., 2d sess., *Testimony before the Committee to Investigate the Relations between Capital and Labor* 4:437.

75. Mancini, *One Dies, Get Another*, 2–3.

76. Lewis, *Sloss Furnaces and the Rise of the Birmingham District*, chap. 17; Letwin, *Challenge of Interracial Unionism*, 17.

77. Worthman, "Working Class Mobility in Birmingham, Alabama."

5. PRISONERS AND REFORM, 1883–1885

1. Ezekiel Archey to R. H. Dawson, May 26, 1884, Gus Moore to Dawson, June 4, 1884, Correspondence of the Inspectors of the Penitentiary, 1883–85, Department of Corrections, ADAH; J. A. Howard to Dawson, Sept. 1886, Reports of Inspectors and Other Officials, ibid.

2. Ezekiel Archey to R. H. Dawson, Jan. 18, 1884, Correspondence of the Inspectors of the Penitentiary, 1883–85, ibid.

3. Owens, *History of Alabama* 1:88–93. Tallulah Bankhead, the famous screen star of the 1930s, was the granddaughter of John Hollis Bankhead and the daughter of Congressman William B. Bankhead. Robert J. Norrell writes, "Bowron's diary of July 14, 1888 reveals that the payoff of $1,200 was to the Alabama Congressman John Hollis Bankhead, formerly the warden of the state prisons" (*James Bowron: The Autobiography of a New South Industrialist* [Chapel Hill, N.C., 1991], 102).

4. Owens, *History of Alabama* 1:471–72, 792–95, 1031.

5. When his brother was thinking of running for the governorship in 1886, Dawson received a letter from Bankhead promising to inquire into the feelings of the mining companies (Bankhead to R. H. Dawson, Aug. 10, 1885, Correspondence of the Inspectors of the Penitentiary, 1883–85, Department of Corrections, ADAH).

6. Dawson to Gov. E. A. O'Neal, April 16, 1883, Letter Book, April 2–Dec. 31, 1883, ibid.

7. Dawson to L. D. Rouse, July 7, 1883, ibid.

8. Dawson to Simon O'Neal, Judge of the Probate, Russell County, May 23, 1883, ibid.

9. The white convicts complained about this (Dawson to H. J. Callen, Judge of Probate, Chilton County, May 19, 1883, ibid.).

10. Dawson to B. F. Porter, June 21, 1883, to B. H. Warren, June 30, 1883, ibid.

11. Dawson to Judge Allston, Aug. 27, 1883, ibid.

12. Entries of July 5, 13, 1883, folder 1, Diary of Reginald Heber Dawson, 1883–1906, ibid.

13. R. H. Dawson to Hon. J. B. Tally, Sept. 16, 1883, and R. H. Dawson to R. A. J. Cumlie, Sept. 25, 1883, Letter Book, July 3, 1881–May 1, 1885, Department of Corrections, ibid.

14. *Convicts at Hard Labor for the County in the State of Alabama on the First Day of March, 1883*, microfiche, ibid. This report, published in 1883, is the first published record of county convicts despite the fact that counties had been leasing and working prisoners since the end of the Civil War.

15. A. T. Henley to R. H. Dawson, Dec. 7, 1883, Correspondence of the Inspectors of the Penitentiary, 1883–85, Department of Corrections, ibid.

16. "Our payroll for the month of October showed six hundred and ninety two free men, and in that month we had 520 convicts. Then the Pratt Co. had other convicts and laborers, and altogether the grand total is one thousand four hundred and thirty seven" (testimony of Justin Collins, Nov. 16, 1883, U.S. Congress, Senate, Committee on Edu-

cation and Labor, 49th Cong., 2d sess., *Testimony before the Committee to Investigate the Relations between Capital and Labor* 4 : 441).

17. Ezekiel Archey to R. H. Dawson, May 26, 1884, Correspondence of the Inspectors of the Penitentiary, 1883–85, Department of Corrections, ADAH.

18. W. D. Lee to R. H. Dawson, Aug. 19, 1884, ibid.

19. R. H. Dawson to A. H. Alston, Jan. 11, 1884, Letter Book, Jan. 11–Aug. 12, 1884, to Hon. T. L. Frazer, Nov. 15, 1883, to Judge James W. Taylor, June 29, 1883, to Hon. William Richardson, Jan. 23, 1884, Letter Book, July 23, 1881–May 1, 1885, ibid.

20. R. H. Dawson to Gov. E. A. O'Neal, April 16, 1883, to B. F. Porter, June 21, 1883, Letter Book, April 2–Dec. 31, 1883, ibid.

21. J. H. Bankhead to Gaius Whitfield, July 18, 1882, R. H. Dawson to W. H. Hubbard, March 14, 1885, Letter Book, July 23, 1881–May 1, 1885, ibid.

22. R. H. Dawson to Hon. William Richardson, Jan. 23, 1884, ibid.

23. "In one or two instances the man has been in the office before I knew he had been granted short time, and in settling with contractors I have no recourse but to take their statement" (R. Andrews to Gov. Thomas Seay, April 15, 1887, Letters, March–June 1887, A-L, Papers of Governor Seay, ibid.).

24. R. H. Dawson to Hon. J. L. Powell, Dec. 18, 1886, Letter Book, Nov. 11, 1886–April 18, 1887, Department of Corrections, ibid.

25. Judge Purifoy to R. H. Dawson, May 8, 1885, Correspondence, March–Dec. 1885, ibid. In this letter the judge explicitly explains to Dawson how he computes costs—"from date of delivery to contractor"—and wishes to know if this is correct.

26. R. H. Dawson to Farriss & McCurdy, labor contractors, re the case of Rachael Thomas, June 23, 1883, Letter Book, April 2–Dec. 31, 1883, ibid. The time for her costs was calculated as though there were only twenty-six days to a month. See also Judge Savage to R. H. Dawson, May 9, 1885, informing him that he "does not count Sundays" in his calculations (Correspondence, March–Dec. 1885, ibid.).

27. *Shelby Sentinel*, May 2, 1878; testimony of J. C. Hunter, *Testimony Taken by the Joint Special Committee*, 19; J. H. Bankhead to Messrs. Steiner Bros., July 15, 1882, Letter Book, July 23, 1881–May 1, 1885, Department of Corrections, ADAH.

28. Correspondence, Papers of Gaius Whitfield, ADAH.

29. *First Biennial Report of the Inspectors of Convicts, 1884–86*, 6–7.

30. R. H. Dawson to Gov. Jones, Jan 6, 1891, Papers of Governor Jones, box 66, ADAH.

31. Albert McAlpine, prisoner at Coalburg, to Wade McAlpine, Nov. 13, 1887, Unorganized Files, box 2, Papers of Governor Seay, ibid.

32. Ezekiel Archey to R. H. Dawson, May 26, 1884, Correspondence of the Inspectors of the Penitentiary, 1883–85, Department of Corrections, ibid.

33. Jane Childes to Col. R. H. Dawson, July 30, 1885, Correspondence, March–Dec. 1885, ibid.

34. Harry Streety to Gov. O'Neal, Aug. 14, 1885, ibid.

35. Judge Kirksey to R. H. Dawson, Jan. 31, 1885, ibid.

36. R. Andrews to Gov. Thomas Seay, April 15, 1887, Letters, March–June 1887, A-L, Papers of Governor Seay, ibid.

37. Sam Black to Gov. Thomas Seay, May 24, 1887, attached to letter from J. D. Douglass to Gov. Thomas Seay, May 28, 1887, Unorganized Files, box 2, Papers of Governor Seay, ADAH

38. Albert McAlpine, prisoner at Coalburg, to Wade McAlpine, Nov. 13, 1887, ibid.

39. R. H. Dawson to Hon. B. H. Warren, Judge of Probate Choctaw County, June 30, 1883, Letter Book, April 2–Dec. 31, 1883, Department of Corrections, ibid.

40. Dawson wrote to Governor O'Neal that "this [short time] has been very rarely allowed them [county convicts] and if it was done more frequently, it would be a great incentive to good conduct" (R. H. Dawson to E. A. O'Neal, April 16, 1883, ibid.).

41. R. H. Dawson to Hon. John A. Steele, Feb. 28, 1884, Letter Book, Jan. 11–Aug. 12, 1884, ibid.

42. A. T. Henley to J. D. Douglass, Sept. 21, 1885, Correspondence, March–Dec. 1885, ibid.

43. R. H. Dawson to J. O. Blair, July 6, 1886, Letter Book, March 26–Nov. 15, 1886, ibid.

44. "There has been no report of county convicts from Marshall co. made to this office since April 1884 and several convicts have applied to me for their 'Time Cards' which I am required to furnish by the last convict act" (R. H. Dawson to Hon. T. A. Street, Feb. 9, 1886, Letter Book, May 2, 1885–March 25, 1886, ibid.).

45. R. H. Dawson to Governor Jones, Dec. 20, 1890, Papers of Governor Jones, box 66, ibid.

46. Albert Ervin to J. D. Douglass, Aug. 25, 1885, Correspondence, March–Dec. 1885, Department of Corrections, ibid.

47. Warren Levett to Dawson, June 1885, ibid.

48. R. H. Dawson to Judge A. D. Sayre, June 13, 1885, Letter Book, May 2, 1885–March 25, 1886, ibid.

49. R. H. Dawson to P. A. Green, June 3, 1885, ibid.

50. R. H. Dawson to W. G. Robertson, June 13, 1885, ibid.

51. Thomas Skinner to R. H. Dawson, Feb. 6, 1884, R. H. Skinner to R. H. Dawson, Dec. 1, 1883, Correspondence of the Inspectors of the Penitentiary, 1883–85, ibid.

52. R. H. Dawson to R. C. Bradley, June 3, 1885, Letter Book, May 2, 1885–March 25, 1886, ibid.; *Steele v. State,* 61 Ala. Reports.

53. R. H. Dawson to A. T. Henley and W. D. Lee to Gov. Thomas Seay, May 11, 1889, Correspondence, Papers of Governor Seay, ADAH.

54. A. T. Henley to R. H. Dawson, Aug. 10, 1885, Reports of Inspectors and Other Officials, ibid.

6. Working and Surviving in Prison Mines

1. Brophy, *A Miner's Life,* 37. For coal mining in the late nineteenth century, see ibid., 38–50; Priscilla Long, *Where the Sun Never Shines: A History of America's Bloody Coal Industry* (New York, 1989), 36–42; Keith Dix, *Work Relations in the Coal Industry: The Hand-Loading Era, 1880–1930* (Morgantown, W.Va., 1977), and *What's a Coal Miner to Do? The Mechanization of Coal Mining* (Pittsburgh, 1988).

2. Lichtenstein, *Twice the Work of Free Labor,* 146–47; Shapiro, *A New South Rebellion,* 66–69, 73.

3. A. T. Henley to Judge Jas. T. Beck, March 2, 1892, Letter Book, Oct. 1, 1890–July 6, 1892, Department of Corrections, ADAH.

4. A. T. Henley to J. L. Dean, Aug. 7, 1891, attached to letter from A. T. Henley to Gov. Thomas G. Jones, Aug. 13, 1891, Papers of Governor Jones, box 27, folder C, ibid.

5. "Rules for Working Prisoners in the Mines," approved by Gov. E. A. O'Neal, Jan. 17, 1885, Correspondence of the Inspectors of the Penitentiary, 1883–85, Department of Corrections, ibid.

6. Testimony of W. E. Cockrell in U.S. Congress, Senate, Committee on Education and Labor, 49th Cong., 2d sess., *Testimony before the Committee to Investigate the Relations between Capital and Labor* 4:430; A. T. Henley to Judge Jas. T. Beck, March 2, 1892, Letter

Book, Oct. 1, 1890–July 6, 1892, Department of Corrections, ADAH.

7. R. H. Dawson to Gov. Thomas G. Jones, June 1891, Letter Book, Oct. 1, 1890–July 6, 1892, Department of Corrections, ADAH.

8. Dawson acknowledged that there was probably more lethal gas in the Rock Slope "than in any of the mines at Pratt Mines" (ibid.; Report of Dr. J. M. Hayes in *First Biennial Report of the Inspectors of Convicts, 1884- 86*, 237–38.

9. Testimony of anonymous prisoner at Slope No. 2, in Alabama, General Assembly, *Testimony before the Joint Committee of the General Assembly, Appointed to Examine into the Convict System of Alabama, Session of 1888–89* (Montgomery, Ala., 1889), 113–15.

10. A. T. Henley to Judge Jas. T. Beck, March 2, 1892, Letter Book, Oct. 1, 1890–July 6, 1892, Department of Corrections, ADAH.

11. Report of R. M. Cunningham, M.D., and Report of Dr. F. P. Lewis, Physician at Coalburg, *First Biennial Report of the Inspectors of Convicts, 1884- 86*, 245, 259, 7; Testimony of anonymous prisoner at Slope No. 2, *Testimony before the Joint Committee of the General Assembly, Appointed to Examine into the Convict System of Alabama, 1888–89*, 114.

12. A. T. Henley to Judge Jas. T. Beck, March 2, 1892, Letter Book, Oct. 1, 1890–July 6, 1892, Department of Corrections, ADAH.

13. Report of Dr. J. M. Hayes, *First Biennial Report of the Inspectors of Convicts, 1884–86*, 233–34.

14. Entries of Oct. 7, 1885, March 7, 1887, Minutes of the Board of Directors, 1883–1913, Department of Corrections, ADAH.

15. Archey to Dawson, Jan. 18, 1884, Correspondence of the Inspectors of the Penitentiary, 1883–85, ibid.

16. Drew Gilpin Faust, "Culture, Conflict, and Community: The Meaning of Power on an Ante-Bellum Plantation," *Journal of Social History* 14:1 (1980): 83–98. See also Raymond A. and Alice Bauer, "Day to Day Resistance to Slavery," *Journal of Negro History* 27 (Oct. 1942): 388–419.

17. Charles B. Dew, "Disciplining Slave Ironworkers in the Antebellum South: Coercion, Conciliation, and Accommodation," *American Historical Review* 79:2 (April 1974): 398–418, quote on 398, and *Bond of Iron: Master and Slave at Buffalo Forge* (New York, 1995). Ronald Lewis, on the other hand, emphasizes that slaves forced to mine coal in Alabama also worked under a quota system. If they failed to produce, they were whipped (*Black Coal Miners in America: Race, Class, and Community Conflict, 1780–1980* [Lexington, Ky., 1987], 9–11).

18. Archey to Dawson, Jan. 18, 1884, Correspondence of the Inspectors of the Penitentiary, 1883–85, Department of Corrections, ADAH.

19. *Testimony before the Joint Committee of the General Assembly, Appointed to Examine into the Convict System of Alabama, 1888–89*, 113–14; Ezekiel Archey to R. H. Dawson, May 26, 1884, Correspondence of the Inspectors of the Penitentiary, 1883–85, Department of Corrections, ADAH.

20. A. T. Henley to R. H. Dawson, June 2, 1885, Reports of Inspectors and Other Officials, Department of Corrections, ADAH.

21. John T. Milner to R. H. Dawson, June 10, 1885, Correspondence, March–Dec. 1885, ibid.

22. Anonymous letter from Prisoners at the Shaft to Gov. Thomas Seay, May 17, 1887, Unorganized Files, box 2, Papers of Governor Seay, ibid.

23. R. H. Dawson to Gov. Seay, May 31, 1887, ibid.

24. R. H. Dawson to A. T. Henley, Oct. 25, 1887, Letter Book, April 19, 1887–Feb. 17, 1888, Department of Corrections, ibid.

25. "When twenty five percent of the men who have turned the machine have died in two years or to be so broken down as to become worthless there is something wrong" (ibid.).

26. Ibid., March 22, 1886, Letter Book, March 26–Nov. 15, 1886, ibid.

27. "Report and Evidence in the Matter of the Death of Alexander Crews," *First Biennial Report of the Inspectors of Convicts, 1884–86*, 277–347, 281.

28. J. D. Douglass to W. D. Lee, July 11, 1888, Letter Book, Feb.–Sept. 1888, Department of Corrections, ADAH.

29. A. T. Henley to R. H. Dawson, Oct. 22, 1887, Reports of Inspectors and Other Officials, ibid.

30. James Scott, *Domination and the Arts of Resistance: Hidden Transcripts* (New Haven, 1990), chap. 1.

31. R. H. Dawson to W. D. Lee, Oct. 6, 1887, Letter Book, April 19, 1887–Feb. 17, 1888, Department of Corrections, ADAH.

7. FEMALE PRISONERS

1. Brenda A. Stevenson, "Gender Convention, Ideals, and Identity among Antebellum Virginia Slave Women," in *More than Chattel: Black Women and Slavery in the Americas*, ed. David Barry Gaspar and Darlene Clark Hine (Bloomington, Ind., 1996), 169–90, 171.

2. See the following annual reports of the penitentiary inspectors, all published in Montgomery: *Annual Report of the Inspectors of the Alabama Penitentiary from Oct. 1, 1869, to Oct. 1, 1870; . . . from March 1 to Sept. 30, 1873; . . . from Oct. 1, 1873, to Sept. 30, 1874; . . . March 4, 1875* (1875); . . . . *for Year Ending Sept. 30, 1877; Biennial Report of the Inspectors of the Alabama Penitentiary from Sept. 30, 1880, to Sept. 30, 1882*.

3. *Eutaw Whig and Observer*, Oct. 28, 1875.

4. *Annual Report of the Inspectors of the Alabama Penitentiary for Year Ending Sept. 30, 1877*.

5. *Biennial Report of the Inspectors of the Alabama Penitentiary from Sept. 30, 1880, to Sept. 30, 1882*, 21.

6. Between 1894–96 no white females were placed in county camps. See also *Third Biennial Report of the Inspectors of Convicts, 1888–90*, 162–63.

7. For a similar observation about antebellum conceptions of female virtue, see Bynum, *Unruly Women*, 93.

8. Victoria Bynum, "On the Lowest Rung: Court Control over Poor White and Free Black Women," *Southern Exposure* 12 (Nov.–Dec. 1884): 40–44, quote on 42.

9. Of these thirty-six, seven were cooks, nine were nurses, six were housekeepers, and the rest were field hands and house servants. It is difficult to determine if these women were part of family units that included men. "Housekeeper" meant someone who stayed at home, whereas nurses, cooks, laundresses, field hands, and servants worked for someone else. The rest of the convictions were for larceny, arson, and perjury (*Third Biennial Report of the Inspectors of Convicts, 1888–90*, 160–63).

10. *Annual Report of the Inspectors of the Alabama Penitentiary from Oct. 1, 1869, to Oct. 1, 1870*, p. 8–9.

11. Petition for the Pardon of Charley Jemison and Petition for the Pardon of Louisa Stewart, both in Pardon and Parole Records, Hale County, 1898 and 1906, respectively, ADAH. It appears that Aarons was held responsible for the death of the child.

12. Bynum, "On the Lowest Rung," 44; Petition for the Pardon of Louisa Stewart, ibid., 1906.

13. For infanticide, see Linda Gordon, *Woman's Body, Woman's Right: Birth Control in America* (1976; rept. New York, 1977), 32–35. Deborah Gray White discusses the "atypical" incidences of infanticide among slave women in *Ar'n't I a Woman? Female Slaves in the Plantation South* (New York, 1985), 87–88.

14. Laura Edwards has shown how close quarters in a black neighborhood in North Carolina led to neighbors knowing about domestic crimes, particularly spouse abuse (*Gendered Strife and Confusion: The Political Culture of Reconstruction* [Urbana, Ill., 1997], 63).

15. Butler, *Gendered Justice*, 212–13.

16. Quoted in ibid., 213.

17. E. C. Meredith to Judge S. H. Sprott, May 27, 1899, Petition for the Pardon of Julia Ann May, Pardon and Parole Records, Greene County, ADAH.

18. Edwards, *Gendered Strife and Confusion*, 56–57.

19. See Herbert Gutman, "Afro-American Kinship before and after Emancipation in North America," in *Interest and Emotion*, ed. Hans Medick and David Warren Sebean (Cambridge, 1986).

20. "Major Ann Pollard paid a $5 fine and sailed out of the Mayor's Court room" (*Montgomery Advertiser*, Nov. 21, 1875).

21. W. W. Dugger to Gov. Thomas Seay, Jan. 25, 1888, Pardon Files, Papers of Governor Seay, ADAH.

22. Petition for Sydney Boddie and attached letter from P. Callahan, March 29, 1873, Pardon and Parole Records, Marengo County, ibid.

23. Rafter, *Partial Justice*, 137.

24. Judge Luther Smith to Gov. Lewis, Jan. 3, 1874, Petition for the Pardon of Susan Ross, Pardon and Parole Records, Marengo County, ADAH.

25. *Biennial Report of the Inspectors of the Alabama Penitentiary from Sept. 30, 1880, to Sept. 30, 1882*, 40–45.

26. Of the men listed in the hospital report, forty-four were married (twenty-five of those African Americans), and thirty-five were single (ibid., 40–45).

27. R. B Smyer to Governor Johnston, July 18, 1899, Pardon Request of Julia Ann May, Pardon and Parole Records, Greene County, ADAH.

28. Letter from Judge Anderson, April 3, 1895, Petition of Hannah Rembert, ibid., Marengo County.

29. Anonymous letter from Troy, Ala., to Governor Seay, 1888, Governor Seay, Pardon Files, ibid.

30. The first women's prison, the Indiana Women's Prison, opened in 1874. A Reformatory Prison for Women opened in Massachusetts in 1877, and a New York "House of Refuge" for women opened in 1887 (Estelle B. Freedmen, *Their Sisters' Keepers: Women's Prison Reform in America, 1830–1930* [Ann Arbor, Mich., 1981], 46–52 and chap. 3, which compares women-only prisons of the late nineteenth century with gender-mixed institutions).

31. Ibid., 152.

32. *Biennial Report of the Inspectors of the Alabama Penitentiary from Sept. 30, 1878, to Sept. 30, 1880*, 34–37, 42–45.

33. Rafter, *Partial Justice*, chap. 6, which focuses on black women in southern prisons.

34. *Biennial Report of the Inspectors of the Alabama Penitentiary from Sept. 30, 1880, to Sept. 30, 1882*, 10, table Z.

35. Ibid., 72–75.

36. Ibid., 72–115, 128.

37. *Testimony before the Joint Committee of the General Assembly, Appointed to Examine into the Convict System of Alabama, 1888–89*, 125.

38. Board of Inspectors to Warden Bankhead, Aug. 25, 1883, Minutes of the Board of Inspectors, 1883–1913, Department of Corrections, ADAH.

39. Entry of July 11, 1883, Reginald Heber Dawson, Diaries, 1883–1906, folder 1, ibid.

40. "Had two babies at mines—oldest going on five years. State furnishes baby with clothes. Father of children got at mine was a convict" (*Testimony before the Joint Committee of the General Assembly, Appointed to Examine into the Convict System of Alabama, 1888–89*, 125).

41. Ibid., 125.

42. Darlene Clark Hine, "Rape and the Inner Lives of Black Women in the Middle West: Preliminary Thoughts on the Culture of Dissemblance," in Hine, King, and Reed, *We Specialize in the Wholly Impossible*, 292–97, 294.

43. *First Biennial Report of the Inspectors of Convicts, 1884–86*, 17.

44. Freedmen, *Their Sisters' Keepers*.

45. R. H. Dawson to Gov. Thomas Seay, March 4, 1889, Letter Book, Sept. 11, 1888–May 17, 1889, Department of Corrections, ADAH. These were not idle observations. On March 15, 1889, Dawson ordered Lizzie Sterrett confined in a dark cell for five days on bread and water for stabbing another woman prisoner with a knife and raising an ax against the yardmaster (entry of March 15, 1889, Minutes of the Board of Inspectors, 1883–1913, ibid.).

46. R. H. Dawson to Governor Seay, Report for the quarter ending Oct. 1, 1889, Administrative Files, Papers of Governor Seay, ibid.

47. Ibid.

48. For example, Lizzie Sterrett was often punished for fighting with other women prisoners (entries of March 15, July 22, 1889, Minutes of the Board of Inspectors, 1883–1913, Department of Corrections, ibid.).

49. Hannah Rembert to Governor Johnston, April 12, 1899, Pardon and Parole Records, Marengo County, ibid.

50. Julia Ann May to Gov. Joseph Johnston, Feb. 26, 1899, ibid., Greene County.

51. Hannah Rembert to Governor Johnston, April 12, 1899, ibid., Marengo County.

52. Francis Woods to Col. Snodgrass, May 10, 1886, John B. Tally, Judge of Probate in Scottsboro, to R. H. Dawson, July 7, 1886, Report of Inspectors and Other Officials, Department of Corrections, ibid. For the vulnerability of poor black and white women to the legal system, see Bynum, "On the Lowest Rung," 40–44.

53. Petition for Bettie Perkins, 1881, Pardon and Parole Records, Marengo County, ADAH.

54. Testimony of Thomas Williams, in *Testimony before the Joint Committee of the General Assembly, Appointed to Examine into the Convict System of Alabama, 1888–89*.

55. B. M. Huey to Col. M. D. Graham, Aug. 19, 1876, pardon request form Wm. H. Redding, Pardon and Parole Records, Perry County, ADAH; *Eutaw Whig and Observer*, Nov. 22, 1877.

56. A. T. Henley to R. H. Dawson, Sept. 1, 1891, Reports of Inspectors and Other Officials, Department of Corrections, ADAH.

57. Ibid. For clothing and black women's self-expression in the late nineteenth century, see Patricia K. Hunt, "Clothing as an Expression of History: The Dress of African-American Women in Georgia, 1880–1915," in Hine, King, and Reed, *We Specialize in the Wholly Impossible*, 393–404.

58. A. T. Henley to R. H. Dawson, Aug. 31, 1891, Reports of Inspectors and Other Officials, Department of Corrections, ADAH.

59. , Ibid., Nov. 1, 1891.

60. Ibid., Oct. 1, 1891.

61. Freedman, *Their Sister's Keepers*, 89–106.

62. A. T. Henley to R. H. Dawson, Aug. 5, 1890, Reports of Inspectors and Other Officials, Department of Corrections, ADAH, contains a lengthy account of the entire incident.

63. According to the 1888–90 *Biennial Report,* Julia Pearson had only been convicted in Jefferson County on July 26, 1890. She had been sentenced to thirty days, with an additional eighty-six days to pay the $42.90 in costs. The attempted assault took place the weekend before Aug. 4, 1890.

64. Melton A. McLaurin, *Celia: A Slave* (1991; New York, 1993), tells the story of Celia, a slave woman, who killed her master after he had raped her repeatedly over a period of years. The jury refused to accept rape as an acceptable defense. See also Peter W. Bardaglio, *Reconstructing the Household: Families, Sex, and the Law in the Nineteenth Century South* (Chapel Hill, N.C., 1998). According to Laura Edwards, freedwomen in Granville, N.C., who pressed criminal charges of rape were most successful against black defendants (*Gendered Strife and Confusion*, 200–207).

65. For slave women's resistance to sexual assault, see Brenda Stevenson, *Life in Black and White: Family and Community in the Slave South* (New York, 1997).

66. Petition for Bettie Perkins, 1881, Pardon and Parole Records, Marengo County, ADAH.

67. Martha Aarons to Mr. Stallworth, Feb. 5, 1889, Reports of Inspectors and Other Officials, Department of Corrections, ibid.

68. J. W. McLigill to Governor Johnston, Sept. 26, 1898, Pardon and Parole Records, Hale County, ibid.

69. The refusal to act like prisoners also echoes the determination of slaves in urban settings to act as free as possible, despite their formal status. See John T. O'Brien, "Factory, Church, and Community: Blacks in Antebellum Richmond," *Journal of Southern History* 44 (Nov. 1978): 509–36.

70. Thomas Williams to Governor Johnston, n.d., Pardon and Parole Records, Hale County, ADAH.

8. PRISONERS CONFRONT TCI

1. P. J. Rogers to R. H. Dawson, Nov. 14, 1888, Reports of Inspectors and Other Officials, Department of Corrections, ADAH.

2. Robert David Ward and William Warren Rogers, *Labor Revolt in Alabama: The Great Strike of 1894* (University, Ala., 1965), 16; Going, *Bourbon Democracy in Alabama*, 178–81. After expenses, the state cleared a profit of over $36,000, making Alabama's profit from leasing larger than any other state's.

3. The "Shaft is located upon a hill in the northern part of town," and the Slope was about one mile away (R. M. Cunningham, "The Convict System of Alabama in Its Relation to Health and Disease," *Proceedings of the Annual Congress of the National Prison Association of the United States, 1889*, 130–32).

4. In 1890 A. T. Henley wrote to Dawson that "I found Chaplain Nicholson preaching to a very small number of convicts in the school room while a large number of them were in the court yard and cells. I issued an order to Warden Sherling to require every

convict not on the sick list to go to service" (Henley to Dawson, July 1, 1890, Reports of Inspectors and Other Officials, Department of Corrections, ADAH).

5. Going, *Bourbon Democracy in Alabama*, 175.

6. G. B. McCormack to R. H. Dawson, Dec. 24, 1889, Reports of Inspectors and Other Officials, Department of Corrections, ADAH.

7. J. Bowron, Secretary and Treasurer of TCI, to Gov. Thomas G. Jones, Jan. 8, 16, 1894, Papers of Governor G. Jones, drawer 66, box 28, ibid.

8. A. T. Henley to R. H. Dawson, Feb. 21, 1890, Reports of Inspectors and Other Officials, Department of Corrections, ibid.

9. Many prisoners were raised from third to second class, a change resulting in increased revenue for the state (Report for July from Henley to Dawson, Aug. 1, 1890, and Lee to Dawson, Aug. 1, 1890, ibid.).

10. Henley to J. D. Douglass, Aug. 2, 1890, ibid.

11. Lee to Dawson, Aug. 1, 1890, ibid.

12. Ibid., Aug. 11, 1890.

13. Report for August from Henley to Dawson, Sept. 1, 1890, ibid.

14. *Testimony before the Joint Committee of the General Assembly, Appointed to Examine into the Convict System of Alabama, 1888–89*, 117.

15. P. J. Rogers to Dawson, Nov. 6, 1890, Reports of Inspectors and Other Officials, Department of Corrections, ADAH.

16. Department of Corrections to P. J. Rogers, General Manager, Pratt Mines, March 16, 1889, Letter Book, Sept. 11, 1888–May 17, 1889, ibid.

17. "From what the convicts tell me I am of the opinion that we should insist upon the men being worked in McArdle Slope alone, for I am sure that the gas in the Rock Slope is dangerous & unless we take this stand somebody will be seriously injured there before long" (Henley to Dawson, March 11, 1889, Reports of Inspectors and Other Officials, ibid.

18. Report for Quarter ending July 1, 1889, Correspondence, Papers of Governor Seay, ibid.

19. Dawson to Seay, Aug. 1, 1889, ibid.

20. Ibid., Aug. 19, 1889.

21. Ibid., Aug. 27, 1889.

22. Ibid., Sept. 3, 1889.

23. Dawson to Seay, July 1, 1890, Letter Book, Dec. 11, 1889–Sept. 30, 1890, Department of Corrections, ibid.

24. See *Third Biennial Report of the Inspectors of Convicts, 1888–90*, 18.

25. "Rogers has been unable to locate the crime on anybody, but the evidence was unmistakable that it was attempted" (Henley to Dawson, Dec. 3, 1890, Reports of Inspectors and Other Officials, Department of Corrections, ADAH).

26. Dawson to Gov. Thomas Jones, June 1891, Letter Book, Oct. 1, 1890–July 6, 1892, ibid.

27. Ibid.

28. Ibid.

29. Lee to Dawson, March 19, 1890, ibid.

30. Henley to Dawson, May 1, 1890, ibid.

31. Henley's Report for May 1890, June 1, 1890, ibid.

32. Henley to Dawson, Feb. 21, 1890, ibid.

33. Henley to Dawson, Aug. 1, 1889, Feb. 21, 1890, Henley to J. D. Douglass, March 5, 1890, Lee to Dawson, March 29, 1890, ibid.

34. Henley to Dawson, Jan. 18, 1891, ibid.

35. Henley to Dawson, May 19, 1891, with attached copy of evidence before the coroner, ibid.

36. Henley to Dawson, June 1, 1891, ibid.

37. Lee to Dawson, June 2, 1891, Henley to Dawson, Sept. 1, 1891, ibid.

38. "There was no reason why fifty should not have gone out . . . the reason why more did not go was due only to the fact that no more were told of the outlet which had been made by the leader, Jim Massey, a very bad negro" (Lee to Dawson, July 8, March 10, 1892, ibid.

39. Henley to Dawson, June 1, 1892, ibid.

40. Lee to Dawson, Oct. 10, 1892, ibid.

41. Jerome Cochran, State Health Officer, to Governor Jones, Aug. 1, 1893, Papers of Governor G. Jones, box 26, folder C, ibid.; Dawson to Governor Jones, May 4, 1893, ibid., box 23, folder D.

42. Ike Berry admitted to knowing about the plot and doing nothing to prevent it. Dawson also withdrew his recommendation that Berry be pardoned (Dawson to Seay, June 11, 1888, Letter Book, Feb.–Sept. 1888, ibid.). For the list of prisoners involved in the mutiny and refused short time, see Report from J. D. Douglass to the Board of Inspectors, July 31, 1888, ibid.

43. Sydney Holman to Gov. Thomas Jones, Dec. 6, 1891, attached to Dawson to Governor Jones, Dec. 15, 1891, Papers of Gov. Jones, box, June 16, 1891–June 15, 1892, folder H, ibid.

44. Charley Jackson was Sydney Holman's "buddy," and he worked with him in the room off the sixth right heading (Henley to Dawson, April 6, 1892, Reports of Inspectors and Other Officials, Department of Corrections, ibid.).

45. Ibid.

46. Testimony of Ezekiel Archey, in U.S. Congress, Senate, Committee on Education and Labor, 49th Cong., 2d sess., *Testimony before the Committee to Investigate the Relations between Capital and Labor* 4:435.

47. Ibid., 436.

48. Although writing anonymously, he did say that he had been imprisoned for a little over a year; thus, he was referring to recent times (*Testimony before the Joint Committee of the General Assembly, Appointed to Examine into the Convict System of Alabama, 1888–89*, 116.

49. Ibid., 122.

50. The exact amount was $7,034.25 ("An Address by W. D. Lee, Inspector of Convicts, before the National Prison Congress at Cincinnati, Ohio," Exhibit 8 in *Third Biennial Report of the Inspectors of Convicts, 1888–90*, 62.

51. Henley to Dawson, May 14, 1891, Reports of Inspectors and Other Officials, Department of Corrections, ADAH.

52. Ibid.; Report for May 1891 dated June 1, 1891, ibid.

53. Cunningham, "The Convict System of Alabama in Relation to Health and Disease," 132–33.

54. Ibid.; Tutwiler, "Prison Schools in Alabama," 215.

55. Dawson to P. J. Rogers, June 4, 1894, Letter Book, Jan. 8, 1892–June 6, 1895, Department of Corrections, ADAH.

56. Report for July 1890 from Henley to Dawson, Aug. 1, 1890, Reports from Inspectors and Other Officials, ibid.

57. Henley to Dawson, Sept. 1, 1891, ibid.

58. Dawson to P. J. Rogers, June 4, 1894, Letter Book, Jan. 8, 1892–June 6, 1895, ibid.

59. Minutes of the Convict Board of Managers, 30, ibid. Money earned from extra labor was restricted to $1 a week because of the disciplinary threat posed by gambling.

60. Henley to Dawson, May 14, 1891, Reports of Inspectors and Other Officials, Department of Corrections, ADAH.

61. Ibid., May 5, 1891.

62. Ibid.

63. *Third Biennial Report of the Inspectors of Convicts, 1888–90*, 28–29.

64. Herbert Aptheker, *American Negro Slave Revolts* (1943; rept. New York, 1983); Gary Y. Okihiro, *In Resistance: Studies in African, Caribbean, and Afro-American History* (Amherst, Mass., 1986).

65. Bauer, "Day to Day Resistance to Slavery." John Dollard had shown the dual roles black citizens were forced to play; he argued that seemingly nonthreatening behavior was, in reality, motivated by indirect aggression. Accommodation, Dollard wrote, "involves the renunciation of protest or aggression . . . and the organizations of the character so that protest does not appear, but acceptance does" (*Caste and Class in a Southern Town*, 3d ed. [New York, 1957], 255).

66. Bauer, "Day to Day Resistance to Slavery"; Dollard, *Caste and Class in a Southern Town*. Tellingly, Ulrich B. Phillips called his chapter on slave resistance and rebellions "Slave Crime" (*American Negro Slavery* [1918; rept. Baton Rouge, La., 1966], chap. 22, see also chap. 15, "Plantation Labor").

67. The exception would be Eugene Genovese, *Roll, Jordan, Roll*. Genovese recognizes that slave communities gave individuals the strength to survive the dehumanizing brutality of the slave regime. But he does believe the slaves accepted white values, especially in his discussion of the black church and slave morals. In his book *The Black Family in Slavery and Freedom*, Herbert Gutman stresses the legacy of cultural values over time and the persistence of the black family structure regardless of one's master or the extent of one's interactions with white people. Gutman stresses the autonomy of black culture and the inadequacy of linking black behavior to white treatment. He does not, however, discuss black and white interactions. For him, resistance consists of creating an autonomous cultural and psychological sphere. He, like the Bauers, would conclude that the appearance of acceptance or accommodation was less important than the internal world of the black community black people themselves created.

68. Dollard, *Caste and Class in a Southern Town*, 260.

69. Michael Buroway, *The Politics of Production* (London, 1985), 37–39.

9. A MORTAL CRISIS

1. "Report of Work Done by Inspector Lee during the Month of June, 1888," details conditions at Newcastle. Lee to Dawson, Feb. 1, 1889, and Henley to Dawson, Feb. 1, 1889, detail excessive whipping at Newcastle; Lee to Dawson, Feb. 11, 25, 1889, and Henley to Dawson, Feb. 28, 1889, report prisoners working without shoes at both Coalburg and Newcastle. Henley's letter also attributes sickness and diarrhea at Coalburg to its tainted water supply (Reports of Inspectors and Other Officials, Department of Corrections, ADAH).

2. Henley to J. D. Douglas, June 27, 1889, ibid.

3. In the spring of 1890, for example, the Jefferson County convicts working on a road crew under the direction of S. Y. Carradine "annoyed" him with their constant

requests for time cards. Carradine asked Dawson's secretary, J. D. Douglas, to send them to him for quick distribution (Carradine to Douglas, May 28, 1890, ibid.).

4. Lee to Dawson, Feb. 1, 1889, ibid.

5. Henley to Dawson, Feb. 1, May 8, 1889, Lee to Dawson, Feb. 25, March 21, 1889, ibid.

6. Henley to Dawson, Feb. 1, 1889, ibid.

7. Ibid., Feb. 28, March 13, 1889.

8. Henley to Douglass, July 7, 1890, to Dawson, Aug. 1, 1890, ibid.

9. Lee to Dawson, Feb. 1, 1889, ibid.

10. Henley to Dawson, April 8, 1889, ibid.

11. Ibid., April 11, 1889.

12. Ibid., June 17, 18, 1889.

13. "County Convicts at Coalburg, March 1, 1893," list sent from the Convict Bureau to Gov. Thomas Jones, Papers of Governor Jones, ibid.; *Third Biennial Report of the Inspectors of Convicts*, 96–97.

14. Henley to Dawson, May 5, 1891, Reports of Inspectors and Other Officials, Department of Corrections, ibid.

15. Ibid., May 14, 1891.

16. Dawson to Gov. Jones, May 4, 1893, Papers of Governor Jones, box 23, folder D, ibid.; H. W. Perry, Manager of the Sloss Iron and Steel Co., to Gov. Jones, June 9, 1893, ibid., folder P.

17. J. C. King, Hard Labor Agent, to Gov. Thomas G. Jones, March 22, 1893, ibid., box 25.

18. Sam Will John to Gov. Thomas G. Jones, April 1, 1893, ibid.

19. H. W. Perry to Gov. Thomas G. Jones, April 9, 1893, ibid.

20. Henley and R. Aug. Jones, M.D., to Gov. Thomas G. Jones, April 9, 1893, ibid.

21. Thomas Seddon to Gov. Thomas G. Jones, April 17, 1893, ibid.

22. J. W. Locke to Dawson, April 23, 1893, ibid., box 23.

23. Ibid., April 30, 1893.

24. Ibid., May 13.

25. J. D. Douglass to Gov. Thomas G. Jones, May 19, 1893, ibid., box 26.

26. W. H. Perry to Gov. Thomas G. Jones, June 9, 1893, ibid., box 23.

27. Dr. Jerome Cochran to Gov. Thomas G. Jones, Aug. 1, 1893, ibid., box 26.

28. Dawson to Gov. Thomas G. Jones, March 10, 1894, ibid., box 29.

29. Thomas D. Parke, M.D., Health Officer of Jefferson County, *Report on Coalburg Prison*, Ordered by the Committee of Health of Jefferson County Medical Society, 1895, microfiche, ibid.

30. Ibid.

31. *First Biennial Report of the Board of Inspectors of Convicts, 1894–96*, 64.

32. Ibid., 65.

33. Dr. F. P. Lewis to J. T. Hill, Dec. 15, 1890, Papers of Governor Jones, box 66, ADAH.

34. *First Biennial Report of the Board of Inspectors of Convicts, 1894–96*, 68.

35. Ibid., 73.

36. Ibid.

37. *Facts about Coalburg Prison: Dr. Parke's Report Reviewed*, Report prepared by Mr. Castleman and Dr. Lewis, microfiche, ADAH.

38. "Coalburg Prison," Health Officer of Jefferson County to the Board of Convict Inspectors, Dec. 3, 1895, microfiche, ibid.

39. "Am almost convinced that the farm and saw mill are about the only places fit

to work convicts" (Lee to Dawson, March 19, 1890, Reports of Inspectors and Other Officials, Department of Corrections, ibid.).

40. Dawson to Gov. Thomas G. Jones, March 1, 1893, Papers of Governor Jones, box 24, ibid.

41. Memorandum of agreement between Col. Thomas Williams and Dawson, Jan. 10, 1893, ibid.

42. Dawson to Gov. Thomas G. Jones, May 4, 1893, ibid., letter box 23.

43. *First Biennial Report of the Board of Inspectors of Convicts, 1894–96,* 4.

44. Ibid., 8.

45. Ibid., 19–43.

46. *Report of the Joint Committee of the General Assembly of Alabama upon the Convict System of Alabama* (Montgomery, Ala., 1901), 6–7.

47. Ibid., 8–11.

48. Ibid., 15.

49. Ibid., 17–18.

50. Ibid., 11–12.

51. J. D. Hand to Col. S. B. Trapp, May 13, 1900, G. W. Sherling to Trapp, July 14, 1900, 1900 Correspondence, Department of Corrections, ADAH.

52. Saunders & Rose of Pensacola to Gov. Johnston, Aug. 30, 1900, Rock City Hosiery Mills to Board Prison Commissioners, Aug. 2, 1900, ibid.

53. Rucker, Vice President of Sloss, to Trapp, July 24, 1900, Horse Shoe Lumber Co. to Trapp, July 23, 25, 1900, ibid.

54. P. J. Rogers to Trapp, July 12, 14, 20, 1900, Eliza Ann Tipton, wife of a prisoner, to Trapp, July 2, 1900, ibid.

55. *Report of the Joint Committee of the General Assembly of Alabama upon the Convict System of Alabama, 1901,* 13.

56. Ibid., 29–30.

57. Ibid., 28–29.

58. Rogers et al., *Alabama,* 296–306.

59. Lee to Dawson, Jan. 21, 1890, Reports of Inspectors and Other Officials, Department of Corrections, ADAH.

60. Samuel L. Webb, "A Jacksonian Democrat in Postbellum Alabama: The Ideology and influence of Journalist Robert McKee, 1869–1896," *Journal of Southern History* 62 (May 1996): 239–74, quote on 273.

61. Rogers et al., *Alabama,* 310.

62. Ibid., 311.

63. Ibid., 314–15; Letwin, *Challenge of Interracial Unionism,* 96–99.

64. For Johnson's background as president of Sloss, see Lewis, *Sloss Furnaces and the Rise of the Birmingham District,* 136, 251–52.

65. Mancini, *One Dies, Get Another,* 111.

66. Lewis, *Sloss Furnaces and the Rise of the Birmingham District,* 310–11.

67. Ibid., 312; Richard Straw, "Soldiers and Miners in a Strike Zone: Birmingham, 1908," *Alabama Review* 38 (Oct. 1985): 289–308.

68. Lewis, *Sloss Furnaces and the Rise of the Birmingham District,* 504.

69. Ward and Rogers, *Convicts, Coal, and the Banner Mine Tragedy,* 118; Mancini, *One Dies, Get Another,* 112–13.

70. Lewis, *Sloss Furnaces and the Rise of the Birmingham District,* 322–33; Ward and Rogers, *Convicts, Coal, and the Banner Mine Tragedy.*

71. "$1,073,286.16 Goes to State from Convicts," *Montgomery Advertiser,* Oct. 3, 1912, "Tuskegee Clipping File," Microfilm Department, Duke University. The article

states that "most of the returns to the department come from the hire of convicts by concerns operating mines in the Birmingham district."

72. Jack Kytle, "A Dead Convict Don't Cost Nothin," in *Up before Daylight: Life Histories from the Alabama Writers' Project, 1938–1939* ed. James Seay Brown Jr. (University, Ala., 1982). Jack Saunders was a seventy-six-year-old white man who had guarded prisoners at Alabama convict mines for forty-five years.

73. Ward and Roger, *Banner Mine Tragedy,* 116, 48–49; Lewis, *Sloss Furnaces and the Rise of the Birmingham District,* 412–13; Mancini, *One Dies, Get Another,* 114–15. The deplorable living and working conditions in Alabama prisons continued until 1973 when federal judge Frank Johnson placed Alabama's entire prison system under federal control (Larry Yackle, *Reform and Regret: The Story of Federal Judicial Involvement in the Alabama Prison System* [New York, 1989], 12).

10. BLACK LEADERSHIP RESPONDS

1. *Third Biennial Report of the Inspectors of Convicts, 1888–90,* 26.

2. *Harper's Weekly,* June 18, 1904, quoted in Giddings, *When and Where I Enter,* 27.

3. Thomas F. Gossett, *Race: The History of an Idea in America* (Dallas, 1963), 253–86.

4. John S. Perry, *Prison Labor: An Argument Made before the Senate Committee and Also before the Assembly Committee of the Legislature of the State of New York on Prisons, March 2, 1882,* 2d ed. (Albany, 1882), Pamphlet Collection, NYPL.

5. Not all northern prisons embraced income-producing labor as an essential part of prison reform. In eastern Pennsylvania, for example, the warden denied the privilege of working to prisoners who loved to work, thus punishing them (Z. R. Brockway, "The Piece Price Plan for Convict Labor," *Proceedings of the National Prison Association, First Annual Report, 2d Series,* (Chicago, 1884), 61, 1884.

6. Remarks of Warden Cassidy of the Eastern Penitentiary of Pennsylvania, ibid., 25–26.

7. *Prison Labor: An Address Delivered by Charles E. Felton, of Chicago, Ill., before the National Prison Congress at Atlanta, Ga., Nov. 11, 1886* (Chicago, 1887), Pamphlet Collection, NYPL.

8. Carroll D. Wright, "Prison Labor," *Proceedings of the Annual Congress of the National Prison Association of the United States, Held at Hartford, Conn., September 23–27, 1899* (Pittsburgh, 1900).

9. Ibid., 12–13.

10. Ibid., *1890,* 86–87.

11. *Proceedings of the Annual Congress of the National Prison Association of the United States, Held at Boston, July 14–19, 1888* (Chicago, 1888), 82.

12. *Proceedings of the Annual Congress of the National Prison Association of the U.S., Held at Pittsburgh, Oct. 10–14, 1891* (Pittsburgh, 1892).

13. Minutes of the Seventh Annual Session of the Alabama State Teachers' Association, Selma, Ala., April 11–13, 1888, H. Councill Trenholm Papers, box 30a, pp. 38–39, Moorland-Spingarn Research Center, Howard University. I would like to thank Adam Fairclough for bringing this document to my attention.

14. "Booker T. Washington on Apportionment," *Montgomery Advertiser,* Feb. 4, 1891.

15. *Montgomery Herald,* July 23, 1887. Duke, like Ida B. Wells of Memphis and Charles Manley of Wilmington, was forced out of town for implying that black men and white women had voluntary sexual relations.

16. D. E. Tobias to Booker T. Washington, July 17, 1899, in Harlan, *Booker T. Washington Papers* 161.

17. Ibid., 162–63.

18. Ibid., 161.

19. W. E. B. Du Bois, "The Negro and Crime," in Aptheker, *Writings by W. E. B. Du Bois in Periodicals Edited by Others* 1 : 57.

20. Ibid.

21. Ibid., 111.

22. W. E. B. Du Bois, "The Spawn of Slavery: The Convict Lease System in the South," ibid., 1 : 110.

23. Ibid., 113.

24. W. E. B. Du Bois, "The Negro South and North," ibid., 257.

25. Clarissa Olds Keeler, *The Crime of Crimes, or The Convict System Unmasked* (Washington, D.C., 1907), Pamphlet Collection, NYPL.

26. Mary Church Terrell, "Peonage in the United States: The Convict Lease System and Chain Gangs," in Beverly Washington Jones, *Quest for Equality: The Life and Writings of Mary Eliza Church Terrell, 1863–1954* (New York, 1990), 255.

27. Ibid., 257.

28. William West, Ashford, Ala., to Governor Jones, July 18, 1894, and Judge Dan Gordon to R. H. Dawson, July 25, 1894, attached together, Papers of Governor Jones, box 32, folder W, ADAH.

29. Terrell, "Peonage in the United States," 263.

30. Ibid., 273.

31. Kelly Miller, "Crime among Negroes," in *Out of the House of Bondage* (1914; rept. New York, 1971), 95–102.

32. Monroe N. Work, "Negro Criminality in the South," in *The Negro's Progress in Fifty Years*, Annals of the American Academy of Political and Social Science, 49 : 138 (Philadelphia, 1913).

33. Ibid., 77.

34. Ibid., 80.

35. Daniel, *Shadow of Slavery*, 24–28. Daniel describes how signing a contract with a white landlord to pay off one's court costs drew many black laborers into the "vortex" of peonage. Not until 1914 did the Supreme Court decide in *U.S. v. Reynolds* 235 U.S. 150 that holding a person captive to pay for the debt of their court costs was unconstitutional.

36. Daniel, *Shadow of Slavery*, chap. 3, "An Experiment in Leniency," 43–64, describes the first attempt to prosecute peonage in two Alabama counties, Coosa and Tallapoosa, in 1903. In chap. 4, "The Alonzo Bailey Case," 65–81, he describes the efforts of Booker T. Washington, William H. Thomas, a city court judge in Montgomery, and northern supporters to bring the Bailey case to the Supreme Court.

37. For elements of emerging black urban culture that revolved around music, drink, and dance and the middle-class response, see Hunter, *To 'Joy My Freedom*, chaps. 7–8.

11. PATERNALISM, THE LEASE, AND THE LAW

1. Glenn Feldman, "Lynching in Alabama, 1889–1921," *Alabama Review* 48 (April 1995): 114–41.

2. Various reasons have been put forward to explain the preponderance of lynchings in the rural, cotton-growing South. Stewart E. Tolnay and E. M. Beck point out the

correlation between falling cotton prices and lynchings in a community (*A Festival of Violence: An Analysis of Southern Lynchings, 1882–1930* [Urbana, Ill., 1992], 119–65). Fitzhugh Brundage correlates lynchings to areas dependent upon a single crop, such as cotton. He also points out that strong local law enforcement often prevented white mobs from laying hands on their intended victims (*Lynching in the New South: Georgia and Virginia, 1880–1930* [Urbana, Ill., 1993]). Jacqueline Dowd Hall reiterates a psychological motivation first put forward by Ida B. Wells: that lynching was an excuse for white men to exert their power over all blacks and remind them of their sexual power over black women (Jacquelyn Dowd Hall, *Revolt against Chivalry: Jessie Daniel Ames and the Women's Campaign against Lynching* [New York, 1979]).

3. Feldman, "Lynching in Alabama," 127.

4. Entry of Jan. 22, 1895, "4 Years Journal Greensborough District. 1892, 1893, 1894, & 1895," Papers of Winfield Henry Mixon, Presiding Elder, AME Church, MS Collection, Duke University.

5. Under segregation black folklore created characters of superhuman strength such as "Big Road Walker" who "personified courage and independence" (Raymond Gavins, "North Carolina Black Folklore and Song in the Age of Segregation: Toward Another Meaning of Survival," *North Carolina Historical Review* 66 [Oct. 1989]: 423).

6. Lawrence Levine, *Black Culture and Black Consciousness: Afro American Folk Thought from Slavery to Freedom* (New York, 1977), 407–20, 415, 417, 419.

7. Owens, "Hale County," *History of Alabama* 1:680.

8. Entry of Jan. 22, 1895, Mixon Journal, MS Department, Duke University.

9. Kevin Gaines, *Uplifting the Race: Black Leadership, Politics, and Culture since the Turn of the Century* (Chapel Hill, N.C., 1996). For a more positive view of the black middle classes of this period, see Glenda Elizabeth Gilmore, *Gender and Jim Crow: Women and the Politics of White Supremacy in North Carolina, 1896–1920* (Chapel Hill, N.C., 1996)

10. The *Huntsville Gazette* opposed excursions throughout the 1880s. See issues of April 28, 1883, Aug. 11, 1888, and Aug. 10, 1889.

11. Mixon Journal, MS Department, Duke University.

12. Catherine Clinton, "Bloody Terrain: Freedwomen, Sexuality, and Violence during Reconstruction," in *Half Sisters of History*, ed. Catherine Clinton (Durham, N.C., 1994), 140.

13. Ibid., 146.

14. Edwards, *Gendered Strife and Confusion*, 145–61; Leslie Schwalm, *A Hard Fight for We: Women's Transition from Slavery to Freedom in South Carolina* (Urbana, Ill., 1997), 260–66; Giddings, *When and Where I Enter*, chap. 2; Susan A. Mann, "Slavery, Sharecropping, and Sexual Inequality," *SIGNS* 14 (Summer 1989): 774–98, reprinted in Hine, King, and Reed, *We Specialize in the Wholly Impossible*, 281–302; Bynum, *Divided Houses*. Thavolia Glymph also has challenged the notion that black women and men walked in lockstep over the issues of female equality in marriage. She suggests that historians expand their conception of what black women wanted out of freedom beyond the realm of marriage (address before the Association for the Study of Negro Life and History, Charleston, S.C., Oct. 1996).

15. Hazel Carby, *Reconstructing Womanhood: The Emergence of the Afro-American Woman Novelist* (New York, 1987), 6.

16. Hunter, *To 'Joy My Freedom*, chaps. 4, 7, & 8.

17. Mann, "Slavery, Sharecropping, and Sexual Inequality."

18. "The best thinking colored women are not of the opinion that he should be hung and neither do the best element of colored men" (A. D. Wimbs to Gov. Joseph F.

Johnston, June 6, 1899, in the Petition for the Pardon of Charley Hall, Pardon and Parole Records, Hale County, ADAH).

19. Ibid.

20. At the request of local female churchwomen, for example, Rev. Mixon agreed to speak at the National Black Women's Convention in Nashville in April 1895. His journal also reveals numerous conversations with black women who were involved in the club movement of the 1890s.

21. See Edwards's example of Dink Watkins, who asserted her right to divorce by stating, "I am my own woman and will do as I please" (*Gendered Strife and Confusion*, chap. 1 and pp. 145–61).

22. Petition for the Pardon of James Crooms, 1898, Pardon and Parole Records, Perry County, ADAH.

23. McMillen, *Dark Journey*, 204–5.

24. See *Walker v. The State*, 91 Ala. 76, for a description of the case and a record of Tom Walker's appeal.

25. Dr. J. H. Edwards, assistant physician at Pratt City, to Gov. Joseph F. Johnston, Hale County, Pardon and Parole Records, 1866–1915, ADAH. See also *Walker v. The State*, 91 Ala. 76, for Walker's appeal.

26. Letters on behalf of Tom Walker, Hale County, Pardon and Parole Records, 1866–1915, ADAH.

12. PRISONERS IN BIRMINGHAM AND PRATT CITY

1. C. C. Whitson, Talladega, Ala., Attorney at Law, to Gov. Thomas G. Jones, Aug. 29, 1894, Papers of Governor Jones, box 33, folder W, ADAH.

2. Worthman, "Black Workers and Labor Unions in Birmingham, Alabama," 387 n.51.

3. Testimony of Justus Collins, *Testimony before the Committee to Investigate the Relations between Capital and Labor* 4:440; First *Biennial Report of the Inspectors of Convicts, 1884–86*, 21.

4. *Report of the Joint Committee of the General Assembly Appointed to Examine into the Convict System of Alabama, 1888–89*, 26.

5. F. P. Lewis, Physician in Charge, to J. T. Hill, Manager of Coalburg, Dec. 15, 1890, attached to J. T. Hill to Gov. Jones, Jan. 10, 1891, Papers of Governor Jones, box 66, ADAH. TCI released 365 state prisoners and 350 county men (*Third Biennial Report of the Inspectors of Convicts, 1888–90*, List No. 9, 109–20, List No. 10, 117–59).

6. Testimony of J. R. Tankersley, in U.S. Congress, Senate, Committee on Education and Labor, 49th Cong., 2d sess., *Testimony before the Committee to Investigate the Relations between Capital and Labor* 4:434.

7. *Birmingham Weekly Iron Age*, July 19, 1888.

8. Gerald H. Gaither, *Blacks and the Populist Revolt: Ballots and Bigotry in the New South* (University, Ala., 1977), 103–10.

9. Letwin, *Challenge of Interracial Unionism*, 97.

10. Wm. Whitaker, Birmingham, to Gov. Thomas G. Jones, Sept. 2, 1892, Papers of Governor Jones, box 21, folder W, ADAH.

11. *Birmingham Weekly Iron Age*, July 19, 1888.

12. Interview with Alex Bryant, June 26, 1984, by Brenda McCallum, p. 5, "Working Lives" Oral History Collection, MS Division, University of Alabama Library, Tuscaloosa. Census evidence bears out Bryant's memories of Pratt City as a racially mixed community.

The *Birmingham Directory*, 1884–85, Colored Department, 178–260, lists 133 African Americans working and living at the Pratt mines.

13. Ezekiel Archey to R. H. Dawson, Jan. 18, 1884, Correspondence of the Inspectors of the Penitentiary, 1883–85, Department of Corrections, ADAH.

14. Ibid.

15. See the exchange between A. T. Henley and Rev. Sims, *Proceedings of the Annual Congress of the National Prison Association of the United States, 1890*, 120.

16. David Lee Johnston to Booker T. Washington, Pratt Mines, Sept. 25, 1889, in Harlan, *Booker T. Washington Papers* 3:6.

17. Entries of April 26, 28, 1895, Jan. 2, 23, May 6, 8, 24, 1897, Mixon Journal, MS Department, Duke University.

18. Letwin, *Challenge of Interracial Unionism*, 91, 103.

19. Ibid., 91.

20. P. J. Rogers to R. H. Dawson, Dec. 8, 1890, Reports of Inspectors and Other Officials, Department of Corrections, ADAH.

21. A. T. Henley to R. H. Dawson, Dec. 19, 1890, ibid.

22. In 1891 free miners in Tennessee successfully invaded that state's prison mines and sent the prisoners, C.O.D., to that state's capital (Pete Daniel, "The Tennessee Convict Wars," *Tennessee Historical Quarterly* 34 [Fall 1975]: 273–92).

23. See Letwin, *Challenge of Interracial Unionism*, 91–95, for a full account of the 1890 strike.

24. Ibid., 99.

25. Ibid., 99–100.

26. Ibid., 104.

27. Agent TNV to Governor Jones, June 6, 1894, box 66, Pinkerton Reports of 1894 Strikes, Papers of Governor Jones, ADAH.

28. For the 1894 strike, see Ward and Rogers, *Labor Revolt in Alabama;* Letwin, *Challenge of Interracial Unionism*, 89–123; Lichtenstein, "Racial Conflict and Racial Solidarity in the Alabama Coal Strike of 1894."

29. Agent JHF to Gov. Jones, May 31, 1894, box 66, Pinkerton Reports of 1894 Strikes, Papers of Governor Jones, ADAH.

30. Prisoners had acted as strikebreakers since 1882. But TCI first requested and received permission to move prisoners from the convict mines to free mines during the strike of 1890 (R. H. Dawson to Gov. Jones, Dec. 17, 1890, Letter Book, Oct. 1, 1890–July 6, 1892, Department of Corrections, ibid.

31. Alabama's miners struck for major wage concessions in 1890, 1894, 1904, and 1908. See Richard Straw, "'This Is Not a Strike, It is Simply a Revolution': Birmingham Miners' Struggle for Power" (Ph.D. diss., University of Missouri-Columbia, 1980); Ward and Rogers, *Labor Revolt in Alabama;* Gutman, "The Negro and the United Mine Workers of America." For a recent summary of this literature, see Hill, "The Problem of Race in American Labor History."

32. Straw, "This is Not a Strike, It Is Simply a Revolution," chap. 1; Ward and Rogers, *Labor Revolt in Alabama*, chap. 1.

33. Worthman, "Black Workers and Labor Unions in Birmingham," 66.

34. Interview with Earl Brown, "Working Lives" Oral History Collection, 9, MS Division, University of Alabama Library, Tuscaloosa.

35. Miners in Walker County to Gov. Thomas Seay, Aug. 3, 1889, Correspondence, Papers of Governor Seay, ADAH.

36. Brophy, *A Miner's Life*, 77–82.

37. Ward and Rogers, *Labor Revolt in Alabama*, 60.

38. Entry of Nov. 1, 1894, Minutes of the Board of Managers of Convicts, 1893–95, Department of Corrections, ADAH.

39. W. D. Lee to R. H. Dawson, Aug. 3, 1892, Reports of Inspectors and Other Officials, ibid.

40. *First Biennial Report of the Board of Inspectors of Convicts, 1894–96*, 36–37.

41. Martha Mitchell Bigelow, "Birmingham's Carnival of Crime, 1871–1910," *Alabama Review* 3 (April 1950): 123–33. In addition to urban problems of overcrowding, ex-prisoners, and the lack of police, Bigelow pointed to the more general problem of the "Negroes." "Living in crowded unsanitary quarters and on the lower economic level and only a few years out of slavery, they presented a rich field for crime and violence of all sorts. Indeed, they constituted 40% of the population of the city and furnished about 60% of its criminals" (ibid., 133).

42. Harris, "Reforms of Government Control of Negroes in Birmingham," 589–90.

43. Ibid., 590–91.

44. George L. Thomas, Commissioners' Court, Jefferson County, to Gov. Thomas G. Jones, Papers of Governor Jones, drawer 66, Letters M-Z, Jan. 20–March 6, 1891, ADAH.

45. Shelby Harrison, "A Cash Nexus for Crime," *Survey*, Jan. 6, 1912, pp. 1554–55.

46. Harris, "Reforms of Government Control of Negroes in Birmingham," 596, quoting the *Birmingham Age-Herald* and the *Birmingham News*.

47. Harrison, "A Cash Nexus for Crime," 1554.

48. Harris, "Reforms of Government Control of Negroes in Birmingham," 567, quoting the *Birmingham News*, Oct. 13, 1912.

49. "The Alabama Mining Camp," *Independent* 63 (Oct. 3, 1907): 790–91.

50. Harrison, "A Cash-Nexus for Crime," 1550–51.

51. Ibid., 1556.

52. Ibid., 1548.

53. Harris, "Reforms of Government Control of Negroes in Birmingham," 599, quoting the *Birmingham Age-Herald*.

EPILOGUE

1. Adam Cohen, "Back on the Chain Gang," *Time*, May 15, 1995. See also *Newsweek*, May 15, 1995; *Jet*, Sept. 18, 1995; *Corrections Today*, April 1996; *Economist*, May 13, 1995.

2. "Chain Gangs to Be Banned in Alabama," *Buffalo News*, June 21, 1996. For a further analysis of the legality of the modern chain gang, see "The Return of the Chain Gang," *Harvard Law Review* 109 (1996): 876. Massachusetts has recently introduced chain gangs on its public roads ("Chain Gangs Come to Massachusetts," *New York Times*, June 17, 1999).

3. The United States has 5 percent of the global population and 25 percent of the world's prisoners (*Guardian*, Feb. 15, 2000; "U.S. Prison Population at New High," *New York Times*, April 20, 2000).

4. John DiIulio, *No Escape: The Future of American Corrections* (New York, 1991), 184–85.

5. Scott Christianson, *With Liberty for Some: 500 Years of Imprisonment in America* (Boston, 1998), 285–90; "In 90s, Prison Building by States and U.S. Government Surged," *New York Times*, Aug. 8, 1997; Raymond Hernandez, "Give Them the Maximum: Small Towns Clamor for the Boon a Big Prison Could Bring," ibid., Feb. 26, 1996, B1; Ed-

ward Walsh, "Strapped Small Towns Try to Lock Up Prisons," *Washington Post,* Dec. 24, 1994, A3.

6. With this term journalist Eric Schlosser deliberately drew upon President Eisenhower's warnings of a "military industrial complex" to capture the current relationship between business, the state, and imprisonment ("The Prison Industrial Complex," *Atlantic Monthly,* Dec. 1998, 51–77, quote on 52).

7. Eric Bates, "Private Prisons," *Nation,* Jan. 5, 1998, cover page and 11–18.

8. Financial backing for CCA came from investors who had supported Kentucky Fried Chicken (ibid.). See also Coramae Richey Mann, *Unequal Justice: A Question of Color* (Bloomington, Ind., 1993), 253–54; DiIulio, *No Escape,* 180–211; Christianson, *With Liberty for Some,* 290–95; Keon S. Chi, "Prison Overcrowding and Privatization: Models and Opportunities," in *Criminal Justice,* ed. J. J. Sullivan and J. L. Victor (Guilford, Conn., 1990); Charles H. Logan and Sharla P. Rausch, "Punish and Profit: The Emergence of Private Enterprise Prisons," *Justice Quarterly* 2:3 (1985): 303–18; Christine Bowditch and Ronald S. Everett, "Private Prisons: Problems within the Solution," ibid., 4:3 (1987) 441–53; Charles H. Logan, *Private Prisons: Cons and Pros* (New York, 1990); Douglas McDonald, ed., *Private Prisons and Public Policy* (Rutgers, N.J., 1987).

9. Schlosser, "The Prison Industrial Complex," 65.

10. Bates, "Private Prisons." Bates quotes from a 1992 study by the New Mexico Corrections Department that showed that inmates at a women's prison run by CCA lost "good time" at a rate eight times higher than their male counterparts at a state prison. See also Mick Ryan and Tony Ward, *Privatization and the Penal System: The American Experience and the Debate in Britain* (New York, 1989), 36–37.

11. Fox Butterfield, "Privately Run Juvenile Prison in Louisiana Is Attacked for Abuse of 6 Inmates," *New York Times,* March 16, 2000.

12. Schlosser, "The Prison Industrial Complex," 69.

13. Ibid., 70.

14. Ibid., 68.

15. Christianson, *With Liberty for Some,* 294–95; David Leonhardt, "As Prison Labor Grows, So Does Debate," *New York Times,* March 19, 2000.

16. By the mid-1990s, 62 percent of federal inmates and 21 percent of state prisoners were sentenced for drug offenses (Christianson, *With Liberty for Some,* 278–80, 282–83.

17. Schlosser, "The Prison Industrial Complex," 63; Christianson, *With Liberty for Some,* 293.

18. Christianson, *With Liberty for Some,* 281; William Glaberson, "One in Four Young Black Men Are in Custody, Study Says," *New York Times,* Oct. 4, 1990; Henry Weinstein, "One in Seven Black Men Are Kept from Voting, Study Finds," *Los Angeles Times,* Jan. 30, 1997; Patrick A. Langon, "Racism on Trial: New Evidence to Explain the Racial Composition of Prisons in the United States," *Journal of Criminal Law and Criminology* 76:3 (1985): 666–83.

19. Coramae Richey Mann provides a summary of the literature on this debate (*Unequal Justice,* 249–50) and a much more detailed discussion of the issue of the African-American experience with the criminal justice system in the United States.

20. DiIulio, *No Escape,* 190–92.

21. Ibid., 200.

Index

Accidents. *See* Prison mining

African-American churches, 32–33, 51

African-American Democrats, 35, 36

African-American prisoners. *See* Black prisoners

African-American reformers, 169, 174–82

African Americans: attitudes toward the law, 8–9, 33–35, 184–95; responses to emancipation and Reconstruction, 28–41; and education, 29–30; religious gatherings, 32–33; legal treatment under slavery, 33; expectations of justice, 34–35; and social control, 35–36, 51; and voting, 37; and racial pride, 38; and allegations of larceny, 42–44, 48–49, 53; and nonpayment of wages, 46–48; and labor contracts, 47–48; and lawsuits against employers, 48; and renting land 50, 53; and allegations of criminality, 169, 174–82; and lynching, 183–84, 200; and class divisions, 185–86, 188–89; as prosecutors of crime, 186, 191, 192; and paternalism, 190–91, 192–95. *See also* African-American women; Black prisoners; Female prisoners

African-American women: and political activism, 40–41, 72, 178–80; threatened with arrest, 40–41; and domestic violence, 186; and paternity suits, 190–91. *See also* Female prisoners

Alabama: Republican party in, 13–15, 17, 24–25, 40; Democratic party in, 13–15, 17–18, 23–24, 26–27, 58, 163–65, 199–200; debt crisis in, 63, 65, 66; De-

partment of Corrections, 68, 83–84; taxation in, 76. *See also* Penitentiary

Alabama Beacon, 39, 51

Alabama Farmers' Alliance, 163–64

Alabama State Teachers' Association, 174

Albany system, 169. *See also* Convict labor, in the North

Alonzo Bailey, 182. *See also* Peonage

Aptheker, Herbert, 143–44

Archey, Ezekiel, 2, 20, 21, 38, 69, 81–82, 87–88, 92, 102–4, 140–41, 201–2. *See also* Black prisoners, letters from

Arrests: in Forkland, 14; politically motivated, 39, 44, 56–57, 57–58; in Jefferson County, 207–10

Arson. *See* Black prisoners, and arson

Ayers, Edward, 43

Bankhead, John H., 22, 63, 67, 74, 75, 76, 77; plans to lease prisoners to coal mines, 78, 85–86; allegations of corruption, 82–83; chaining prisoners, 90–91; and female prisoners, 114–15, 122; elected to office, 200

Banner Mine, 166–67

Bass, John G., 18, 19, 21, 65–66, 67, 68, 76, 77

Bauer, Alice and Raymond, 144

Berry, Ike, 109–10

Berry, Mary Frances, 7

Billings, W. P., 14

Birmingham, Ala.: interracial labor movement in, 1, 203–4; condition of county jail, 209–10. *See also* Jefferson County

Black, Jim, 15, 16

Carter G. Woodson Institute Series in Black Studies